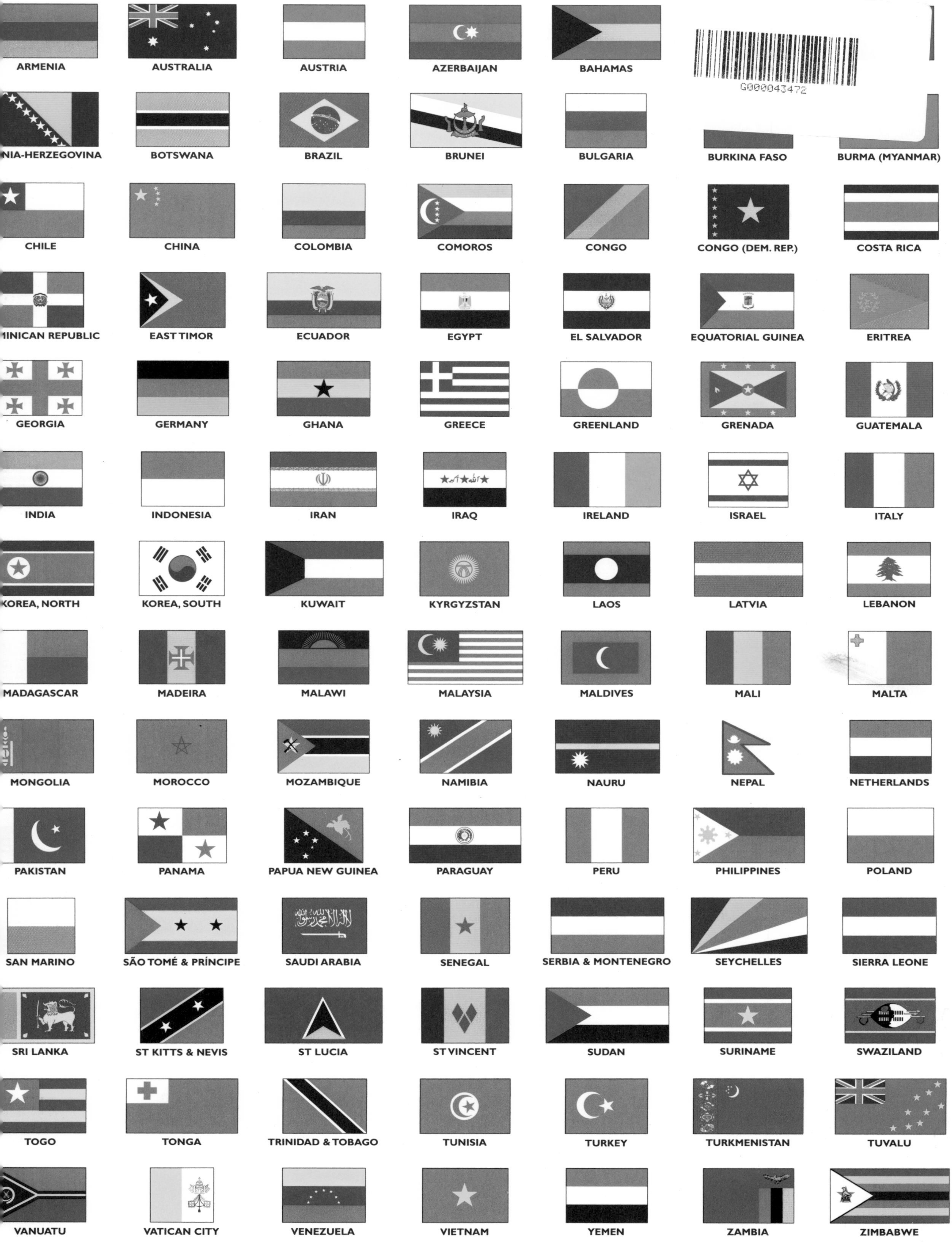
ARMENIA
AUSTRALIA
AUSTRIA
AZERBAIJAN
BAHAMAS
NIA-HERZEGOVINA
BOTSWANA
BRAZIL
BRUNEI
BULGARIA
BURKINA FASO
BURMA (MYANMAR)
CHILE
CHINA
COLOMBIA
COMOROS
CONGO
CONGO (DEM. REP.)
COSTA RICA
IINICAN REPUBLIC
EAST TIMOR
ECUADOR
EGYPT
EL SALVADOR
EQUATORIAL GUINEA
ERITREA
GEORGIA
GERMANY
GHANA
GREECE
GREENLAND
GRENADA
GUATEMALA
INDIA
INDONESIA
IRAN
IRAQ
IRELAND
ISRAEL
ITALY
KOREA, NORTH
KOREA, SOUTH
KUWAIT
KYRGYZSTAN
LAOS
LATVIA
LEBANON
MADAGASCAR
MADEIRA
MALAWI
MALAYSIA
MALDIVES
MALI
MALTA
MONGOLIA
MOROCCO
MOZAMBIQUE
NAMIBIA
NAURU
NEPAL
NETHERLANDS
PAKISTAN
PANAMA
PAPUA NEW GUINEA
PARAGUAY
PERU
PHILIPPINES
POLAND
SAN MARINO
SÃO TOMÉ & PRÍNCIPE
SAUDI ARABIA
SENEGAL
SERBIA & MONTENEGRO
SEYCHELLES
SIERRA LEONE
SRI LANKA
ST KITTS & NEVIS
ST LUCIA
ST VINCENT
SUDAN
SURINAME
SWAZILAND
TOGO
TONGA
TRINIDAD & TOBAGO
TUNISIA
TURKEY
TURKMENISTAN
TUVALU
VANUATU
VATICAN CITY
VENEZUELA
VIETNAM
YEMEN
ZAMBIA
ZIMBABWE

G000043472

PHILIP'S FAMILY WORLD ATLAS

Contents

CITY CENTRE MAPS – KEY TO SYMBOLS

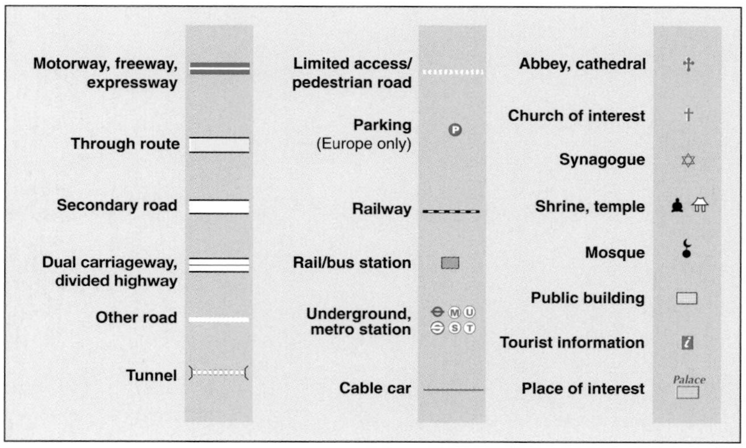

Motorway, freeway, expressway
Through route
Secondary road
Dual carriageway, divided highway
Other road
Tunnel
Limited access/ pedestrian road
Parking (Europe only)
Railway
Rail/bus station
Underground, metro station
Cable car
Abbey, cathedral
Church of interest
Synagogue
Shrine, temple
Mosque
Public building
Tourist information
Place of interest
Palace

Philip's World Atlases are published in association with The Royal Geographical Society (with The Institute of British Geographers).

The Society was founded in 1830 and given a Royal Charter in 1859 for 'the advancement of geographical science'. It holds historical collections of national and international importance, many of which relate to the Society's association with and support for scientific exploration and research from the 19th century onwards. It was pivotal in establishing geography as a teaching and research discipline in British universities close to the turn of the century, and has played a key role in geographical and environmental education ever since.

Today the Society is a leading world centre for geographical learning – supporting education, teaching, research and expeditions, and promoting public understanding of the subject.

The Society welcomes those interested in geography as members. For further information, please visit the website at: www.rgs.org

City Centre Maps – Cartography by Philip's

Page iii, Dublin: The town plan of Dublin is based on Ordnance Survey Ireland by permission of the Government Permit Number 8097. © Ordnance Survey Ireland and Government of Ireland.

Ordnance Survey® Page iii, Edinburgh, and page iv, London: This product includes mapping data licensed from Ordnance Survey® with the permission of the Controller of Her Majesty's Stationery Office. © Crown copyright 2006. All rights reserved. Licence number 100011710.

Vector data: Courtesy of Gräfe and Unser Verlag GmbH, München, Germany (city centre maps of Bangkok, Mexico City, Singapore, Sydney and Tokyo).

Published in Great Britain in 2006 by Philip's,
a division of Octopus Publishing Group,
2–4 Heron Quays, London E14 4JP

Copyright © 2006 Philip's
Cartography by Philip's

ISBN-13 978-0-540-08892-8
ISBN-10 0-540-08892-7

A CIP catalogue record for this book is available from the British Library.

Printed in Hong Kong

All rights reserved. Apart from any fair dealing for the purpose of private study, research, criticism or review, as permitted under the Copyright, Designs and Patents Act, 1988, no part of this publication may be reproduced, stored in a retrieval system, or transmitted in any form or by any means, electronic, electrical, chemical, mechanical, optical, photocopying, recording, or otherwise, without prior written permission. All enquiries should be addressed to the Publisher.

Details of other Philip's titles and services can be found on our website at: www.philips-maps.co.uk

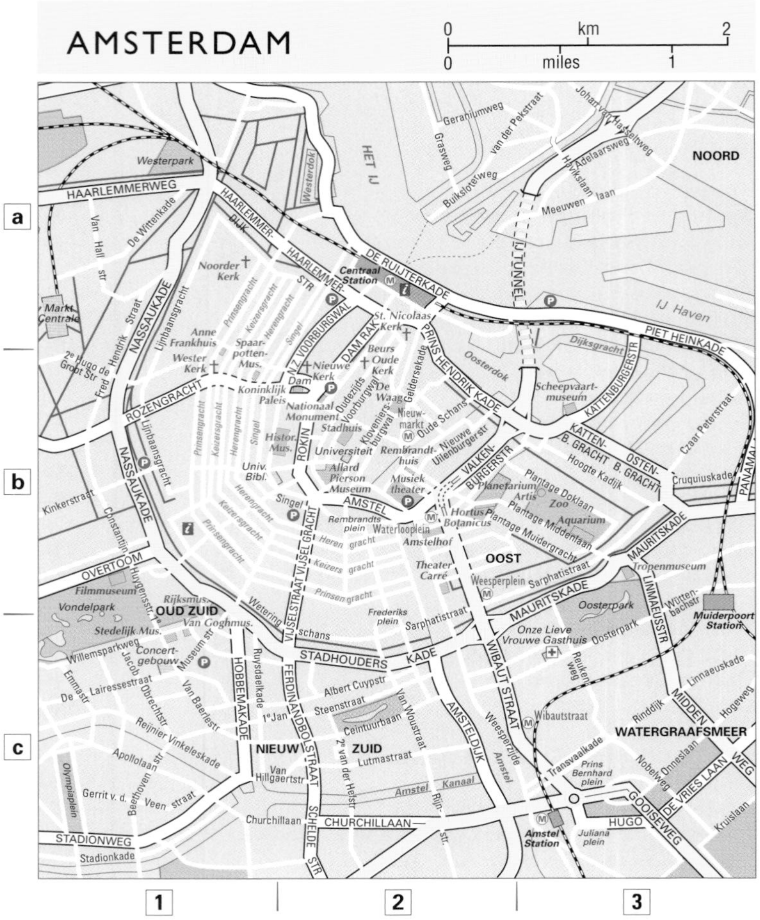

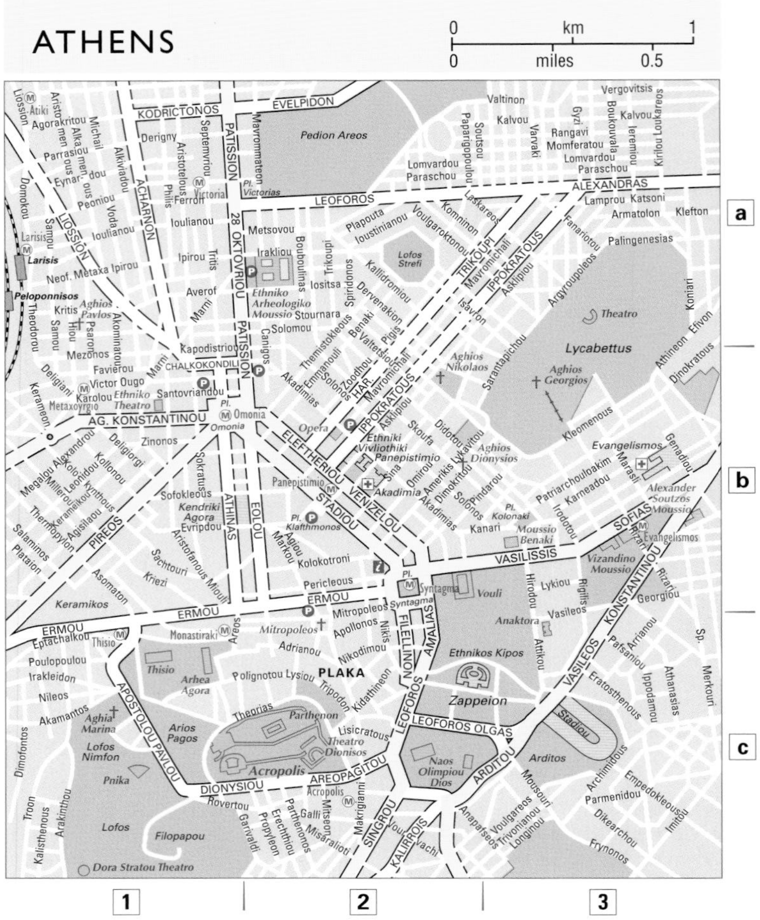

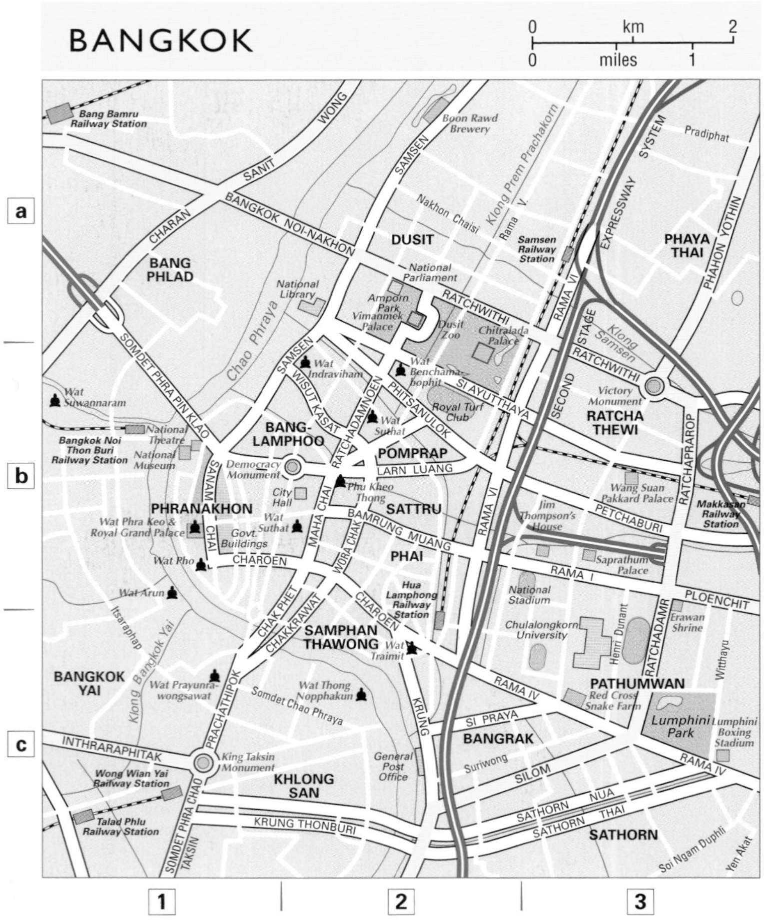

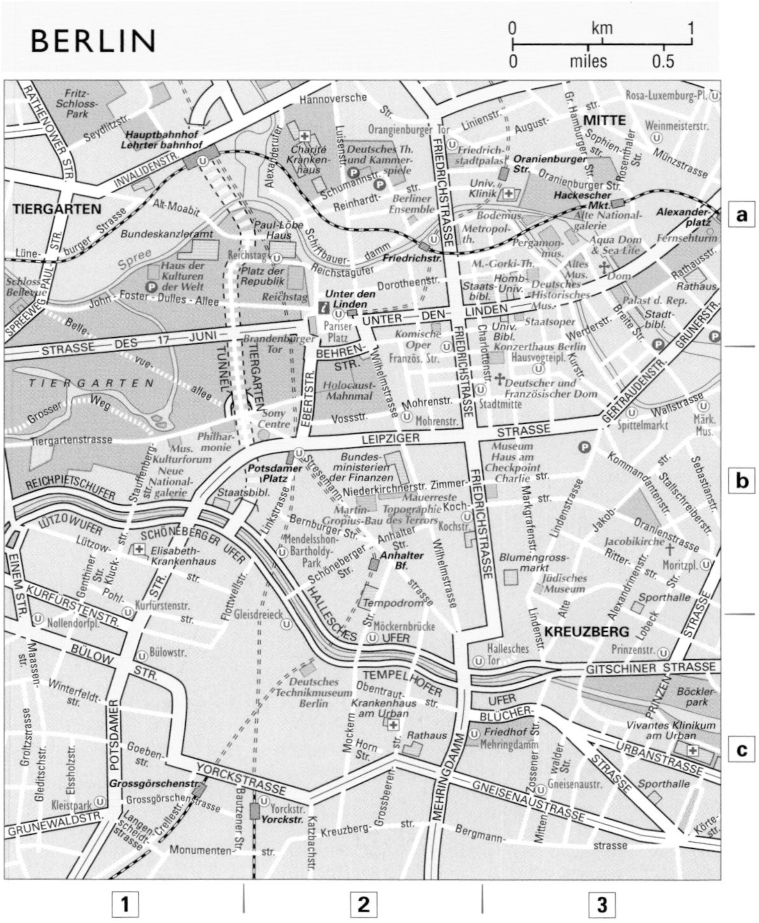

COPYRIGHT PHILIPS

BRUSSELS

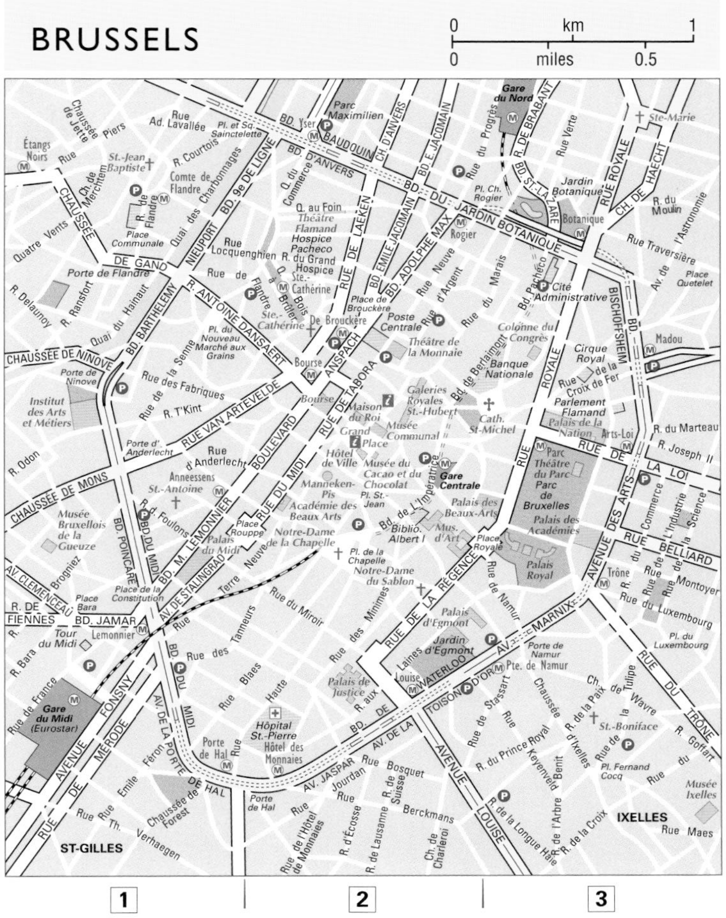

DELHI

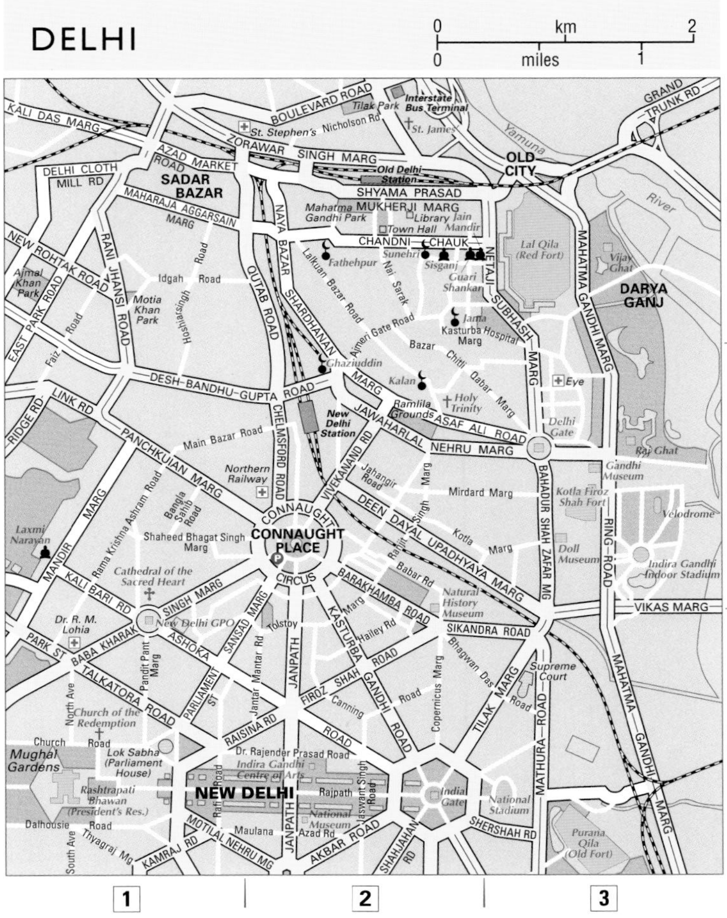

DUBLIN

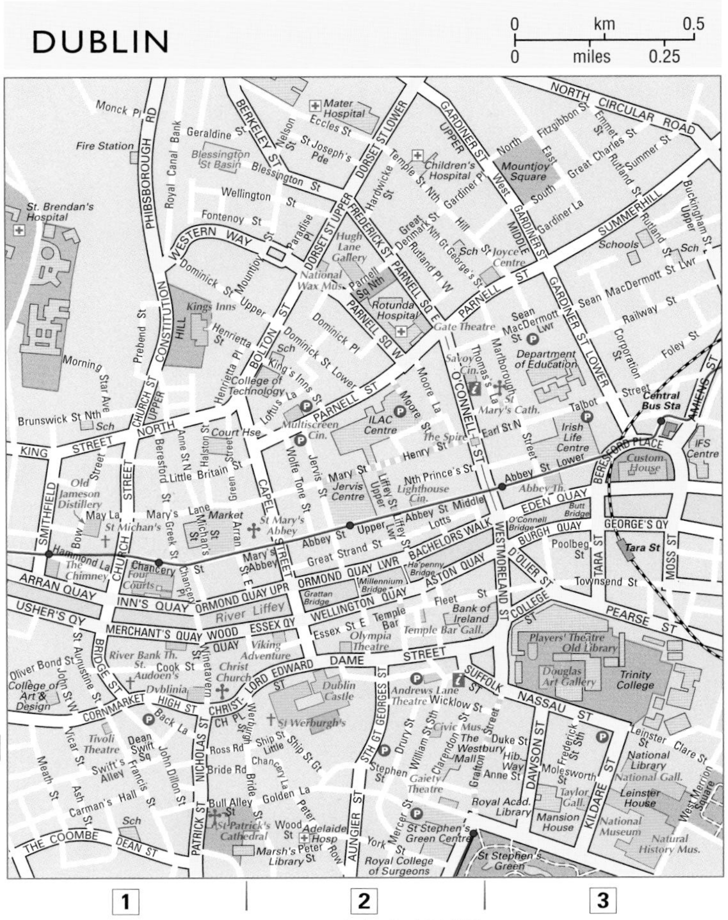

—●— Light Rail (LUAS)

EDINBURGH

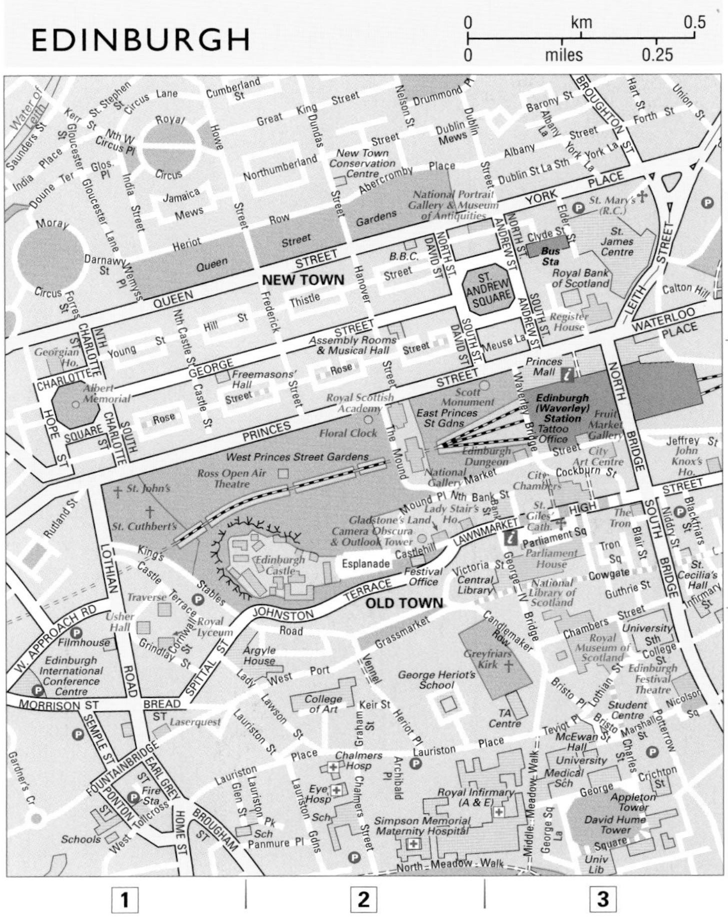

COPYRIGHT PHILIPS

LONDON

0 km 2
0 miles 1

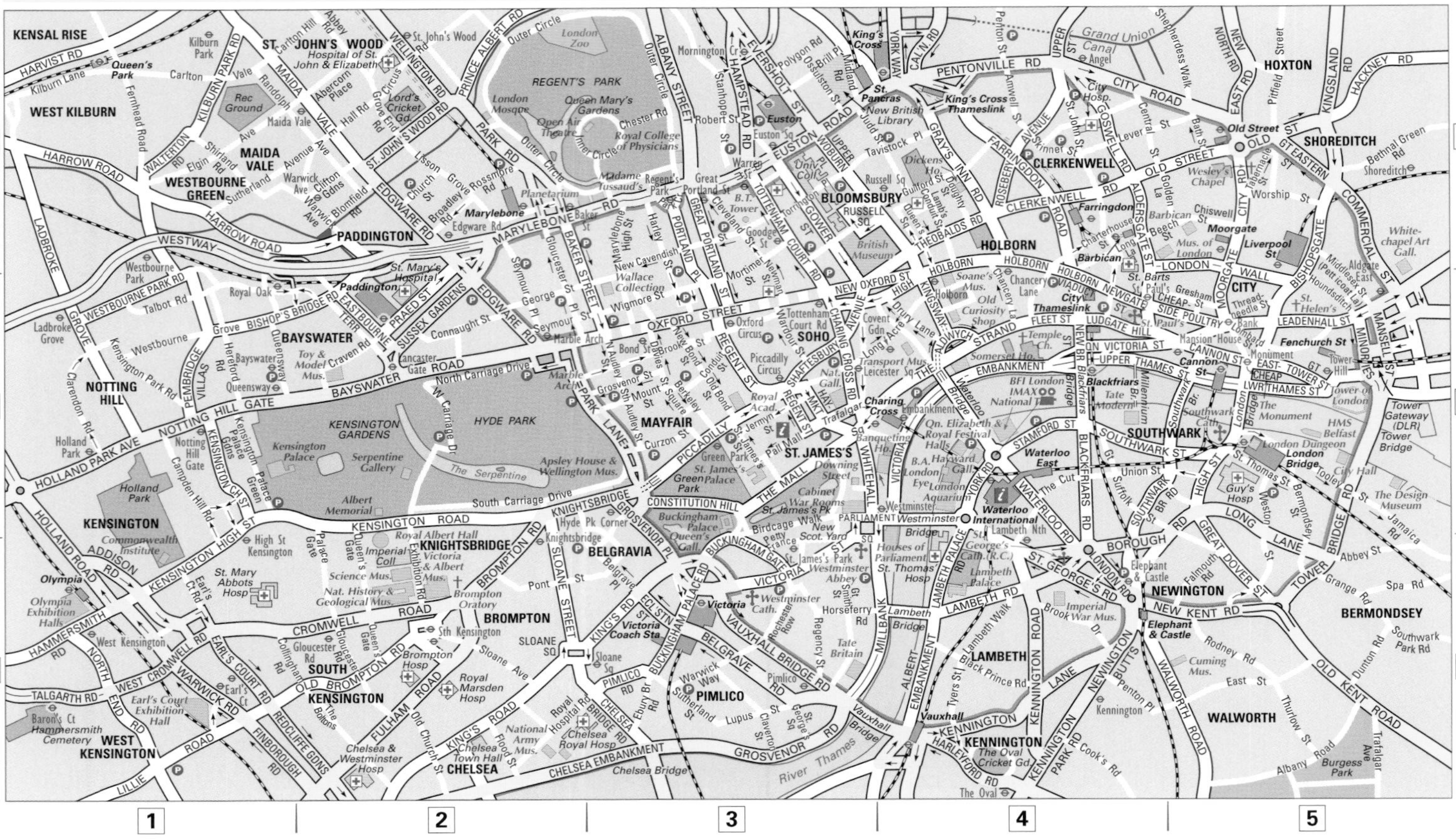

Congestion Charging Zone

LISBON

0 km 1
0 miles 0.5

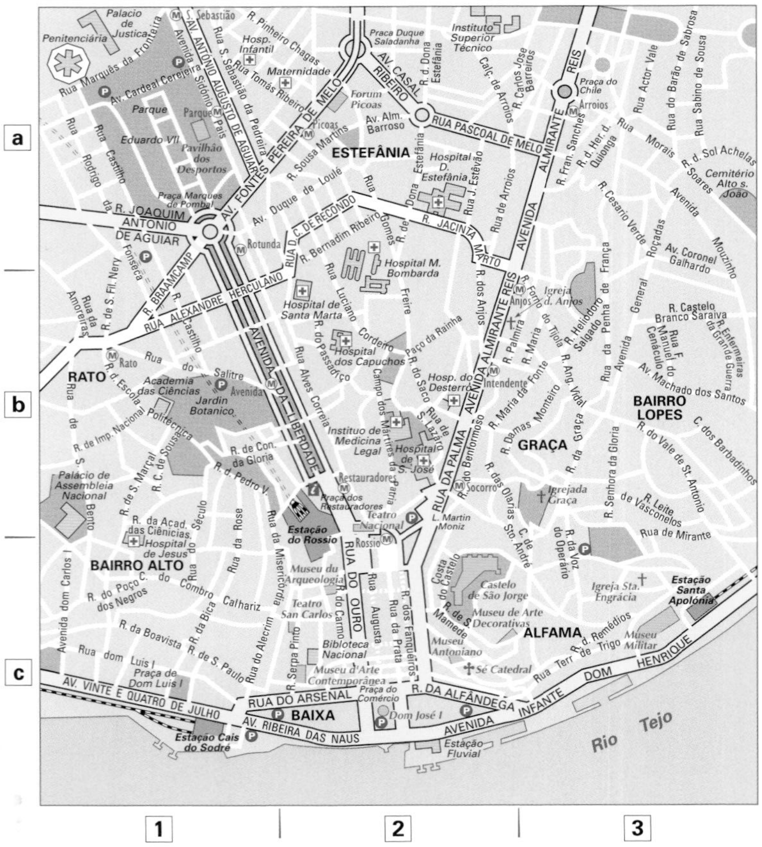

MADRID

0 km 1
0 miles 0.5

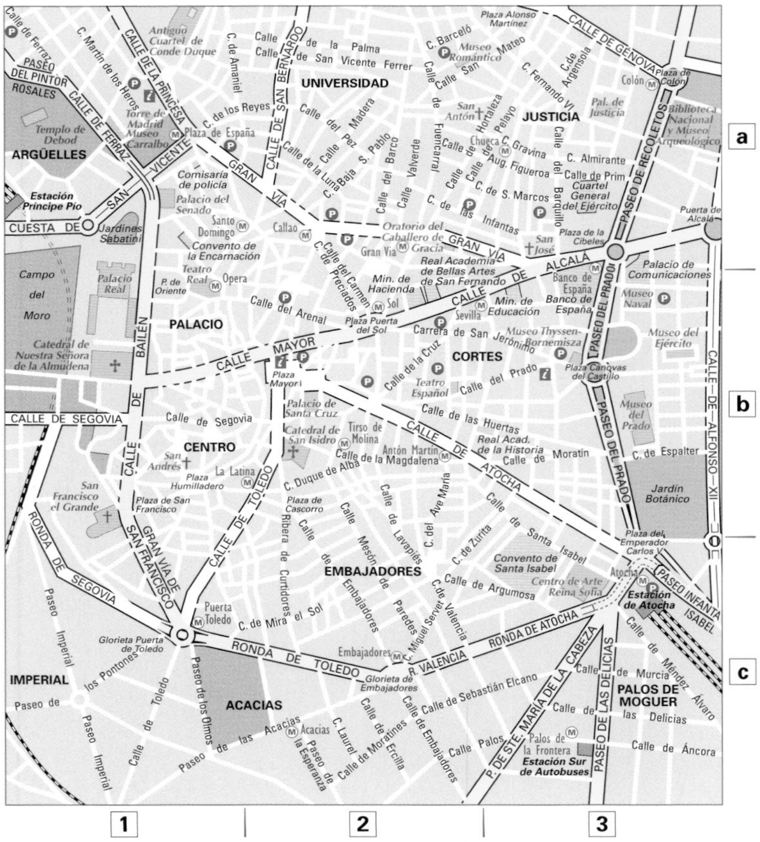

COPYRIGHT PHILIPS

MEXICO CITY

0 km 1
0 miles 0.5

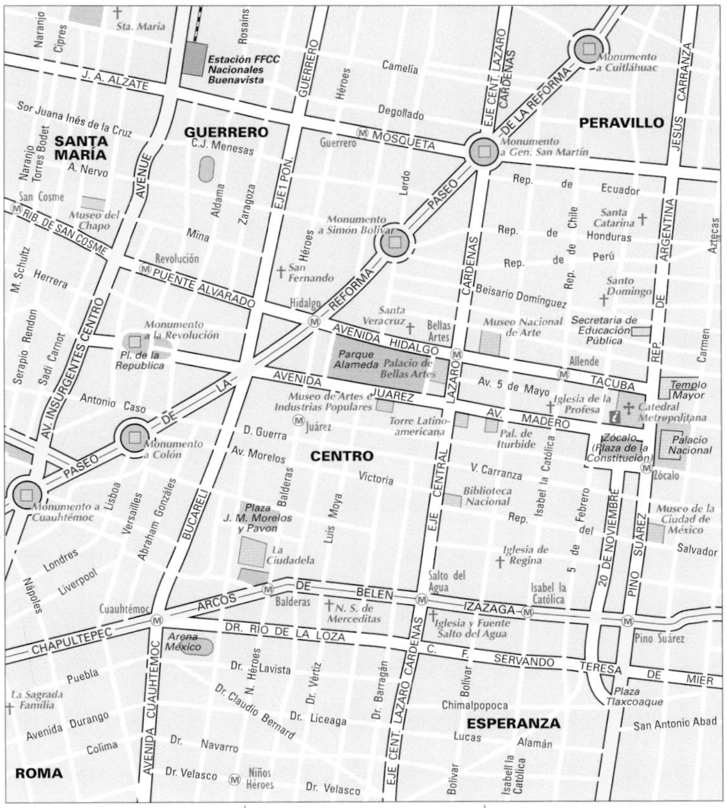

a
b
c
1 2 3

MUMBAI

0 km 2
0 miles 1

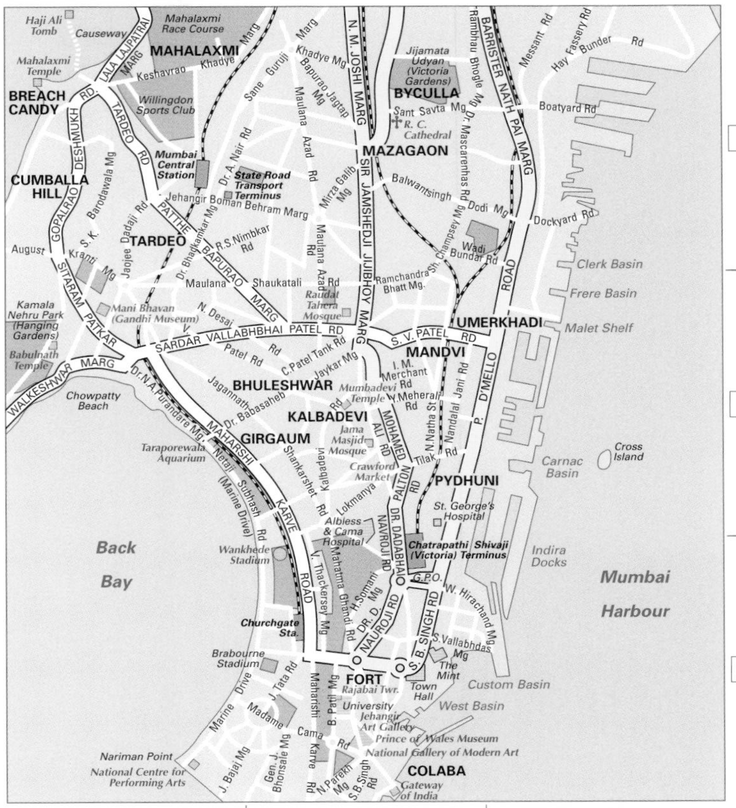

a
b
c
1 2 3

NEW YORK

0 km 2
0 miles 1

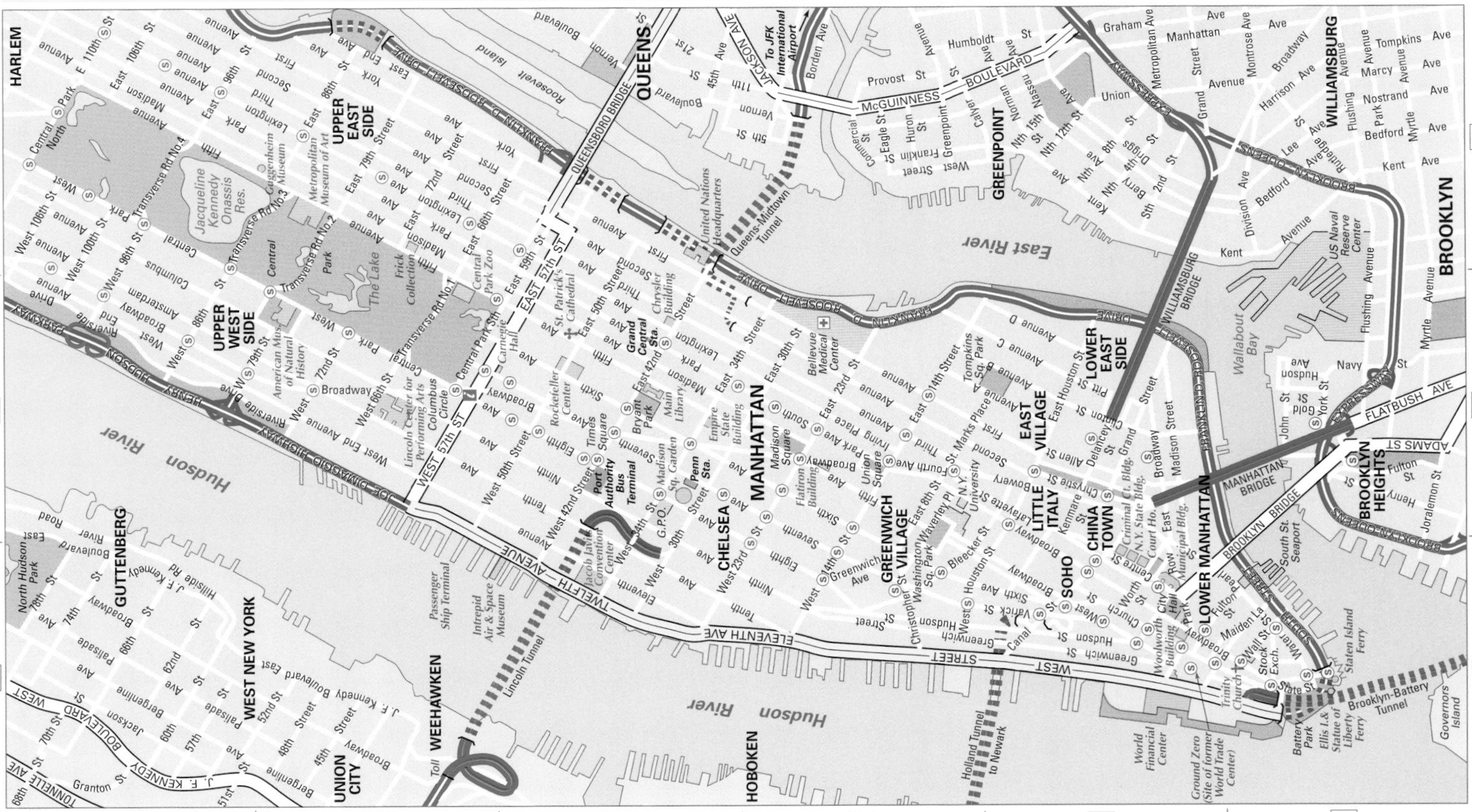

3
2
1
a b c d e f

COPYRIGHT PHILIPS

PARIS, PRAGUE, RIO DE JANEIRO

PARIS

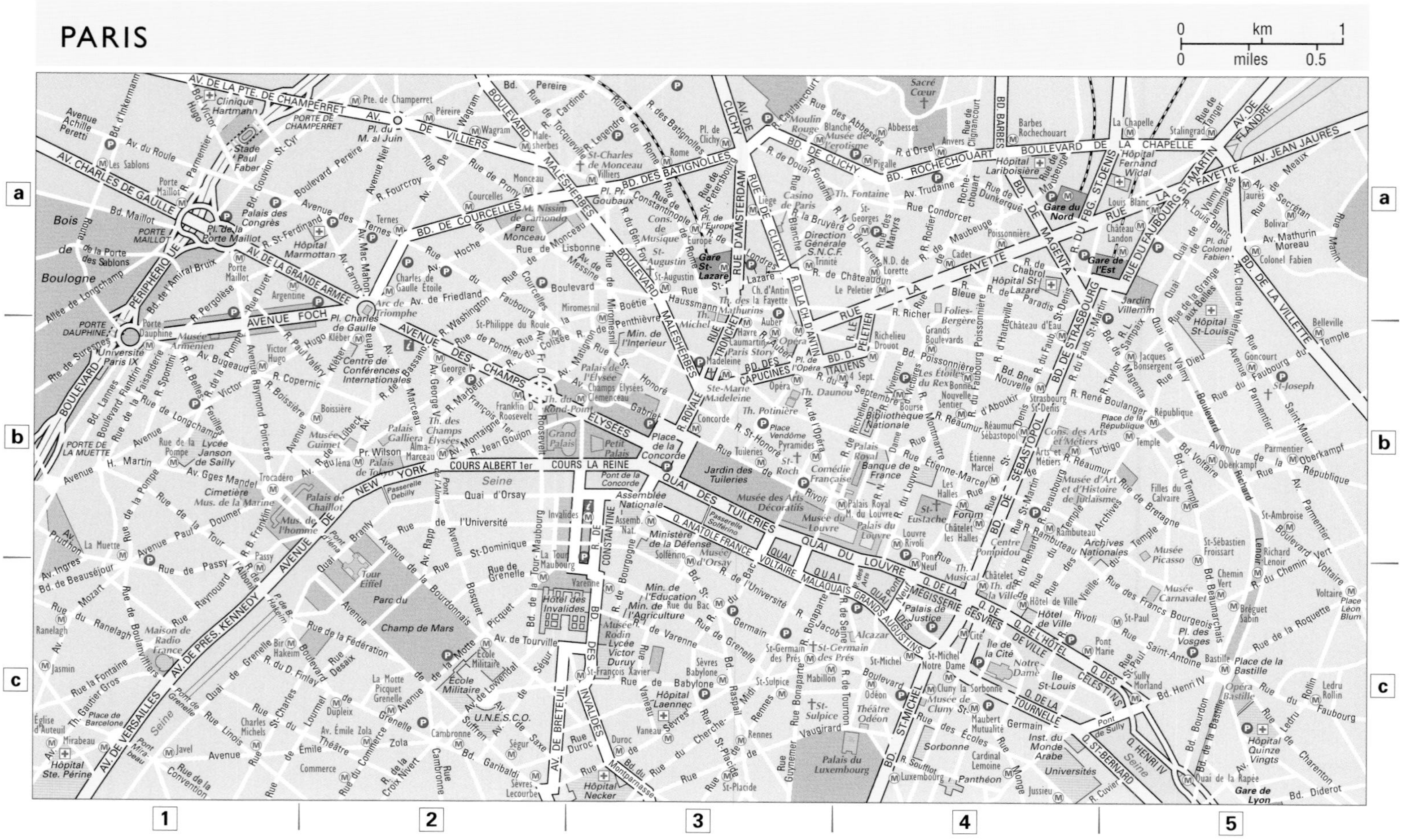

PRAGUE

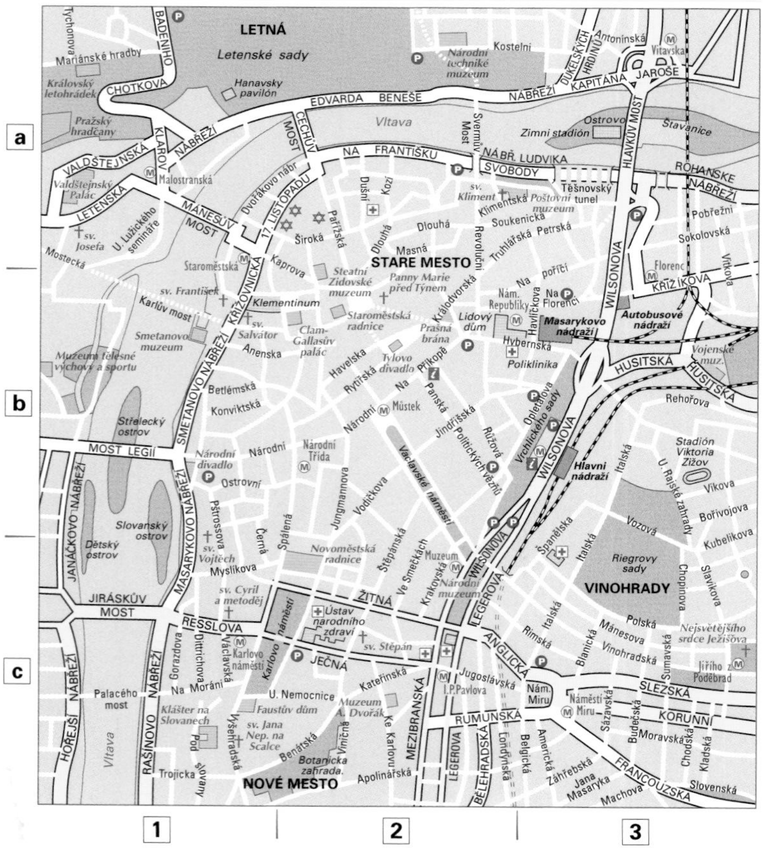

RIO DE JANEIRO

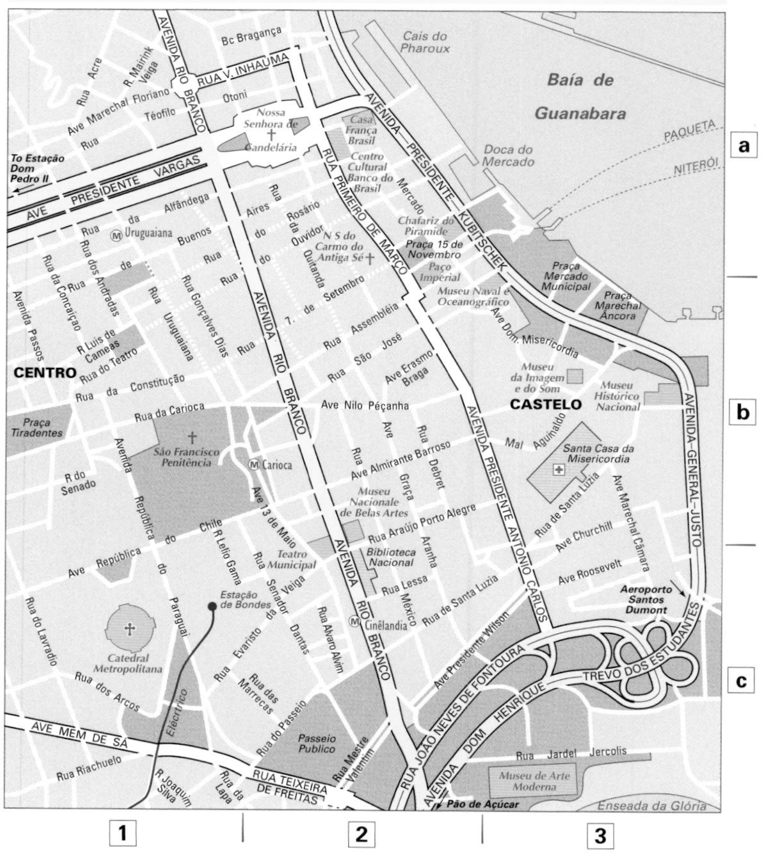

COPYRIGHT PHILIPS

ROME

0 km 1
0 miles 0.5

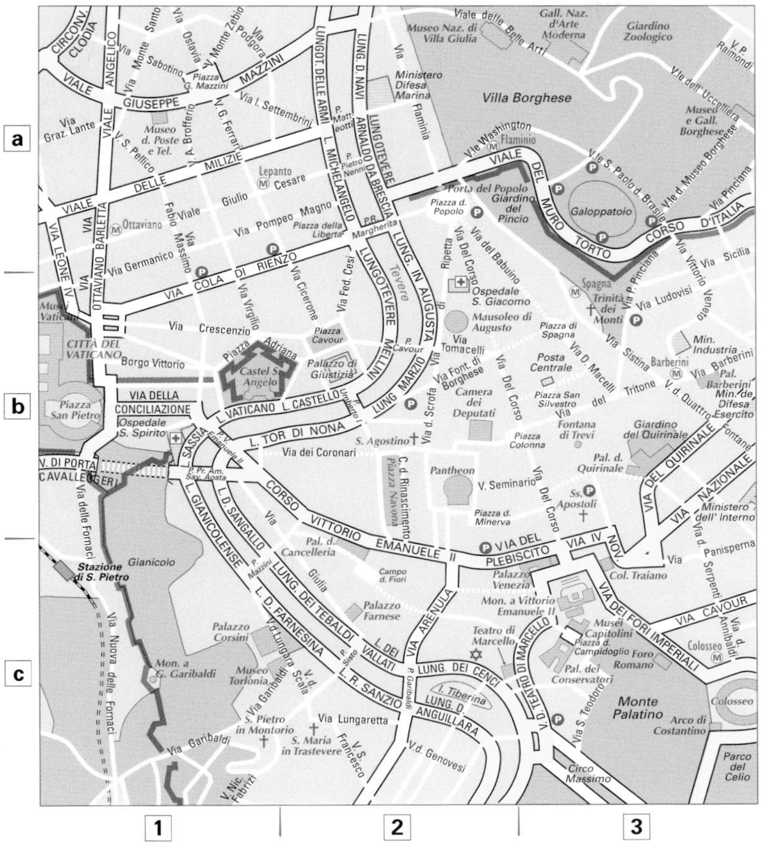

SINGAPORE

0 km 1
0 miles 0.5

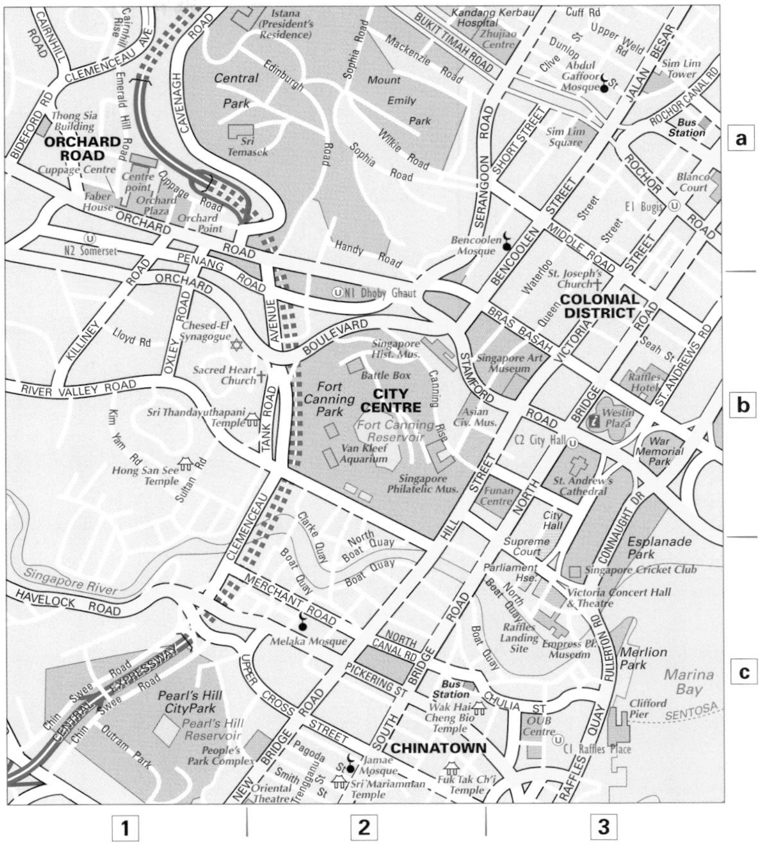

SYDNEY

0 km 2
0 miles 1

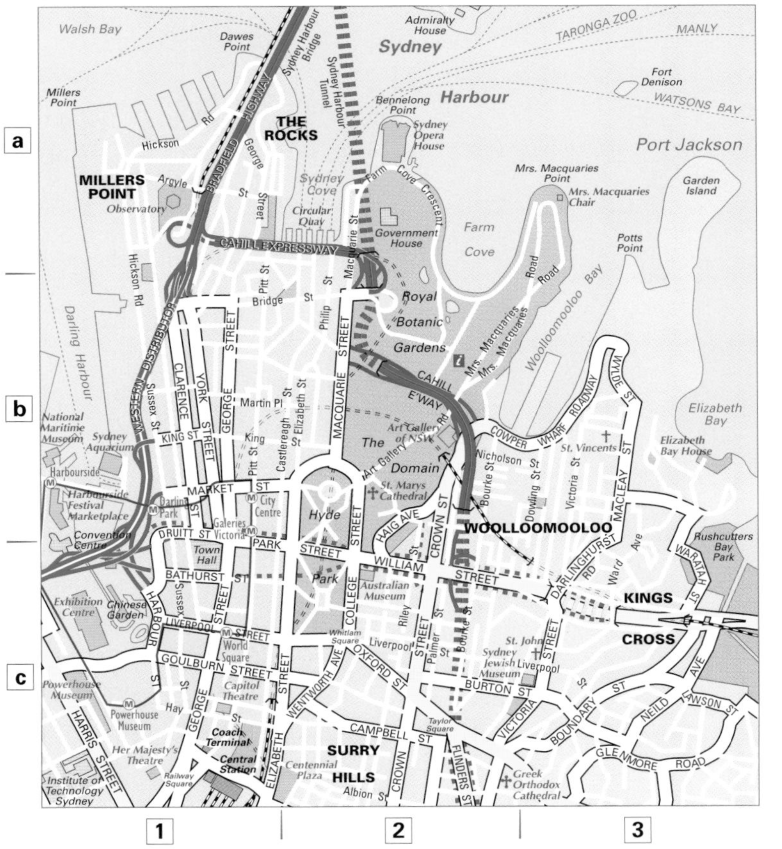

TOKYO

0 km 1
0 miles 0.5

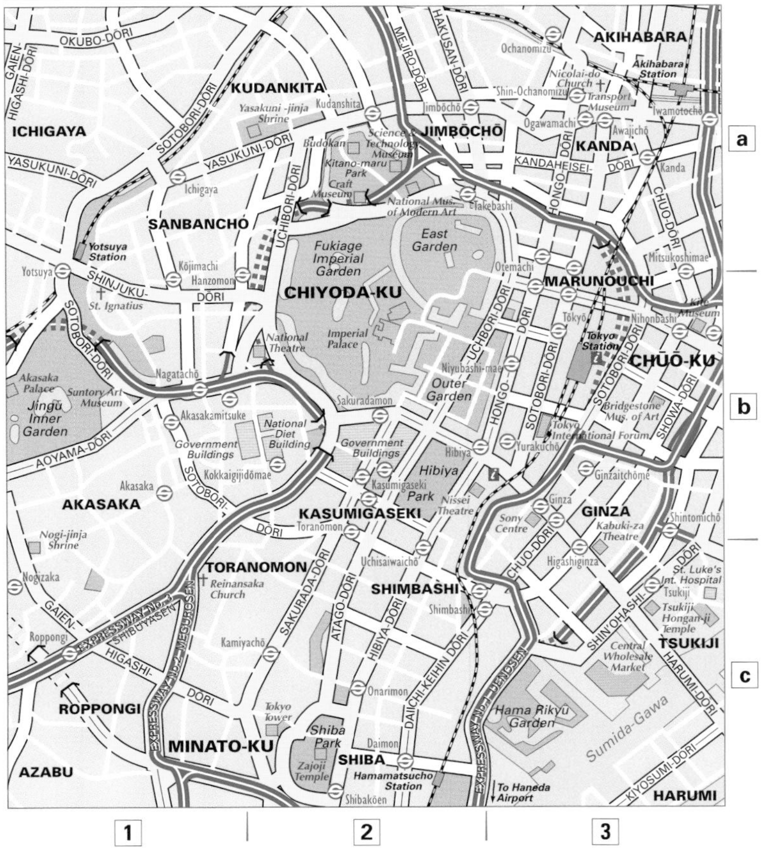

COPYRIGHT PHILIPS

VIII WORLD CITIES: DISTANCES

The table shows air distances in kilometres and miles between 24 major cities. Known as 'great circle' distances, these measure the shortest routes between the cities, which are used by aircraft wherever possible. The maps show the world centred on six cities, and illustrate, for example, why direct flights from Japan to North America and Europe are across the Arctic regions. The maps have been constructed on an Azimuthal Equidistant projection, on which all distances measured through the centre point are true to scale. The red lines are drawn at 5,000, 10,000 and 15,000 km from the central city.

Kms

Kms	Beijing	Bombay (Mumbai)	Buenos Aires	Cairo	Calcutta (Kolkata)	Caracas	Chicago	Hong Kong	Honolulu	Johannesburg	Lagos	London	Los Angeles	Mexico City	Moscow	Nairobi	New York	Paris	Rio de Janeiro	Rome	Singapore	Sydney	Tokyo	Wellington
Beijing																								
Bombay (Mumbai)	4757																							
Buenos Aires	19268	14925																						
Cairo	7544	4355	11814																					
Calcutta (Kolkata)	3269	1664	16524	5699																				
Caracas	14399	14522	5096	10203	15464																			
Chicago	10603	12953	9011	3206	12839	4027																		
Hong Kong	1963	4317	18478	8150	2659	16360	12526																	
Honolulu	8160	12914	12164	14223	11343	9670	6836	8921																
Johannesburg	11710	6974	8088	6267	8459	11019	13984	10732	19206															
Lagos	11457	7612	7916	3915	9216	7741	9612	11845	16308	4505														
London	8138	7190	11131	3508	7961	7507	6356	9623	11632	9071	5017													
Los Angeles	10060	14000	9852	12200	13120	5812	2804	11639	4117	16676	12414	8758												
Mexico City	12460	15656	7389	12372	15280	3586	2726	14122	6085	14585	11071	8936	2493											
Moscow	5794	5031	13477	2902	5534	9938	8000	7144	11323	9161	6254	2498	9769	10724										
Nairobi	9216	4532	10402	3536	6179	11544	12883	8776	17282	2927	3807	6819	15544	14818	6344									
New York	10988	12541	8526	9020	12747	3430	1145	12950	7980	12841	8477	5572	3936	3264	7510	11842								
Paris	8217	7010	11051	3210	7858	7625	6650	9630	11968	8732	4714	342	9085	9200	2486	6485	5836							
Rio de Janeiro	17338	13409	1953	9896	15073	4546	8547	17704	13342	7113	6035	9299	10155	7693	11562	8928	7777	9187						
Rome	8126	6175	11151	2133	7219	8363	7739	9284	12916	7743	4039	1431	10188	10243	2376	5391	6888	1105	9214					
Singapore	4478	3914	15879	8267	2897	18359	15078	2599	10816	8660	11145	10852	14123	16610	8428	7460	15339	10737	15712	10025				
Sydney	8949	10160	11800	14418	9138	15343	14875	7374	8168	11040	15519	16992	12073	12969	14497	12153	15989	16962	13501	16324	6300			
Tokyo	2099	6742	18362	9571	5141	14164	10137	2874	6202	13547	13480	9562	8811	11304	7485	11260	10849	9718	18589	9861	5321	7823		
Wellington	10782	12370	9981	16524	11354	13122	13451	9427	7513	11761	16050	18814	10814	11100	16549	13664	14405	18987	11855	18545	8526	2226	9273	

Miles

Miles	Beijing	Bombay (Mumbai)	Buenos Aires	Cairo	Calcutta (Kolkata)	Caracas	Chicago	Hong Kong	Honolulu	Johannesburg	Lagos	London	Los Angeles	Mexico City	Moscow	Nairobi	New York	Paris	Rio de Janeiro	Rome	Singapore	Sydney	Tokyo	Wellington
Beijing		2956	11972	4688	2031	8947	6588	1220	5070	7276	7119	5057	6251	7742	3600	5727	6828	5106	10773	5049	2783	5561	1304	6700
Bombay (Mumbai)			9275	2706	1034	9024	8048	2683	8024	4334	4730	4467	8700	9728	3126	2816	7793	4356	8332	3837	2432	6313	4189	7686
Buenos Aires				7341	10268	3167	5599	11481	7558	5025	4919	6917	6122	4591	8374	6463	5298	6867	1214	6929	9867	7332	11410	6202
Cairo					3541	6340	6127	5064	8838	3894	2432	2180	7580	7687	1803	2197	5605	1994	6149	1325	5137	8959	5947	10268
Calcutta (Kolkata)						9609	7978	1653	7048	5256	5727	4946	8152	9494	3438	3839	7921	4883	9366	4486	1800	5678	3195	7055
Caracas							2502	10166	6009	6847	4810	4664	3612	2228	6175	7173	2131	4738	2825	5196	11407	9534	8801	8154
Chicago								7783	4247	8689	5973	3949	1742	1694	4971	8005	711	4132	5311	4809	9369	9243	6299	8358
Hong Kong									5543	6669	7360	5980	7232	8775	4439	5453	8047	5984	11001	5769	1615	4582	1786	5857
Honolulu										11934	10133	7228	2558	3781	7036	10739	4958	7437	8290	8026	6721	5075	3854	4669
Johannesburg											2799	5637	10362	9063	5692	1818	7979	5426	4420	4811	5381	6860	8418	7308
Lagos												3118	7713	6879	3886	2366	5268	2929	3750	2510	6925	9643	8376	9973
London													5442	5552	1552	4237	3463	212	5778	889	6743	10558	5942	11691
Los Angeles														1549	6070	9659	2446	5645	6310	6331	8776	7502	5475	6719
Mexico City															6664	9207	2090	5717	4780	6365	10321	8058	7024	6897
Moscow																3942	4666	1545	7184	1477	5237	9008	4651	10283
Nairobi																	7358	4029	5548	3350	4635	7552	6996	8490
New York																		3626	4832	4280	9531	9935	6741	8951
Paris																			5708	687	6671	10539	6038	11798
Rio de Janeiro																				5725	9763	8389	11551	7367
Rome																					6229	10143	6127	11523
Singapore																						3915	3306	5298
Sydney																							4861	1383
Tokyo																								5762
Wellington																								

MEXICO CITY
19° 26′N 99° 04′W

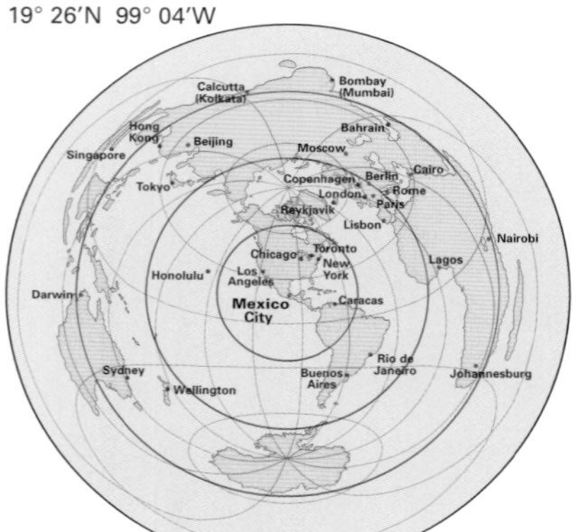

LONDON
51° 28′N 00° 27′W

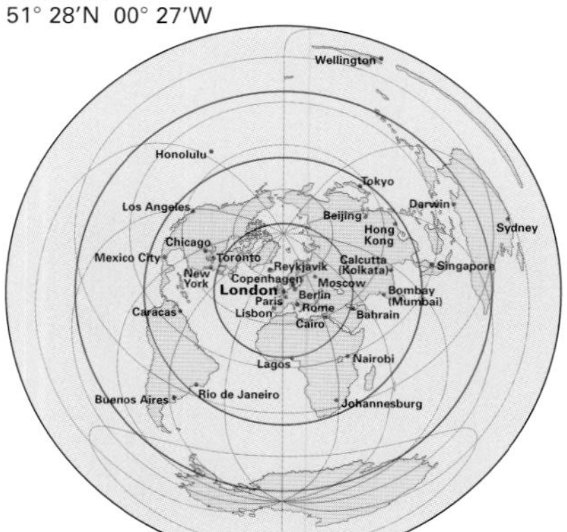

TOKYO
35° 33′N 139° 46′E

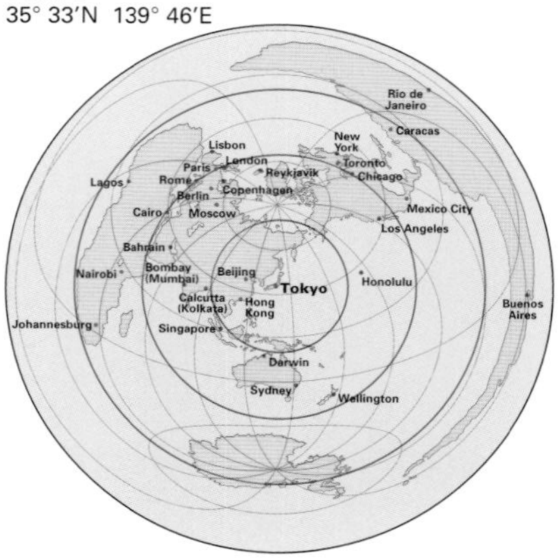

RIO DE JANEIRO
22° 50′S 43° 15′W

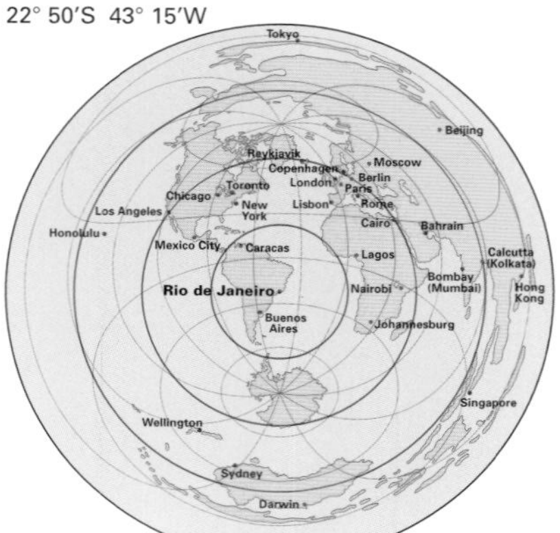

SINGAPORE
1° 21′N 103° 54′E

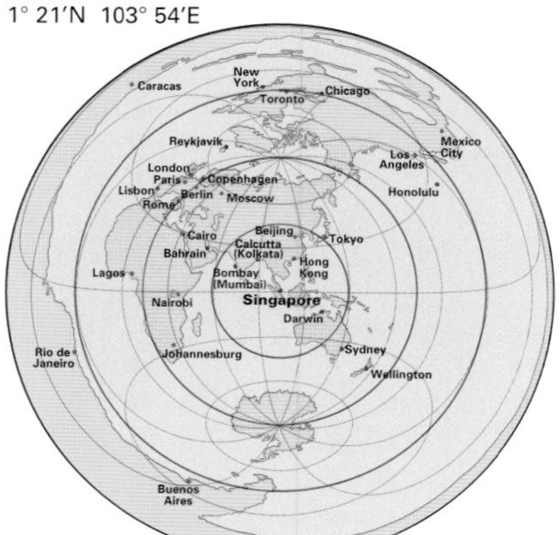

SYDNEY
33° 56′ S 151° 10′E

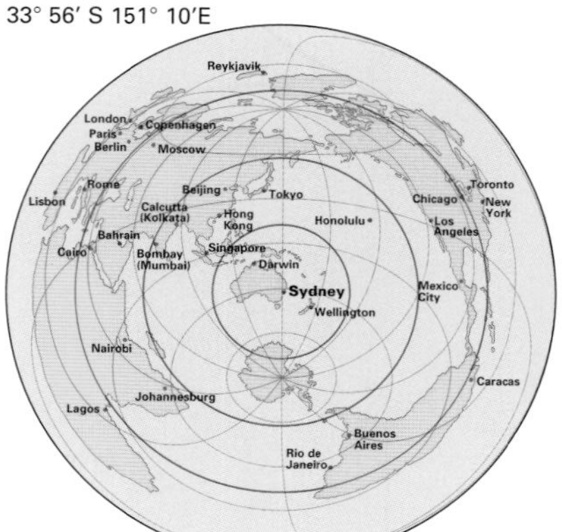

COPYRIGHT PHILIPS

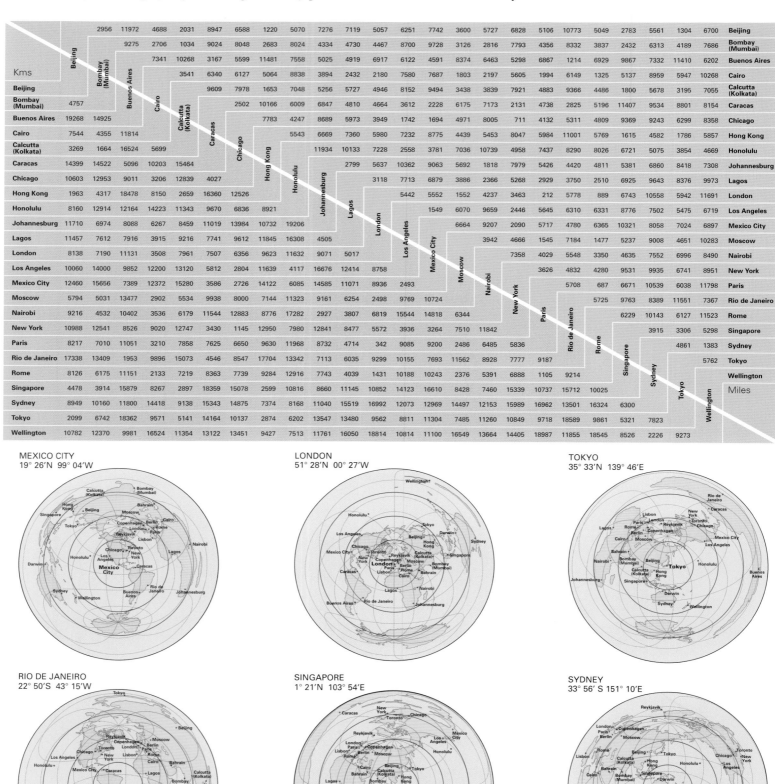

WORLD MAPS

SETTLEMENTS

■ PARIS   ■ Berne   ⊙ Livorno   ⊙ Brugge   ◎ Algeciras   ○ *Frejus*   ○ *Oberammergau*   ○ *Thira*

Settlement symbols and type styles vary according to the scale of each map and indicate the importance of towns on the map rather than specific population figures. Capital cities have red infills.

ADMINISTRATION

International boundaries

International boundaries (undefined or disputed)

Internal boundaries

National park boundaries

International boundaries show the *de facto* situation where there are rival claims to territory

COMMUNICATIONS

Principal roads

Principal railways

Railway tunnels

Road tunnels

Railways under construction

Principal canals

Passes

Airfields

PHYSICAL FEATURES

Perennial streams

Intermittent lakes

▲ 8848 Elevations in metres

Intermittent streams

Swamps and marshes

▼ 8500 Sea depths in metres

Perennial lakes

Permanent ice and glaciers

1134 Height of lake surface above sea level in metres

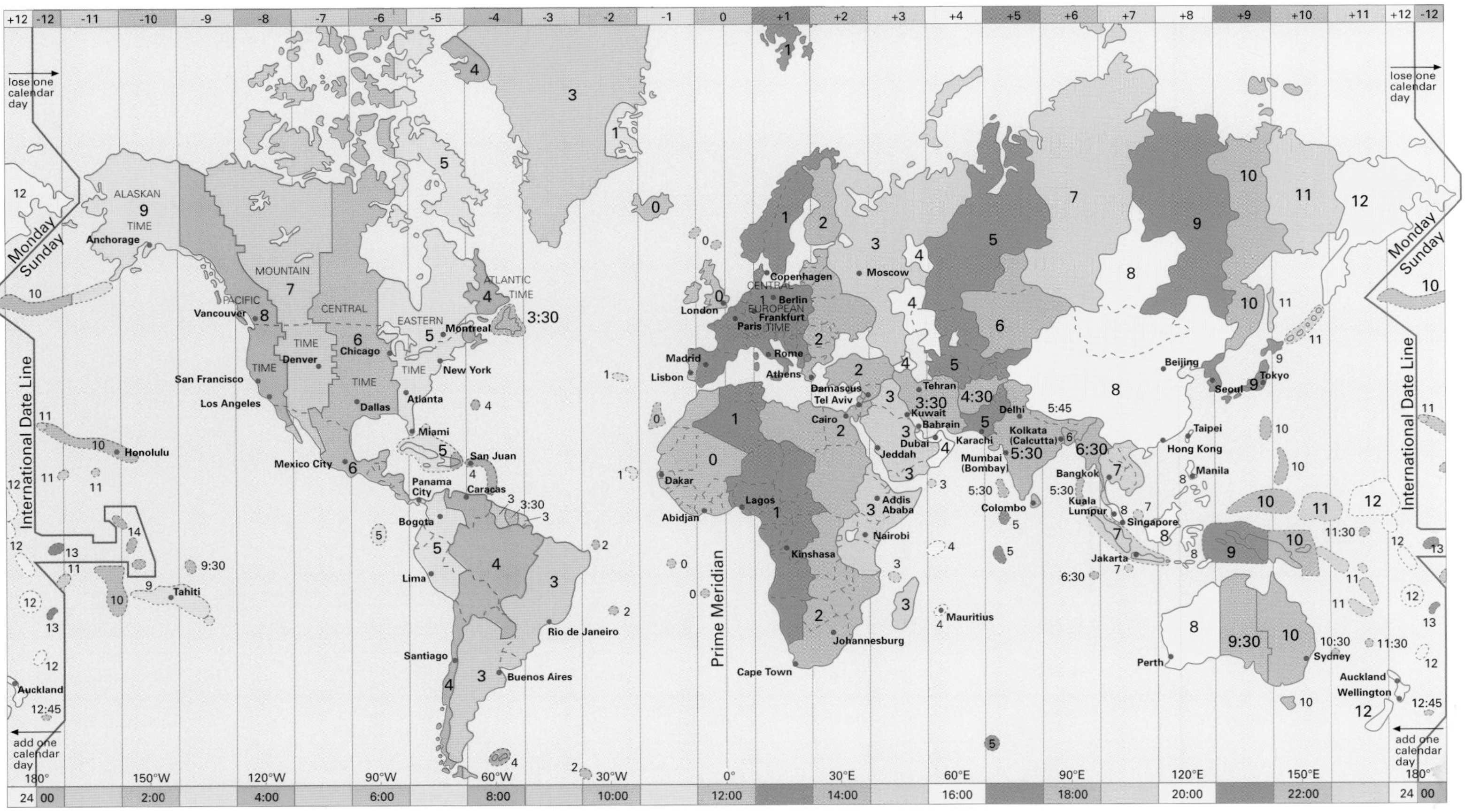

TIME ZONES

Zones using UT (Greenwich Mean Time)

Zones behind UT (Greenwich Mean Time)

Zones ahead of UT (Greenwich Mean Time)

Half-hour zones

10 Hours behind or ahead of UT (Greenwich Mean Time)

International boundaries

Actual solar time, when it is noon at Greenwich, is shown at the foot of the map.

Note: Certain time zones are affected by the incidence of daylight saving time in countries where it is adopted.

Time-zone boundaries

International Date Line

2 THE WORLD : Physical

Equatorial Scale 1:95 000 000

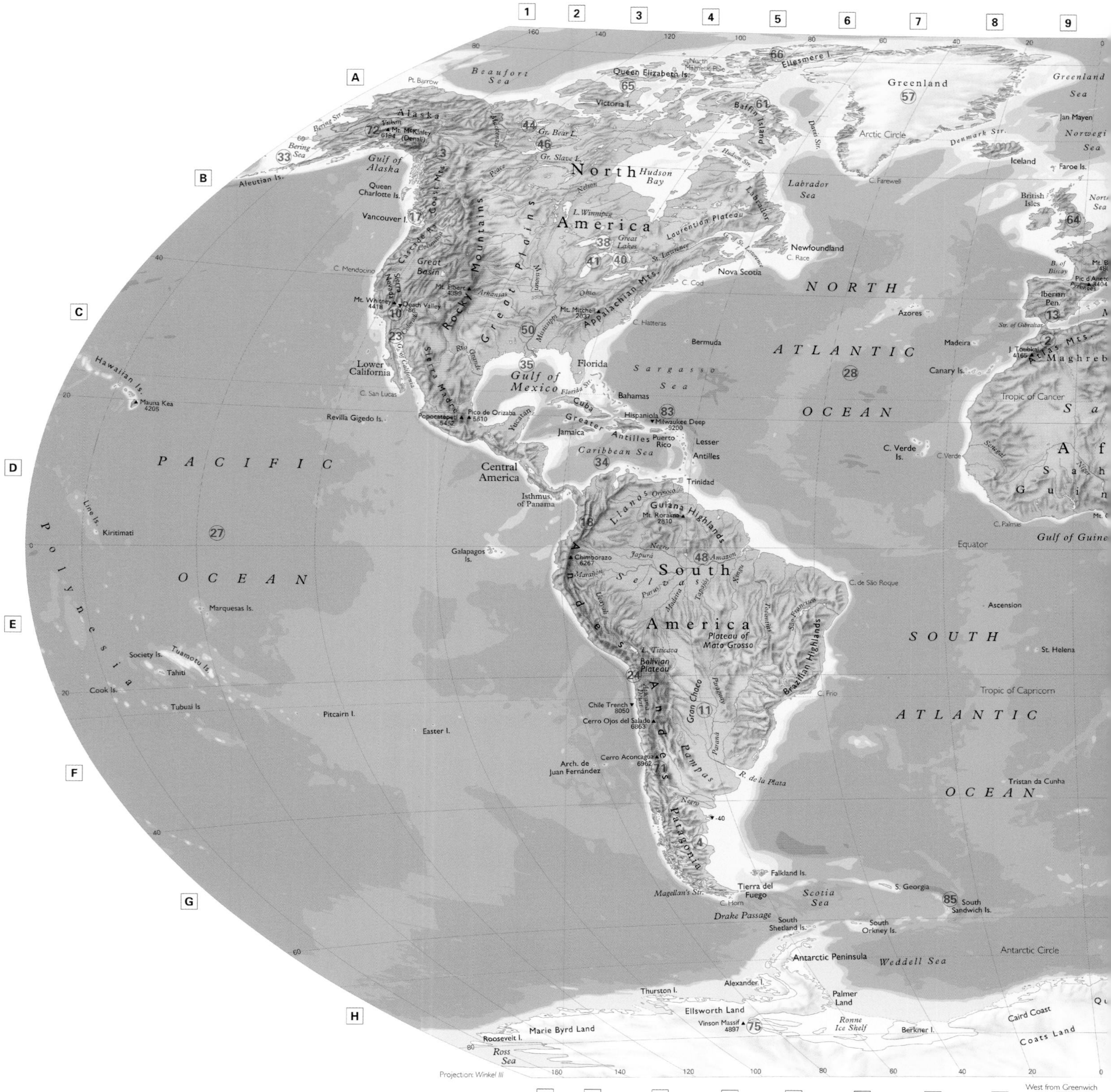

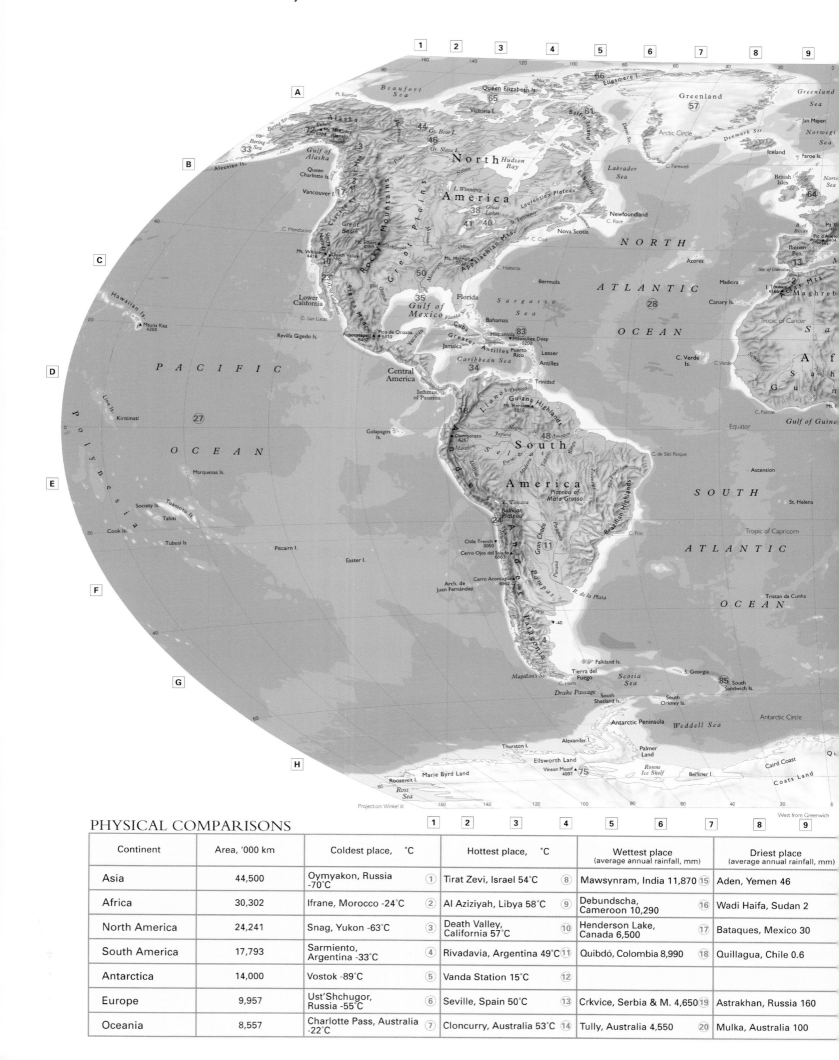

PHYSICAL COMPARISONS

Continent	Area, '000 km	Coldest place, °C	Hottest place, °C	Wettest place (average annual rainfall, mm)	Driest place (average annual rainfall, mm)
Asia	44,500	Oymyakon, Russia -70°C (1)	Tirat Zevi, Israel 54°C (8)	Mawsynram, India 11,870 (15)	Aden, Yemen 46
Africa	30,302	Ifrane, Morocco -24°C (2)	Al Aziziyah, Libya 58°C (9)	Debundscha, Cameroon 10,290 (16)	Wadi Haifa, Sudan 2
North America	24,241	Snag, Yukon -63°C (3)	Death Valley, California 57°C (10)	Henderson Lake, Canada 6,500 (17)	Bataques, Mexico 30
South America	17,793	Sarmiento, Argentina -33°C (4)	Rivadavia, Argentina 49°C (11)	Quibdó, Colombia 8,990 (18)	Quillagua, Chile 0.6
Antarctica	14,000	Vostok -89°C (5)	Vanda Station 15°C (12)		
Europe	9,957	Ust'Shchugor, Russia -55°C (6)	Seville, Spain 50°C (13)	Crkvice, Serbia & M. 4,650 (19)	Astrakhan, Russia 160
Oceania	8,557	Charlotte Pass, Australia -22°C (7)	Cloncurry, Australia 53°C (14)	Tully, Australia 4,550 (20)	Mulka, Australia 100

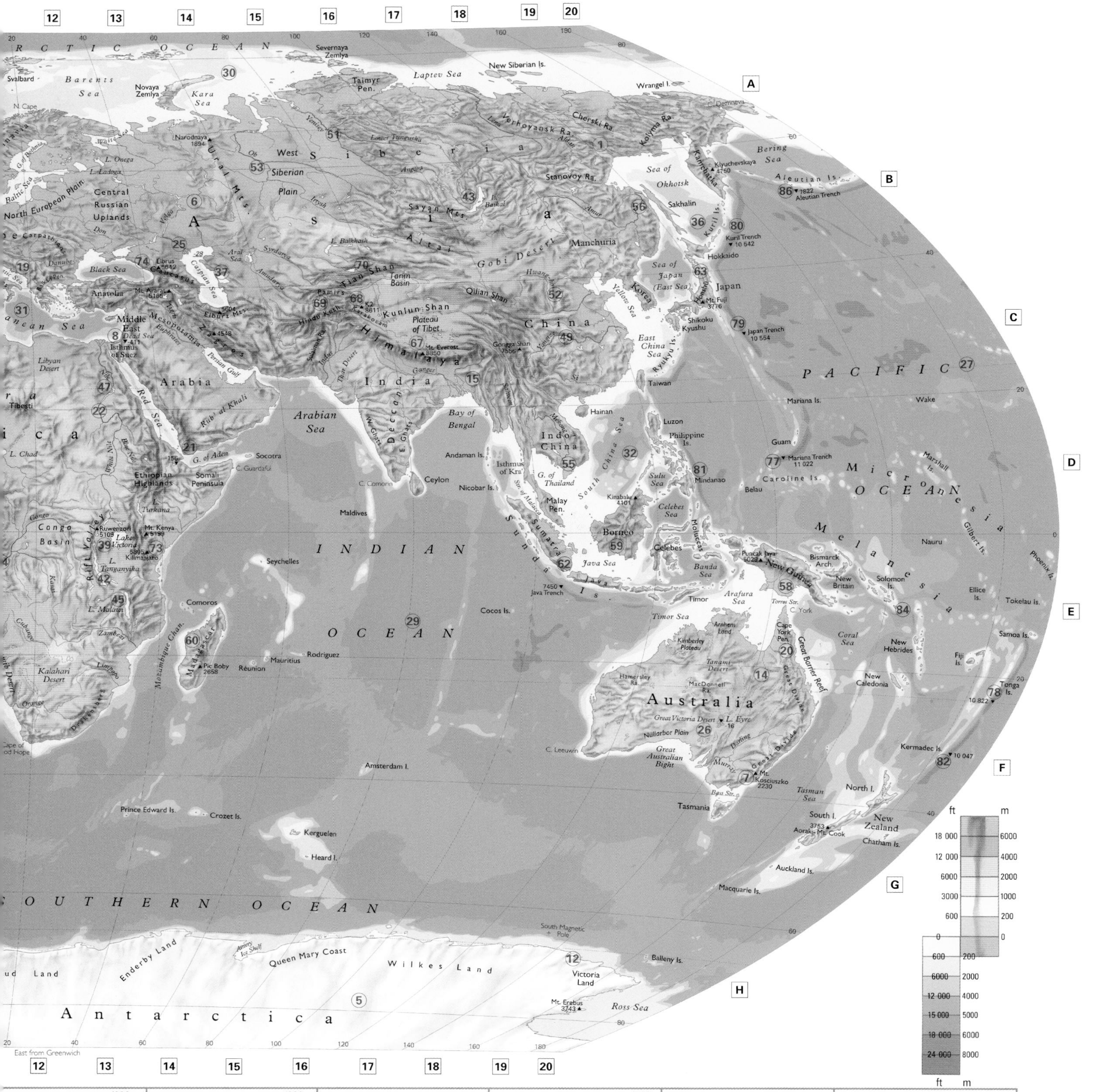

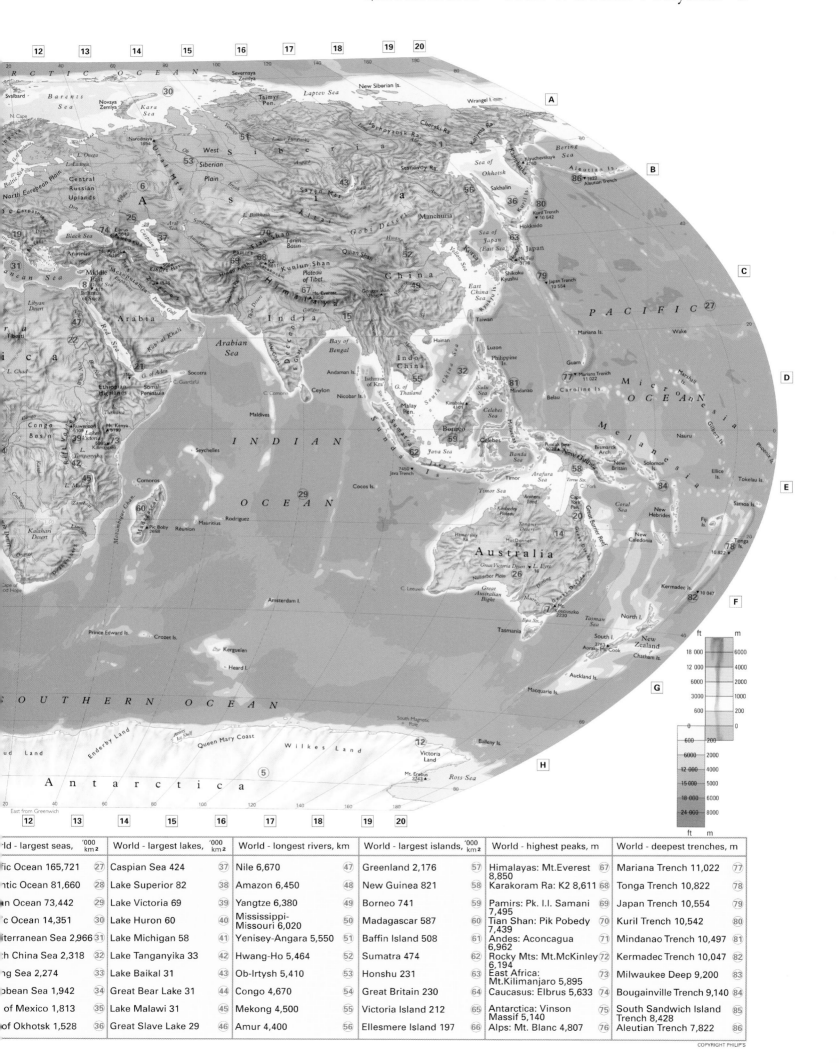

...ld - largest seas, '000 km²		World - largest lakes, '000 km²		World - longest rivers, km		World - largest islands, '000 km²		World - highest peaks, m		World - deepest trenches, m	
...fic Ocean 165,721	27	Caspian Sea 424	37	Nile 6,670	47	Greenland 2,176	57	Himalayas: Mt.Everest 8,850	67	Mariana Trench 11,022	77
...ntic Ocean 81,660	28	Lake Superior 82	38	Amazon 6,450	48	New Guinea 821	58	Karakoram Ra: K2 8,611	68	Tonga Trench 10,822	78
...n Ocean 73,442	29	Lake Victoria 69	39	Yangtze 6,380	49	Borneo 741	59	Pamirs: Pk. I.I. Samani 7,495	69	Japan Trench 10,554	79
...c Ocean 14,351	30	Lake Huron 60	40	Mississippi-Missouri 6,020	50	Madagascar 587	60	Tian Shan: Pik Pobedy 7,439	70	Kuril Trench 10,542	80
...iterranean Sea 2,966	31	Lake Michigan 58	41	Yenisey-Angara 5,550	51	Baffin Island 508	61	Andes: Aconcagua 6,962	71	Mindanao Trench 10,497	81
...h China Sea 2,318	32	Lake Tanganyika 33	42	Hwang-Ho 5,464	52	Sumatra 474	62	Rocky Mts: Mt.McKinley 6,194	72	Kermadec Trench 10,047	82
...ng Sea 2,274	33	Lake Baikal 31	43	Ob-Irtysh 5,410	53	Honshu 231	63	East Africa: Mt.Kilimanjaro 5,895	73	Milwaukee Deep 9,200	83
...bean Sea 1,942	34	Great Bear Lake 31	44	Congo 4,670	54	Great Britain 230	64	Caucasus: Elbrus 5,633	74	Bougainville Trench 9,140	84
...of Mexico 1,813	35	Lake Malawi 31	45	Mekong 4,500	55	Victoria Island 212	65	Antarctica: Vinson Massif 5,140	75	South Sandwich Island Trench 8,428	85
...of Okhotsk 1,528	36	Great Slave Lake 29	46	Amur 4,400	56	Ellesmere Island 197	66	Alps: Mt. Blanc 4,807	76	Aleutian Trench 7,822	86

COPYRIGHT PHILIP'S

THE WORLD : Political

Equatorial Scale 1:95 000 000

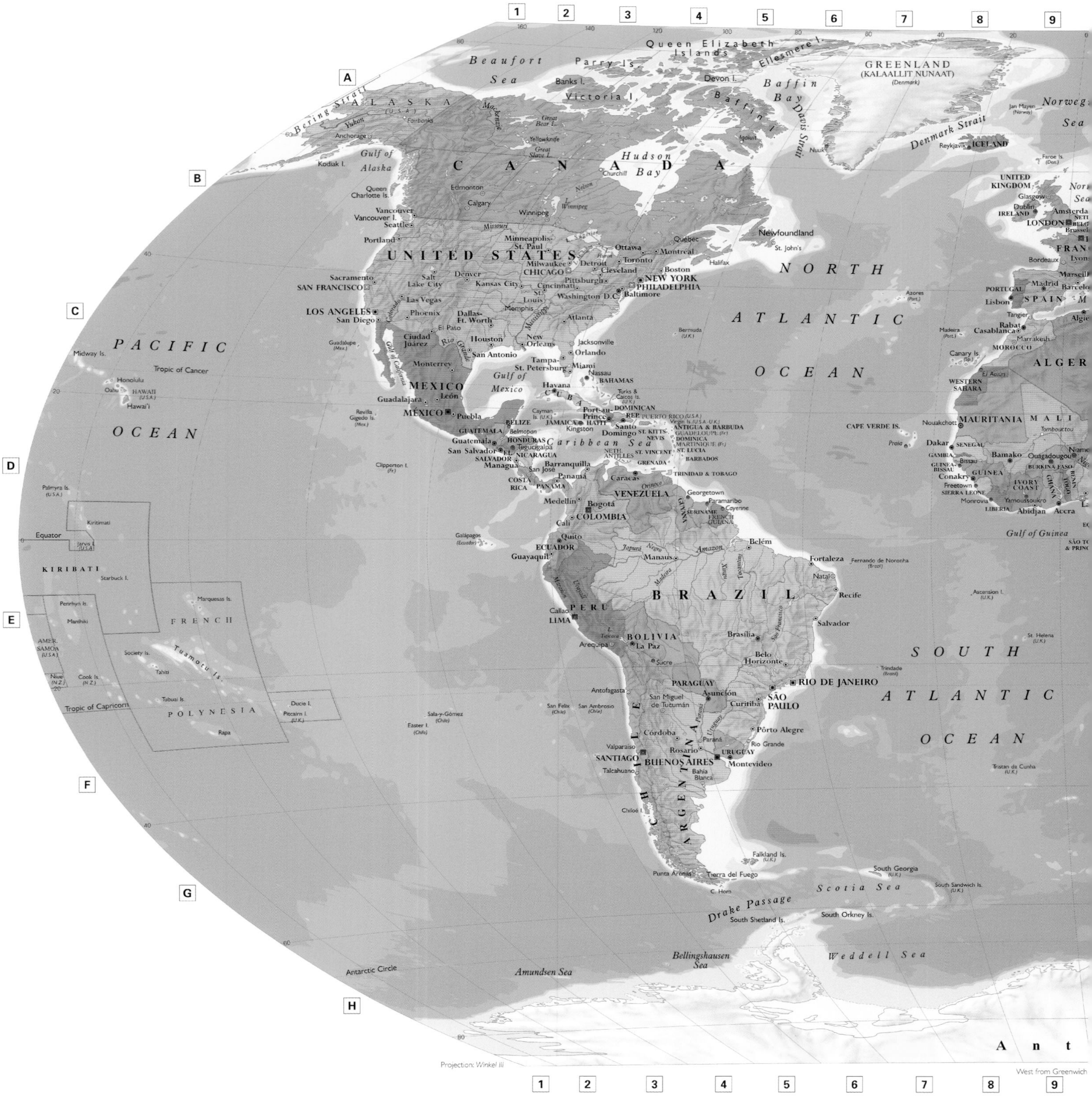

COUNTRY COMPARISONS

Country	Population in thousands 2005 estimate	Area in thous' km²	Country	Population in thousands 2005 estimate	Area in thous' km²	Country	Population in thousands 2005 estimate	Area in thous' km²	Country	Population in thousands 2005 estimate	Area in thous' km²	Country	Population in thousands 2005 estimate
China	1,306,300	9,597	Mexico	106,200	1,958	France	60,700	552	Argentina	39,500	2,780	Uganda	27,300
India	1,080,300	3,287	Philippines	87,900	300	United Kingdom	60,400	242	Poland	38,600	323	Uzbekistan	26,900
United States	295,700	9,629	Vietnam	83,500	332	Italy	58,100	301	Tanzania	36,800	945	Saudi Arabia	26,400
Indonesia	242,000	1,905	Germany	82,400	357	South Korea	48,600	99	Kenya	33,800	580	Iraq	26,100
Brazil	186,100	8,514	Egypt	77,500	1,001	Ukraine	47,000	604	Canada	32,800	9,971	Venezuela	25,400
Pakistan	162,400	796	Ethiopia	73,100	1,104	Burma (Myanmar)	47,000	677	Morocco	32,700	447	Malaysia	24,000
Bangladesh	144,300	144	Turkey	69,700	775	South Africa	44,300	1,221	Algeria	32,500	2,382	North Korea	22,900
Russia	143,400	17,075	Iran	68,000	1,648	Colombia	43,000	1,139	Afghanistan	29,900	652	Taiwan	22,900
Nigeria	128,800	924	Thailand	64,200	513	Spain	40,300	498	Peru	27,900	1,285	Romania	22,300
Japan	127,400	378	Congo, Dem. Rep.	60,800	2,345	Sudan	40,200	2,506	Nepal	27,700	147	Ghana	21,900

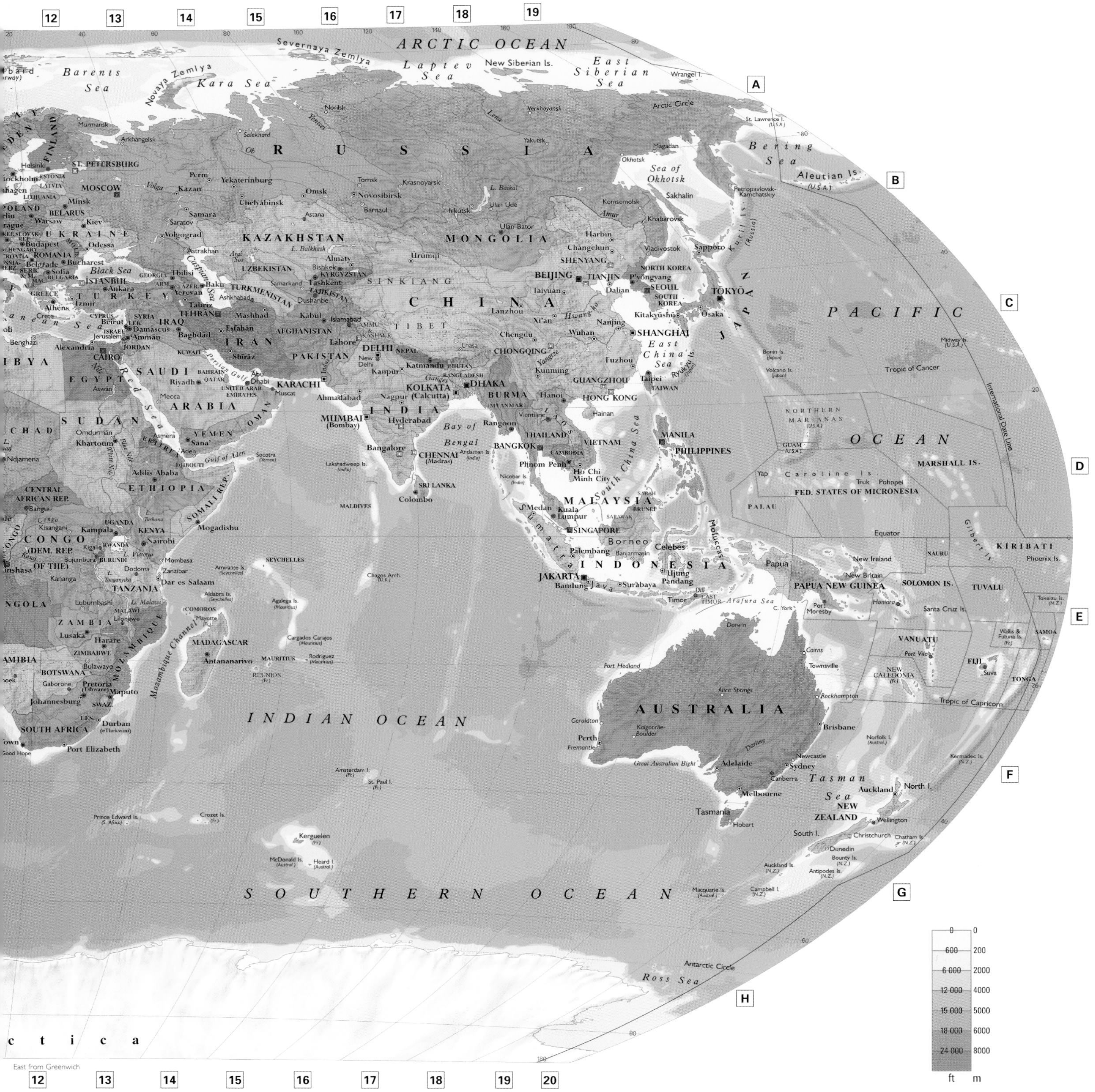

try	Population in thousands 2005 estimate	Area in thous' km²	Country	Population in thousands 2005 estimate	Area in thous' km²	Country	Population in thousands 2005 estimate	Area in thous' km²	Country	Population in thousands 2005 estimate	Area in thous' km²	Country	Population in thousands 2005 estimate	Area in thous' km²
n	20,700	528	Kazakhstan	15,200	2,725	Mali	11,400	1,240	Hungary	10,000	93	Azerbaijan	7,900	87
alia	20,100	7,741	Cambodia	13,600	181	Cuba	11,300	111	Chad	9,700	1,284	Burundi	7,800	28
nka	20,100	66	Burkina Faso	13,500	274	Zambia	11,300	753	Guinea	9,500	246	Benin	7,600	113
mbique	19,400	802	Ecuador	13,400	284	Serbia & Montenegro	10,800	102	Dominican Rep.	9,000	49	Switzerland	7,500	41
	18,400	185	Malawi	12,700	118	Greece	10,700	132	Sweden	9,000	450	Bulgaria	7,500	111
gascar	18,000	587	Niger	12,200	1,267	Portugal	10,600	89	Bolivia	8,900	1,099	Honduras	7,200	112
Coast	17,300	322	Zimbabwe	12,200	394	Belgium	10,400	31	Somalia	8,600	638	Tajikistan	7,200	143
roon	17,000	475	Guatemala	12,000	109	Belarus	10,300	208	Rwanda	8,400	26	Hong Kong (China)	6,900	1
rlands	16,400	42	Angola	11,800	1,247	Czech Republic	10,200	79	Austria	8,200	84	El Salvador	6,700	21
	16,000	757	Senegal	11,700	197	Tunisia	10,100	164	Haiti	8,100	28	Paraguay	6,300	407

COPYRIGHT PHILIP'S

6 POLAR REGIONS

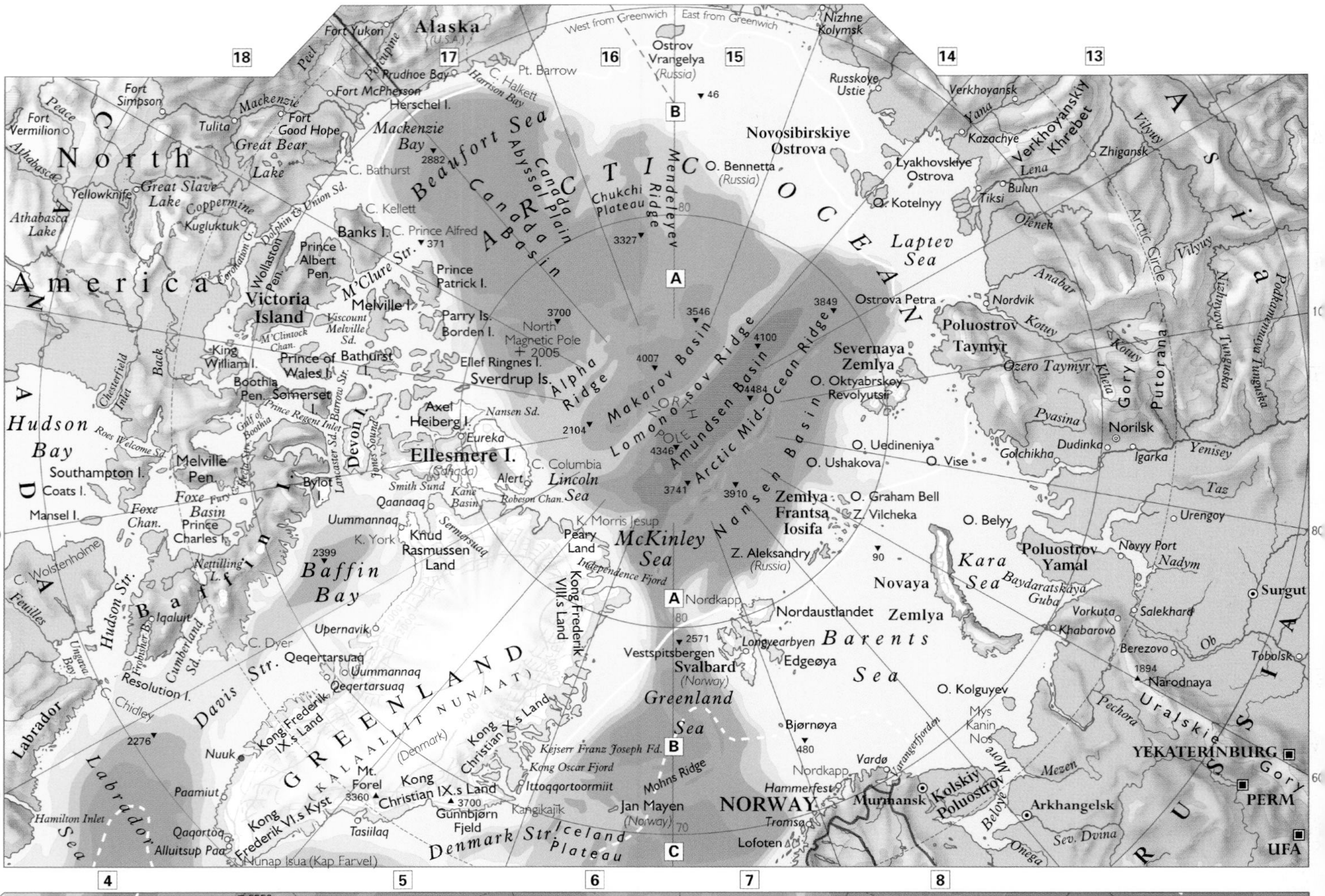

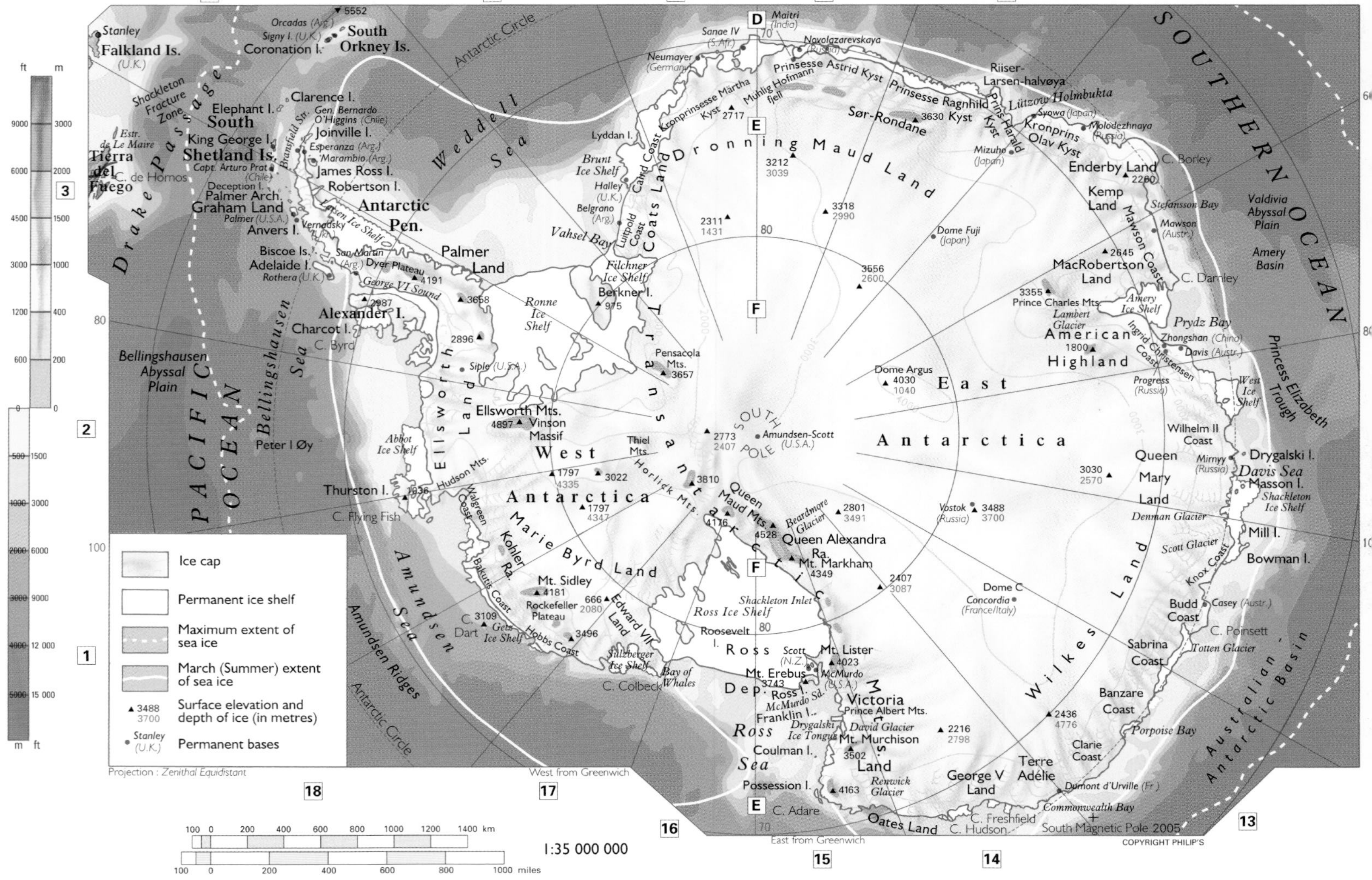

1:10 000 000
50 0 100 200 300 400 km
50 0 50 100 150 200 250 miles
West from Greenwich
20 East from Greenwich
ICELAND
on same scale
Arctic Circle
Ísafjörður
Siglufjörður
Húsavík
Húnaflói
Sauðárkrókur
Akureyri
Breiðafjörður
Seyðisfjörður
ICELAND
Hofsjökull
Langjökull
Vatnajökull
Faxaflói
Akranes
Reykjavík
Keflavík
Mýrdalsjökull
Öræfajökull
NORWEGIAN SEA
BARENTS SEA
Nordkapp
Sørøya
Hammerfest
Varangerhalvøya
Vardø
Vadsø
Varangerfjorden
Rybachiy Poluostrov
Pechenga
Zapolyarnyy
Severomorsk
Murmansk
Tromsø
Senja
Halta
Inarijärvi
Inari
Vesterålen
Lofoten
Narvik
Vestfjorden
Bodø
Kiruna
Kebnekaise
Lappland
Kolskiy Poluostrov
Olenegorsk
Monchegorsk
Kirovsk
Apatity
Kandalaksha
Alakurtti
Gremikha
Ponoy
Umba
Kuzomen
Stora Lulevatten
Gällivare
Rovaniemi
Kemijärvi
Kemijoki
Kandalakshskiy Zaliv
Beloye More
(White Sea)
Mo i Rana
Mosjøen
Vega
Haparanda
Tornio
Kemi
Boden
Luleå
Piteå
Kuusamo
Pya-ozero
Top-ozero
Arkhangelsk
Severodvinsk
Onega
Hailuoto
Oulu
Skellefteå
Storuman
Vilhelmina
Raahe
KARELIA
Belomorsk
Onezhskaya Guba
Vikna
Trondheimsfjorden
Steinkjer
Norrland
Oulujärvi
Kajaani
Segezha
Hitra
Kristiansund
Levanger
Kallsjön
Trondheim
Umeå
Vännäs
Gulf of Bothnia
Kokkola
Iisalmi
Pielinen
Kuopio
Joensuu
Molde
Ålesund
Dovrefjell
Snøhetta
Östersund
Storsjön
Örnsköldsvik
Vaasa
Seinäjoki
Medvezhyegorsk
Povenets
Kondopoga
Florø
Høyanger
Sognefjorden
Jotunheimen
Galdhøpiggen
Bräcke
Ånge
Härnösand
Sundsvall
Jyväskylä
Suoyarvi
Onezhskoye Ozero
Petrozavodsk
Pudozh
Kargopol
Vytegra
Bergen
Flåm
Lillehammer
Hudiksvall
Tampere
Savonlinna
Saimaa
Imatra
Pori
Rauma
Hardangerfjorden
Hamar
Söderhamn
Mora
Falun
Gävle
Hämeenlinna
Lahti
Kouvola
Priozersk
Olonets
Ladozhskoye Ozero
Vyborg
Lodeinoye Pole
Belozersk
Hønefoss
Oslo
Uusikaupunki
Turku
Vantaa
Helsinki
Espoo
Kotka
Kronshtadt
Sankt-Peterburg
Kolpino
Tikhvin
Cherepovets
Haugesund
Drammen
Svealand
Avesta
Sala
Uppsala
Åland
Stavanger
Skien
Larvik
Fredrikstad
Halden
Karlstad
Västerås
Gulf of Finland
Hanko
Tallinn
Narva
Kohtla-Järve
Örebro
Eskilstuna
STOCKHOLM
Hiiumaa
(Dagö)
Gdov
Luga
RUSSIA
Borovichi
Rybinskoye Vdkhr.
Kristiansand
Arendal
Mandal
Lindesnes
Vänern
Vättern
Trollhättan
Norrköping
Linköping
ESTONIA
Pärnu
Tartu
Ozero Chudskoye
Novgorod
Ozero Ilmen
Bologoye
Vyshniy Volochek
Skagerrak
Göteborg
Götaland
Gotland
Saaremaa
(Ösel)
Staraya Russa
Frederikshavn
Skagen
Borås
Jönköping
Västervik
Visby
BALTIC SEA
Gulf of Riga
Valga
Pskov
Dno
Tver
Limfjorden
Aalborg
Varberg
Oskarshamn
Ventspils
Valdayskaya Vozvyshennost
Holstebro
Jylland
Kattegat
Riga
LATVIA
Staritsa
Rzhev
Zelenograd
Randers
Halmstad
Kalmar
Jelgava
Rezekne
Toropets
MOSKVA
(Moscow)
Odintsovo
Århus
DENMARK
Helsingborg
KØBENHAVN
(Copenhagen)
Öland
Karlskrona
Liepāja
Daugava
Daugavpils
Velikiye Luki
Esbjerg
Odense
Sjælland
Malmö
Lund
Fyn
Šiauliai
Panevėžys
Bornholm
Klaipėda
LITHUANIA
Polatsk
Vitsyebsk
Vyazma
Flensburg
Gedser
Rügen
Sovetsk
Nemunas
Lyepyel
Smolensk
Kaluga
Helgoland
Kiel
Stralsund
Sassnitz
Gdynia
Kaliningrad
(Russia)
Kaunas
Vilnius
Orsha
Lübeck
Rostock
Gdańsk
Elblag
Barysaw
Roslavl
Emden
HAMBURG
Świnoujście
Koszalin
Suwałki
MINSK
Mahilyow
Bremen
Szczecin
Olsztyn
Hrodna
BELARUS
Seltso
Bryansk
Orel
Bydgoszcz
Łomża
Baranavichy
Babruysk
Osnabrück
Hannover
Potsdam
BERLIN
Toruń
Białystok
Slutsk
Zhlobin
Münster
Braunschweig
Poznań
Płock
Magdeburg
Homyel
Novhorod-Siverskyy
GERMANY
Frankfurt
WARSZAWA
(Warsaw)
Pinsk
Pripet Marshes
Mazyr
Chernihiv
Dortmund
POLAND
Brest
Konotop
Kassel
Halle
Kalisz
Łódź
Erfurt
Leipzig
Dresden
Radom
Kovel
Korosten
Nizhyn
Sumy
Legnica
Wrocław
Kielce
Lublin
Fulda
Chemnitz
Plauen
Wałbrzych
Opole
Pryluky
Okhtyrka
Frankfurt
Darmstadt
Sněžka
Częstochowa
Katowice
Lutsk
Rivne
UKRAINE
Pereyaslav-Khmelnytskyy
PRAHA
(Prague)
Hradec Králové
Chorzów
Kraków
Zhytomyr
KYYIV
(Kiev)
Heidelberg
Würzburg
Plzeň
Nürnberg
Tychy
Rzeszów
Chervonohrad
CZECH REP.
Ostrava
Tarnów
Przemyśl
Lviv
Berdychiv
Bila Tserkva
Cherkasy
Kremenchuksk Vdskh.
Poltava
Cieszyn
Žilina
Projection: Conical with two standard parallels
COPYRIGHT PHILIP'S
m ft
200 600
500 1500
1000 3000
2000 6000
4000 12 000

8 ENGLAND AND WALES

10 0 10 20 30 40 50 60 70 80 km

1:2 000 000

10 0 10 20 30 40 50 miles

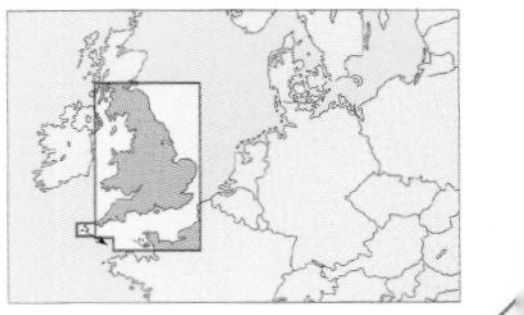

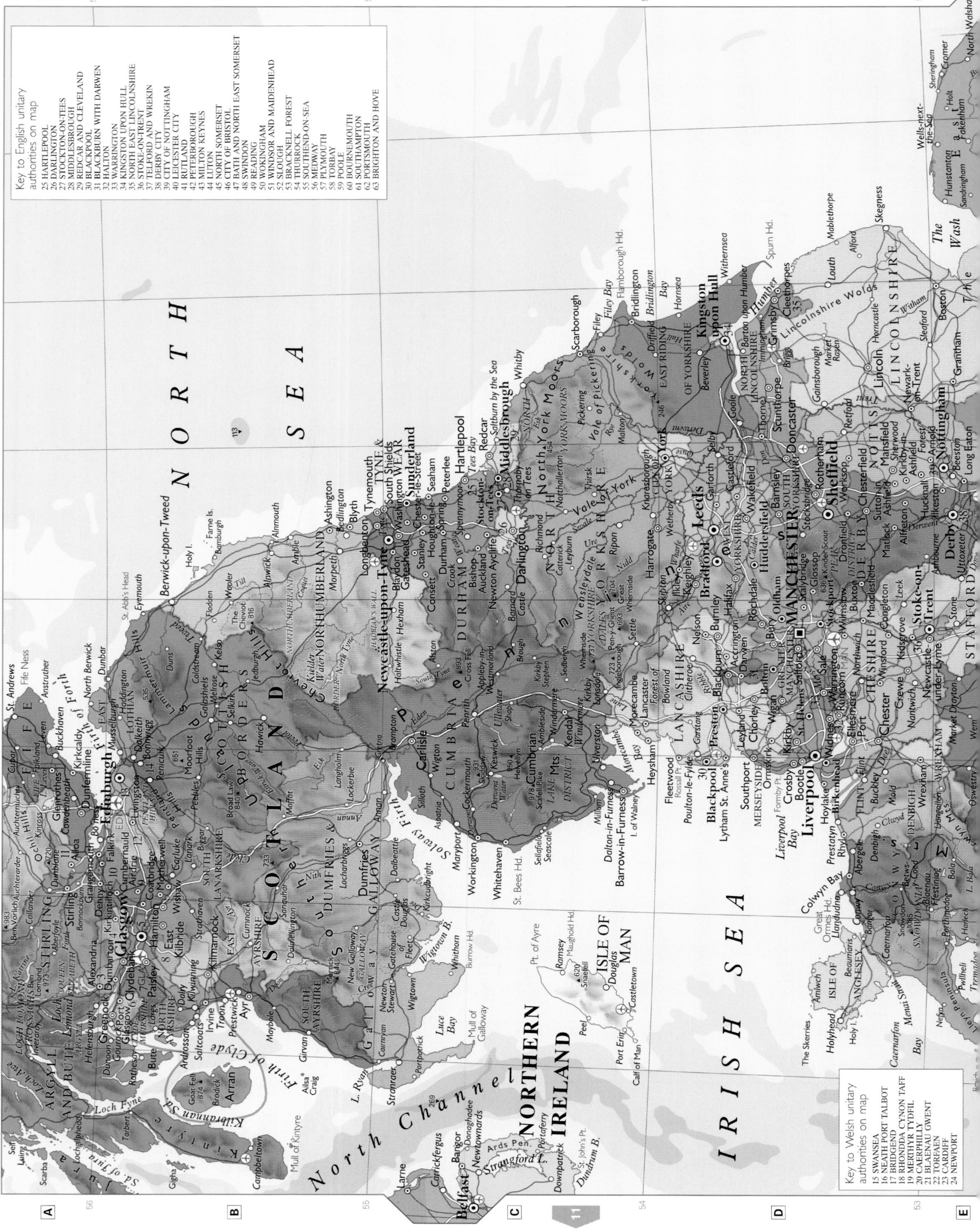

NORTH SEA
IRISH SEA
North Channel
NORTHERN IRELAND
ISLE OF MAN
Key to English unitary authorities on map
25 HARTLEPOOL
26 DARLINGTON
27 STOCKTON-ON-TEES
28 MIDDLESBROUGH
29 REDCAR AND CLEVELAND
30 BLACKPOOL
31 BLACKBURN WITH DARWEN
32 HALTON
33 WARRINGTON
34 KINGSTON UPON HULL
35 NORTH EAST LINCOLNSHIRE
36 STOKE-ON-TRENT
37 TELFORD AND WREKIN
38 DERBY CITY
39 CITY OF NOTTINGHAM
40 LEICESTER CITY
41 RUTLAND
42 PETERBOROUGH
43 MILTON KEYNES
44 LUTON
45 NORTH SOMERSET
46 CITY OF BRISTOL
47 BATH AND NORTH EAST SOMERSET
48 SWINDON
49 READING
50 WOKINGHAM
51 WINDSOR AND MAIDENHEAD
52 SLOUGH
53 BRACKNELL FOREST
54 THURROCK
55 SOUTHEND-ON-SEA
56 MEDWAY
57 PLYMOUTH
58 TORBAY
59 POOLE
60 BOURNEMOUTH
61 SOUTHAMPTON
62 PORTSMOUTH
63 BRIGHTON AND HOVE
Key to Welsh unitary authorities on map
15 SWANSEA
16 NEATH PORT TALBOT
17 BRIDGEND
18 RHONDDA CYNON TAFF
19 MERTHYR TYDFIL
20 CAERPHILLY
21 BLAENAU GWENT
22 TORFAEN
23 CARDIFF
24 NEWPORT

ENGLAND
WALES
FRANCE
ENGLISH CHANNEL
Bristol Channel
Cardigan Bay
Strait of Dover
Baie de la Seine
Baie de la Somme
Lyme Bay
Carmarthen Bay
Bridgwater Bay
CHANNEL ISLANDS (U.K.)
Alderney
Guernsey
Sark
Herm
Jersey
St. Helier
St. Peter Port
ISLE OF WIGHT
LONDON
BIRMINGHAM
Bristol
Cardiff
Southampton
Portsmouth
Plymouth
Brighton
Bournemouth
Swansea
Newport
Coventry
Wolverhampton
Peterborough
Cambridge
Ipswich
Oxford
Gloucester
Exeter
Dover
Calais
Boulogne-sur-Mer
Dieppe
Le Havre
Rouen
Caen
Cherbourg
NORMANDIE
HAUTE-NORMANDIE
Isles of Scilly
ISLES OF SCILLY on same scale
National Parks in England and Wales
Projection: Lambert's Conformal Conic
COPYRIGHT PHILIP'S
West from Greenwich
East from Greenwich
m ft
50 150
100 300
200 600

SCOTLAND

1:2 000 000

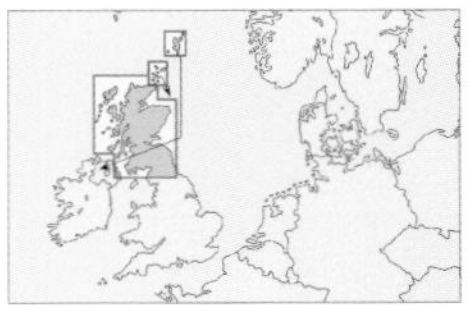

10 0 10 20 30 40 50 60 70 80 km
10 0 10 20 30 40 50 miles
Key to Scottish unitary authorities on map
1 CITY OF ABERDEEN
2 DUNDEE CITY
3 WEST DUNBARTONSHIRE
4 EAST DUNBARTONSHIRE
5 CITY OF GLASGOW
6 INVERCLYDE
7 RENFREWSHIRE
8 EAST RENFREWSHIRE
9 NORTH LANARKSHIRE
10 FALKIRK
11 CLACKMANNANSHIRE
12 WEST LOTHIAN
13 CITY OF EDINBURGH
14 MIDLOTHIAN
ORKNEY IS.
on same scale
SHETLAND IS.
on same scale
SCOTLAND
ATLANTIC OCEAN
NORTH SEA
North Channel
Pentland Firth
Moray Firth
Firth of Forth
Firth of Clyde
Firth of Lorn
Solway Firth
Sea of the Hebrides
Outer Hebrides
Inner Hebrides
The Minch
Little Minch
North West Highlands
Grampian Mountains
Cairngorm Mts.
Monadhliath Mts.
Southern Uplands
Cheviot Hills
Lammermuir Hills
Pentland Hills
Ochil Hills
Sidlaw Hills
HIGHLAND
MORAY
ABERDEENSHIRE
ANGUS
PERTH AND KINROSS
FIFE
STIRLING
ARGYLL AND BUTE
SOUTH AYRSHIRE
EAST AYRSHIRE
SOUTH LANARKSHIRE
DUMFRIES & GALLOWAY
SCOTTISH BORDERS
EAST LOTHIAN
WESTERN ISLES
ORKNEY
SHETLAND
NORTHERN IRELAND
ENGLAND
NORTHUMBERLAND
CUMBRIA
DURHAM
Sutherland
Caithness
Buchan
Lochaber
Morvern
Galloway
Lewis
Harris
North Uist
South Uist
Benbecula
Barra
Skye
Mull
Islay
Jura
Arran
Kintyre
Tiree
Coll
Rhum (Rùm)
Eigg
Stornoway
Thurso
Wick
Inverness
Aberdeen
Dundee
Perth
Stirling
Glasgow
Edinburgh
Fort William
Oban
Ayr
Dumfries
Kirkwall
Lerwick
Carlisle
Newcastle-upon-Tyne
Belfast
Ben Nevis
1342
Ben Macdhui
1309
Loch Lomond
Loch Ness
Glen More
Projection : Lambert's Conformal Conic
West from Greenwich
COPYRIGHT PHILIP'S
m ft

National Parks and Forest Parks in Scotland

1:2 000 000

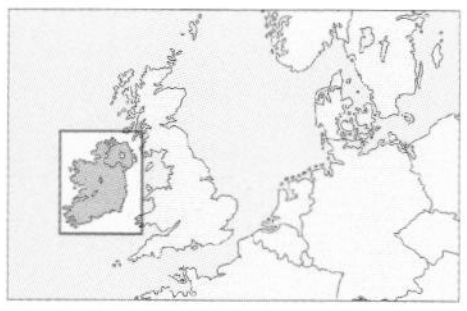

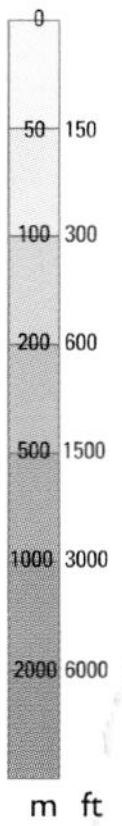

National Parks

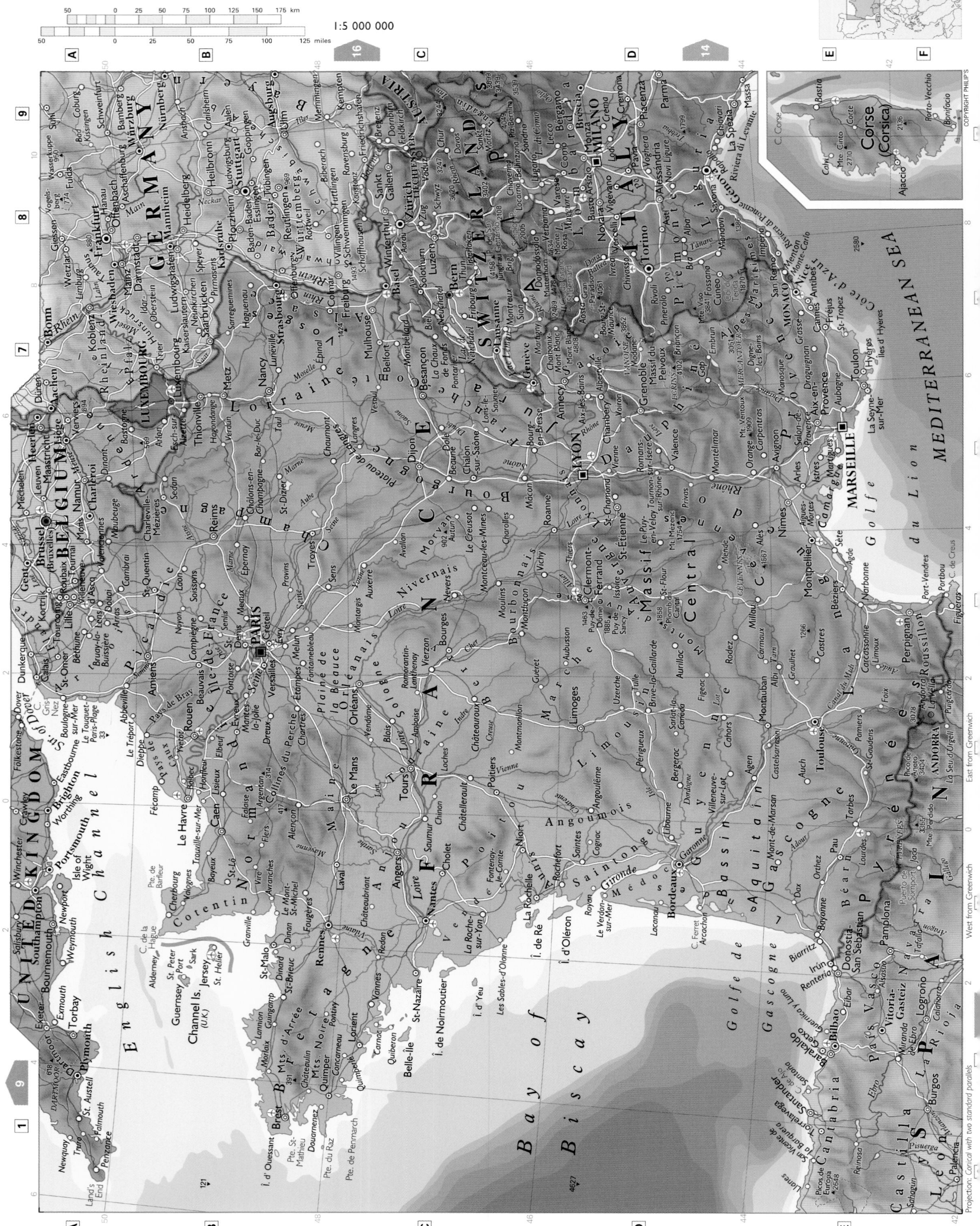

1:5 000 000
50 0 25 50 75 100 125 150 175 km
50 0 25 50 75 100 125 miles
FRANCE
GERMANY
BELGIUM
LUXEMBOURG
SWITZERLAND
ITALY
UNITED KINGDOM
MONACO
ANDORRA
SPAIN
English Channel
Bay of Biscay
Golfe de Gascogne
MEDITERRANEAN SEA
Golfe du Lion
Côte d'Azur
Channel Is. (U.K.)
PARIS
LYON
MARSEILLE
Massif Central
Bassin Aquitain
Pyrénées
Alpes
Bretagne
Normandie
Picardie
Champagne
Lorraine
Bourgogne
Provence
Corse (Corsica)
Bastia
Ajaccio
Bonifacio
Porto-Vecchio
Projection: Conical with two standard parallels
West from Greenwich
East from Greenwich
COPYRIGHT PHILIP'S
m ft
4000 12000
3000 9000
2000 6000
1000 3000
500 1500
200 600
100 300
50 150
0

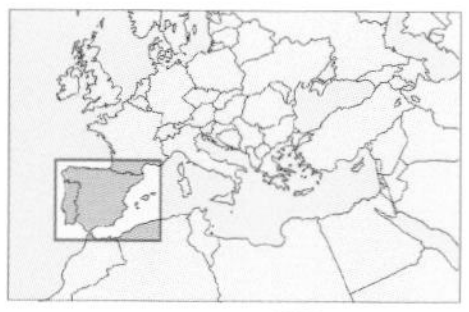

1:5 000 000

50 0 25 50 75 100 125 150 175 km

50 0 25 50 75 100 125 miles

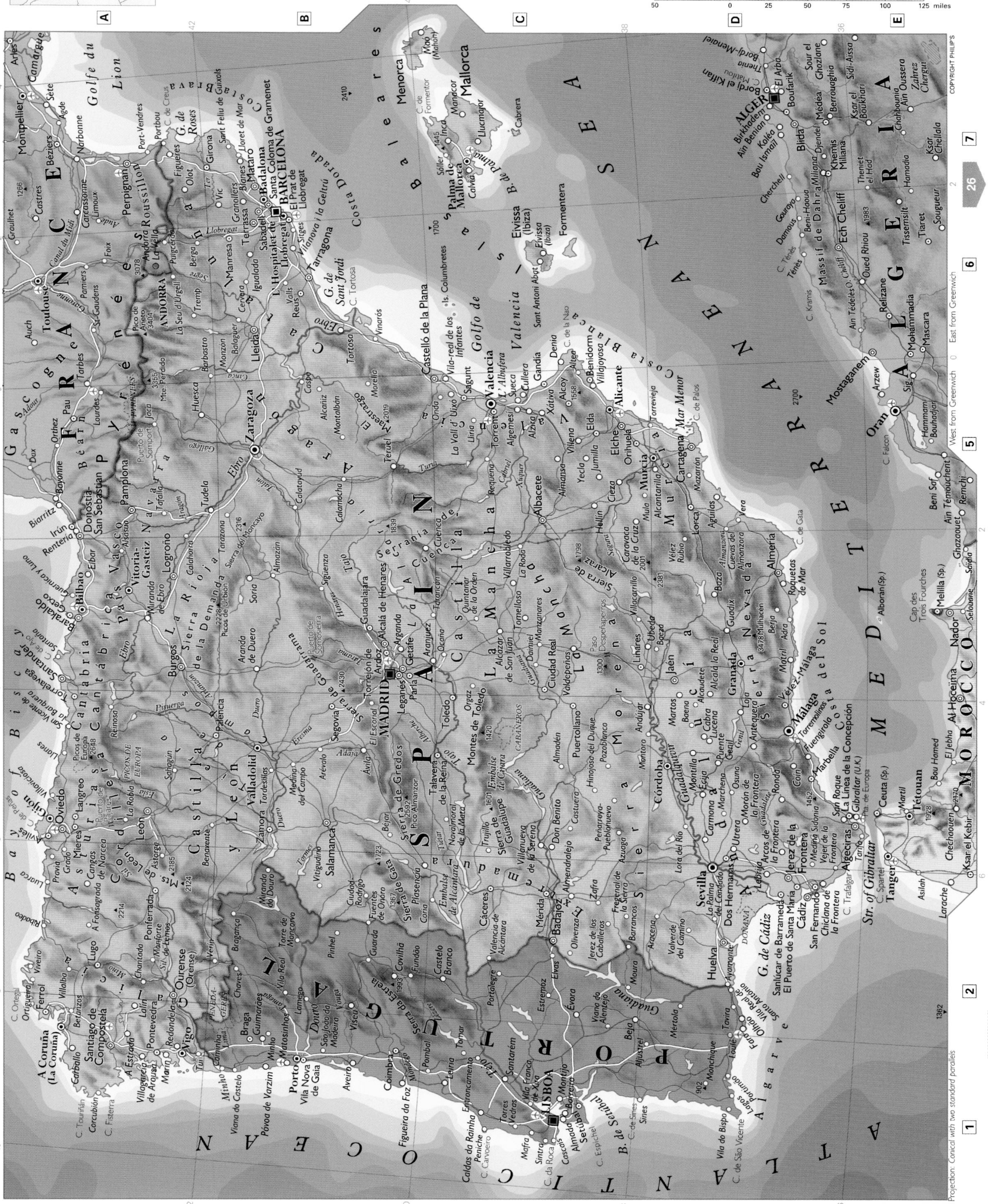

National Parks

m ft
0 — 50 150 — 100 300 — 200 600 — 500 1500 — 1000 3000 — 2000 6000 — 3000 9000 — 4000 12000

COPYRIGHT PHILIP'S

ITALY AND THE BALKAN STATES 1:5 000 000

National Parks

17
8
9
10
11
12
13
B
C
D
E
F
G
17
27
East from Greenwich
COPYRIGHT PHILIP'S
HUNGARY
ROMANIA
SERBIA &
MONTENEGRO
BULGARIA
MACEDONIA
ALBANIA
GREECE
TURKEY
UKRAINE
BLACK SEA
AEGEAN SEA
IONIAN SEA
MEDITERRANEAN SEA
Sea of Crete
Sea of Thrace
Mirtoo Sea
Marmara Denizi
Transilvania
Carpații Meridionali
Walachia
Dobrogea
Stara Planina
Rhodopi Planina
Makedonia
Thrace
Mysia
Lydia
Caria
Peloponnese
Kriti (Crete)
Cyclades
Dodecanese
Vojvodina
Kosovo
Pindos Oros
Str. of Otranto
BEOGRAD (Belgrade)
BUCUREȘTI (Bucharest)
SOFIYA
ATHINA (Athens)
Skopje
Tiranë
Sarajevo
Podgorica
Novi Sad
Timișoara
Craiova
Plovdiv
Varna
Burgas
Constanța
Thessaloniki (Salonica)
İSTANBUL
BURSA
İZMIR (Smyrna)
Edirne
Larisa
Patra
Iraklio
Rhodes
Lesbos
Limnos
Hios
Samos
Evia
Kythira
Karpathos
Kerkyra (Corfu)
Kefalonia (Cephalonia)
Zakynthos (Zante)
Lefkada
Thasos
Samothraki
Gökçeada
Bozcaada
Ionioi Nisoi
Korinthiakos Kolpos
Saronikos Kolpos
Argolikos Kolpos
Lakonikos Kolpos
Messiniakos Kolpos
Thessaloniki Kolpos
Kasandra Kolpos
Orfano Kolpos
Saros Körfezi
Edremit Körfezi
Gökova Körfezi
Canakkale Boğazi
İstanbul Boğazi (Bosporus)
Dunav (Danube)
Dunărea (Danube)
Sava
Drina
Morava
Mureș
Olt
Maritsa
Vardar
Struma
Lecce
Brindisi
Otranto
Galatina
C. d'Otranto
C. Santa Maria di Leuca

16 GERMANY AND CENTRAL EUROPE

50 0 25 50 75 100 125 150 175 km
1:5 000 000
50 0 25 50 75 100 125 miles
NORTH SEA
BALTIC SEA
POLAND
GERMANY
CZECH REP.
SLOVAK REP.
AUSTRIA
HUNGARY
SWITZERLAND
FRANCE
BELGIUM
NETHERLANDS
LUXEMBOURG
ITALY
SLOVENIA
CROATIA
RUSSIA
BERLIN
WARSZAWA (Warsaw)
PRAHA (Prague)
WIEN (Vienna)
BUDAPEST
MÜNCHEN (Munich)
HAMBURG
AMSTERDAM
Projection: Conical with two standard parallels
East from Greenwich
COPYRIGHT PHILIP'S

1:10 000 000

BLACK SEA
MEDITERRANEAN SEA
CASPIAN SEA
AEGEAN SEA
Sea of Azov
TURKEY
GREECE
BULGARIA
ROMANIA
MOLDOVA
UKRAINE
RUSSIA
GEORGIA
ARMENIA
AZERBAIJAN
IRAN
IRAQ
SYRIA
LEBANON
ISRAEL
JORDAN
SAUDI ARABIA
CYPRUS
EGYPT
LIBYA
ALBANIA
MACEDONIA
SERBIA AND MONTENEGRO
HUNGARY
ANKARA
İSTANBUL
BUCUREŞTI (Bucharest)
SOFIYA
ATHINA (Athens)
TBILISI
YEREVAN
BAKI (Baku)
BAGHDAD
DIMASHQ (Damascus)
BAYRUT (Beirut)
AMMAN
EL QÂHIRA (Cairo)
EL ISKANDARÎYA (Alexandria)
Projection: Conical with two standard parallels
East from Greenwich
COPYRIGHT PHILIP'S

km 50 0 100 200 300 400

miles 50 0 50 100 150 200 250

m ft
0
200 600
500 1500
1000 3000
2000 5000
4000 12 000

RUSSIA AND NORTHERN ASIA

1:20 000 000

100 0 100 200 300 400 500 600 700 800 km
100 0 100 200 300 400 500 miles
D
C
B
RUSSIA
1 Adygea
2 Karachey-Cherkessia
3 Kabardino-Balkaria
4 North Ossetia
5 Ingushetia
6 Chechenia
7 Dagestan
8 Mordvinia
9 Chuvashia
10 Mari El
11 Tatarstan
12 Udmurtia
13 Khakassia
AZERBAIJAN
14 Naxçıvan
GEORGIA
15 Ajaria
16 Abkhazia
UKRAINE
17 Crimea
E
F
G
m ft
200 600
2000 6000
4000 12 000
NORWAY
SWEDEN
FINLAND
ESTONIA
LATVIA
LITHUANIA
BELARUS
POLAND
UKRAINE
MOLDOVA
ROMANIA
TURKEY
GEORGIA
ARMENIA
AZERBAIJAN
IRAQ
IRAN
TURKMENISTAN
UZBEKISTAN
KAZAKHSTAN
KYRGYZSTAN
TAJIKISTAN
AFGHANISTAN
RUSSIA
North Sea
Baltic Sea
Gulf of Bothnia
Barents Sea
Kara Sea
Black Sea
Caspian Sea
Aral Sea
MOSKVA
SANKT-PETERBURG
NIZHNIY NOVGOROD
KAZAN
SAMARA
YEKATERINBURG
CHELYABINSK
OMSK
NOVOSIBIRSK
VOLGOGRAD
ROSTOV
KYYIV
MINSK
ASTANA
ALMATY
TOSHKENT
BISHKEK
TEHRĀN
BAKI (Baku)
TBILISI
YEREVAN
Projection: Conical Orthomorphic with two standard parallels
East from Greenwich
6
7
8
9

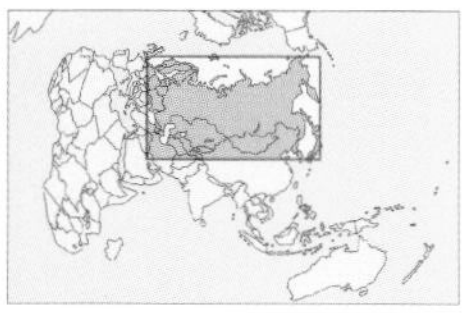

A
B
C
D
E
F
9
10
11
12
13
14
15
16
17
18
19
20
21
OCEAN
Laptev Sea
East Siberian Sea
Chukchi Sea
Bering Sea
Sea of Okhotsk
Sea of Japan
(East Sea)
Severnaya Zemlya
Ostrov Shmidta
Ostrov Komsomolets
Ostrov Oktyabrskoy Revolyutsii
Ostrov Pioner
Ostrov Bolshevik
Mys Arkticheskiy
Mys Chelyuskin
Proliv Vilkitskogo
Poluostrov Taymyr
Gory Byrranga
Oz. Taymyr
Novosibirskiye Ostrova
Ostrov Kotelnyy
Ostrov Belkovskiy
Ostrov Stolbovoy
Lyakhovskiye Ostrova
Proliv Dmitriya Lapteva
Ostrov Faddeyevskiy
Ostrov Novaya Sibir
Ostrova Delonga
Ostrov Bennetta
Ostrov Genrietty
Ostrov Zhannetty
Ostrov Zhokhova
Ostrov Vrangelya
Ostrova Medvezhi
Ostrov Ayon
Mys Dezhneva (East C.)
St. Lawrence I. (U.S.A.)
Anadyrskiy Zaliv
Chukotskoye Nagorye
Koryakskoye Nagorye
Kolymskoye Nagorye
Khrebet Cherskogo
Verkhoyanskiy Khrebet
DALNEVOSTOCHNY
SAKHA
RUSSIA
Poluostrov Kamchatka
Sredinnyy Khrebet
Komandorskiye Ostrova
Petropavlovsk-Kamchatskiy
Kurilskiye Ostrova
Sakhalin
Tatarskiy Proliv
La Perouse Str.
Stanovoy Khrebet
Yablonovyy Khrebet
Khrebet Dzhugdzur
Khrebet Sikhote Alin
Sayan
Vostochnyy Sayan
Hentiyn Nuruu
Hangayn Nuruu
MONGOLIA
Gobi
CHINA
Da Hinggan Ling
Dongbei (Manchuria)
NORTH KOREA
SOUTH KOREA
JAPAN
Hokkaido
Honshū
Arctic Circle
Tiksi
Yakutsk
Magadan
Okhotsk
Anadyr
Pevek
Cherskiy
Bratsk
Irkutsk
Krasnoyarsk
Ulan Ude
Chita
Khabarovsk
Komsomolsk
Vladivostok
Yuzhno-Sakhalinsk
Blagoveshchensk
Ulaanbaatar
HARBIN
CHANGCHUN
SHENYANG
BEIJING
PYONGYANG
SEOUL
BUSAN
SAPPORO
KYOTO
OSAKA
KOBE
COPYRIGHT PHILIP'S

CHINA AND THE FAR EAST

1:15 000 000

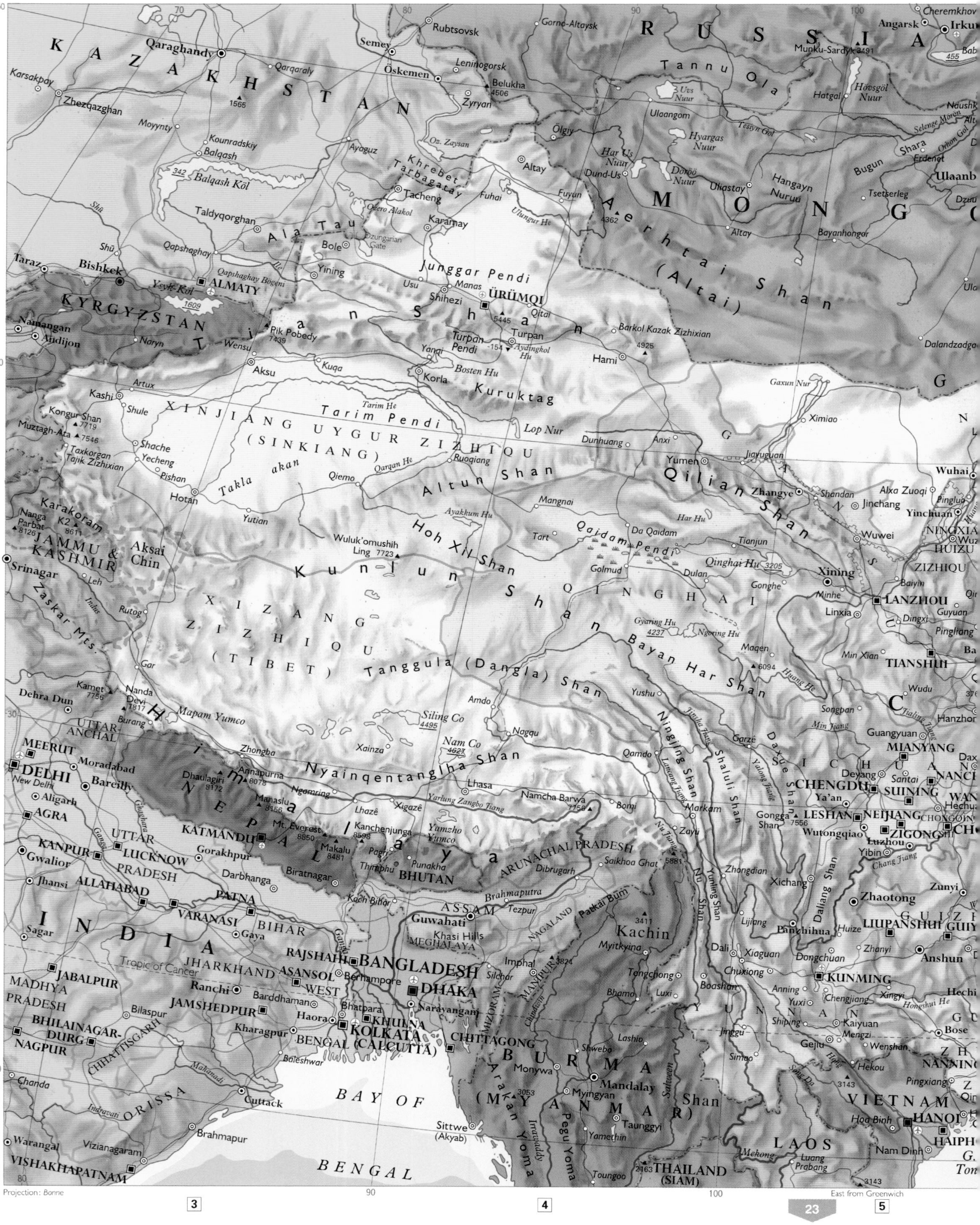

0 200 600 2000 6000 4000 12 000 6000 18 000
m ft

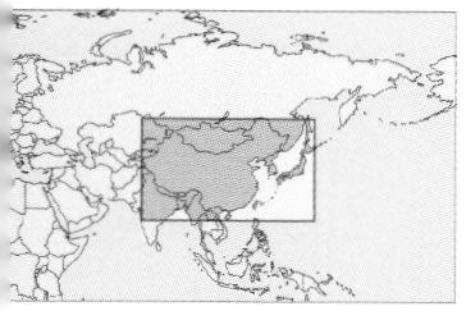

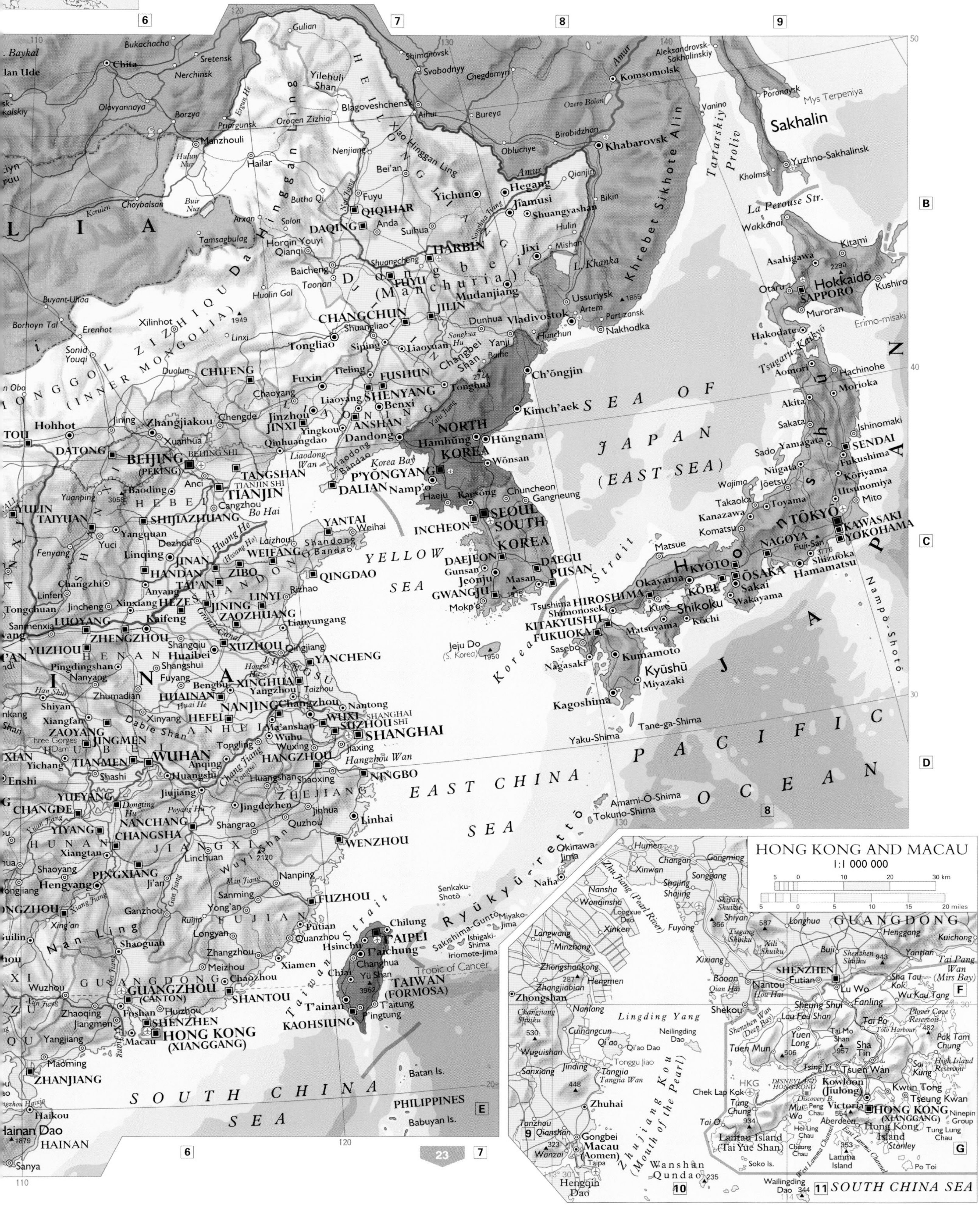
6
7
8
9
B
C
D
E
F
G
Baykal
Ulan Ude
Chita
Bukachacha
Sretensk
Nerchinsk
Olovyannaya
Borzya
Priargunsk
Manzhouli
Hulun Nur
Hailar
Buir Nur
Choybalsan
Kerulen
Arxan
Solon
Tamsagbulag
Gulian
Yilehuli Shan
Oroqen Zizhiqi
Blagoveshchensk
Aihui
Shimanovsk
Svobodnyy
Chegdomyn
Bureya
Amur
Komsomolsk
Aleksandrovsk-Sakhalinskiy
Ozero Bolon
Birobidzhan
Obluchye
Khabarovsk
Vanino
Tartarskiy Proliv
Sakhalin
Poronaysk
Mys Terpeniya
Yuzhno-Sakhalinsk
Kholmsk
La Perouse Str.
Wakkanai
Kitami
Asahigawa
Hokkaidō
Otaru
SAPPORO
Kushiro
Muroran
Erimo-misaki
Hakodate
Tsugaru-Kaikyō
Aomori
Hachinohe
Morioka
Akita
Sakata
Ishinomaki
SENDAI
Fukushima
Yamagata
Sado
Niigata
Kōriyama
Utsunomiya
Jōetsu
Wajima
Toyama
Mito
Takaoka
Kanazawa
TŌKYŌ
KAWASAKI
YOKOHAMA
Komatsu
Honshu
NAGOYA
Fuji-San
3776
Shizuoka
Hamamatsu
KYŌTO
ŌSAKA
KOBE
Sakai
Wakayama
Okayama
HIROSHIMA
Matsue
Shikoku
Kōchi
Kure
Shimonoseki
Tsushima
KITAKYUSHU
FUKUOKA
Matsuyama
Sasebo
Nagasaki
Kumamoto
Kyūshū
Miyazaki
Kagoshima
Yaku-Shima
Tane-ga-Shima
Nampō-Shotō
JAPAN
Amami-Ō-Shima
Tokuno-Shima
Okinawa-Jima
Naha
Ryūkyū-rettō
Senkaku-Shotō
Sakishima-Guntō
Miyako-Jima
Ishigaki-Shima
Iriomote-Jima
SEA OF JAPAN (EAST SEA)
PACIFIC OCEAN
Khrebet Sikhote Alin
Qianjin
Bikin
Hulin
Mishan
L. Khanka
Ussuriysk
1855
Partizansk
Artem
Vladivostok
Nakhodka
Hunchun
Yichun
Hegang
Jiamusi
Shuangyashan
Jixi
Heilong Jiang
Xiao Hinggan Ling
Da Hinggan Ling
Nenjiang
Bei'an
Fuyu
QIQIHAR
Butha Qi
DAQING
Anda
Suihua
Horqin Youyi Qianqi
HARBIN
Shuangcheng
Heilongjiang
Baicheng
Taonan
Songhua Jiang
FUYU
Jilin
Manchuria
Mudanjiang
JILIN
CHANGCHUN
Dunhua
Shuangliao
Siping
Liaoyuan
Songhua Hu
Tongliao
Changbei Shan
Yanji
Baihe
2744
Ch'ŏngjin
Kimch'aek
Hŭngnam
Hamhŭng
NORTH KOREA
Wŏnsan
P'YŎNGYANG
Namp'o
Haeju
Kaesŏng
Chuncheon
Gangneung
SEOUL
SOUTH KOREA
INCHEON
DAEJEON
DAEGU
PUSAN
Gunsan
Jeonju
Masan
GWANGJU
Mokp'o
Jeju Do (S. Korea)
1950
Korea Strait
Buyant-Uhaa
Huolin Gol
Xilinhot
1949
Borhoyn Tal
Erenhot
Linxi
Sonid Youqi
NEI MONGGOL ZIZHIQU (INNER MONGOLIA)
Duolun
CHIFENG
Fuxin
Tieling
FUSHUN
Tonghua
SHENYANG
Benxi
Liaoning
Chaoyang
Liaoyang
ANSHAN
Jinzhou
JINXI
Yingkou
Dandong
Qinhuangdao
Liaodong Wan
Liaodong Bandao
Korea Bay
DALIAN
Hohhot
Jining
Zhangjiakou
Chengde
Xuanhua
DATONG
BEIJING (PEKING)
BEIJING SHI
TANGSHAN
TIANJIN
TIANJIN SHI
Anci
Baoding
Yuanping
3058
HEBEI
Cangzhou
Bo Hai
YULIN
TAIYUAN
SHIJIAZHUANG
Yangquan
Yuci
Dezhou
Huang He
Laizhou
YANTAI
Weihai
Shandong Bandao
Fenyang
Linqing
JINAN
WEIFANG
ZIBO
QINGDAO
HANDAN
TAI'AN
Changzhi
Anyang
Linfen
SHANDONG
LINYI
Rizhao
Xinxiang
HEZE
JINING
ZAOZHUANG
Jincheng
Tongchuan
LUOYANG
Sanmenxia
Kaifeng
Grand Canal
Lianyungang
ZHENGZHOU
Shangqiu
XUZHOU
YUZHOU
HENAN
Huaibei
Qingjiang
Shangshui
YANCHENG
Pingdingshan
Nanyang
Fuyang
Bengbu
XINGHUA
JIANGSU
Yangzhou
Taizhou
Han Shui
Zhumadian
HUAINAN
Shiyan
Huai He
HEFEI
NANJING
Changzhou
Nantong
Xiangfan
Xinyang
WUXI
SUZHOU
SHANGHAI
SHANGHAI SHI
Dabie Shan
ANHUI
Ma'anshan
Wuhu
ZAOYANG
JINGMEN
Three Gorges Dam
HUBEI
Tongling
Wuxing
Jiaxing
Hangzhou Wan
HANGZHOU
XIAN
Yichang
TIANMEN
WUHAN
Anqing
Chang Jiang (Yangtze)
Enshi
Shashi
Huangshi
Huangshan
Shaoxing
NINGBO
ZHEJIANG
YUEYANG
Dongting Hu
Poyang Hu
Jiujiang
Jingdezhen
Jinhua
Linhai
CHANGDE
NANCHANG
Shangrao
Quzhou
YIYANG
CHANGSHA
WENZHOU
HUNAN
JIANGXI
Xiangtan
Linchuan
2120
Wuyi Shan
Shaoyang
PINGXIANG
Hengyang
Ji'an
Nanping
Min Jiang
Sanming
FUZHOU
Yong'an
Ganzhou
FUJIAN
Putian
Quanzhou
Xing'an
Nan Ling
Ruijin
Longyan
Shaoguan
Zhangzhou
Xiamen
Meizhou
Chaozhou
SHANTOU
GUANGDONG
GUANGZHOU (CANTON)
Wuzhou
Huizhou
Zhaoqing
Jiangmen
Foshan
SHENZHEN
HONG KONG (XIANGGANG)
Macau
Yangjiang
Maoming
ZHANJIANG
Haikou
Hainan Dao
1879
HAINAN
Sanya
Taiwan Strait
Chilung
T'AIPEI
Hsinchu
T'aichung
Changhua
Chiai
Yü Shan
3952
TAIWAN (FORMOSA)
Tropic of Cancer
T'ainan
T'aitung
KAOHSIUNG
P'ingtung
Batan Is.
PHILIPPINES
Babuyan Is.
YELLOW SEA
EAST CHINA SEA
SOUTH CHINA SEA
23
HONG KONG AND MACAU
1:1 000 000
Humen
Xinwan
Changan
Gongming
Songgang
Zhu Jiang (Pearl River)
Nansha
Shajing
Wanqinsha
Longxue Dao
Xinken
Fuyong
Shiyan Shuiku
Shiyan
366
587
Longhua
GUANGDONG
Henggang
Kuichong
Tiegang Shuiku
Xili Shuiku
Langwang
Minzhong
Xixiang
Buji
Shenzhen Shuiku
943
Yantian
Tai Pang Wan (Mirs Bay)
Zhongshankong
287
Hengmen
Zhongshan
Baoan
Qian Hai
SHENZHEN
Futian
Nantou
Hou Hai
Lu Wo
Sha Tau Kok
Wu Kau Tang
Lingding Yang
Shekou
Sheung Shui
Fanling
Plover Cove Reservoir
Changjiang Shuiku
Nanlang
Shenzhen Wan (Deep Bay)
Lau Fau Shan
Tai Po
Tolo Harbour
Tai Mo Shan
957
Pak Tam Chung
482
530
Cuihangcun
Qi'ao
Qi'ao Dao
Neilingding Dao
Yuen Long
Tuen Mun
506
Sha Tin
Wuguishan
Tonggu Jiao
Tsing Yi
Tsuen Wan
Sai Kung
High Island Reservoir
Sanxiang
Jinding
Tangjia
Tangjia Wan
HKG
Kowloon (Jiulong)
Kwun Tong
448
Zhujiang Kou (Mouth of the Pearl)
Chek Lap Kok
Tseung Kwan
Zhuhai
Tung Chung
934
Mui Wo
Peng Chau
Victoria
HONG KONG (XIANGGANG)
Ninepin Group
Tanzhou
Qianshan
Gongbei
Macau (Aomen)
Taipa
Tai O
Lantau Island (Tai Yue Shan)
Hei Ling Chau
Aberdeen
Hong Kong Island
Tung Lung Chau
Cheung Chau
Lamma Island
353
Stanley
West Lamma Channel
East Lamma Channel
323
Wanzai
Hengqin Dao
Soko Is.
Po Toi
Wanshan Qundao
235
Wailingding Dao
344
10
11
SOUTH CHINA SEA

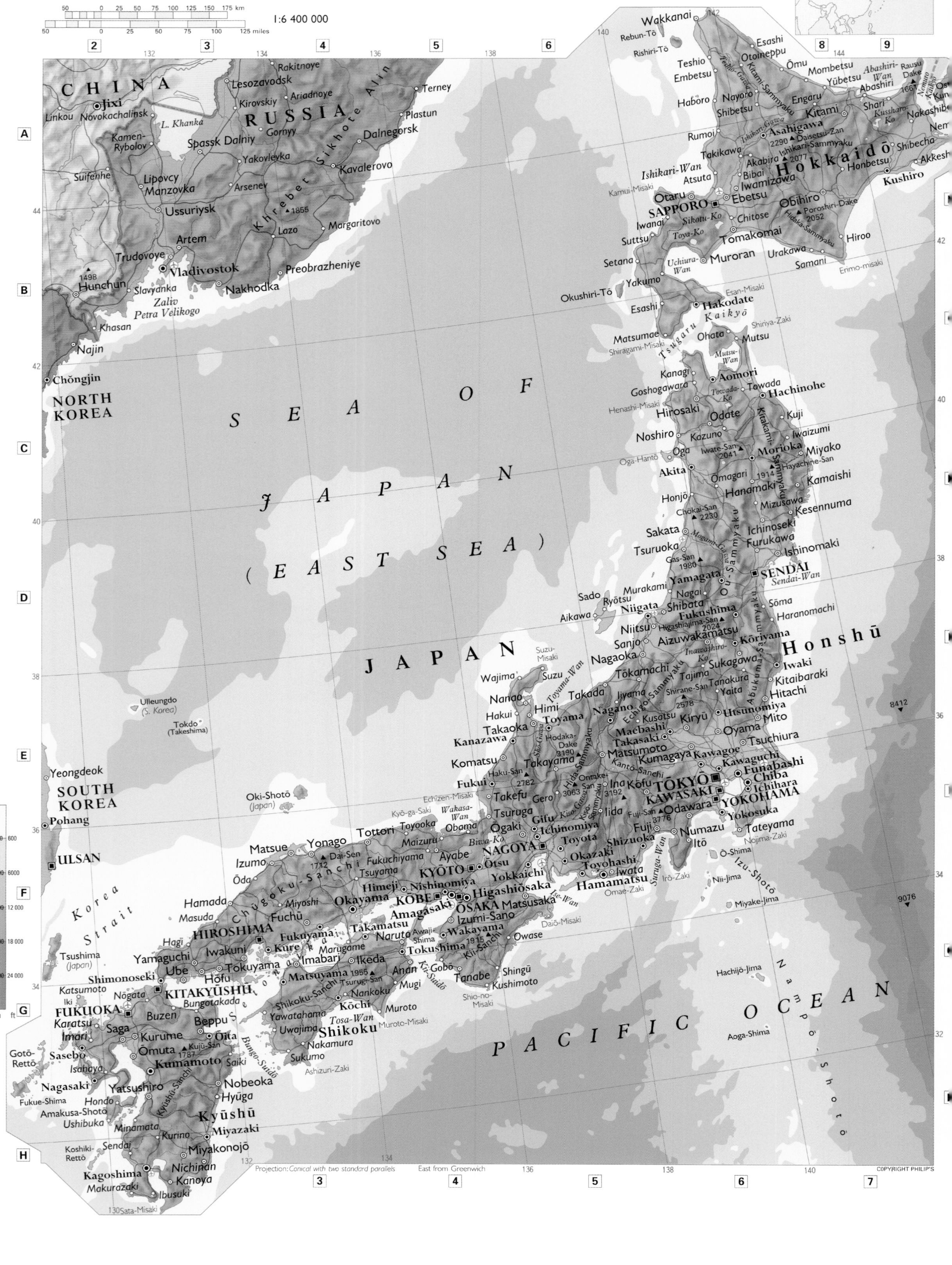
1:6 400 000
CHINA
RUSSIA
NORTH KOREA
SOUTH KOREA
JAPAN
SEA OF JAPAN (EAST SEA)
PACIFIC OCEAN
Hokkaidō
Honshū
Shikoku
Kyūshū
Wakkanai
Rebun-Tō
Rishiri-Tō
Esashi
Otoineppu
Teshio
Embetsu
Ōmu
Mombetsu
Yūbetsu
Abashiri
Rausu Dake
Haboro
Nayoro
Shibetsu
Engaru
Kitami
Shari
Nakashibetsu
Rumoi
Asahigawa
Daisetsu-Zan
Takikawa
Akabira
Bibai
Shibecha
Honbetsu
Akkeshi
Ishikari-Wan
Atsuta
Iwamizawa
Kushiro
Otaru
SAPPORO
Ebetsu
Obihiro
Iwanai
Shikotsu-Ko
Chitose
Toya-Ko
Suttsu
Tomakomai
Hiroo
Setana
Uchiura-Wan
Muroran
Urakawa
Samani
Erimo-misaki
Okushiri-Tō
Yakumo
Esashi
Hakodate
Esan-Misaki
Tsugaru Kaikyō
Matsumae
Shirakami-Misaki
Ohata
Mutsu
Shiriya-Zaki
Mutsu-Wan
Aomori
Kanagi
Goshogawara
Towada
Towada-Ko
Hachinohe
Henashi-Misaki
Hirosaki
Odate
Kuji
Noshiro
Kazuno
Iwaizumi
Oga-Hantō
Oga
Iwate-San
Morioka
Miyako
Hayachine-San
Akita
Omagari
Kamaishi
Honjō
Hanamaki
Mizusawa
Chōkai-San
Kesennuma
Sakata
Ichinoseki
Furukawa
Tsuruoka
Ishinomaki
Gas-San
Yamagata
SENDAI
Sendai-Wan
Murakami
Nagai
Sado
Ryōtsu
Aikawa
Niigata
Shibata
Fukushima
Sōma
Haranomachi
Niitsu
Higashiazuma-San
Aizuwakamatsu
Sanjo
Kōriyama
Nagaoka
Inawashiro-Ko
Suzu-Misaki
Tōkamachi
Sukagawa
Iwaki
Wajima
Suzu
Toyama-Wan
Tajima
Tanakura
Kitaibaraki
Nanao
Himi
Takada
Iiyama
Shirane-San
Yaita
Hitachi
Hakui
Toyama
Nagano
Utsunomiya
Mito
Takaoka
Kusatsu
Kiryū
Kanazawa
Hodaka-Dake
Maebashi
Oyama
Takasaki
Tsuchiura
Komatsu
Matsumoto
Kumagaya
Kawagoe
Haku-San
Takayama
Kawaguchi
Funabashi
Fukui
Ontake-San
Ina
Kōfu
TŌKYŌ
Chiba
Takefu
Gero
Ichihara
KAWASAKI
YOKOHAMA
Echizen-Misaki
Tsuruga
Iida
Fuji-San
Odawara
Kyō-ga-Saki
Wakasa-Wan
Yokosuka
Toyooka
Obama
Ōgaki
Ichinomiya
Fuji
Numazu
Tateyama
Tottori
Maizuru
Biwa-Ko
Gifu
Shizuoka
Itō
Nojima-Zaki
Matsue
Yonago
Dai-Sen
NAGOYA
Toyota
Suruga-Wan
Ō-Shima
Izumo
Fukuchiyama
Ayabe
Ōtsu
Okazaki
Izu-Shotō
Ōda
Tsuyama
KYŌTO
Yokkaichi
Toyohashi
Iwata
Irō-Zaki
Nii-Jima
Chūgoku-Sanchi
Himeji
Nishinomiya
Hamamatsu
Omae-Zaki
Hamada
KŌBE
Higashiōsaka
Ise-Wan
Miyake-Jima
Masuda
Miyoshi
Okayama
Amagasaki
ŌSAKA
Matsusaka
Fuchū
Izumi-Sano
Daiō-Misaki
HIROSHIMA
Fukuyama
Takamatsu
Naruto
Wakayama
Hagi
Iwakuni
Kure
Marugame
Awaji-Shima
Tokushima
Owase
Yamaguchi
Imabari
Kii-Sanchi
Tokuyama
Ikeda
Shingū
Ube
Matsuyama
Anan
Gobō
Hachijō-Jima
Shimonoseki
Hōfu
Tsurugi-San
Tanabe
Kushimoto
Katsumoto
Nōgata
KITAKYŪSHŪ
Shikoku-Sanchi
Nankoku
Mugi
Kii-Suidō
Shio-no-Misaki
Iki
Bungotakada
Kōchi
FUKUOKA
Buzen
Yawatahama
Tosa-Wan
Muroto
Muroto-Misaki
Karatsu
Saga
Beppu
Uwajima
Imari
Kurume
Ōita
Nakamura
Aoga-Shima
Gotō-Rettō
Sasebo
Ōmuta
Kuju-San
Bungo-Suidō
Sukumo
Isahaya
Kumamoto
Saiki
Ashizuri-Zaki
Nagasaki
Yatsushiro
Nobeoka
Fukue-Shima
Hondo
Hyūga
Amakusa-Shotō
Kyushu-Sanchi
Ushibuka
Minamata
Kurino
Miyazaki
Koshiki-Rettō
Sendai
Miyakonojō
Kagoshima
Nichinan
Makurazaki
Kanoya
Ibusuki
Sata-Misaki
Nampō-shotō
Korea Strait
Tsushima (Japan)
Oki-Shotō (Japan)
Ulleungdo (S. Korea)
Tokdo (Takeshima)
Yeongdeok
Pohang
ULSAN
Chŏngjin
Najin
Khasan
Zaliv Petra Velikogo
Hunchun
Slavyanka
Vladivostok
Nakhodka
Preobrazheniye
Trudovoye
Artem
Lazo
Margaritovo
Ussuriysk
Khrebet Sikhote Alin
Lipovcy
Manzovka
Arsenev
Suifenhe
Kamen-Rybolov
Spassk Dalniy
Yakovlevka
Kavalerovo
Dalnegorsk
L. Khanka
Gornyy
Plastun
Linkou
Novokachalinsk
Jixi
Kirovskiy
Ariadnoye
Terney
Lesozavodsk
Rakitnoye
Projection: Conical with two standard parallels
East from Greenwich
COPYRIGHT PHILIP'S

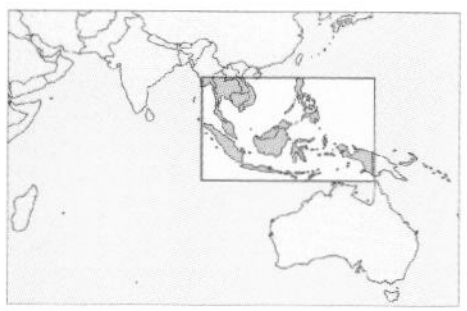

1:20 000 000

100 0 100 200 300 400 500 600 700 800 km

100 0 100 200 300 400 500 miles

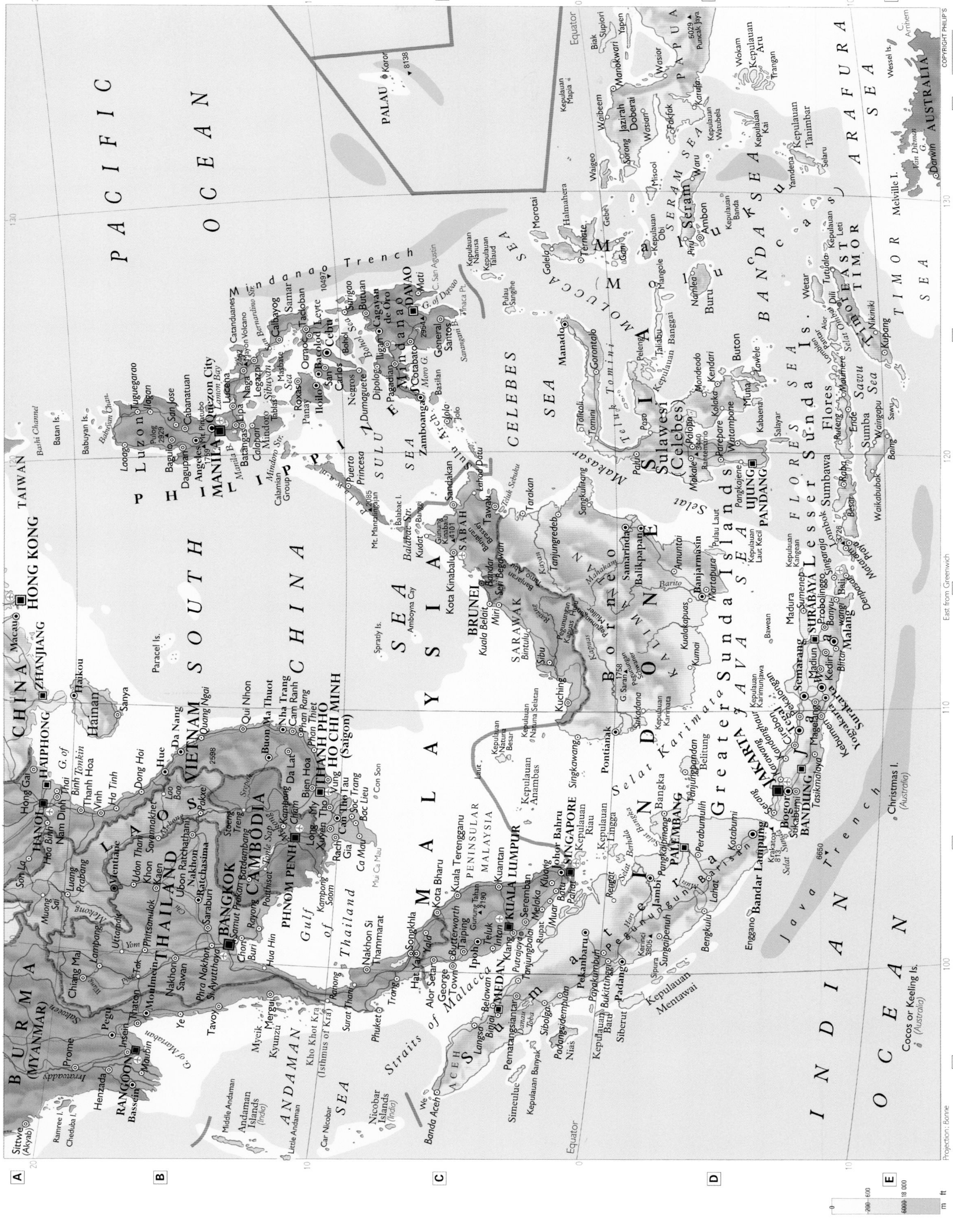
PACIFIC
OCEAN
SOUTH
CHINA
SEA
INDIAN
OCEAN
CELEBES
SEA
SULU
SEA
JAVA
SEA
BANDA
SEA
FLORES
SEA
TIMOR
SEA
ARAFURA
SEA
ANDAMAN
SEA
MOLUCCA
SEA
SERAM
SEA
PHILIPPINES
MALAYSIA
INDONESIA
THAILAND
CAMBODIA
LAOS
VIETNAM
BURMA (MYANMAR)
CHINA
TAIWAN
HONG KONG
BRUNEI
SINGAPORE
AUSTRALIA
PALAU
EAST TIMOR
MANILA
BANGKOK
HANOI
PHNOM PENH
KUALA LUMPUR
JAKARTA
RANGOON
THANH PHO HO CHI MINH (Saigon)
Borneo
Sumatera
Sulawesi (Celebes)
Jawa
Luzon
Mindanao
Java Trench
Mindanao Trench
Equator
Projection: Bonne
COPYRIGHT PHILIP'S
East from Greenwich

30

0 200 600 6000 m

0 600 18 000 ft

1:17 500 000

Projection: Alber's Equal Area with two standard Parallels

East from Greenwich

17 18 27 28

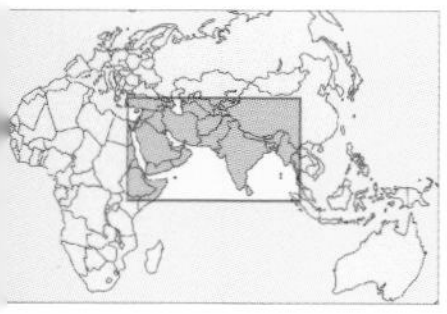

6 7 8 20 9

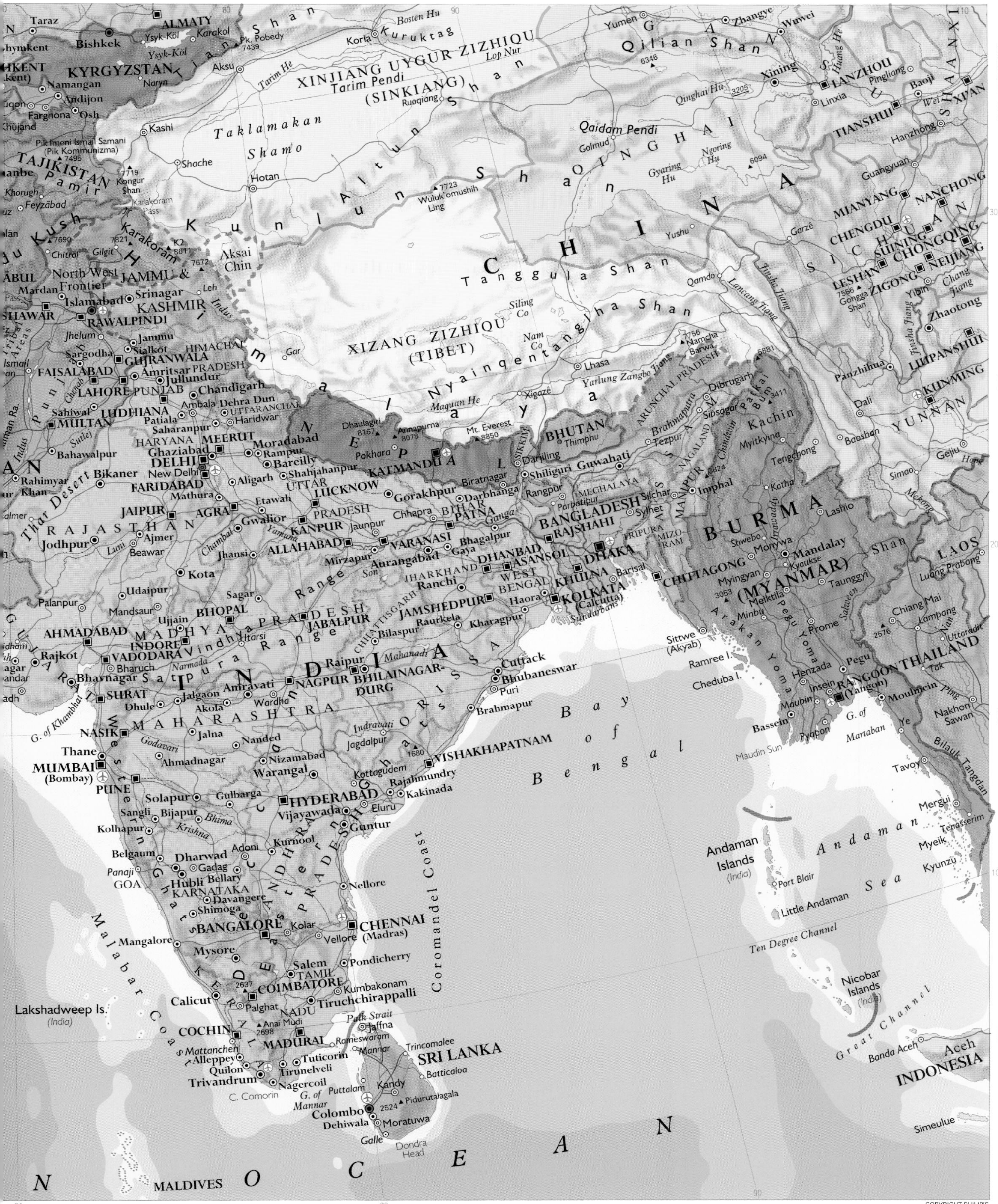

B C D E 21 23

6 7 8

COPYRIGHT PHILIP'S

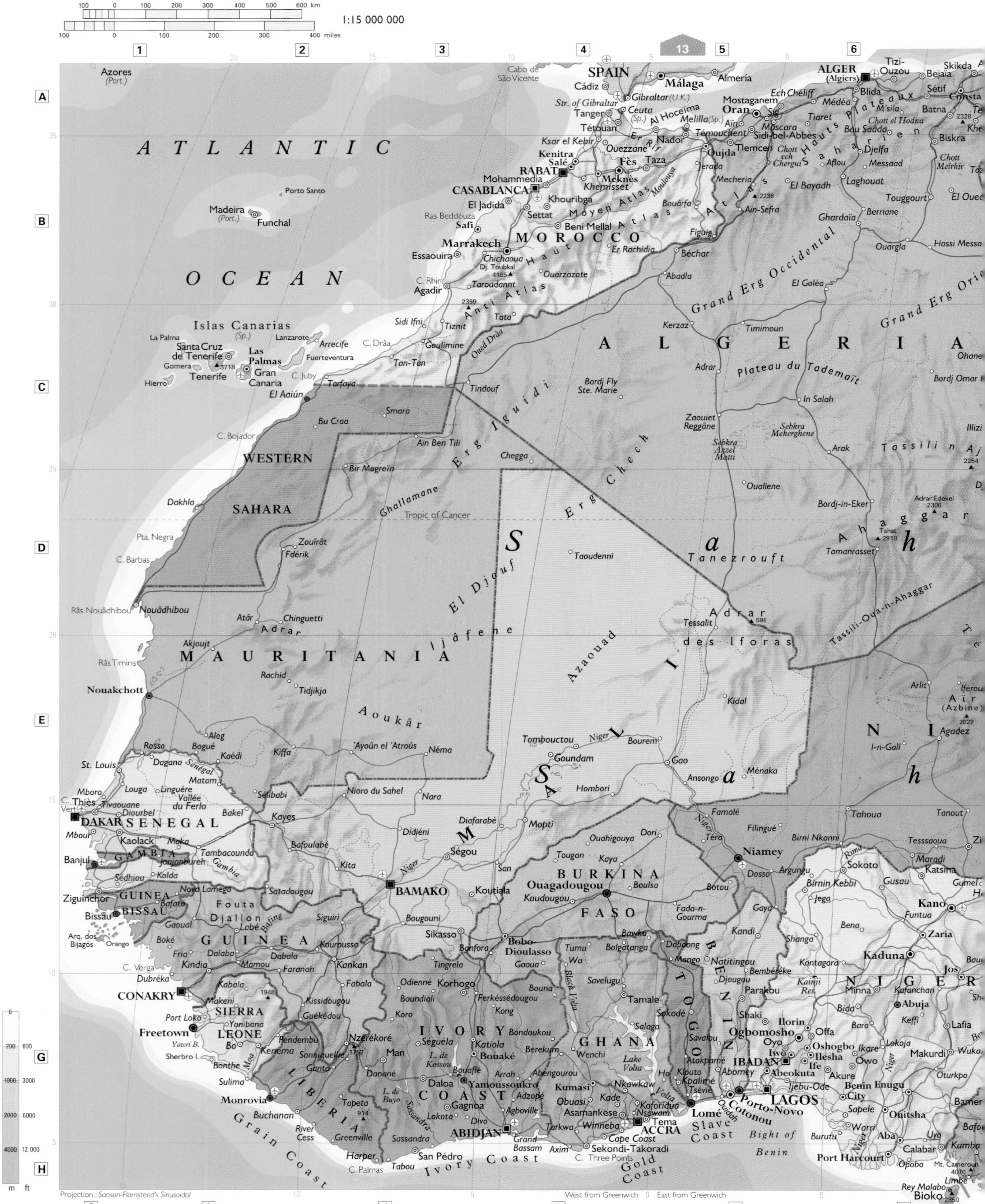
100 0 100 200 300 400 500 600 km
100 0 100 200 300 400 miles
1:15 000 000
13
1 2 3 4 5 6
A B C D E F G H
2 3 4 5 6 7
Azores (Port.)
ATLANTIC
OCEAN
Porto Santo
Madeira (Port.)
Funchal
Islas Canarias (Sp.)
La Palma
Santa Cruz de Tenerife
Gomera
3718
Tenerife
Hierro
Las Palmas
Gran Canaria
Lanzarote
Arrecife
Fuerteventura
C. Juby
C. Drâa
Cabo de São Vicente
SPAIN
Cádiz
Málaga
Almería
Str. of Gibraltar
Gibraltar (U.K.)
Ceuta (Sp.)
Tanger
Tétouan
Al Hoceïma
Melilla (Sp.)
Nador
Ksar el Kebir
Ouezzane
Er Rif
Kenitra
Salé
RABAT
Fès
Taza
Meknès
Khemisset
Mohammedia
CASABLANCA
Khouribga
El Jadida
Settat
Ras Beddouza
Safi
Moyen Atlas
Beni Mellal
Marrakech
Essaouira
Chichaoua
Dj. Toubkal 4165
Haut Atlas
MOROCCO
Er Rachidia
Ouarzazate
Taroudannt
C. Rhir
Agadir
Anti Atlas
2359
Sidi Ifni
Tiznit
Tata
Goulimine
Tan-Tan
Oued Drâa
Tarfaya
El Aaiún
Tindouf
Smara
Bu Craa
C. Bojador
Aïn Ben Tili
WESTERN SAHARA
Bir Mogreïn
Erg Iguidi
Chegga
Dakhla
Ghallamane
Tropic of Cancer
Pta. Negra
Zouîrât
Fdérik
C. Barbas
Râs Nouâdhibou
Nouâdhibou
Atâr
Chinguetti
Adrar
Akjoujt
Râs Timiris
MAURITANIA
Rachid
Tidjikja
Nouakchott
Aoukâr
Aleg
Rosso
Bogué
Kaédi
Kiffa
'Ayoûn el 'Atroûs
Néma
St. Louis
Dagana
Sénégal
Matam
Mboro
Louga
Linguère
Vallée du Ferlo
Sélibabi
C. Vert
Thiès
Tivaouane
Diourbel
Bakel
DAKAR
SENEGAL
Mbour
Kaolack
Maka
Tambacounda
Banjul
GAMBIA
Janjanbureh
Gambia
Sédhiou
Kolda
Ziguinchor
GUINEA-BISSAU
Bafata
Bissau
Nova Lamego
Arq. dos Bijagós
Orango
Fouta Djallon
Labé
Gaoual
GUINEA
Boké
Fria
Dalaba
Dabola
Mamou
Faranah
Kindia
C. Verga
Dubréka
CONAKRY
Kabala
1948
Makeni
SIERRA LEONE
Port Loko
Yonibana
Freetown
Yawri B.
Sherbro I.
Bo
Kenema
Pendembu
Bonthe
Sulima
Monrovia
LIBERIA
Buchanan
River Cess
Greenville
Grain Coast
Harper
C. Palmas
Tabou
Kayes
Nioro du Sahel
Nara
Diéma
Kita
Bafoulabé
Satadougou
Siguiri
Kourussa
Kankan
Fabala
Kissidougou
Guékédou
Nzérékoré
1752
Sanniquellie
Ganta
Tapeta
914
Danané
Man
Diafarabé
Mopti
Djéni
MALI
Ségou
San
Niger
BAMAKO
Koutiala
Bougouni
Sikasso
Banfora
Tingrela
Odienné
Korhogo
Boundiali
Ferkéssédougou
Kong
Koro
Séguéla
Katiola
Bouaké
IVORY COAST
L. de Kossou
Bouaflé
Yamoussoukro
Daloa
Gagnoa
L. de Buyo
Sassandra
Lakota
Divo
Agboville
Adzopé
Abengourou
ABIDJAN
Grand Bassam
San Pédro
Ivory Coast
Bondoukou
Bouna
Dj. Fly Ste. Marie
Bordj Fly Ste. Marie
Taoudenni
El Djouf
Erg Chech
Azaouad
Tombouctou
Goundam
Bourem
Gao
Ansongo
Ménaka
Hombori
Kidal
Tessalit
Adrar des Iforas
598
Tanezrouft
Ouallene
Bordj-in-Eker
Tamanrasset
Tahat 2918
Ahaggar
Adrar Edekel 2306
Tassili-Oua-n-Ahaggar
Tassili n Ajjer
2254
ALGERIA
ALGER (Algiers)
Tizi-Ouzou
Bejaïa
Blida
Médéa
Sétif
Batna
M'sila
Chott el Hodna
2328
Biskra
Bou Saâda
Hauts Plateaux
Djelfa
Messaad
Ech Cheliff
Mostaganem
Oran
Sig
Aïn
Mascara
Tiaret
Sidi-bel-Abbès
Témouchent
Tlemcen
Oujda
Chott ech Chergui
Aflou
Jerada
Mecheria
Saharien Atlas
El Bayadh
Laghouat
2236
Aïn-Sefra
Bouârfa
Figuig
Béchar
Abadla
Touggourt
El Oued
Chott Melrhir
Berriane
Ghardaïa
Ouargla
Hassi Messaoud
Grand Erg Occidental
Grand Erg Oriental
El Goléa
Kerzaz
Timimoun
Adrar
Plateau du Tademaït
Bordj Omar Driss
In Salah
Zaouiet Reggâne
Sebkra Mekerghene
Sebkra Azzel Matti
Arak
Illizi
Ohanet
NIGER
Arlit
Iferouane
Aïr (Azbine)
2022
Agadez
In-Gall
Tahoua
Tanout
Famalé
Filingué
Niamey
Birni Nkonni
Tesssaoua
Zinder
Téra
Dosso
Argungu
Dori
Ouahigouya
Kaya
Tougan
BURKINA FASO
Ouagadougou
Koudougou
Boulsa
Botou
Fada-n-Gourma
Gaya
Bobo-Dioulasso
Gaoua
Tumu
Wa
Bolgatanga
Bawku
Dapaong
Kandi
Mango
Natitingou
Djougou
Bembèrèkè
Parakou
Savelugu
Tamale
Salaga
Black Volta
GHANA
Bouna
Berekum
Wenchi
Lake Volta
Sokodé
TOGO
BENIN
Savalou
Atakpamé
Abomey
Kpalimé
Tsévié
Ho
Kumasi
Obuasi
Kade
Nkawkaw
Koforidua
Nsawam
Asamankese
Winneba
Tarkwa
Cape Coast
ACCRA
Tema
Sekondi-Takoradi
Axim
C. Three Points
Gold Coast
Lomé
Ouidah
Cotonou
Porto-Novo
LAGOS
Slave Coast
Bight of Benin
Sokoto
Maradi
Katsina
Birnin Kebbi
Gusau
Gumel
Jega
Kano
Funtua
Bena
Zaria
Shanga
Kaduna
Kontagora
Kainji Res.
NIGERIA
Minna
Kafanchan
Jos
Abuja
Bida
Shaki
Ilorin
Offa
Baro
Keffi
Lafia
Ogbomosho
Oyo
Oshogbo
Ikare
Lokoja
Makurdi
Wukari
Iwo
Ilesha
Owo
IBADAN
Ife
Abeokuta
Akure
Ijebu-Ode
Benin City
Enugu
Sapele
Onitsha
Warri
Aba
Burutu
Port Harcourt
Calabar
Uyo
Opobo
Mt. Cameroun 4070
Limbe
Rey Malabo
Bioko
2850
Bamenda
Kumba
Bafoussam
Rima
Niger
Volta
Bafing
Moa
Sassandra
Projection : Sanson-Flamsteed's Sinusoidal
West from Greenwich 0 East from Greenwich
m ft
0
200 600
1000 3000
2000 6000
4000 12 000

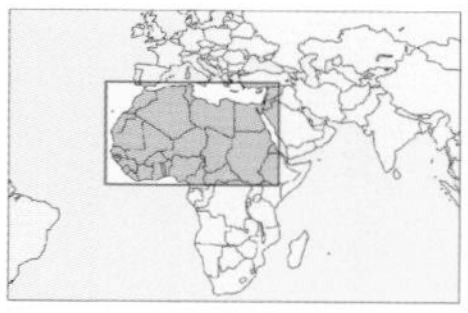

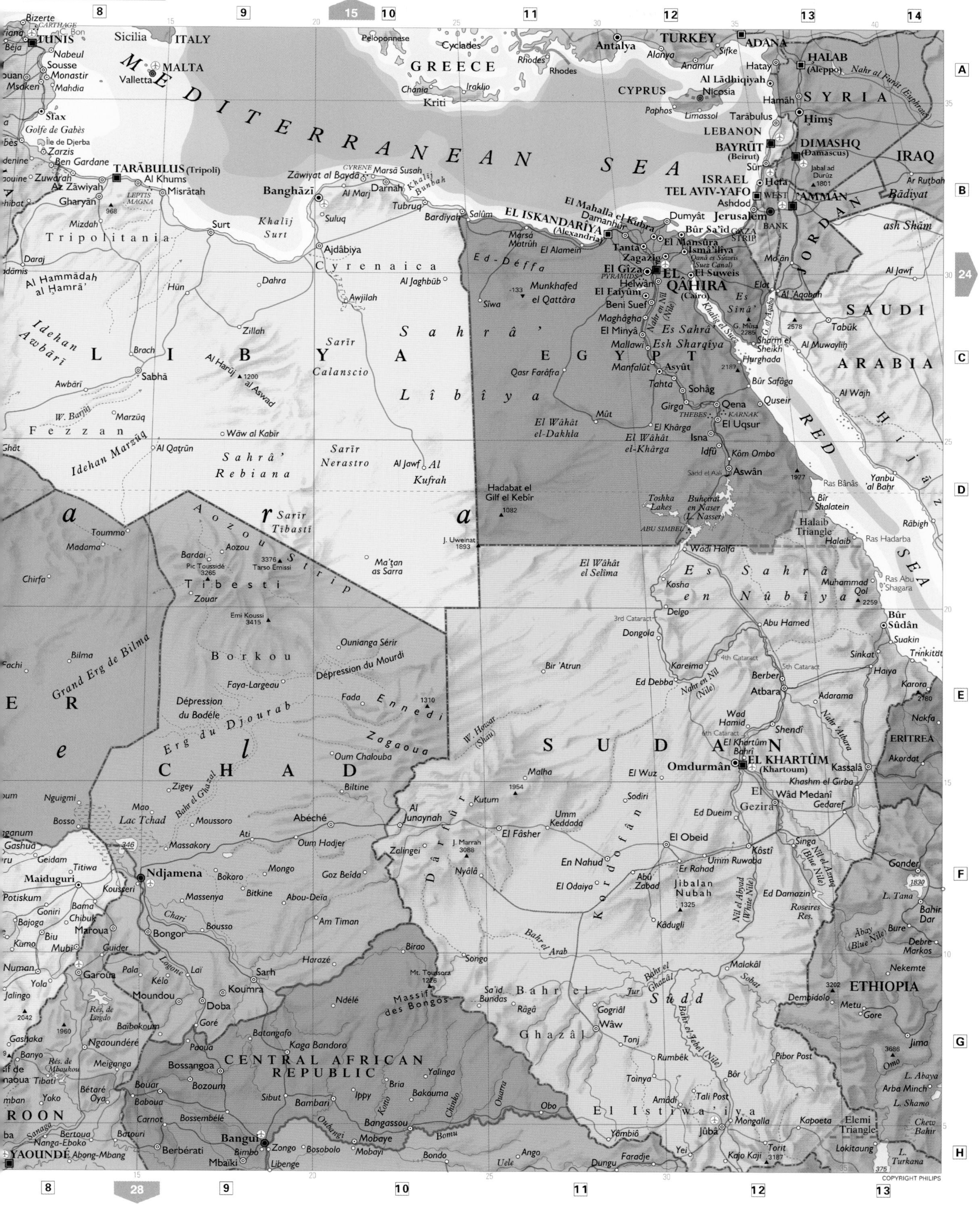

COPYRIGHT PHILIPS

100 0 100 200 300 400 500 600 km

1:15 000 000

100 0 100 200 300 400 miles

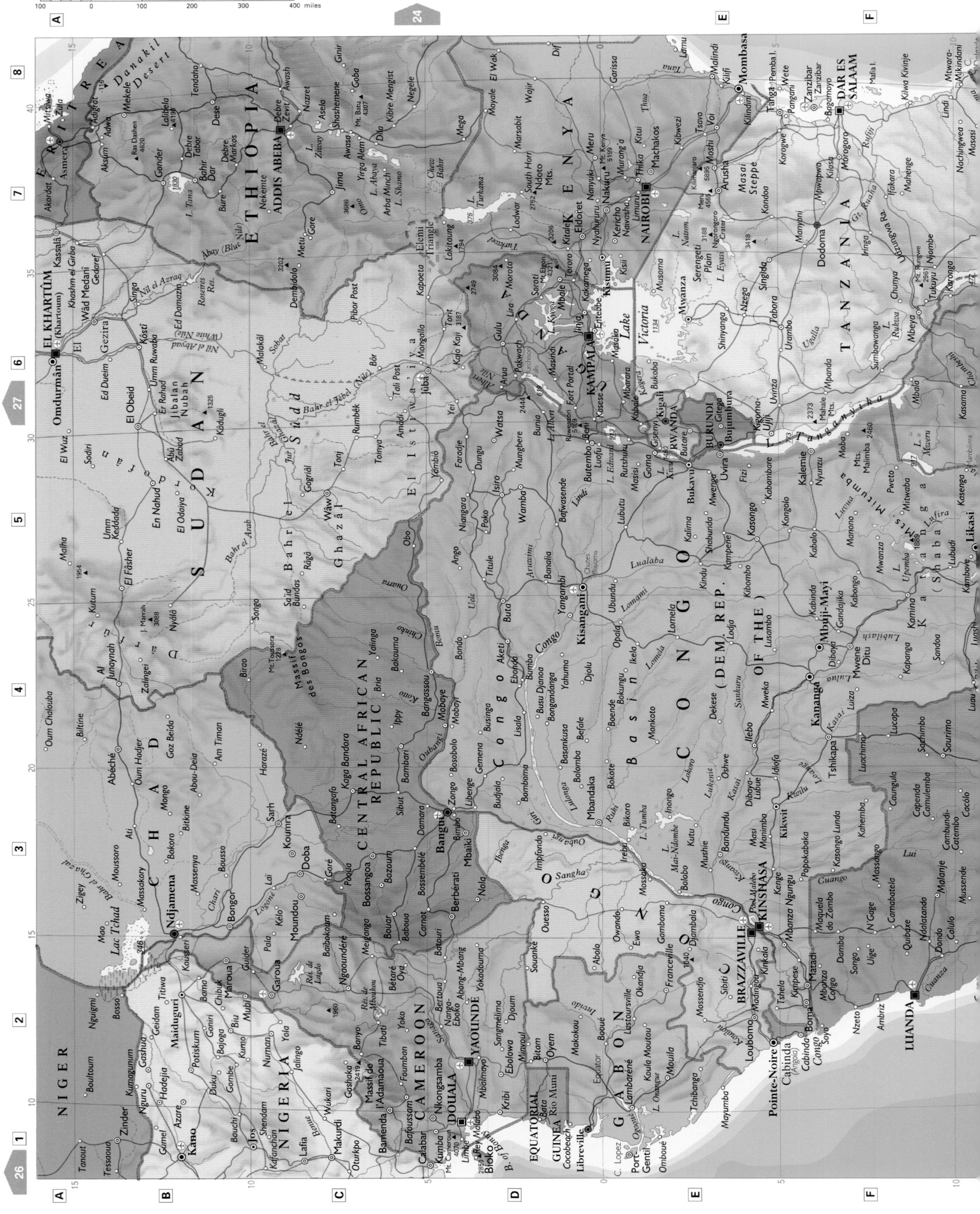

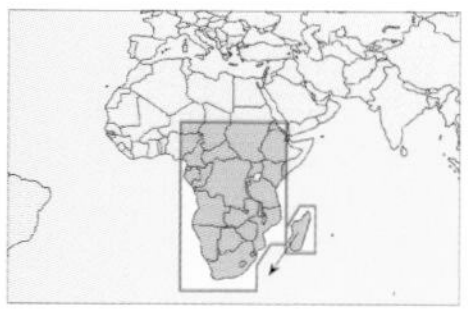

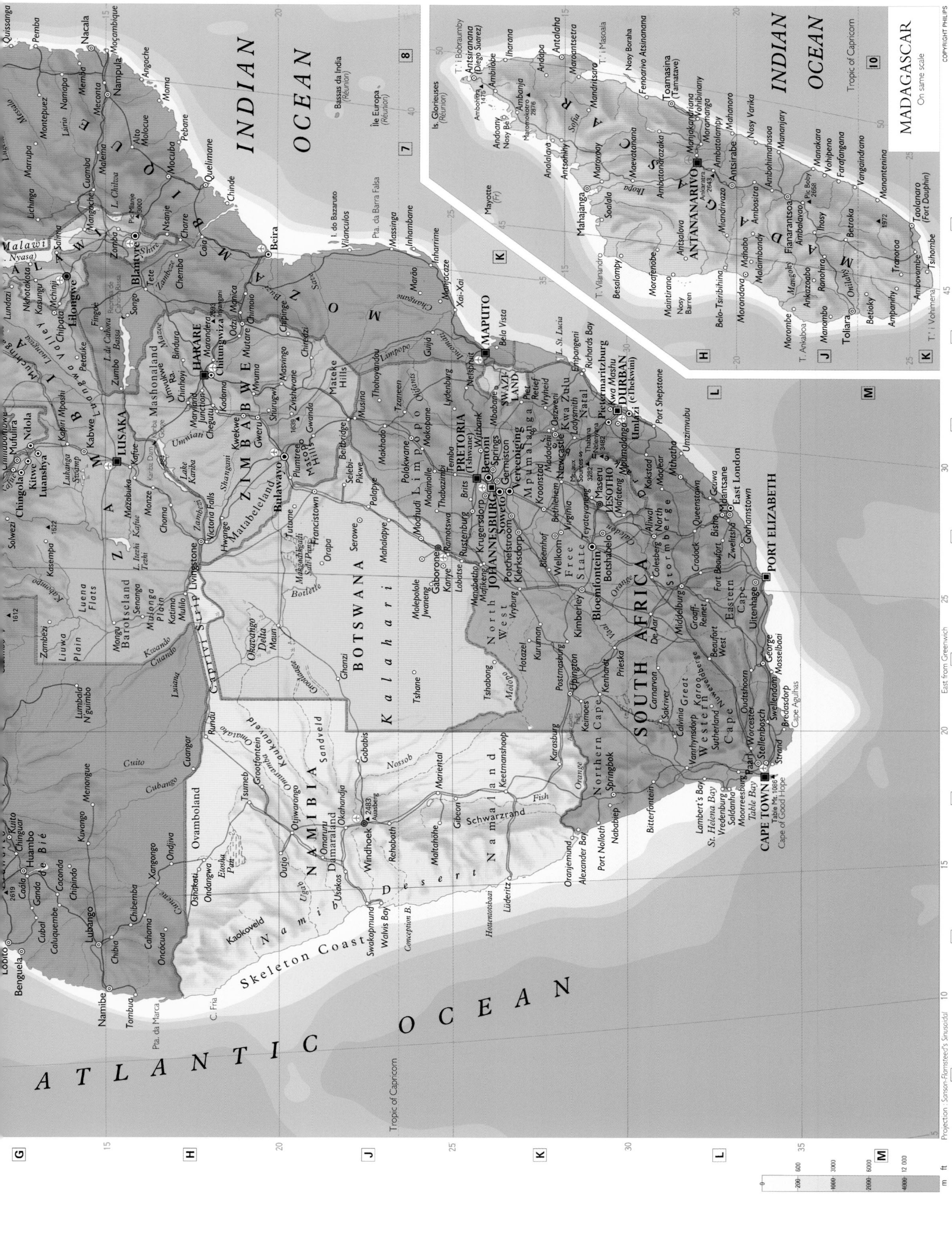
ATLANTIC OCEAN
INDIAN OCEAN
SOUTH AFRICA
NAMIBIA
BOTSWANA
ZIMBABWE
ZAMBIA
MOZAMBIQUE
MADAGASCAR
LESOTHO
SWAZILAND
Kalahari
Namib Desert
Skeleton Coast
Caprivi Strip
Okavango Delta
Tropic of Capricorn
CAPE TOWN
PORT ELIZABETH
DURBAN
JOHANNESBURG
PRETORIA
MAPUTO
HARARE
LUSAKA
Bulawayo
Windhoek
Gaborone
Bloemfontein
Lilongwe
Blantyre
Beira
ANTANANARIVO
Toamasina
Toliara
Mahajanga
Fianarantsoa
Walvis Bay
Lüderitz
East London
Kimberley
Maseru
Livingstone
Victoria Falls
Cape of Good Hope
Cape Agulhas
Île Europa
Bassas da India
Mayotte
MADAGASCAR
On same scale
COPYRIGHT PHILIPS
Projection : Sanson-Flamsteed's Sinusoidal
East from Greenwich
m ft
0
200 600
1000 3000
2000 6000
4000 12 000

1:20 000 000
km
miles
Equator
Maluku
Sulawesi (Celebes)
Palu
Kep. Sula
Seram Sea
Seram (Ceram)
Buru
Ambon
Misool
Sorong
Vogelkop Peninsula
Biak
Fakfak
Jayapura
Papua
Pegunungan Maoke
Puncak Jaya 5029
Bismarck Sea
Wewak
Bismarck Archipelago
Kavieng
Rabaul
New Ireland
New Britain
PAPUA NEW GUINEA
Madang
Mount Hagen
Mt. Wilhelm 4508
Lae
New Guinea
INDONESIA
Mamuju
Palopo
Kendari
Butung
Banda Sea
Weber 7260 Basin
Kep. Kai
Kep. Aru
Kep. Tanimbar
Watampone
Parepare
UJUNG PANDANG (MAKASAR)
Flores Sea
Wetar
Babar
Leti
Dili
Alor
EAST TIMOR
Timor
Flores
Ende
Sumbawa
Raba
Sumba
Savu Sea
Kupang
Timor Sea
Arafura Sea
Pulau Dolak
Fly
Gulf of Papua
Port Moresby
Owen Stanley Range
Solomon Sea
D'Entrecasteaux Islands
Louisiade Archipelago
Torres Strait
Badu I.
Moa I.
C. York
Prince of Wales I.
Coral Sea Basin
Cape York Peninsula
Weipa
Great Barrier Reef
Melville I.
C. Croker
C. Arnhem
Darwin
Arnhem Land
Groote Eylandt
Gulf of Carpentaria
North Australia Basin
Joseph Bonaparte Gulf
C. Londonderry
Katherine
Larrimah
Daly Waters
Wyndham
L. Argyle
Kimberley 970
Halls Creek
Derby
Broome
Wellesley Is.
Cooktown
Mitchell
Cairns
1611
Normanton
Forsayth
Flinders
Queensland Plateau
Townsville
Charters Towers
Whitsunday Is.
Mackay
L. Dalrymple
Barkly Tableland
NORTHERN TERRITORY
Tanami Desert
Tennant Creek
Kajabbi
Mount Isa
Cloncurry
Hughenden
Dajarra
Winton
Great Sandy Desert
Port Hedland
L. Mackay
MacDonnell Ranges
Alice Springs
Mt. Zeil 1510
QUEENSLAND
Longreach
Emerald
Rockhampton
Gladstone
Great Dividing Range
1312
Yaraka
Diamantina
Dampier
Karratha
N. W. Cape
Pannawonica
Lake Disappointment
Gibson Desert
Mt. Bruce 1235
Hamersley Range
Newman
Paraburdoo
AUSTRALIA
Uluru (Ayers Rock) 867
Mt. Woodroffe 1440
Musgrave Ranges
Simpson Desert
Sturt Stony Desert
216
Grey Range
Charleville
Quilpie
Roma
Maryborough
Gympie
BRISBANE
Toowoomba
Cooper Creek
Thargomindah
Cunnamulla
Dirranbandi
WESTERN AUSTRALIA
SOUTH AUSTRALIA
Carnarvon
L. Carnegie
Great Victoria Desert
Coober Pedy
Lake Eyre
Marree
Warrego
Bourke
Walgett
Moree
Shark Bay
Meekatharra
Murchison
Mount Magnet
Leonora
Lake Torrens
St. Mary Pk. 1168
Flinders Ranges
Broken Hill
NEW SOUTH WALES
Tamworth
Round Mt.
Tarcoola
Lake Gairdner
Cobar
Darling
Dubbo
Newcastle
Lake Barlee
Kalgoorlie-Boulder
Geraldton
Nullarbor Plain
Penong
Port Augusta
Whyalla
Eyre Pen.
Port Pirie
Orange
Bathurst
SYDNEY
Wollongong
Murray
Mildura
Hay
Griffith
Goulburn
INDIAN OCEAN
Darling Range
Norseman
Northam
PERTH
Esperance
Great Australian Bight
Port Lincoln
Spencer Gulf
Gulf St. Vincent
ADELAIDE
Swan Hill
Wagga Wagga
Canberra A.C.T.
Mt. Kosciuszko 2230
Shepparton
Albury-Wodonga
Bendigo
Snowy Mts.
Bombala
Kangaroo I.
Encounter B.
Horsham
VICTORIA
Ballarat
MELBOURNE
C. Howe
5632
Bunbury
Naturaliste Plateau
C. Leeuwin
Augusta
Albany
South Australian Basin
Mount Gambier
Geelong
Warrnambool
Sale
Bass Strait
Flinders I.
Furneaux Group
King I.
Tasman Abyssal
Burnie
Launceston
Mt. Ossa 1617
TASMANIA
Hobart
S.E.Cape
SOUTHERN OCEAN
South Tasman Plateau
m
ft
Projection: Lambert's Equivalent Azimuthal
East from Greenwich

10
11
12
13
14
15
16
A
B
C
D
E
F
G
H
J
Ontong Java Plateau
Solomon Rise
Melanesia
Bougainville
Balbi
Choiseul
SOLOMON ISLANDS
Santa Isabel
Lavella
New Georgia Is.
Vangunu
Russell Is.
Florida Is.
Malaita
Honiara
2439
San Cristóbal (Makira)
Guadalcanal
Pocklington Reef
Bellona
Rennell
South Solomon Trench
7223
Reef Is.
Duff Is.
Nendo
Santa Cruz Is.
9165
Vanikoro
Fataka
Tikopia
Vitiaz Trench
Tabiteuea
Beru
Nikunau
Gilbert Is.
Tamana
Arorae
KIRIBATI
Baker (U.S.A.)
Equator
6195
McKean
Abariringa
Birnie
Enderbury
Phoenix Is.
Nikumaroro
Orona
Rawaki
Carondelet
Manra
Namumea
Nanumanga
Niutao
Nui
Vaitupu
TUVALU (Ellice Is.)
Funafuti
Fongafale
Nukulaelae
Niulakita
Atafu
Tokelau Is. (N.Z.)
Nukunonu
Fakaofo
Rotuma
Is. Torres
Vanua Lava
Is. Banks
Gaua
Espíritu Santo
1879
VANUATU (New Hebrides)
Malakula
Epi
Shepherd Is.
Port Vila
Efate
Erromango
Tanna
Aneityum
West Fiji Basin
Îles D'Entrecasteaux
Îles Bélep
Îles Chesterfield
New Caledonia (Fr.)
1628
Î. Lifou
Î. Maré
Nouméa
Î. des Pins
Îles Loyauté
7569
South New Hebrides Trench
Î. Matthew
Ceve-i-Ra
Mata-Utu
Uvea
Wallis & Futuna (Fr.)
Horn
Alofi
SAMOA
Savai'i
Apia
'Upolu
Pago Pago
American Samoa (U.S.A.)
Tutuila
Vanua Levu
Taveuni
Viti Levu
1323
Suva
FIJI
Kadavu
Niuafo'ou
Niua Group
Niuatoputapu
Lau Group
Lau Basin
Lau Ridge
Vava'u Group
Late
Ha'apai Group
TONGA
Niue (N.Z.)
Nuku'alofa
Tongatapu Group
Eua
Ata
Tonga Trench
10 882
PACIFIC OCEAN
5303
South Fiji Basin
Tropic of Capricorn
Lord Howe Seamount Chain
New Caledonia Trough
Norfolk Ridge
Norfolk I. (Austral.)
Norfolk Basin
Lord Howe I. (Austral.)
734
Lord Howe Rise
Raoul I.
Kermadec Is. (N.Z.)
Macauley I.
Curtis I.
Kermadec Trench
Colville Ridge
10 047
Tasman Sea
Southwest Pacific Basin
North C.
Kaitaia
Whangarei
AUCKLAND
North Island
Hamilton
Bay of Plenty
Tauranga
Challenger Plateau
New Plymouth
Rotorua
Ruapehu
2797
Gisborne
NEW ZEALAND
Wanganui
Napier
Palmerston North
Masterton
Wellington
Nelson
Blenheim
Cook Strait
5267
International Date Line
Greymouth
South Island
Aoraki Mt. Cook
3753
Southern Alps
Christchurch
Chatham Rise
Queenstown
Timaru
Chatham I.
Chatham Is. (N.Z.)
Pitt I.
Dunedin
Invercargill
Stewart I.
West from Greenwich
COPYRIGHT PHILIP'S
10
11
12
13
14
15
16
17
18

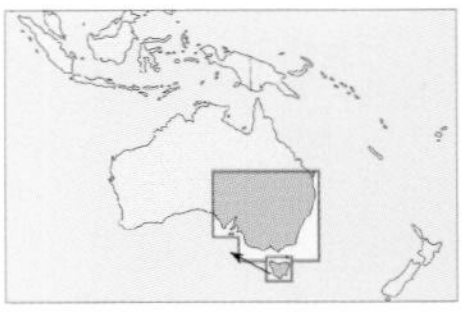

1:8 000 000

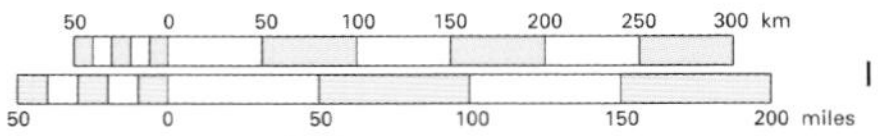
50 0 50 100 150 200 250 300 km
50 0 50 100 150 200 miles

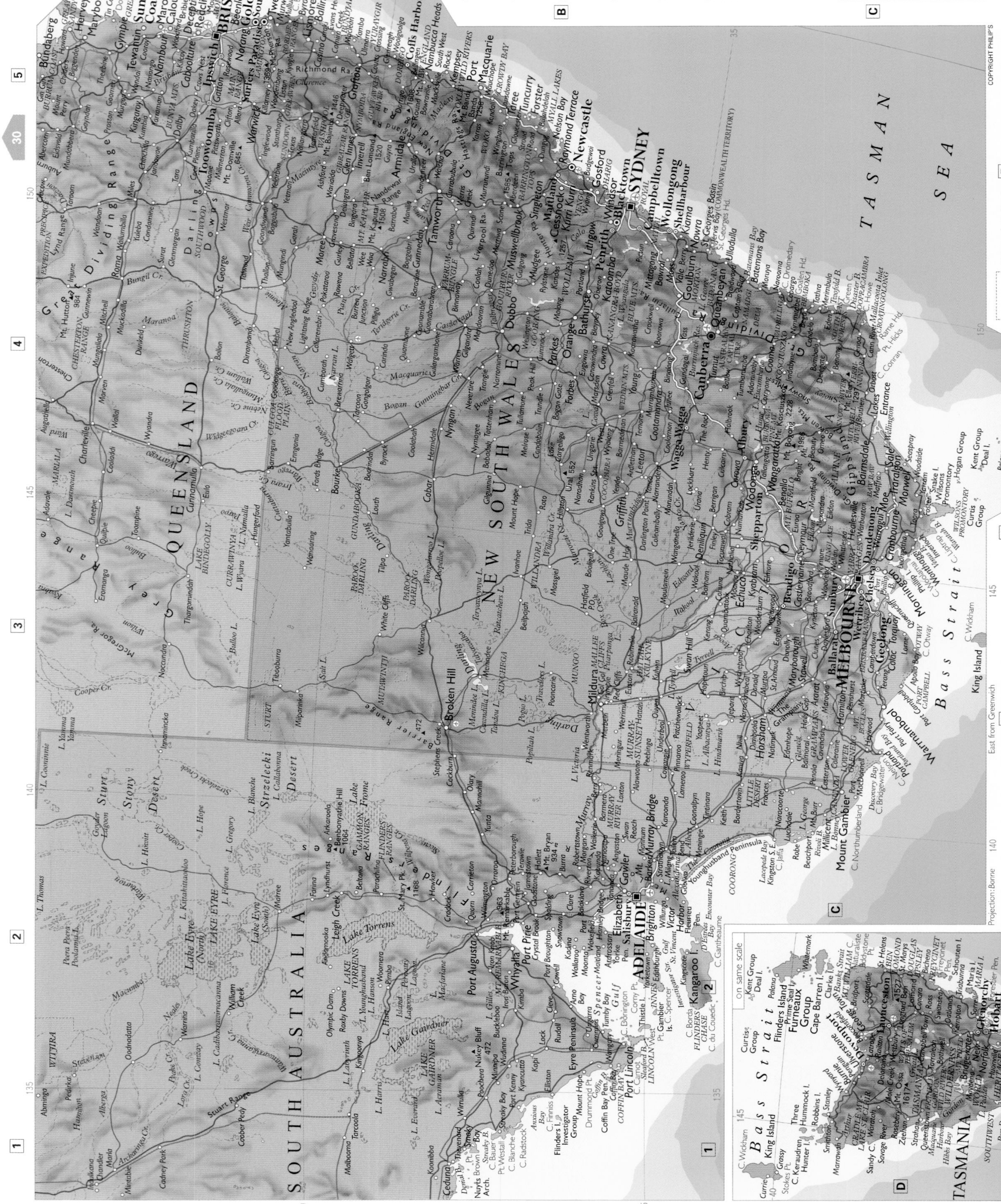
SOUTH-EAST AUSTRALIA
QUEENSLAND
NEW SOUTH WALES
SOUTH AUSTRALIA
TASMANIA
TASMAN SEA
Bass Strait
SYDNEY
MELBOURNE
ADELAIDE
BRISBANE
Canberra
Hobart
Newcastle
Wollongong
Geelong
Gold Coast
Broken Hill
Mildura
Port Augusta
Kangaroo I.
King Island
Flinders Island
Great Dividing Range
Lake Eyre (North)
Lake Torrens
Lake Gairdner
Sturt Stony Desert
Strzelecki Desert
National Parks
Projection: Bonne
East from Greenwich
COPYRIGHT PHILIP'S

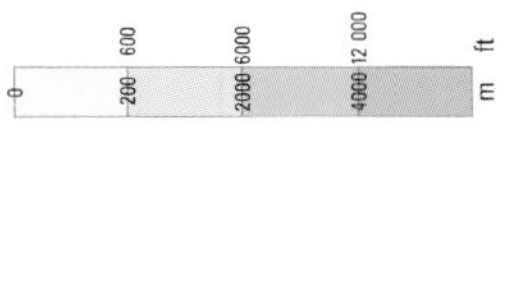
0 200 600 2000 6000 4000 12 000
m ft

1:6 000 000

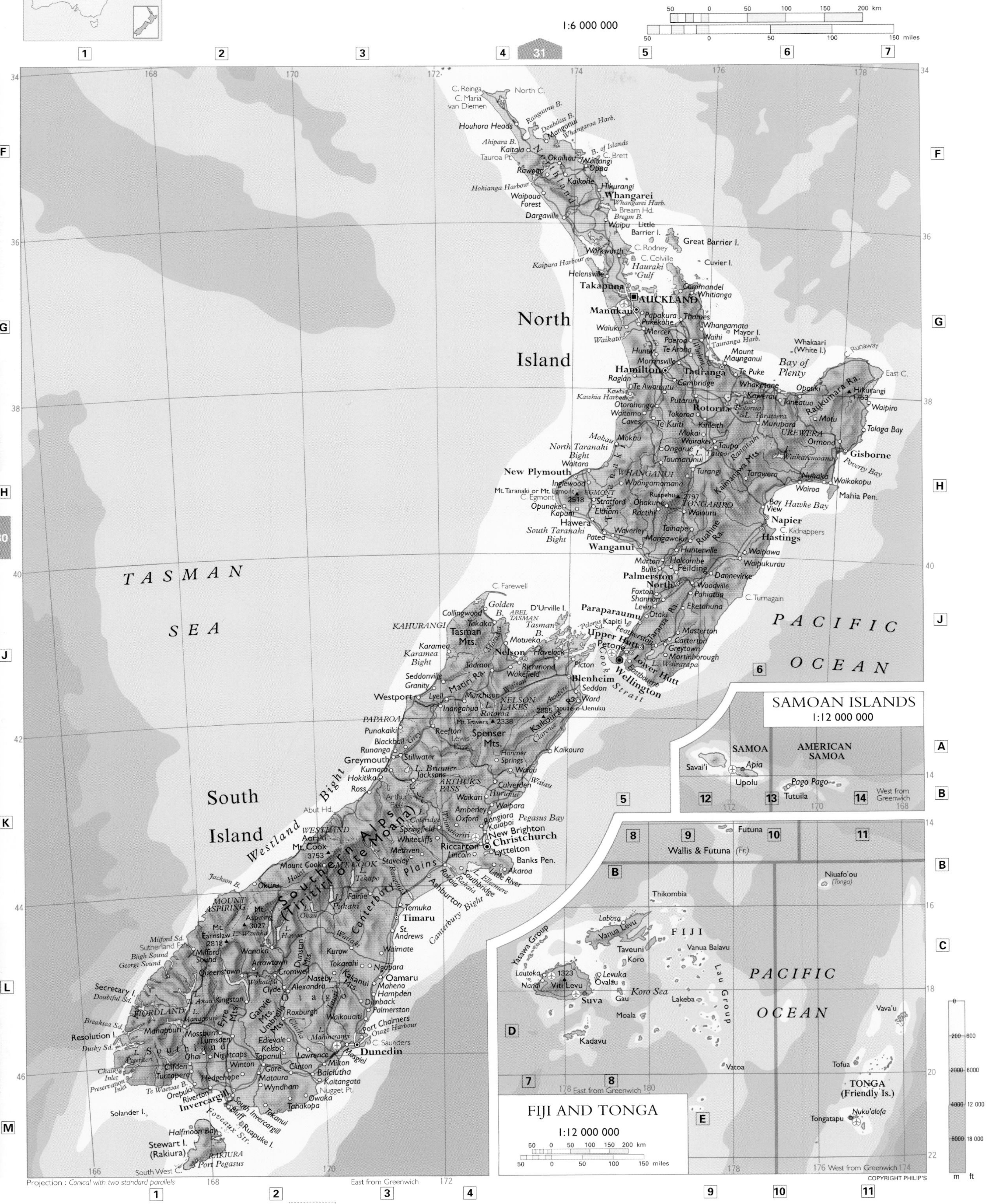

TASMAN SEA
PACIFIC OCEAN
North Island
South Island
C. Reinga
North C.
C. Maria van Diemen
Houhora Heads
Rangaunu B.
Doubtless B.
Mangonui
Whangaroa Harb.
Ahipara B.
Kaitaia
B. of Islands
C. Brett
Tauroa Pt.
Okaihau
Waitangi
Opua
Rawene
Kaikohe
Hokianga Harbour
Hikurangi
Whangarei
Whangarei Harb.
Waipoua Forest
Bream Hd.
Bream B.
Dargaville
Waipu
Little Barrier I.
Great Barrier I.
C. Rodney
Warkworth
C. Colville
Kaipara Harbour
Hauraki Gulf
Cuvier I.
Helensville
Takapuna
Coromandel
AUCKLAND
Whitianga
Manukau
Papakura
Thames
Pukekohe
Whangamata
Waiuku
Mercer
Mayor I.
Waihi
Tauranga Harb.
Waikato
Paeroa
Te Aroha
Huntly
Mount Maunganui
Morrinsville
Whakaari (White I.)
Runaway
Hamilton
Tauranga
Te Puke
Bay of Plenty
East C.
Raglan
Cambridge
Whakatane
Opotiki
Te Awamutu
Hikurangi 1753
Kawhia Harbour
Kawerau
Putaruru
Rotorua
Otorohanga
Waitomo Caves
Tokoroa
L. Rotorua
L. Tarawera
Murupara
Raukumara Ra.
Waipiro
Te Kuiti
Kinleith
Motu
Tolaga Bay
Mokau
Mokai
UREWERA
Wairakei
Taupo
Ruatoria
Ormond
North Taranaki Bight
Ongarue
L. Taupo
Waikaremoana
Gisborne
Waitara
Taumarunui
Poverty Bay
New Plymouth
WHANGANUI
Turangi
Tarawera
Nuhaka
Inglewood
Whangamomona
Waikokopu
Mt. Taranaki or Mt. Egmont 2518
EGMONT
Ruapehu 2797
TONGARIRO
Wairoa
C. Egmont
Mahia Pen.
Opunake
Stratford
Ohakune
Bay View
Hawke Bay
Kaponga
Eltham
Raetihi
Waiouru
Hawera
Napier
Kaimanawa Mts.
South Taranaki Bight
Patea
Waverley
Taihape
C. Kidnappers
Hastings
Wanganui
Mangaweka
Ruahine Ra.
Hunterville
Waipawa
Marton
Halcombe
Waipukurau
Bulls
Feilding
Palmerston North
Dannevirke
Foxton
Woodville
Shannon
Pahiatua
Levin
C. Turnagain
Otaki
Eketahuna
Paraparaumu
Kapiti I.
Featherston
Masterton
Upper Hutt
Carterton
Greytown
Martinborough
Petone
Lower Hutt
L. Wairarapa
Wellington
Cook Strait
C. Farewell
Golden B.
ABEL TASMAN
D'Urville I.
Collingwood
Takaka
Tasman B.
KAHURANGI
Tasman Mts.
Motueka
Pelorus Sd.
Karamea
Karamea Bight
Nelson
Havelock
Tadmor
Richmond
Picton
Wakefield
Blenheim
Seddonville
Granity
Seddon
Westport
Lyell
Matiri Ra.
Murchison
NELSON LAKES
Ward
Inangahua
L. Rotoroa
Tapuae-o-Uenuku 2885
PAPAROA
Mt. Travers 2338
Kaikoura Ra.
Punakaiki
Reefton
Spenser Mts.
Clarence
Blackball
Kaikoura
Runanga
Stillwater
Hanmer Springs
Greymouth
Kumara
L. Brunner
Jacksons
Hokitika
Waiau
ARTHUR'S PASS
Ross
Culverden
Abut Hd.
Waikari
Amberley
Waipara
Pegasus Bay
Oxford
Rangiora
Kaiapoi
WESTLAND
New Brighton
Aoraki Mt. Cook 3753
Southern Alps (Tiritiri o te Moana)
Christchurch
Whitecliffs
Riccarton
Lyttelton
Methven
Lincoln
Banks Pen.
Staveley
Akaroa
Mount Cook
MT. COOK
Rakaia
L. Ellesmere
Westland Bight
Jackson B.
Southbridge
Little River
Okuru
Haast
Tekapo
Ashburton
Fairlie
Canterbury Plains
Canterbury Bight
Pukaki
MOUNT ASPIRING
Mt. Aspiring 3027
Temuka
Timaru
Ohau
Milford Sd.
Mt. Earnslaw 2818
St. Andrews
Sutherland Falls
Waimate
Bligh Sound
Milford Sound
Wanaka
Dunstan Mts.
Kurow
George Sound
Arrowtown
Tokarahi
Ngapara
Cromwell
Queenstown
Naseby
Kakanui Mts.
Oamaru
Secretary I.
Wakatipu
Alexandra
Maheno
Doubtful Sd.
Clyde
Otago
Hampden
Te Anau
Kingston
Dunback
FIORDLAND
Eyre Mts.
Garvie Mts.
Roxburgh
Palmerston
Breaksea Sd.
Manapouri
Umbrella Mts.
Waikouaiti
Mossburn
Port Chalmers
Resolution I.
Lumsden
Otago Harbour
Dusky Sd.
Southland
Edievale
C. Saunders
Nightcaps
Kelso
Dunedin
Ohai
Tapanui
Mosgiel
Winton
Lawrence
Milton
Clifden
Gore
Clinton
Balclutha
Chalky Inlet
Tuatapere
Hedgehope
Mataura
Kaitangata
Preservation Inlet
Te Waewae B.
Wyndham
Nugget Pt.
Orepuki
Riverton
Owaka
Invercargill
Tahakopa
South Invercargill
Bluff
Tokanui
Solander I.
Foveaux Str.
Ruapuke I.
Halfmoon Bay
Stewart I. (Rakiura)
RAKIURA
Port Pegasus
South West C.
SAMOAN ISLANDS
1:12 000 000
SAMOA
AMERICAN SAMOA
Savai'i
Apia
Upolu
Pago Pago
Tutuila
West from Greenwich
Wallis & Futuna (Fr.)
Futuna
Niuafo'ou (Tonga)
Thikombia
Labasa
Vanua Levu
FIJI
Yasawa Group
Taveuni
Vanua Balavu
Koro
Lautoka
Nandi
Viti Levu 1323
Levuka
Ovalau
Suva
Koro Sea
Gau
Lakeba
Lau Group
PACIFIC OCEAN
Moala
Vava'u
Kadavu
Vatoa
Tofua
TONGA (Friendly Is.)
Tongatapu
Nuku'alofa
East from Greenwich
FIJI AND TONGA
1:12 000 000
Projection : Conical with two standard parallels
COPYRIGHT PHILIP'S

National Parks

Equatorial Scale 1:54 000 000

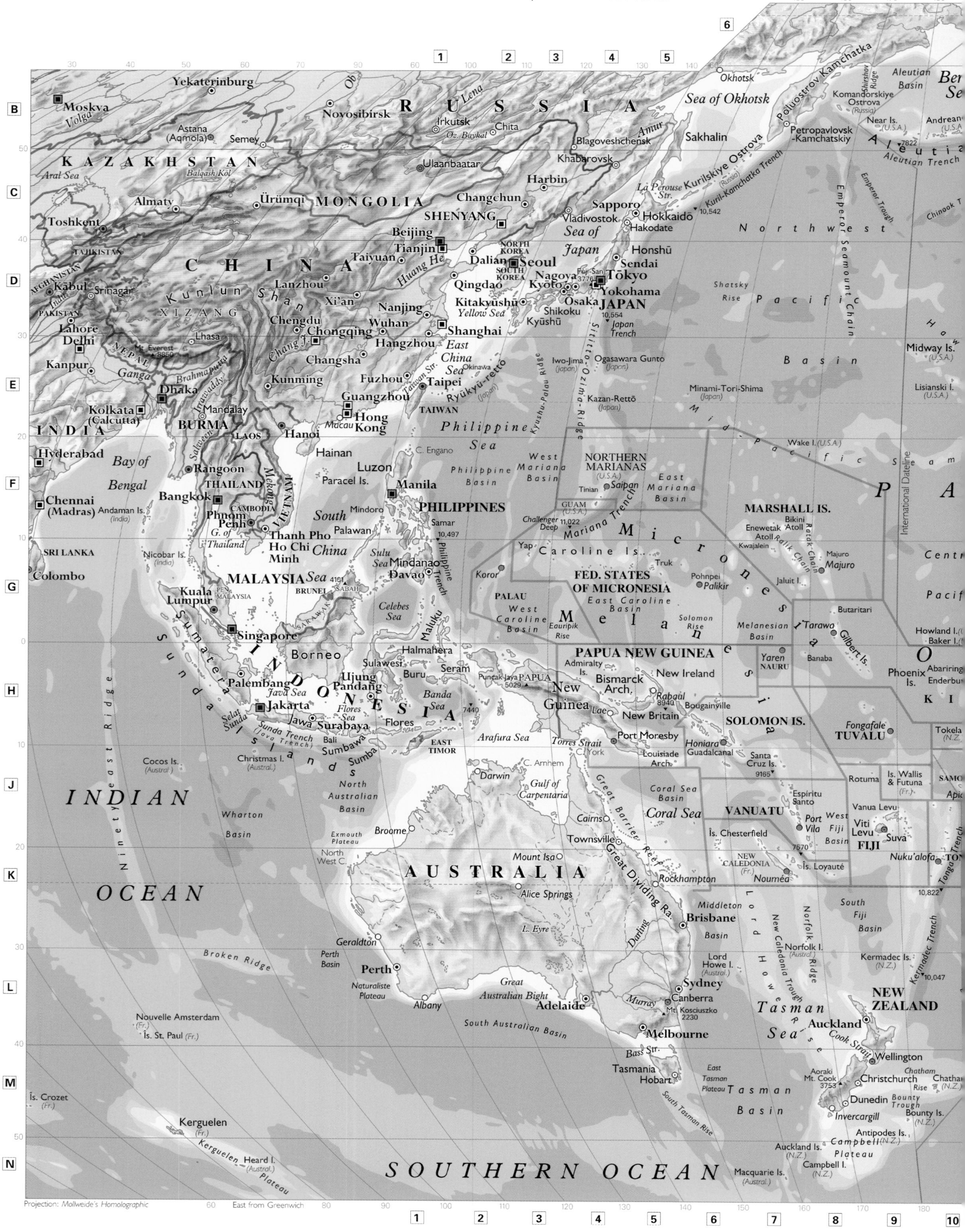

RUSSIA
Moskva
Volga
Yekaterinburg
Ob
Novosibirsk
Lena
Irkutsk
Oz. Baykal
Chita
Astana (Aqmola)
Semey
KAZAKHSTAN
Balqash Köl
Aral Sea
Ulaanbaatar
Blagoveshchensk
Amur
Khabarovsk
Harbin
Sea of Okhotsk
Okhotsk
Sakhalin
Poluostrov Kamchatka
Petropavlovsk-Kamchatskiy
Komandorskiye Ostrova (Russia)
Shirshov Ridge
Aleutian Basin
Bering Sea
Near Is. (U.S.A.)
Andreanof Is. (U.S.A.)
Aleutian Is.
Aleutian Trench
7822
Kurilskiye Ostrova (Russia)
Kuril-Kamchatka Trench
10,542
La Pérouse Str.
Emperor Trough
Emperor Seamount Chain
Chinook Trough
Northwest Pacific Basin
Shatsky Rise
Almaty
Ürümqi
MONGOLIA
Toshkent
TAJIKISTAN
AFGHANISTAN
Kābul
Srinagar
Indus
PAKISTAN
Lahore
Delhi
Kanpur
Ganga
NEPAL
Mt. Everest 8850
Lhasa
Brahmaputra
XIZANG
Kunlun Shan
CHINA
Lanzhou
Xi'an
Chengdu
Chongqing
Chang Jiang
Kunming
Changsha
Wuhan
Nanjing
Hangzhou
Shanghai
Fuzhou
Taipei
TAIWAN
Taiwan Str.
Guangzhou
Hong Kong
Macau
Hanoi
Hainan
Taiyuan
Huang He
Beijing
Tianjin
SHENYANG
Changchun
Dalian
Qingdao
Yellow Sea
East China Sea
Okinawa
Ryūkyū-rettō (Japan)
NORTH KOREA
SOUTH KOREA
Seoul
Vladivostok
Sea of Japan
Sapporo
Hokkaidō
Hakodate
Honshū
Sendai
Fuji-San 3776
Tōkyō
Yokohama
Nagoya
Kyōto
Ōsaka
Kitakyūshū
Shikoku
Kyūshū
JAPAN
10,554
Japan Trench
Iwo-Jima (Japan)
Ogasawara Gunto (Japan)
Kazan-Rettō (Japan)
Shichito-Iozima Ridge
Kyushu-Palau Ridge
Minami-Tori-Shima (Japan)
Midway Is. (U.S.A.)
Lisianski I. (U.S.A.)
Wake I. (U.S.A.)
Mid-Pacific Seamounts
International Dateline
INDIA
Kolkata (Calcutta)
Dhaka
Mandalay
Irrawaddy
Salween
BURMA
Rangoon
LAOS
Mekong
THAILAND
Bangkok
CAMBODIA
Phnom Penh
VIETNAM
Thanh Pho Ho Chi Minh
G. of Thailand
Hyderabad
Bay of Bengal
Chennai (Madras)
Andaman Is. (India)
Nicobar Is. (India)
SRI LANKA
Colombo
Paracel Is.
Luzon
C. Engano
Manila
PHILIPPINES
Mindoro
Samar
10,497
Palawan
South China Sea
Sulu Sea
Mindanao
Davao
Philippine Trench
Philippine Sea
Philippine Basin
West Mariana Basin
NORTHERN MARIANAS (U.S.A.)
Saipan
Tinian
East Mariana Basin
GUAM (U.S.A.)
Challenger Deep 11,022
Mariana Trench
Micronesia
Yap
Caroline Is.
Truk
FED. STATES OF MICRONESIA
Pohnpei
Palikir
Koror
PALAU
West Caroline Basin
East Caroline Basin
Eauripik Rise
MARSHALL IS.
Bikini Atoll
Enewetak Atoll
Kwajalein
Ratak Chain
Ralik Chain
Majuro
Jaluit I.
Butaritari
Tarawa
Gilbert Is.
Banaba
Howland I. (U.S.A.)
Baker I. (U.S.A.)
Phoenix Is.
Enderbury
Abariringa
KIRIBATI
MALAYSIA
PEN. MALAYSIA
Kuala Lumpur
BRUNEI
SABAH
SARAWAK
4101
Celebes Sea
Maluku
Singapore
Sumatera
Borneo
Halmahera
Sulawesi
Buru
Seram
Ujung Pandang
Palembang
Java Sea
Jakarta
Jawa
Surabaya
Bali
Flores Sea
Flores
Sumbawa
Sumba
Banda Sea
7440
INDONESIA
EAST TIMOR
Selat Sunda
Sunda Trench (Java Trench)
Sunda Islands
Christmas I. (Austral.)
Cocos Is. (Austral.)
Ninetyeast Ridge
Puncak Jaya 5029
PAPUA
New Guinea
Lae
Melanesia
PAPUA NEW GUINEA
Admiralty Is.
Bismarck Arch.
New Ireland
Rabaul
8940
New Britain
Bougainville
Port Moresby
Solomon Rise
Melanesian Basin
Yaren
NAURU
SOLOMON IS.
Honiara
Guadalcanal
Louisiade Arch.
Santa Cruz Is.
9165
Torres Strait
C. York
Arafura Sea
C. Arnhem
Darwin
Gulf of Carpentaria
Coral Sea Basin
Coral Sea
Great Barrier Reef
Cairns
Townsville
VANUATU
Espiritu Santo
Port Vila
Is. Chesterfield
NEW CALEDONIA (Fr.)
Nouméa
Is. Loyauté
7570
TUVALU
Fongafale
Tokelau (N.Z.)
Rotuma
Is. Wallis & Futuna (Fr.)
SAMOA
Apia
Vanua Levu
Viti Levu
Suva
FIJI
West Fiji Basin
Nuku'alofa
TONGA
Tonga Trench
10,822
INDIAN OCEAN
Wharton Basin
North Australian Basin
Exmouth Plateau
Broome
North West C.
AUSTRALIA
Mount Isa
Alice Springs
L. Eyre
Great Dividing Ra.
Darling
Rockhampton
Brisbane
Middleton Basin
Lord Howe Rise
New Caledonia Trough
Norfolk Ridge
Norfolk I. (Austral.)
South Fiji Basin
Kermadec Is. (N.Z.)
Kermadec Trench
10,047
Lord Howe I. (Austral.)
Geraldton
Perth
Perth Basin
Naturaliste Plateau
Albany
Great Australian Bight
Adelaide
Murray
Sydney
Canberra
Mt. Kosciuszko 2230
Melbourne
South Australian Basin
Broken Ridge
Bass Str.
Tasmania
Hobart
East Tasman Plateau
Tasman Sea
Tasman Basin
South Tasman Rise
NEW ZEALAND
Auckland
Cook Strait
Wellington
Aoraki Mt. Cook 3753
Christchurch
Chatham Rise
Chatham Is. (N.Z.)
Dunedin
Invercargill
Bounty Trough
Bounty Is. (N.Z.)
Antipodes Is. (N.Z.)
Campbell Plateau
Auckland Is. (N.Z.)
Campbell I. (N.Z.)
Macquarie Is. (Austral.)
Nouvelle Amsterdam (Fr.)
Is. St. Paul (Fr.)
Is. Crozet (Fr.)
Kerguelen (Fr.)
Kerguelen Plateau
Heard I. (Austral.)
SOUTHERN OCEAN
Projection: Mollweide's Homolographic
East from Greenwich

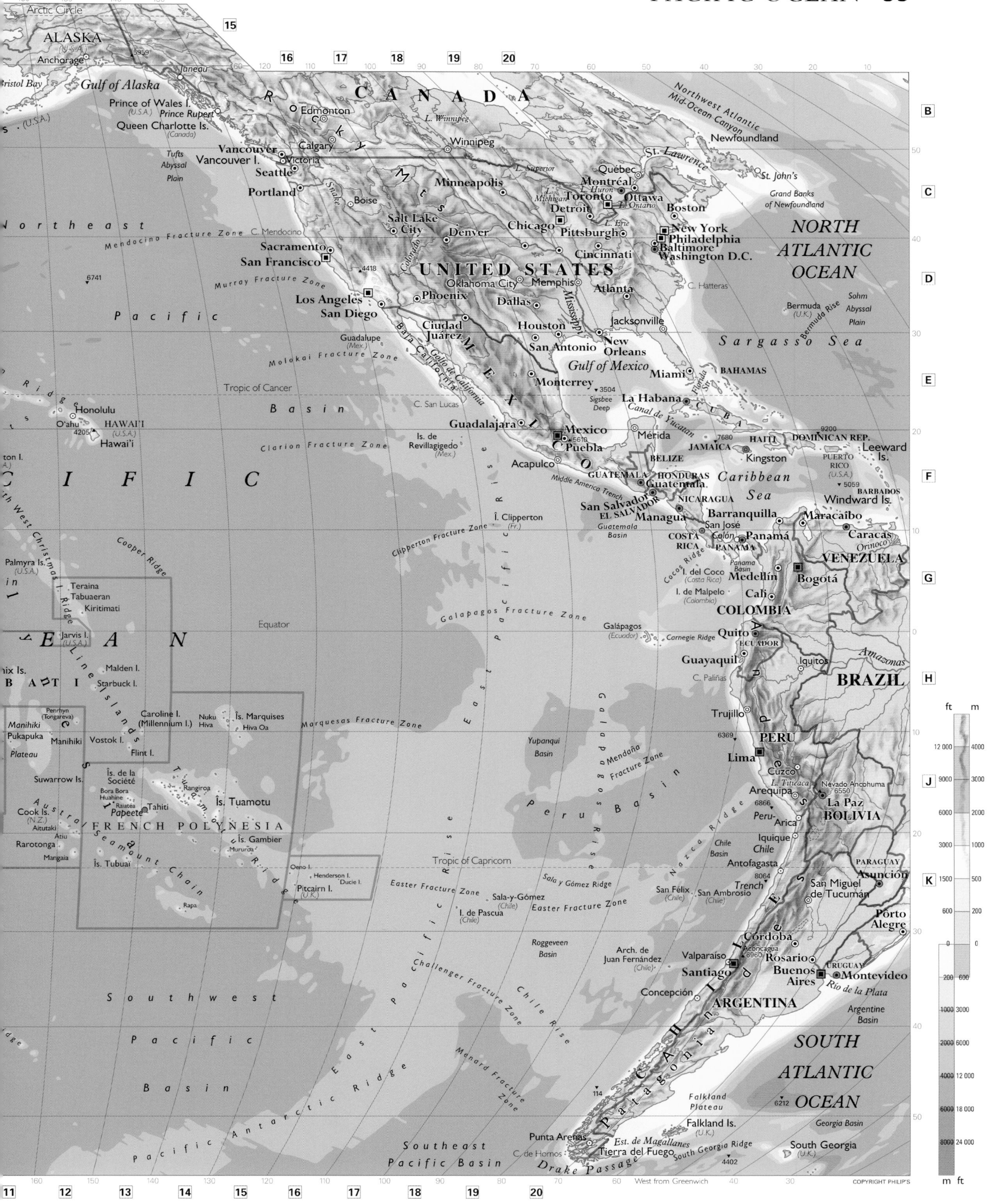
Arctic Circle
ALASKA
(U.S.A.)
Anchorage
5959
Juneau
Bristol Bay
Gulf of Alaska
Prince of Wales I.
(U.S.A.)
Prince Rupert
Queen Charlotte Is.
(Canada)
Tufts
Abyssal
Plain
Vancouver
Vancouver I.
Victoria
Seattle
Portland
C A N A D A
R O C K Y
M t s
Edmonton
Calgary
L. Winnipeg
Winnipeg
Northwest Atlantic
Mid-Ocean Canyon
Newfoundland
St. Lawrence
L. Superior
Minneapolis
Québec
Montréal
St. John's
Grand Banks
of Newfoundland
L. Huron
L. Michigan
Toronto
Ottawa
L. Ontario
Boston
Detroit
L. Erie
Boise
Snake
Salt Lake
City
Denver
Chicago
Pittsburgh
New York
Philadelphia
Baltimore
Washington D.C.
Cincinnati
NORTH
ATLANTIC
OCEAN
N o r t h e a s t
Mendocino Fracture Zone
C. Mendocino
Sacramento
San Francisco
4418
Colorado
UNITED STATES
Oklahoma City
Memphis
Atlanta
C. Hatteras
Sohm
Abyssal
Plain
6741
Murray Fracture Zone
Los Angeles
San Diego
Phoenix
Dallas
Mississippi
Bermuda
(U.K.)
Bermuda Rise
P a c i f i c
Ciudad
Juárez
Houston
Jacksonville
San Antonio
New
Orleans
S a r g a s s o   S e a
Guadalupe
(Mex.)
Baja California
Golfo de California
M E X I C O
Molokai Fracture Zone
Gulf of Mexico
Miami
Florida Str.
BAHAMAS
Monterrey
Tropic of Cancer
3504
Sigsbee
Deep
La Habana
C U B A
Honolulu
C. San Lucas
B a s i n
Canal de Yucatán
O'ahu
HAWAI'I
(U.S.A.)
4205
Hawai'i
Guadalajara
Mexico
5610
Puebla
Mérida
9200
7680
JAMAICA
HAITI
DOMINICAN REP.
Leeward
Is.
Kingston
Clarion Fracture Zone
Is. de
Revillagigedo
(Mex.)
Acapulco
BELIZE
PUERTO
RICO
(U.S.A.)
P A C I F I C
GUATEMALA
HONDURAS
Guatemala
Caribbean
Sea
5059
BARBADOS
Middle America Trench
San Salvador
EL SALVADOR
NICARAGUA
Windward Is.
Managua
Barranquilla
Maracaibo
Caracas
Î. Clipperton
(Fr.)
Guatemala
Basin
San José
COSTA
RICA
Colón
Panamá
PANAMA
Orinoco
Clipperton Fracture Zone
Cooper Ridge
Palmyra Is.
(U.S.A.)
Cocos Ridge
Panama
Basin
VENEZUELA
Teraina
Tabuaeran
Kiritimati
I. del Coco
(Costa Rica)
Medellín
Bogotá
I. de Malpelo
(Colombia)
Cali
COLOMBIA
Galapagos Fracture Zone
Equator
Jarvis I.
(U.S.A.)
O C E A N
Line Islands
Galápagos
(Ecuador)
Carnegie Ridge
Quito
ECUADOR
Amazonas
Malden I.
Starbuck I.
Guayaquil
Iquitos
C. Pariñas
BRAZIL
Penrhyn
(Tongareva)
Manihiki
Pukapuka
Manihiki
Plateau
Caroline I.
(Millennium I.)
Vostok I.
Flint I.
Nuku
Hiva
Îs. Marquises
Hiva Oa
Marquesas Fracture Zone
East Pacific Rise
Yupanqui
Basin
Trujillo
6369
PERU
Lima
Mendaña Fracture Zone
Galápagos Rise
Suwarrow Is.
Îs. de la
Société
Bora Bora
Huahine
Raiatea
Tahiti
Papeete
Rangiroa
Îs. Tuamotu
Cook Is.
(N.Z.)
Aitutaki
Atiu
Rarotonga
Mangaia
FRENCH POLYNESIA
Austral Seamount Chain
Tuamotu Ridge
Îs. Gambier
Mururoa
Îs. Tubuai
P e r u   B a s i n
Nazca Ridge
Cuzco
L. Titicaca
Nevado Ancohuma
6550
Arequipa
6866
La Paz
Peru-
Arica
BOLIVIA
Chile
Basin
Iquique
Chile
Antofagasta
Tropic of Capricorn
Oeno I.
Henderson I.
Ducie I.
Pitcairn I.
(U.K.)
Rapa
Easter Fracture Zone
Sala y Gómez Ridge
Sala-y-Gómez
(Chile)
Easter Fracture Zone
I. de Pascua
(Chile)
San Félix
(Chile)
San Ambrosio
(Chile)
8064
Trench
San Miguel
de Tucumán
PARAGUAY
Asunción
Porto
Alegre
Roggeveen
Basin
Arch. de
Juan Fernández
(Chile)
Córdoba
Aconcagua
6960
Valparaíso
Rosario
Santiago
Buenos
Aires
URUGUAY
Montevideo
Río de la Plata
Challenger Fracture Zone
Chile Rise
Concepción
ARGENTINA
Argentine
Basin
A N D E S
S o u t h w e s t
P a c i f i c
B a s i n
Pacific Antarctic Ridge
Menard Fracture Zone
PATAGONIA
SOUTH
ATLANTIC
OCEAN
114
Falkland
Plateau
6212
Falkland Is.
(U.K.)
Georgia Basin
Punta Arenas
Est. de Magallanes
Tierra del Fuego
South Georgia Ridge
South Georgia
(U.K.)
4402
S o u t h e a s t
P a c i f i c   B a s i n
C. de Hornos
Drake Passage
West from Greenwich
COPYRIGHT PHILIP'S
ft
m
12 000
4000
9000
3000
6000
2000
3000
1000
1500
500
600
200
0
0
200
600
1000
3000
2000
6000
4000
12 000
6000
18 000
8000
24 000
m
ft
B
C
D
E
F
G
H
J
K
11
12
13
14
15
16
17
18
19
20

1:15 000 000

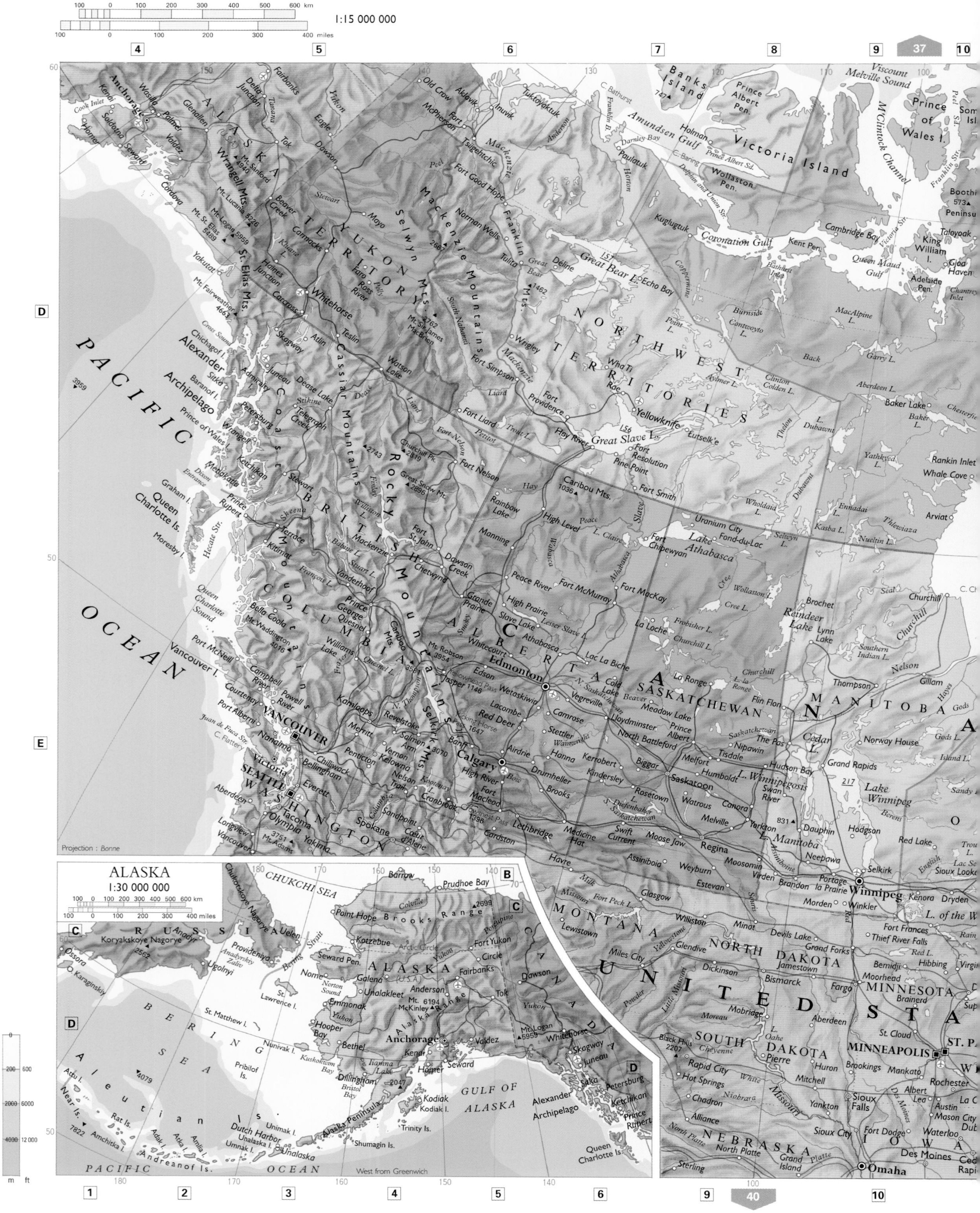

PACIFIC OCEAN
ALASKA
YUKON TERRITORY
NORTHWEST TERRITORIES
BRITISH COLUMBIA
ALBERTA
SASKATCHEWAN
MANITOBA
MONTANA
NORTH DAKOTA
SOUTH DAKOTA
MINNESOTA
NEBRASKA
IOWA
WASHINGTON
UNITED STATES
Victoria Island
Banks Island
Prince of Wales I.
Melville Sound
Amundsen Gulf
Coronation Gulf
Queen Maud Gulf
Great Bear L.
Great Slave L.
Lake Athabasca
Reindeer Lake
Lake Winnipeg
Lake Manitoba
Rocky Mountains
Mackenzie Mountains
Coast Mountains
Cassiar Mountains
Selwyn Mts.
St. Elias Mts.
Wrangell Mts.
Selkirk Mts.
Mt. Logan 5959
Mt. Robson 3954
Anchorage
Fairbanks
Whitehorse
Dawson
Juneau
Inuvik
Yellowknife
Edmonton
Calgary
Vancouver
Victoria
Seattle
Regina
Saskatoon
Winnipeg
Minneapolis
Omaha
Queen Charlotte Is.
Vancouver I.
Alexander Archipelago
Hudson Bay
Projection : Bonne
ALASKA
1:30 000 000
CHUKCHI SEA
BERING SEA
GULF OF ALASKA
Aleutian Is.
Brooks Range
Alaska Range
Arctic Circle
West from Greenwich
RUSSIA
CANADA
37
40

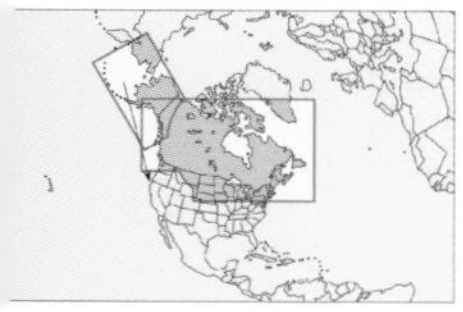

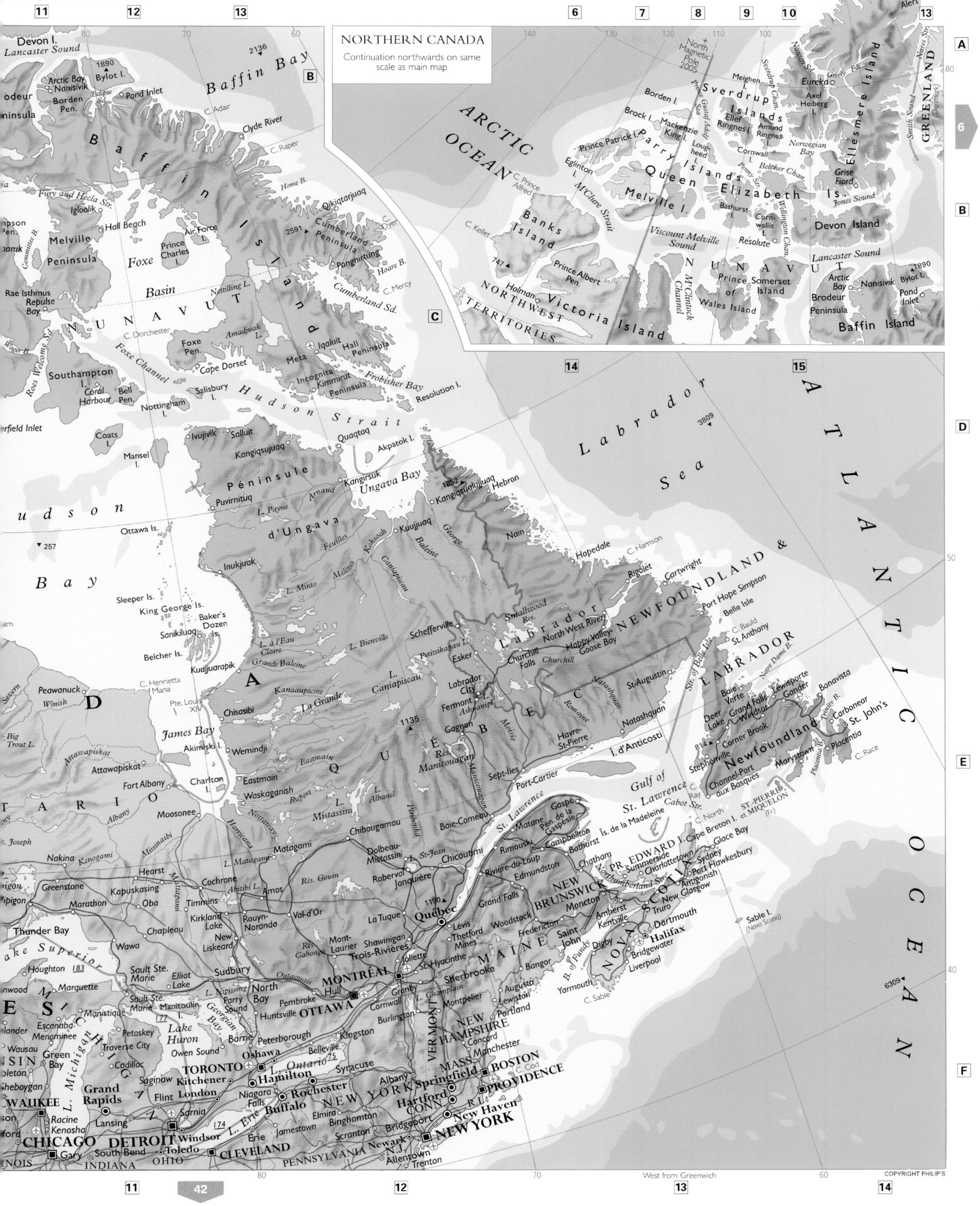
NORTHERN CANADA
Continuation northwards on same scale as main map
ARCTIC OCEAN
Sverdrup Islands
Queen Elizabeth Is.
Parry Islands
Melville I.
Banks Island
Victoria Island
Prince Patrick I.
Borden I.
Brock I.
Mackenzie King I.
Lougheed I.
Ellef Ringnes I.
Amund Ringnes I.
Meighen I.
Axel Heiberg I.
Eureka
Ellesmere Island
Alert
C. Columbia
Greely Fd.
Nansen Sd.
Nares Str.
Smith Sound
GREENLAND (Denmark)
Norwegian Bay
Grise Fiord
Jones Sound
Devon Island
Cornwall I.
Belcher Chan.
Penny Str.
Wellington Chan.
Bathurst I.
Cornwallis I.
Resolute
Lancaster Sound
Viscount Melville Sound
M'Clure Strait
M'Clintock Channel
Prince of Wales Island
Somerset Island
Arctic Bay
Nanisivik
Bylot I.
Pond Inlet
Brodeur Peninsula
Baffin Island
Prince Albert Pen.
Holman
Eglinton I.
C. Prince Alfred
C. Kellet
North Magnetic Pole 2005
Prince Gustaf Adolf Sea
Sverdrup Chan.
NUNAVUT
NORTHWEST TERRITORIES
Devon I.
Lancaster Sound
Baffin Bay
Baffin Island
Clyde River
C. Adair
C. Raper
Home B.
Qikiqtarjuaq
Cumberland Peninsula
Pangnirtung
Cumberland Sd.
Hoare B.
C. Mercy
C. Dyer
Fury and Hecla Str.
Igloolik
Hall Beach
Melville Peninsula
Foxe Basin
Prince Charles I.
Air Force I.
Nettilling L.
Amadjuak L.
Rae Isthmus
Repulse Bay
C. Dorchester
Foxe Pen.
Foxe Channel
Cape Dorset
Iqaluit
Hall Peninsula
Meta Incognita Peninsula
Kimmirut
Frobisher Bay
Resolution I.
Southampton I.
Coral Harbour
Bell Pen.
Salisbury I.
Nottingham I.
Hudson Strait
Coats I.
Mansel I.
Ivujivik
Salluit
Kangiqsujuaq
Quaqtaq
Akpatok I.
Kangirsuk
Ungava Bay
Péninsule d'Ungava
Puvirnituq
Kangiqsualujjuaq
Hebron
Kuujjuaq
Hudson Bay
Ottawa Is.
Inukjuak
Sleeper Is.
King George Is.
Baker's Dozen Is.
Sanikiluaq
Belcher Is.
Kuujjuarapik
C. Henrietta Maria
Peawanuck
Winisk
James Bay
Akimiski I.
Attawapiskat
Fort Albany
Charlton I.
Moosonee
Chisasibi
Wemindji
Eastmain
Waskaganish
L. Mistassini
Chibougamau
L. Minto
L. à l'Eau Claire
Grande Baleine
L. Bienville
La Grande
L. Caniapiscau
Schefferville
Labrador City
Fermont
Gagnon
Rés. Manicouagan
Nain
Hopedale
C. Harrison
Rigolet
Cartwright
Labrador
Smallwood Res.
North West River
Happy Valley-Goose Bay
Churchill Falls
NEWFOUNDLAND & LABRADOR
Port Hope Simpson
Belle Isle
C. Bauld
St. Anthony
Str. of Belle Isle
St-Augustin
Natashquan
Havre-St-Pierre
Î. d'Anticosti
Sept-Îles
Port-Cartier
Baie-Comeau
QUÉBEC
Labrador Sea
ATLANTIC OCEAN
Deer Lake
Corner Brook
Stephenville
Channel-Port aux Basques
Grand Falls-Windsor
Gander
Lewisporte
Bonavista
Carbonear
St. John's
Marystown
Placentia
C. Race
Newfoundland
Gulf of St. Lawrence
Cabot Str.
C. Ray
Gaspé
Pen. de la Gaspésie
Matane
Rimouski
Campbellton
Bathurst
Chatham
Îs. de la Madeleine
PR. EDWARD I.
Charlottetown
Summerside
Cape Breton I.
Sydney
Glace Bay
Port Hawkesbury
Antigonish
New Glasgow
Truro
Amherst
Moncton
NEW BRUNSWICK
Fredericton
Saint John
Woodstock
Edmundston
Grand Falls
NOVA SCOTIA
Halifax
Dartmouth
Bridgewater
Liverpool
Kentville
Digby
Yarmouth
C. Sable
Sable I. (Nova Scotia)
ST.-PIERRE et MIQUELON (Fr.)
Chicoutimi
Jonquière
Roberval
Dolbeau-Mistassini
Québec
Lévis
Thetford Mines
La Tuque
Shawinigan
Trois-Rivières
Mont-Laurier
Joliette
St-Hyacinthe
Sherbrooke
Granby
MONTRÉAL
Hull
OTTAWA
Cornwall
Kingston
Pembroke
Huntsville
Peterborough
Barrie
Owen Sound
Parry Sound
North Bay
Sudbury
Elliot Lake
Sault Ste. Marie
Wawa
Chapleau
Timmins
Kirkland Lake
Rouyn-Noranda
Val-d'Or
Amos
Cochrane
Hearst
Kapuskasing
Oba
Matagami
L. Matagami
Nakina
Greenstone
Marathon
Thunder Bay
Lake Superior
Houghton
Marquette
Manitoulin I.
Georgian Bay
Lake Huron
Lake Michigan
MICHIGAN
TORONTO
Oshawa
Hamilton
Kitchener
London
Sarnia
Windsor
DETROIT
Toledo
CLEVELAND
CHICAGO
Gary
South Bend
Lansing
Flint
Saginaw
Grand Rapids
Traverse City
Cadillac
Petoskey
L. Ontario
L. Erie
Niagara Falls
Buffalo
Rochester
Syracuse
Erie
Jamestown
Elmira
Binghamton
Scranton
NEW YORK
Albany
Burlington
Montpelier
VERMONT
NEW HAMPSHIRE
Concord
Manchester
MAINE
Augusta
Lewiston
Portland
Bangor
BOSTON
PROVIDENCE
Springfield
Hartford
New Haven
Bridgeport
Newark
Allentown
Trenton
PENNSYLVANIA
OHIO
INDIANA
C. Cod
B. of Fundy
Racine
Kenosha
Green Bay
Escanaba
Menominee
Manistique
Wausau
L. Nipissing
Ottawa
Sault Ste. Marie
West from Greenwich
COPYRIGHT PHILIP'S

50 0 50 100 150 200 km

1:6 000 000

50 0 50 100 150 miles

A B C D E F

40

BRITISH COLUMBIA
ALBERTA
SASKATCHEWAN
CANADA
MONTANA
WYOMING
IDAHO
WASHINGTON
OREGON
NEVADA
ROCKY MOUNTAINS
Columbia Basin
Blue Mountains
Bighorn Mountains
Wind River Range
Absaroka Range
Bitterroot Range
Lemhi Range
Sawtooth Range
Salmon River Mountains
Clearwater Mountains
Cabinet Mountains
Great Basin
Great Salt Lake
Great Salt Lake Desert
Uinta Mountains
Cascade Range
Coast Ranges
Klamath Mts.
Snake River Plain
Columbia Plateau
Olympic Mts.
VANCOUVER
SEATTLE
PORTLAND
SACRAMENTO
Salt Lake City
Boise
Spokane
Great Falls
Helena
Billings
Casper
Missoula

36

B C D E F G

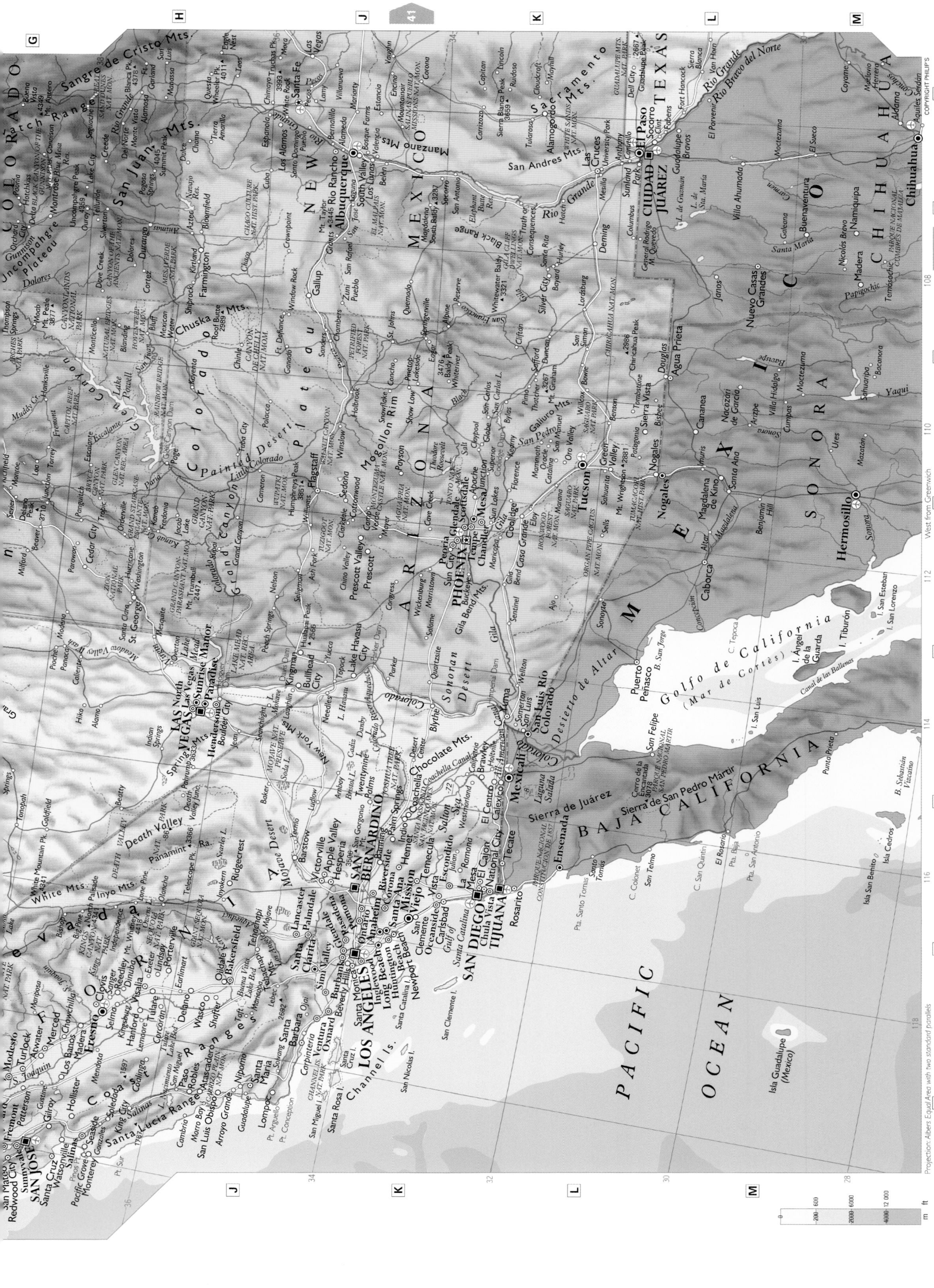

COLORADO
NEW MEXICO
ARIZONA
TEXAS
CHIHUAHUA
SONORA
MEXICO
BAJA CALIFORNIA
PACIFIC OCEAN
Golfo de California (Mar de Cortés)
Colorado Plateau
Sangre de Cristo Mts.
San Juan Mts.
Mogollon Rim
Grand Canyon
Mojave Desert
Sonoran Desert
Death Valley
Channel Is.
LOS ANGELES
SAN DIEGO
TIJUANA
LAS VEGAS
PHOENIX
Tucson
Albuquerque
Santa Fe
El Paso
CIUDAD JUÁREZ
Chihuahua
Hermosillo
Mexicali
Ensenada
SAN JOSE
Fresno
SAN BERNARDINO
State Capitals
National Parks
Projection: Albers Equal Area with two standard parallels
West from Greenwich
COPYRIGHT PHILIP'S

50 0 50 100 150 200 km

1:6 000 000

50 0 50 100 150 miles

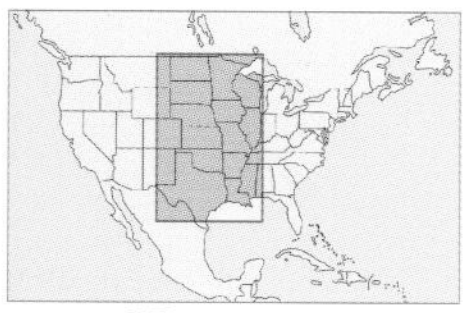

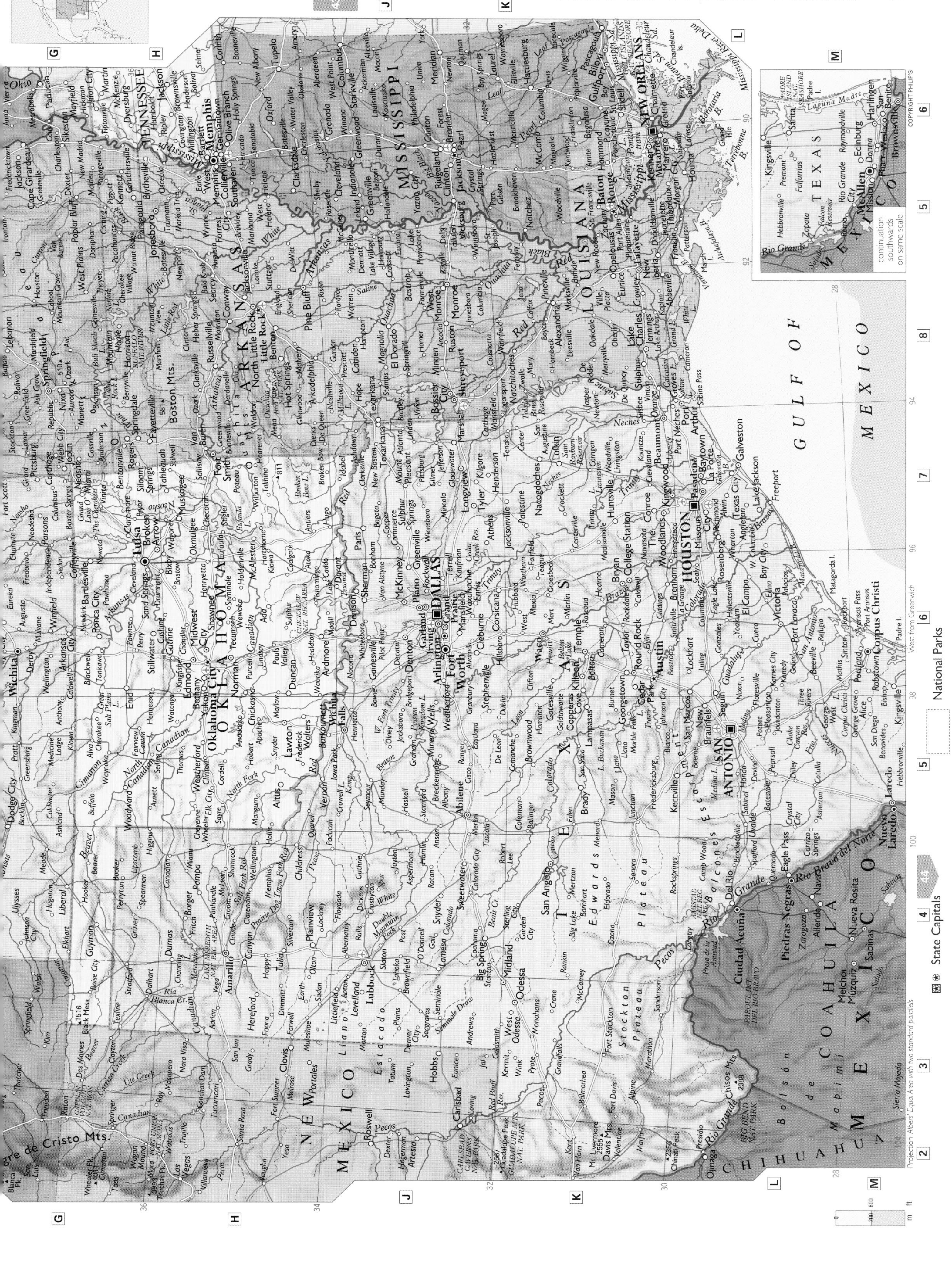
OKLAHOMA
ARKANSAS
MISSISSIPPI
LOUISIANA
TENNESSEE
TEXAS
NEW MEXICO
MEXICO
COAHUILA
CHIHUAHUA
GULF OF MEXICO
Oklahoma City
Tulsa
Dallas
Fort Worth
Houston
San Antonio
Austin
Memphis
Little Rock
Jackson
Baton Rouge
New Orleans
Shreveport
Lubbock
Amarillo
Wichita
continuation southwards on same scale
State Capitals
National Parks
West from Greenwich
Projection: Albers' Equal Area with two standard parallels
COPYRIGHT PHILIP'S

50 0 50 100 150 200 km

1:6 000 000

50 0 50 100 150 miles

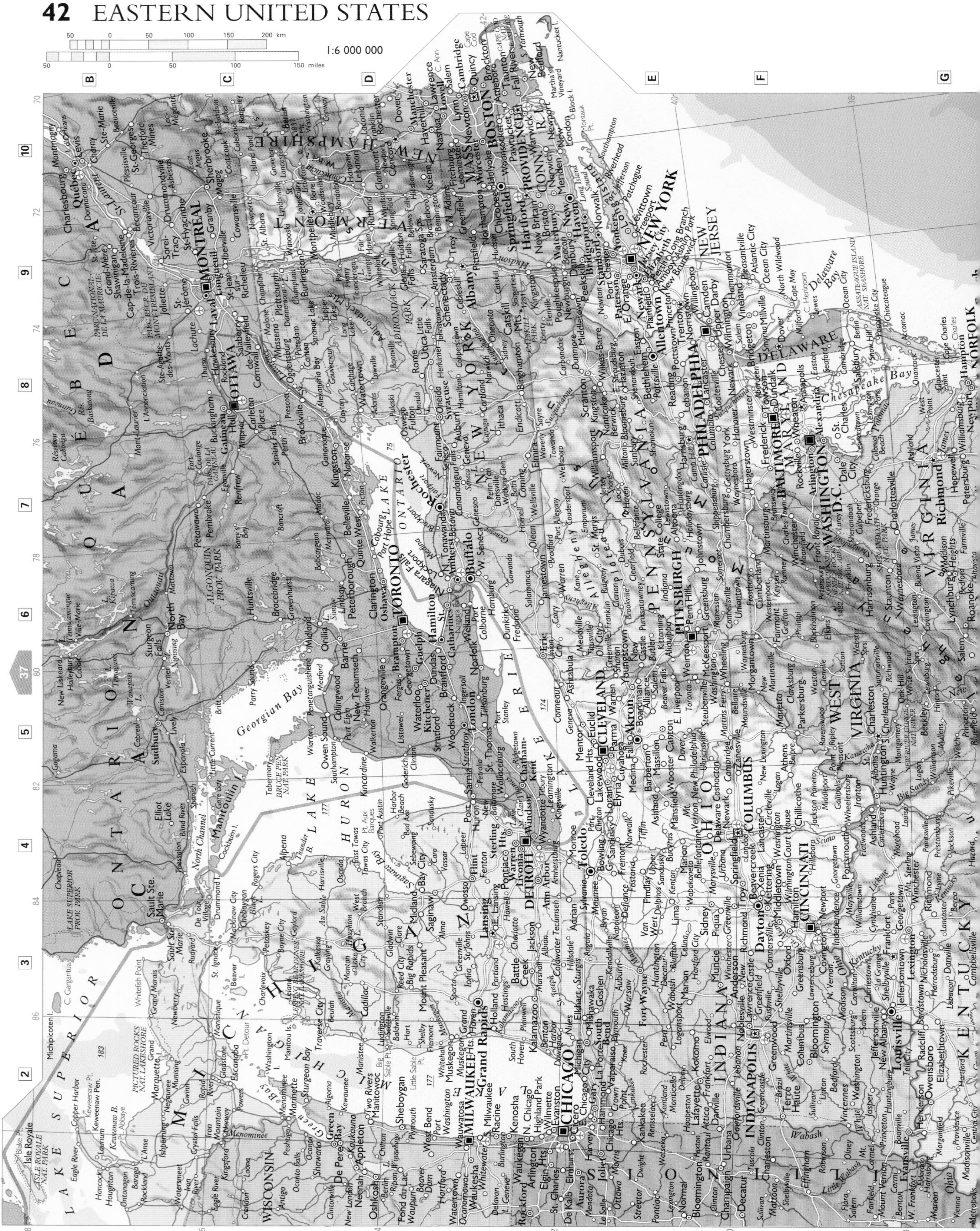

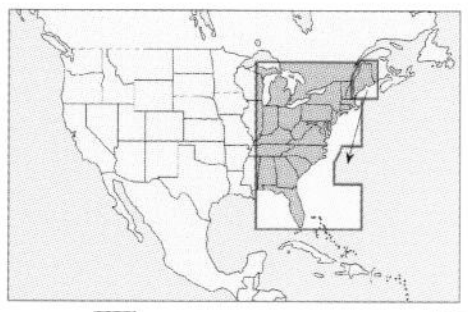

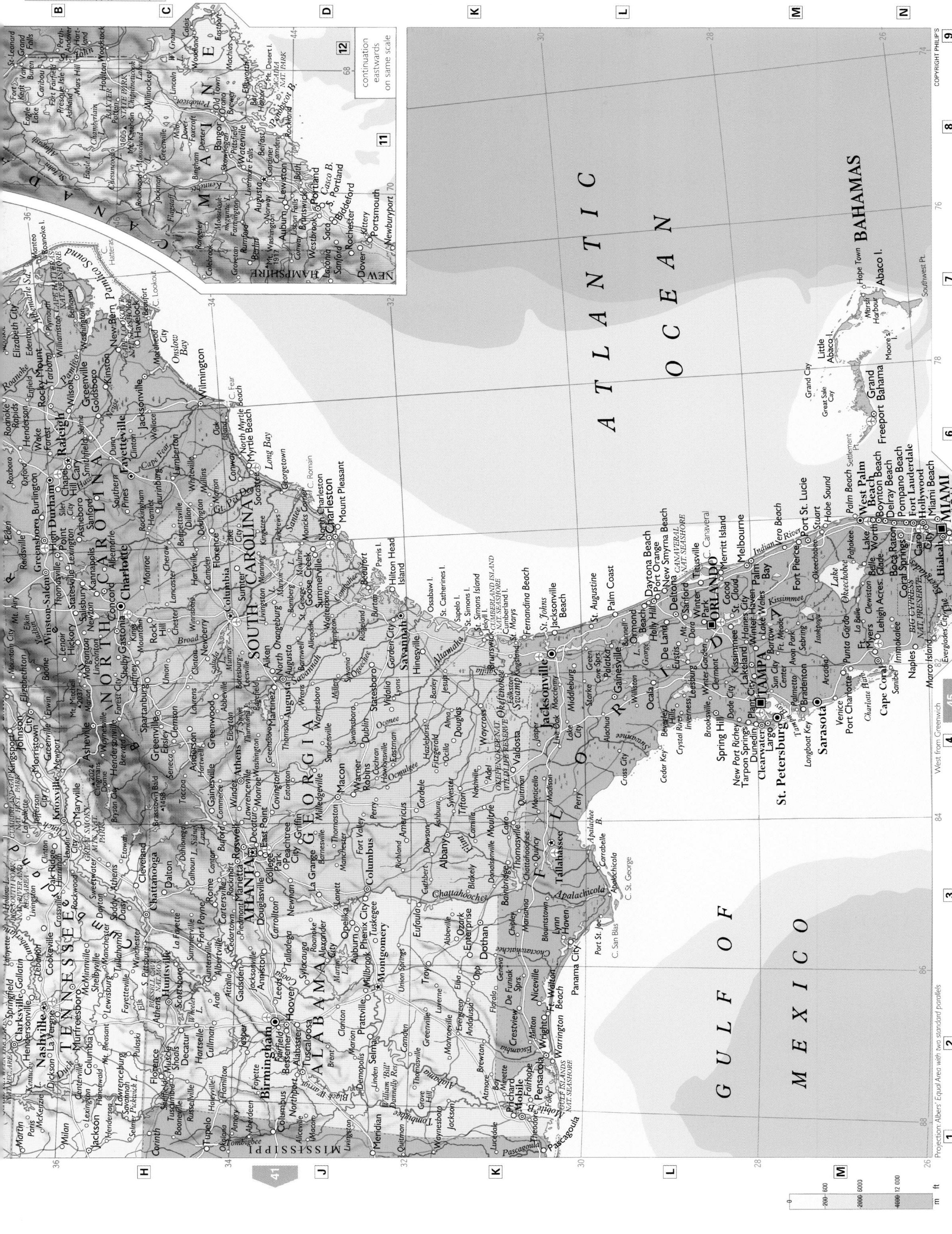
ATLANTIC OCEAN
GULF OF MEXICO
BAHAMAS
NORTH CAROLINA
SOUTH CAROLINA
GEORGIA
FLORIDA
ALABAMA
TENNESSEE
MISSISSIPPI
MAINE
NEW HAMPSHIRE
Atlanta
Charlotte
Raleigh
Columbia
Jacksonville
Orlando
Tampa
St. Petersburg
Miami
Savannah
Charleston
Birmingham
Montgomery
Tallahassee
Nashville
Knoxville
Chattanooga
Mobile
Pensacola
Augusta
Portland
Bangor
continuation eastwards on same scale
State Capitals
National Parks
Projection: Albers' Equal Area with two standard parallels
West from Greenwich
m ft
COPYRIGHT PHILIP'S

MEXICO, CENTRAL AMERICA AND THE WEST INDIES

1:15 000 000

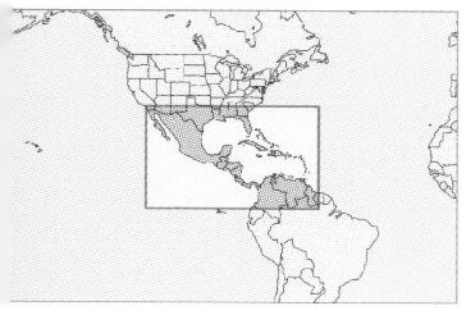

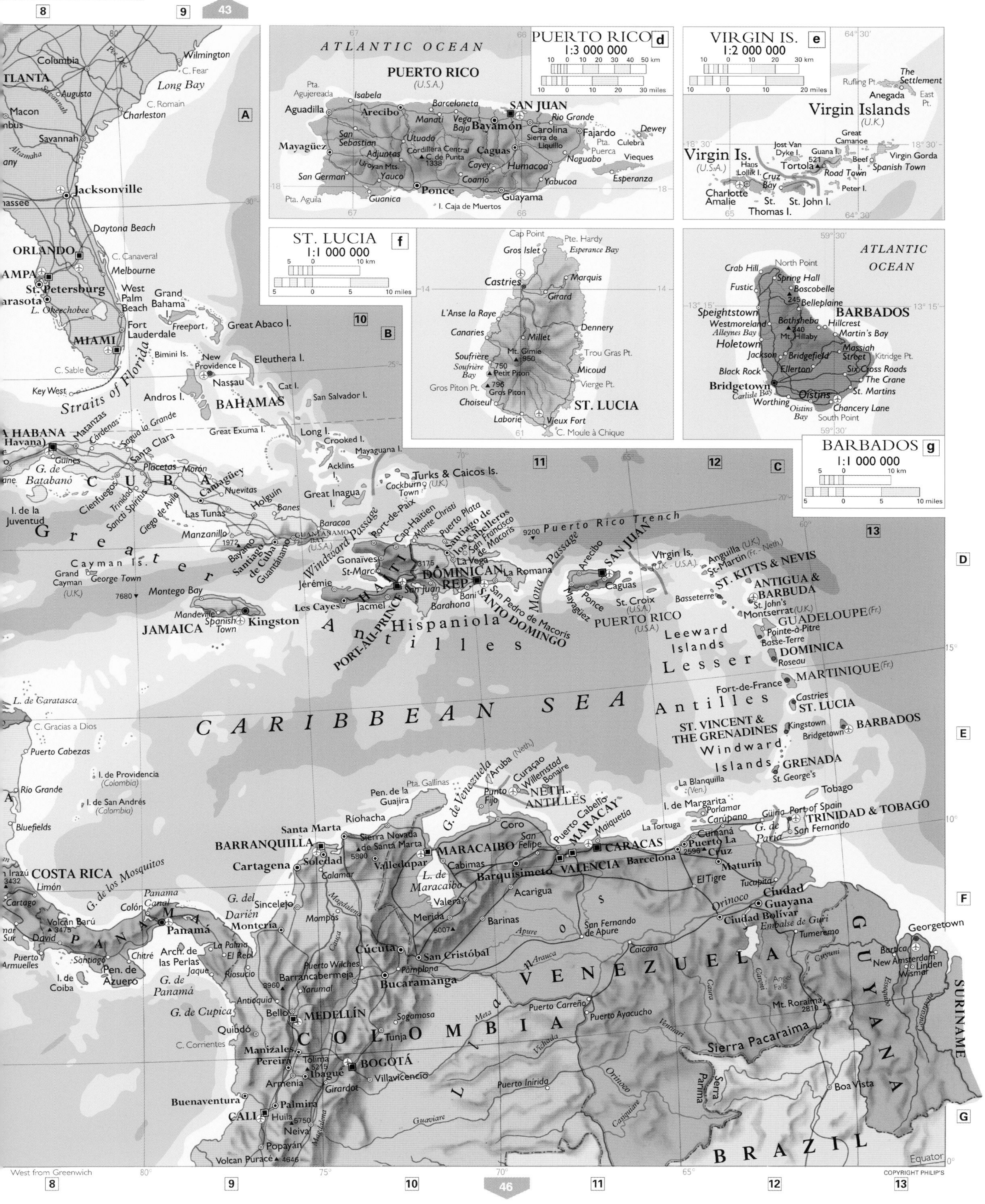
8
9
43
PUERTO RICO d
1:3 000 000
ATLANTIC OCEAN
PUERTO RICO
(U.S.A.)
Pta. Agujereada
Isabela
Aguadilla
Arecibo
Barceloneta
SAN JUAN
Manatí
Vega Baja
Bayamón
Carolina
Rio Grande
Fajardo
Sierra de Luquillo
Dewey
Culebra
Pta. Puerca
Vieques
Mayagüez
San Sebastian
Adjuntas
Utuado
Cordillera Central
C. de Punta 1338
Caguas
Uroyan Mts.
Cayey
Humacoa
Naguabo
San German
Yauco
Coamo
Yabucoa
Esperanza
Pta. Aguila
Guanica
Ponce
Guayama
I. Caja de Muertos
VIRGIN IS. e
1:2 000 000
The Settlement
Anegada
East Pt.
Rufling Pt.
Virgin Islands
(U.K.)
Great Camanoe
Jost Van Dyke I.
Guana I.
Beef I.
Virgin Gorda
Spanish Town
Virgin Is.
(U.S.A.)
Hans Lollik I.
Tortola
521
Road Town
Cruz Bay
Peter I.
Charlotte Amalie
St. Thomas I.
St. John I.
ST. LUCIA f
1:1 000 000
Cap Point
Pte. Hardy
Gros Islet
Esperance Bay
Castries
Marquis
Girard
L'Anse la Raye
Canaries
Dennery
Millet
Mt. Gimie 950
Soufrière
Soufrière Bay
Trou Gras Pt.
Micoud
Petit Piton 750
Gros Piton 796
Vierge Pt.
Gros Piton Pt.
Choiseul
ST. LUCIA
Laborie
Vieux Fort
C. Moule à Chique
ATLANTIC OCEAN
North Point
Crab Hill
Spring Hall
Fustic
Boscobelle
Belleplaine
245
Speightstown
Westmoreland
Alleynes Bay
Bathsheba
Hillcrest
BARBADOS
Holetown
Mt. Hillaby 340
Martin's Bay
Jackson
Bridgefield
Massiah Street
Kitridge Pt.
Black Rock
Ellerton
Six Cross Roads
The Crane
Bridgetown
Carlisle Bay
Worthing
Oistins
Oistins Bay
St. Martins
Chancery Lane
South Point
BARBADOS g
1:1 000 000
Wilmington
C. Fear
Columbia
Pee Dee
ATLANTA
Augusta
Long Bay
Macon
C. Romain
Charleston
Savannah
Altamaha
Jacksonville
Daytona Beach
ORLANDO
C. Canaveral
Melbourne
TAMPA
St. Petersburg
West Palm Beach
Grand Bahama I.
Freeport
L. Okeechobee
Great Abaco I.
Fort Lauderdale
MIAMI
Bimini Is.
New Providence I.
Eleuthera I.
C. Sable
Nassau
Key West
Straits of Florida
Andros I.
Cat I.
San Salvador I.
BAHAMAS
LA HABANA (Havana)
Matanzas
Cárdenas
Great Exuma I.
Long I.
Crooked I.
Mayaguana I.
G. de Batabanó
Güines
Sagua la Grande
Santa Clara
Placetas
Morón
Camagüey
Acklins I.
Turks & Caicos Is. (U.K.)
Cockburn Town
CUBA
Nuevitas
Great Inagua I.
Cienfuegos
Trinidad
Sancti Spíritus
Ciego de Avila
Holguín
Las Tunas
Banes
I. de la Juventud
Greater Antilles
Manzanillo
Baracoa
GUANTÁNAMO BAY (U.S.A.)
Windward Passage
Port-de-Paix
Cap-Haïtien
Monte Christi
Puerto Plata
Santiago de los Caballeros
San Francisco de Macorís
Puerto Rico Trench
9200
Cayman Is.
Grand Cayman
George Town
(U.K.)
Bayamo
Santiago de Cuba
Guantánamo
1972
Gonaïves
St-Marc
HAITI
3175
DOMINICAN REP.
La Vega
La Romana
Mona Passage
Arecibo
SAN JUAN
Virgin Is. (U.K. - U.S.A.)
Anguilla (U.K.)
St-Martin (Fr. - Neth.)
ST. KITTS & NEVIS
ANTIGUA & BARBUDA
St. John's
Montego Bay
7680
Jérémie
San Juan
Bani
Caguas
Mayagüez
Ponce
St. Croix (U.S.A.)
Basseterre
Montserrat (U.K.)
GUADELOUPE (Fr.)
Pointe-à-Pitre
Basse-Terre
Les Cayes
Jacmel
Barahona
San Pedro de Macorís
SANTO DOMINGO
PUERTO RICO (U.S.A.)
Leeward Islands
DOMINICA
Roseau
Mandeville
Spanish Town
Kingston
JAMAICA
PORT-AU-PRINCE
Hispaniola
Lesser Antilles
MARTINIQUE (Fr.)
Fort-de-France
Castries
ST. LUCIA
L. de Caratasca
CARIBBEAN SEA
ST. VINCENT & THE GRENADINES
Kingstown
Bridgetown
BARBADOS
C. Gracias a Dios
Windward Islands
Puerto Cabezas
GRENADA
St. George's
I. de Providencia (Colombia)
Pta. Gallinas
Aruba (Neth.)
Curaçao
Willemstad
Bonaire
NETH. ANTILLES
La Blanquilla (Ven.)
Tobago
Rio Grande
I. de San Andrés (Colombia)
Pen. de la Guajira
G. de Venezuela
Punto Fijo
I. de Margarita
Porlamar
Carúpano
Güiria
Port of Spain
TRINIDAD & TOBAGO
San Fernando
Bluefields
Ríohacha
Coro
Puerto Cabello
MARACAY
Maiquetia
La Tortuga
G. de Paria
Santa Marta
Sierra Nevada de Santa Marta
5800
MARACAIBO
San Felipe
CARACAS
Cumaná
Puerto La Cruz
2596
BARRANQUILLA
Soledad
Valledupar
Cabimas
Barquisimeto
VALENCIA
Barcelona
Maturín
Cartagena
Calamar
L. de Maracaibo
El Tigre
Tucupita
Irazú 3432
COSTA RICA
Limón
G. de los Mosquitos
Panama Canal
G. del Darién
Sincelejo
Valera
Acarigua
Orinoco
Ciudad Guayana
Cartago
Colón
Montería
Mérida
Ciudad Bolívar
Embalse de Guri
Volcan Barú 3475
David
PANAMA
Panamá
Mompós
Barinas
San Fernando de Apure
Apure
Tumeremo
Georgetown
Chitré
Arch. de las Perlas
La Palma
El Real
Cúcuta
San Cristóbal
Caicara
Bartica
New Amsterdam
Linden
Wismar
Puerto Armuelles
Santiago
Pen. de Azuero
Jaqué
Puerto Wilches
Pamplona
Arauca
VENEZUELA
I. de Coiba
G. de Panamá
Riosucio
3960
Barrancabermeja
Yarumal
Bucaramanga
Caura
Caroni
Angel Falls
GUYANA
SURINAME
Antioquia
Puerto Carreño
Puerto Ayacucho
Mt. Roraima 2810
G. de Cupica
Bello
MEDELLÍN
Sogamoso
Meta
Ventuari
Quibdó
Tunja
COLOMBIA
Vichada
Sierra Pacaraima
C. Corrientes
Manizales
Pereira
Tolima 5215
Ibagué
BOGOTÁ
Villavicencio
Armenia
Girardot
Puerto Inírida
Serra Parima
Boa Vista
Buenaventura
Palmira
CALI
Huila 5750
Neiva
Popayán
Guaviare
Volcan Puracé 4646
BRAZIL
Equator
West from Greenwich
COPYRIGHT PHILIP'S
10
11
12
13
46
A
B
C
D
E
F
G

1:16 000 000

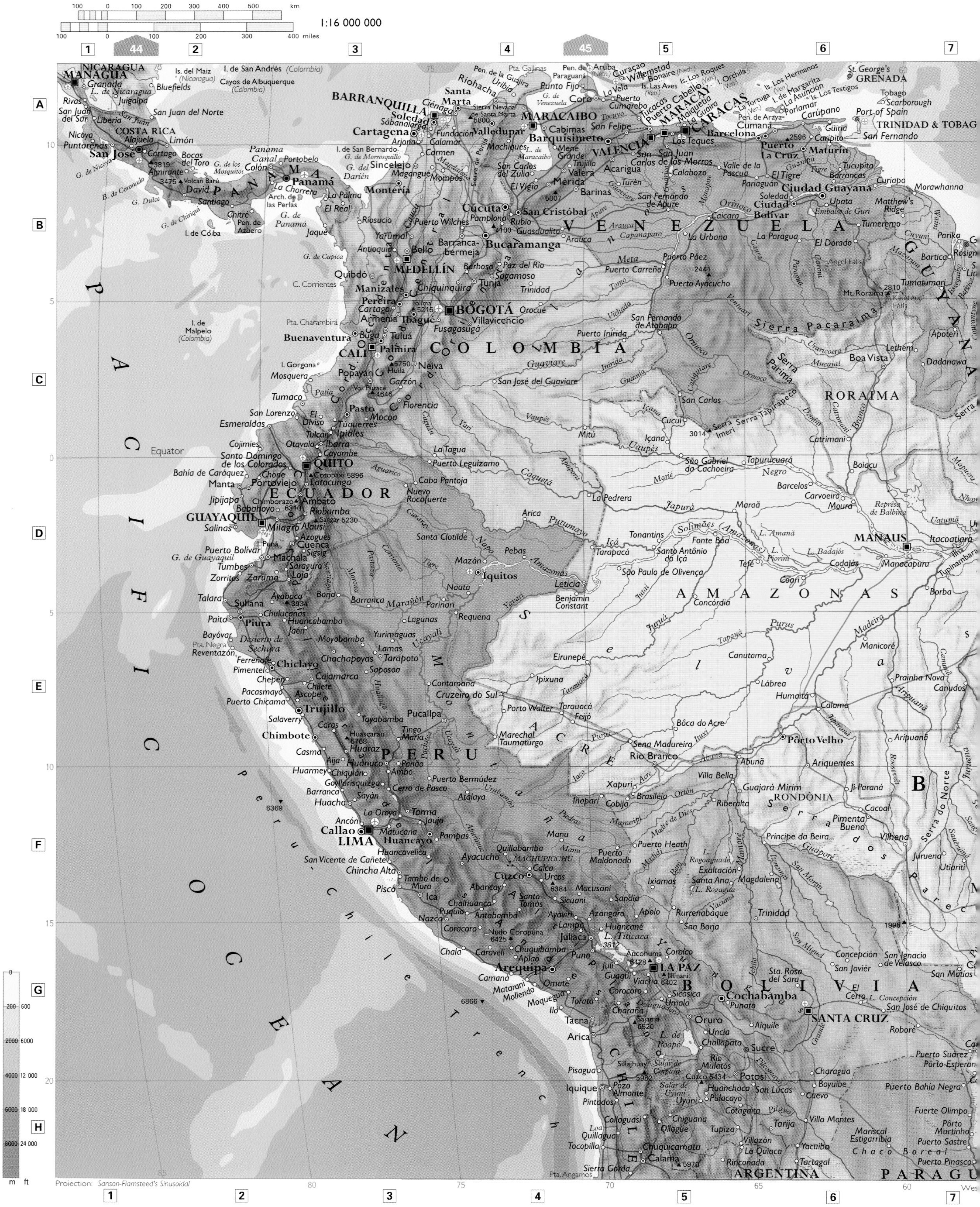

km 100 0 100 200 300 400 500
100 0 100 200 300 400 miles
1 44 2 3 4 45 5 6 7
A B C D E F G H
NICARAGUA
MANAGUA
Granada
L. de Nicaragua
Juigalpa
Bluefields
Is. del Maiz (Nicaragua)
I. de San Andrés (Colombia)
Cayos de Albuquerque (Colombia)
Rivas
San Juan del Sur
Liberia
San Juan del Norte
Nicoya
Puntarenas
COSTA RICA
Alajuela
Limón
San José
Cartago
Bocas del Toro
G. de los Mosquitos
Colón
Portobelo
Panama Canal
PANAMA
Panamá
La Chorrera
Arch. de las Perlas
G. de Panamá
David
Santiago
Chitré
Pen. de Azuero
I. de Coiba
G. de Chiriquí
G. de Nicoya
B. de Coronado
G. Dulce
Volcán Barú
La Palma
El Real
Jaqué
BARRANQUILLA
Cartagena
Santa Marta
Ciénaga
Soledad
Sabanalarga
Riohacha
Uribia
Pen. de la Guajira
Pta. Gallinas
Sierra Nevada de Santa Marta
Valledupar
Fundación
Calamar
Arjona
Carmen
Magangué
Mompós
Sincelejo
Montería
I. de San Bernardo
G. de Morrosquillo
G. del Darién
Riosucio
Yarumal
Antioquia
Bello
MEDELLÍN
Barrancabermeja
Bucaramanga
Cúcuta
Pamplona
Rubio
San Cristóbal
Guasdualito
Arauca
Quibdó
G. de Cupica
C. Corrientes
Manizales
Pereira
Cartago
Armenia
Ibagué
Chiquinquirá
Barbosa
Tunja
Sogamoso
Paz del Rio
BOGOTÁ
Villavicencio
Fusagasugá
Tolima
Pta. Charambirá
I. de Malpelo (Colombia)
Buenaventura
Buga
Tuluá
CALI
Palmira
Neiva
Huila
I. Gorgona
Mosquera
Popayán
Garzón
Vol. Puracé
Florencia
Tumaco
Pasto
Mocoa
San Lorenzo
Esmeraldas
Tulcán
Ipiales
Túquerres
COLOMBIA
Guaviare
San José del Guaviare
Mitú
Vaupés
Yari
Caquetá
Apaporis
Cojimies
Otavalo
Ibarra
Cayambe
Equator
Santo Domingo de los Colorados
QUITO
Cotopaxi
Latacunga
Bahía de Caráquez
Chone
Portoviejo
Manta
ECUADOR
Ambato
Chimborazo
Riobamba
Sangay
Jipijapa
Babahoyo
GUAYAQUIL
Salinas
Milagro
Alausí
Azogues
Cuenca
Sigsig
I. Puná
Puerto Bolívar
G. de Guayaquil
Machala
Tumbes
Saraguro
Loja
Zorritos
Zaruma
Talara
Sullana
Ayabaca
Piura
Chulucanas
Huancabamba
Jaén
Paita
Bayóvar
Pta. Negra
Reventazón
Desierto de Sechura
Moyobamba
Chiclayo
Ferreñafe
Pimentel
Chepén
Pacasmayo
Puerto Chicama
Cajamarca
Chilete
Ascope
Trujillo
Salaverry
Chimbote
Casma
Huascarán
Huaraz
Caraz
Aija
Huánuco
Huarmey
Chiquián
Goyllarisquizga
Barranca
Huacho
Sayán
Cerro de Pasco
Ambo
Panao
Tarma
La Oroya
Jauja
Ancón
Callao
LIMA
Matucana
Huancayo
Huancavelica
San Vicente de Cañete
Chincha Alta
Pisco
Ica
Nazca
Tambo de Mora
PERU
Yurimaguas
Lamas
Tarapoto
Saposoa
Chachapoyas
Tayabamba
Tingo María
Pucallpa
Contamana
Cruzeiro do Sul
Puerto Bermúdez
Atalaya
Requena
Lagunas
Parinari
Nauta
Iquitos
Mazán
Pebas
Leticia
Benjamin Constant
Barranca
Borja
Marañón
Ucayali
Huallaga
Pampas
Ayacucho
Quillabamba
MACHUPICCHU
Cuzco
Calca
Urcos
Sicuani
Abancay
Chalhuanca
Puquio
Santo Tomás
Antabamba
Coracora
Nudo Coropuna
Chala
Caraveli
Camaná
Arequipa
Matarani
Mollendo
Moquegua
Omate
Ilo
Tacna
Arica
Ayaviri
Lampa
Juliaca
Puno
Azángaro
L. Titicaca
Huancané
Juli
Guaqui
Viacha
LA PAZ
Ancohuma
Illimani
Corocoro
Charaña
Sajama
Oruro
L. de Poopó
Uncia
Challapata
Sucre
Potosí
Rio Mulatos
Salar de Coipasa
Salar de Uyuni
Uyuni
Pulacayo
Huanchaca
Cotagaita
Tupiza
Villazón
La Quiaca
Tarija
Pisagua
Iquique
Pozo Almonte
Pintados
Collaguasi
Ollagüe
Chiguana
Quillagua
Tocopilla
Chuquicamata
Calama
Sierra Gorda
Pta. Angamos
CHILE
ARGENTINA
BOLIVIA
Cochabamba
Punata
SANTA CRUZ
Aiquile
Sicasica
Umala
Apolo
Rurrenabaque
San Borja
Riberalta
Guajará Mirim
Villa Bella
Trinidad
Magdalena
Exaltación
Santa Ana
Puerto Heath
Puerto Maldonado
Iñapari
Cobija
Xapuri
Brasiléia
Rio Branco
Sena Madureira
Feijó
Tarauacá
Marechal Taumaturgo
Porto Walter
ACRE
Ipixuna
Eirunepé
Lábrea
Canutama
Humaitá
Pôrto Velho
Abunã
Ariquemes
Ji-Paraná
RONDÔNIA
Pimenta Bueno
Cacoal
Vilhena
Principe da Beira
Concepción
San Javier
San Ignacio de Velasco
San Matías
San José de Chiquitos
Roboré
Charagua
Boyuibe
Cuevo
Villa Montes
Yacuiba
Tartagal
Rinconada
Mariscal Estigarribia
Chaco Boreal
Puerto Suárez
Pôrto Esperança
Puerto Bahia Negra
Fuerte Olimpo
Pôrto Murtinho
Puerto Sastre
Puerto Pinasco
PARAGU
MARACAIBO
L. de Maracaibo
Cabimas
Barquisimeto
San Felipe
Machiques
Coro
Punto Fijo
Paraguaná
Pen. de Paraguaná
G. de Venezuela
La Vela
Puerto Cumarebo
Aruba
Curaçao
Willemstad
Bonaire
Is. Las Aves
Is. Los Roques
I. Orchila
Tucacas
Puerto Cabello
MARACAY
VALENCIA
CARACAS
La Guaira
Maiquetía
Los Teques
San Carlos del Zulia
El Vigía
Mérida
Valera
Trujillo
Acarigua
San Carlos
San Juan de los Morros
Calabozo
Barinas
Guanare
Turén
San Fernando de Apure
Valle de la Pascua
El Tigre
Barcelona
Puerto La Cruz
Cumaná
Carúpano
Pen. de Araya
Guiria
Caripito
Maturín
La Tortuga
I. de Margarita
La Asunción
Porlamar
Is. Los Hermanos
Is. Los Testigos
Tucupita
Barrancas
Pariaguán
Ciudad Guayana
Ciudad Bolívar
Soledad
Upata
Caicara
Embalse de Guri
Tumeremo
VENEZUELA
La Urbana
La Paragua
El Dorado
Puerto Páez
Puerto Carreño
Puerto Ayacucho
Angel Falls
Mt. Roraima
Kaieteur Falls
Sierra Pacaraima
San Fernando de Atabapo
Puerto Inírida
Sierra Parima
Serra Tapirapecó
San Carlos
Cucuí
Içana
Serra Imeri
Orinoco
Meta
Tomo
Vichada
Apure
Arauca
Capanaparo
Ventuari
Caroní
Caura
Cuyuni
Trinidad & Tobag
Port of Spain
San Fernando
Tobago
Scarborough
St. George's
GRENADA
Morawhanna
Matthew's Ridge
Bartica
Rosignol
Parika
Tumatumari
Apoteri
Lethem
Dadanawa
GUYANA
Boa Vista
RORAIMA
Catrimani
Boiaçu
Barcelos
Carvoeiro
Moura
Negro
São Gabriel da Cachoeira
Topurucuará
Uaupés
Japurá
Maraã
La Pedrera
La Tagua
Puerto Leguízamo
Cabo Pantoja
Nuevo Rocafuerte
Arica
Putumayo
Santa Clotilde
Tonantins
Fonte Boa
Santo Antônio do Içá
Tarapacá
São Paulo de Olivença
Tefé
Coari
Codajás
Manacapuru
MANAUS
Itacoatiara
Solimões (Amazonas)
Amazonas
AMAZONAS
Juruá
Purus
Concórdia
Manicoré
Borba
Madeira
Prainha Nova
Canudos
Aripuanã
Calama
Bôca do Acre
Serra do Norte
Juruena
Utiariti
PACIFIC OCEAN
Peru - Chile Trench
Projection: Sanson-Flamsteed's Sinusoidal
m ft
200 600
2000 6000
4000 12 000
6000 18 000
8000 24 000

TRINIDAD AND TOBAGO
1:2 500 000
West from Greenwich
Tobago
Charlotteville
North Pt.
Little Tobago
Castara
Main Ridge
Roxborough
Plymouth
Scarborough
Buccoo Reef
Crown Pt.
Rockly Bay
Blanchisseuse
Sans Souci
Matelot
Chupara Pt.
La Vache Pt.
Maracas Bay Village
Dragon's Mouths
Corozal Pt.
Monos I.
Maraval
Northern Range
Mt. Aripo
Toco
Galera Pt.
Redhead
Salybia
VENEZUELA
Pen. de Paria
Macuro
Güiria
Port of Spain
San Juan
Tunapuna
Valencia
Arima
Caroni
Guaico
Sangre Grande
Matura Bay
ATLANTIC OCEAN
Golfo de Paria
Chaguanas
Talparo
Upper Manzanilla
Nariva Swamp
Cocos Bay
Trinidad
Point Lisas
Otaheite Bay
Couva
Gasparillo
Rio Claro
Guatuaro Pt.
San Fernando
Brighton
Guapo Bay
La Brea
Pitch Lake
Princes Town
Pierreville
Mayaro Bay
Point Fortin
Penal
Basse Terre
Guayaguayare
Cedros Bay
Bonasse
Palo Seco
Siparia
Trinity Hills
Galeota Pt.
Icacos Pt.
Erin Pt.
La Lune
Moruga
Serpent's Mouth
Pta. Bombedor
VENEZUELA
ATLANTIC
OCEAN
Equator
Nickerie
Paramaribo
Nieuw Amsterdam
Moengo
St-Laurent
Iracoubo
Sinnamary
Kourou
Cayenne
Albina
Kaw
C. Orange
St-Georges
Oiapoque
FRENCH GUIANA
Camopi
Amapá
I. de Maracá
Serra Tumucumaque
AMAPÁ
Merirumã
Serra do Navio
Macapá
I. Caviana
I. Mexiana
C. Maguarinho
Mazagão
Afuá
I. de Marajó
Soure
Curuçá
Salinópolis
Bragança
I. Grande de Gurupá
Chaves
Vigia
BELÉM
Almeirim
Gurupá
Breves
Óbidos
Monte Alegre
Prainha
Pôrto de Moz
Curralinho
Abaetetuba
Castanhal
Viseu
Turiaçu
Amazonas (Amazon)
Alenquer
Cametá
Santarém
Belterra
Altamira
Baião
Aveiro
Brasília Legal
Tucuruí
Represa de Tucuruí
Itaituba
PARÁ
Alcântara
São Luís
Barreirinhas
Tutóia
Luís Correia
Camocim
Pinheiro
Rosário
Itapecuru-Mirim
Parnaíba
Granja
Itapipoca
Caucaia
FORTALEZA
Viana
Santa Inês
Brejo
Piracuruca
Sobral
Maranguape
Cascavel
Bacabal
Coroatá
Piripiri
Codó
Baturité
Aracati
Caxias
Ipu
Quixadá
Russas
Açailândia
Pedreiras
Campo Maior
Areia Branca
Macau
Ceará Mirim
Marabá
MARANHÃO
Imperatriz
Teresina
Crateús
CEARÁ
Mossoró
C. de São Roque
Natal
Barra do Corda
Senador Pompeu
RIO GRANDE DO NORTE
São João do Araguaia
Carajás
Tocantinópolis
Pôrto Franco
Colinas
Amarante
Valença do Piauí
Iguatu
Caraúbas
Caicó
Currais Novos
Canguaretama
Mamanguape
Estreito
Floriano
Oeiras
Picos
Cajàzeiras
Cedro
Sousa
Patos
Alagoa Grande
Cabedelo
Carolina
Loreto
Nova Iorque
PIAUÍ
Chapada do Araripe
Crato
Juàzeiro do Norte
PARAÍBA
Campina Grande
João Pessoa
Araguaína
Riachão
Uruçuí
Ouricuri
Salgueiro
Caruaru
RECIFE
Olinda
Jaboatão
Conceição do Araguaia
Paulistana
PERNAMBUCO
Pesqueira
São João do Piauí
Vitória de Santo Antão
Araguacema
Pedro Afonso
Santa Filomena
Serra dos Dois Irmãos
Petrolina
São Francisco
Garanhuns
Petrolândia
Palmares
Caracol
Novo Remanso
Nova Casa Nova
Juàzeiro
Palmeira dos Índios
Rio Largo
Maceió
Represa de Sobradinho
Paulo Afonso
Arapiraca
ALAGOAS
Penedo
Palmas
Parnaguá
Senhor-do-Bonfim
Propriá
SERGIPE
Capela
Aracaju
São Cristóvão
Estância
Pôrto Nacional
TOCANTINS
Barra
Xique-Xique
Jacobina
Mundo Novo
Queimadas
Serrinha
Santa Isabel do Morro
Gurupi
Peixe
Taguatinga
Barreiras
BAHIA
Ibotirama
Feira de Santana
Alagoinhas
Itaberaba
Cachoeira
Santo Amaro
SALVADOR
Paranã
Campos Belos
São Domingos
Santa Maria da Vitória
Bom Jesus da Lapa
Serra do Sincorá
Castro Alves
Valença
Nazaré
B. de Todos os Santos
Jequié
Barragem de Serra da Mesa
Niquelândia
Posse
Carinhanha
Caetité
Brumado
Ubaitaba
Vitória da Conquista
Itabuna
Ilhéus
Uruaçu
Aruanã
Condeúba
Januária
Monte Azul
Canavieiras
Formosa
Taguatinga
BRASÍLIA
São Francisco
Pedra Azul
Belmonte
Santo Antônio
Barra do Garças
Goiás
Anápolis
Luziânia
Jaíba
Montes Claros
Salinas
Jequitinhonha
Pôrto Seguro
Rondonópolis
GOIÂNIA
GOIÁS
Vianópolis
Araçuaí
Itamaraju
Alto Araguaia
Morrinhos
Paracatu
Pirapora
Teófilo Otoni
Nanuque
Prado
Caravelas
Jataí
Rio Verde
Ipameri
Patos de Minas
Catalão
Diamantina
Mucuri
Coxim
Quirinópolis
Itumbiara
Araguari
Corinto
Governador Valadares
Conceição da Barra
São Mateus
MINAS GERAIS
Uberlândia
Patrocínio
Curvelo
Ipatinga
Nova Venécia
Colatina
Linhares
Ituiutaba
Prata
Araxá
Ibiá
Sete Lagoas
Itabira
Paranaíba
Uberaba
BELO HORIZONTE
Sabará
Caratinga
Campo Grande
Santa Fé do Sul
Frutal
Ponte Nova
Cariacica
Vitória
Água Clara
São José do Barretos
Igarapava
Divinópolis
Vila Velha
Três Lagoas
Rio Prêto
Franca
Passos
Conselheiro Lafaiete
Ouro Prêto
Ubá
Cachoeiro de Itapemirim
Ribas do Rio Pardo
Andradina
Araçatuba
Ribeirão Prêto
Guaxupé
São João del Rei
Barbacena
Itaperuna
Panorama
Penápolis
Catanduva
Araraquara
Poços de Caldas
Juiz de Fora
Campos
Dourados
Presidente Epitácio
SÃO PAULO
Lins
São Carlos
Três Rios
Presidente Prudente
Marília
Bauru
Jaú
Caldas
Mogi-Mirim
São Lourenço
Nova Friburgo
Ponta Porã
Assis
Piracicaba
Limeira
Volta Redonda
RIO DE JANEIRO
Petrópolis
Botucatu
CAMPINAS
Niterói
Cabo Frio
Pedro Juan Caballero
RIO DE JANEIRO
Mato Grosso
Planalto do Mato Grosso
MATO GROSSO
MATO GROSSO DO SUL
São Paulo (Braz.)
Rocas
Fernando de Noronha (Braz.)
Trindade (Braz.)
COPYRIGHT PHILIP'S

1:16 000 000

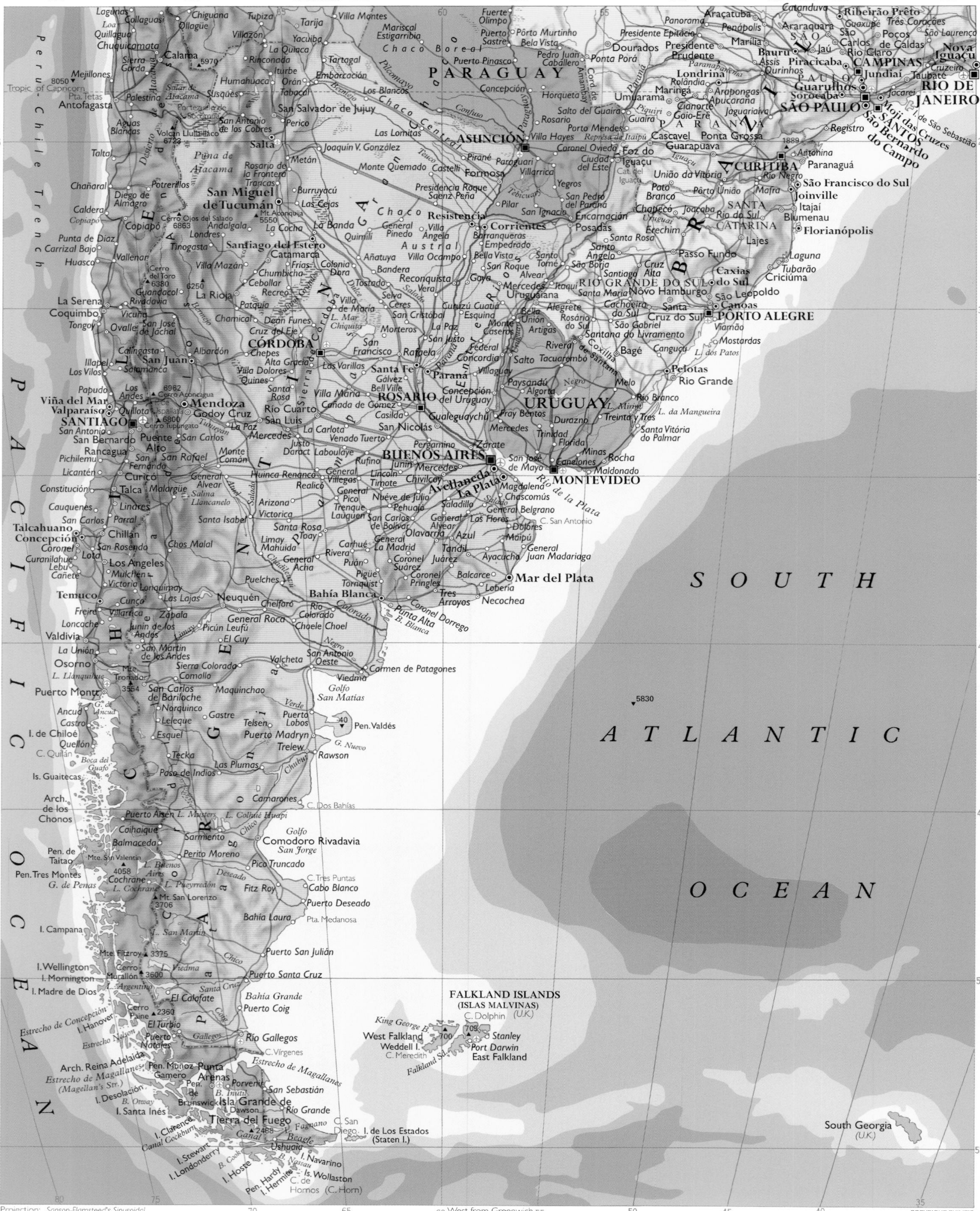

Tropic of Capricorn
Peru - Chile Trench
PACIFIC OCEAN
SOUTH ATLANTIC OCEAN
PARAGUAY
URUGUAY
ASUNCIÓN
MONTEVIDEO
BUENOS AIRES
SÃO PAULO
RIO DE JANEIRO
CAMPINAS
CURITIBA
PÔRTO ALEGRE
CÓRDOBA
ROSARIO
SANTIAGO
Chaco Boreal
Chaco Central
Chaco Austral
Rio de la Plata
FALKLAND ISLANDS
(ISLAS MALVINAS)
(U.K.)
West Falkland
East Falkland
Stanley
South Georgia
(U.K.)
Tierra del Fuego
Isla Grande de Tierra del Fuego
Estrecho de Magallanes
C. de Hornos (C. Horn)
I. de Los Estados (Staten I.)
Golfo San Matías
Golfo San Jorge
Pen. Valdés
I. de Chiloé
Mar del Plata
Bahía Blanca
Mendoza
San Miguel de Tucumán
Comodoro Rivadavia
Río Gallegos
Punta Arenas
Ushuaia
Puerto Montt
Valparaíso
Concepción
Antofagasta
Florianópolis
5830
West from Greenwich

Projection: Sanson-Flamsteed's Sinusoidal

COPYRIGHT PHILIP'S

INDEX

The index contains the names of all the principal places and features shown on the maps. The alphabetical order of names composed of two or more words is governed primarily by the first word and then by the second. This is an example of the rule:

New South Wales □	**32**	**B4**
New York □	**42**	**D8**
New Zealand ■	**33**	**J6**
Newark, *Del., U.S.A.*	**42**	**F8**
Newark, *N.J., U.S.A.*	**42**	**E8**

Physical features composed of a proper name (Erie) and a description (Lake) are positioned alphabetically by the proper name. The description is positioned after the proper name and is usually abbreviated:

Erie, L.	**42**	**D5**
Everest, Mt.	**25**	**C7**

Where a description forms part of a settlement name or administrative name, however, it is always written in full and put in its true alphabetical position:

Lake Charles	**41**	**K8**
Mount Isa	**30**	**E6**

The number in bold type which follows each name in the index refers to the number of the map page where that place or feature will be found. This is usually the largest scale at which the place or feature appears.

The letter and figure which are immediately after the page number give the grid square on the map page, within which the feature is situated. The letter represents the latitude and the figure the longitude. In some cases the feature itself may fall within the specified square, while the name is outside.

Rivers are indexed to their mouths or confluences and carry the symbol → after their names. The following symbols are also used in the index: ■ country, ⧄ overseas territory or dependency, □ first order administrative area, △ national park or reserve.

A

B

Bingham 43 C11
Binghamton 42 D8
Binjai 23 C1
Binnaway 32 B4
Bioko 28 D1
Bîr Shalatein 24 C2
Biratnagar 25 C7
Birchip 32 C3
Birjand 24 B4
Birkenhead 8 D4
Birmingham, U.K. 9 E6
Birmingham, U.S.A. 43 J2
Birmingham Int. (BHX) 9 E6
Birnie 31 A16
Birr 11 C4
Birrie → 32 A4
Bisbee 39 L9
Biscay, B. of 12 D1
Biscayne B. 43 N5
Bishkek 18 E8
Bisho 29 L5
Bishop, Calif., U.S.A. 39 H4
Bishop, Tex., U.S.A. 41 M6
Bishop Auckland 8 C6
Bishop's Stortford 9 F8
Biskra 26 B7
Bismarck 40 B4
Bismarck Arch. 30 A9
Bison 40 C3
Bissau 26 F2
Bitola 15 D9
Bitter Creek 38 F9
Bitterfontein 29 L3
Bitterroot → 38 C6
Bitterroot Range 38 D6
Biwa-Ko 22 F5
Biwabik 40 B8
Bixby 41 H7
Biysk 18 D9
Black →, Ariz., U.S.A. 39 K8
Black →, Ark., U.S.A. 41 H9
Black →, La., U.S.A. 41 K9
Black →, Wis., U.S.A. 40 D9
Black Canyon of the Gunnison △ 39 G10
Black Forest = Schwarzwald 16 D4
Black Forest 40 F2
Black Hd. 11 C2
Black Hills 40 D3
Black L. 42 C3
Black Mesa 41 G3
Black Mts. 9 F4
Black Range 39 K10
Black River 44 a
Black River Falls 40 C9
Black Rock 45 g
Black Sea 17 B5
Black Volta → 26 G5
Black Warrior → 43 J2
Blackball 33 K3
Blackburn 8 D5
Blackfoot 38 E7
Blackfoot → 38 C7
Blackfoot Res. 38 E8
Blackpool 8 D4
Blacksburg 42 G5
Blacksod B. 11 B1
Blackstairs Mt. 11 D5
Blackstone 42 G7
Blackwater →, Meath, Ireland 11 C4
Blackwater →, Waterford, Ireland 11 D4
Blackwater →, U.K. 11 B5
Blackwell 41 G6
Blaenau Ffestiniog 8 E4
Blaenau Gwent □ 9 F4
Blagoveshchensk 19 D13
Blaine, Minn., U.S.A. 40 C8
Blaine, Wash., U.S.A. 38 B2
Blair 40 E6
Blair Atholl 10 E5
Blairgowrie 10 E5
Blake Pt. 40 A10
Blakely 43 K3
Blanc, Mont 12 D7
Blanca Peak 39 H11
Blanche, C. 32 B1
Blanche, L. 32 A2
Blanco 41 K5
Blanco, C. 38 E1
Blandford Forum 9 G5
Blanding 39 H9
Blanquilla 45 E12
Blantyre 29 H6
Blarney 11 E3
Blaydon 8 C6
Blayney 32 B4
Blenheim 33 J4
Bletchley 9 F7
Blida 26 A6
Bligh Sound 33 L1
Bliss 38 E6
Blitar 23 D3
Block I. 42 E10
Bloemfontein 29 K5
Bloemhof 29 K5
Blois 12 C4
Bloody Foreland 11 A3
Bloomer 40 C9
Bloomfield, Iowa, U.S.A. 40 E8
Bloomfield, N. Mex., U.S.A. 39 H10
Bloomfield, Nebr., U.S.A. 40 D6
Bloomington, Ill., U.S.A. 40 E10
Bloomington, Ind., U.S.A. 42 F2
Bloomington, Minn., U.S.A. 40 C8
Bloomsburg 42 E7
Blountstown 43 K3
Blue Earth 40 D8
Blue Mesa Res. 39 G10
Blue Mountain Pk. 44 a
Blue Mts., Jamaica 44 a
Blue Mts., U.S.A. 38 D4
Blue Nile = Nîl el Azraq → 27 E12
Blue Rapids 40 F6
Blue Ridge Mts. 43 G5
Bluefield 42 G5
Bluefields 45 E8
Bluff, N.Z. 33 M2
Bluff, U.S.A. 39 H9
Bluffton 42 E3
Blumenau 48 B7
Blunt 40 C5
Bly 38 E3
Blyth 8 B6
Blythe 39 K6
Blytheville 41 H10
Bo Hai 21 C6
Boardman 42 E5
Bobadah 32 B4
Bobo-Dioulasso 26 F5
Bóbr → 16 B7
Boca Raton 43 M5
Bochum 16 C3
Boddam 10 B7
Boden 7 D8
Bodensee 12 C8
Bodmin 9 G3
Bodmin Moor 9 G3
Bodø 7 D6
Boerne 41 L5
Bogalusa 41 K10
Bogan → 32 A4
Bogan Gate 32 B4
Bogata 41 J7
Boggabilla 32 A5
Boggabri 32 B5
Boggeragh Mts. 11 D3
Bognor Regis 9 G7
Bogong, Mt. 32 C4
Bogor 23 D2
Bogotá 46 C4
Böhmerwald 16 D6
Bohol □ 23 C4
Bohol Sea 23 C4
Boise 38 E5
Boise City 41 G3
Bojnūrd 24 B4
Bokhara → 32 A4
Bole 20 B3
Bolgatanga 26 F5
Bolivar, Mo., U.S.A. 41 G8
Bolivar, Tenn., U.S.A. 41 H10
Bolivia ■ 46 G6
Bollon 32 A4
Bologna 14 B4
Bolshevik, Ostrov 19 B11
Bolt Head 9 G4
Bolton 8 D5
Bolzano 14 A4
Boma 28 F2
Bombala 32 C4
Bombay = Mumbai 25 D6
Bon, C. 14 F4
Bonaire 45 E11
Bonang 32 C4
Bonar Bridge 10 D4
Bonavista 37 E14
Bo'ness 10 E5
Bonham 41 J6
Bonifacio 12 F8
Bonifacio, Bouches de 14 D3
Bonn 16 C3
Bonne Terre 41 G9
Bonners Ferry 38 B5
Bonney, L. 32 C3
Bonny, Bight of 28 D1
Bonnyrigg 10 F5
Booker 41 G4
Booligal 32 B3
Boonah 32 A5
Boone, Iowa, U.S.A. 40 D8
Boone, N.C., U.S.A. 43 G5
Booneville, Ark., U.S.A. 41 H8
Booneville, Miss., U.S.A. 43 H1
Boonville, Ind., U.S.A. 42 F2
Boonville, Mo., U.S.A. 40 F8
Boonville, N.Y., U.S.A. 42 D8
Boorindal 32 B4
Boorowa 32 B4
Boothia, Gulf of 37 B11
Boothia Pen. 36 B10
Bootle 8 D4
Bora Bora 35 J12
Borah Peak 38 D7
Borås 7 F6
Borda, C. 32 C2
Bordeaux 12 D3
Borden I. 37 B11
Borden Pen. 37 B11
Border Ranges △ 32 A5
Bordertown 32 C3
Borehamwood 9 F7
Borger 41 H4
Borhoyn Tal 21 B6
Borneo 23 C3
Bornholm 7 F7
Borrisokane 11 D3
Borth 9 E3
Bosaso 24 D3
Boscastle 9 G3
Boscobelle 45 g
Bosnia-Herzegovina ■ 14 B7
Bosporus = İstanbul Boğazı 15 D13
Bosque Farms 39 J10
Bossier City 41 J8
Bosten Hu 20 B3
Boston, U.K. 8 E7
Boston, U.S.A. 42 D10
Boston Mts. 41 H8
Bothnia, G. of 7 E8
Bothwell 32 D4
Botletle → 29 J4
Botoşani 17 A3
Botswana ■ 29 J4
Bottineau 40 A4
Bouaké 26 G4
Bouar 28 C3
Bougainville I. 31 B10
Bouillante 44 b
Boulder, Colo., U.S.A. 40 E2
Boulder, Mont., U.S.A. 38 C7
Boulder City 39 J6
Boulogne-sur-Mer 12 A4
Bountiful 38 F8
Bounty Is. 34 M9
Bounty Trough 34 M9
Bourbonnais 12 C5
Bourg-en-Bresse 12 C6
Bourges 12 C5
Bourgogne □ 12 C6
Bourke 32 B4
Bourne 8 E7
Bournemouth 9 G6
Bouvetøya 4 G10
Bovill 38 C5
Bow → 36 D8
Bow Island 38 B8
Bowbells 40 A3
Bowdle 40 C5
Bowen Mts. 32 C4
Bowie, Ariz., U.S.A. 39 K9
Bowie, Tex., U.S.A. 41 J6
Bowland, Forest of 8 D5
Bowling Green, Ky., U.S.A. 42 G2
Bowling Green, Ohio, U.S.A. 42 E4
Bowman 40 B3
Bowmore 10 F2
Bowral 32 B5
Bowraville 32 B5
Box Cr. → 32 B3
Boyce 41 K8
Boyle 11 C3
Boyne → 11 C5
Boyne City 42 C3
Boynton Beach 43 M5
Boysen Res. 38 E9
Bozeman 38 D8
Bracadale, L. 10 D2
Bräcke 7 E7
Brackettville 41 L4
Bracknell 9 F7
Bracknell Forest □ 9 F7
Bradenton 43 M4
Bradford, U.K. 8 D6
Bradford, U.S.A. 42 E6
Bradley 41 J8
Brady 41 K5
Braga 13 B1
Brahmapur 25 D7
Brahmaputra → 20 D3
Braich-y-pwll 8 E3
Braidwood 32 C4
Brăila 15 B12
Brainerd 40 B7
Braintree 9 F8
Brampton 8 C5
Branco → 46 D6
Brandenburg 16 B6
Brandenburg □ 16 B6
Brandon 36 E10
Brandon B. 11 D1
Brandon Mt. 11 D1
Branson 41 G8
Brasil, Planalto 2 E7
Brasília 47 G9
Braşov 15 B11
Brassey, Banjaran 23 C3
Brasstown Bald 43 H4
Bratislava 16 D8
Bratsk 19 D11
Brattleboro 42 D9
Braunschweig 16 B5
Braunton 9 F3
Brawley 39 K6
Bray 11 C5
Brazil 42 F2
Brazil ■ 47 F9
Brazos → 41 L7
Brazzaville 28 E3
Breaksea Sd. 33 L1
Bream B. 33 F5
Bream Hd. 33 F5
Brechin 10 E6
Breckenridge, Colo., U.S.A. 38 G10
Breckenridge, Minn., U.S.A. 40 B6
Breckenridge, Tex., U.S.A. 41 J5
Breckland 9 E8
Brecon 9 F4
Brecon Beacons 9 F4
Brecon Beacons △ 9 F4
Breda 16 C2
Bredasdorp 29 L4
Bregenz 16 E4
Bremen 16 B4
Bremerhaven 16 B4
Bremerton 38 C2
Brenham 41 K6
Brennerpass 16 E5
Brent 43 J2
Brentwood 9 F8
Bréscia 12 D9
Breslau = Wrocław 16 C8
Bressay 10 A7
Brest, Belarus 18 D3
Brest, France 12 B1
Bretagne □ 12 B2
Breton Sd. 41 L10
Brett, C. 33 F5
Brevard 43 H4
Brewarrina 32 B4
Brewer 43 C11
Brewster 38 B4
Brewton 43 K2
Briançon 12 D7
Bribie I. 32 A5
Bridgefield 45 g
Bridgend 9 F4
Bridgeport, Calif., U.S.A. 39 G4
Bridgeport, Conn., U.S.A. 42 E9
Bridgeport, Nebr., U.S.A. 40 E3
Bridgeport, Tex., U.S.A. 41 J6
Bridger 38 D9
Bridgeton 42 F8
Bridgetown 45 g
Bridgewater, Australia 32 D4
Bridgewater, Canada 37 E13
Bridgewater, C. 32 C3
Bridgnorth 9 E5
Bridgwater 9 F5
Bridgwater B. 9 F4
Bridlington 8 C7
Bridlington B. 8 C7
Bridport, Australia 32 D4
Bridport, U.K. 9 G5
Brigg 8 D7
Brigham City 38 F7
Bright 32 C4
Brighton, Australia 32 C2
Brighton, U.K. 9 G7
Bríndisi 15 D7
Brinkley 41 H9
Brisbane 32 A5
Brisbane → 32 A5
Bristol, U.K. 9 F5
Bristol, Conn., U.S.A. 42 E9
Bristol, Tenn., U.S.A. 43 G4
Bristol B. 36 D4
Bristol Channel 9 F3
Bristol L. 39 J5
Bristow 41 H6
British Columbia □ 36 D7
British Isles 2 B9
British Virgin Is. ☑ 45 e
Brits 29 K5
Brittany = Bretagne □ 12 B2
Britton 40 C6
Brive-la-Gaillarde 12 D4
Brixham 9 G4
Brno 16 D8
Broad → 43 J5
Broad B. 10 C2
Broad Haven 11 B2
Broad Law 10 F5
Broads △ 9 E9
Broads, The 8 E9
Broadus 40 C2
Brochet 36 D9
Brock I. 37 B11
Brocken 16 C5
Brockport 42 D7
Brockton 42 D10
Brockway 40 B2
Brodeur Pen. 37 B11
Brodick 10 F3
Brogan 38 D5
Broken Arrow 41 G7
Broken Bow, Nebr., U.S.A. 40 E5
Broken Bow, Okla., U.S.A. 41 H7
Broken Bow Lake 41 H7
Broken Hill 32 B3
Broken Ridge 34 L1
Bromley □ 9 F8
Bromsgrove 9 E5
Brookhaven 41 K9
Brookings, Oreg., U.S.A. 38 E1
Brookings, S. Dak., U.S.A. 40 C6
Brooklyn Park 40 C8
Brooks 36 D8
Brooks Range 36 C5
Brooksville 43 L4
Brookville 42 E6
Broom, L. 10 D3
Broome 30 D3
Brora 10 C5
Brora → 10 C5
Brosna → 11 C4
Brothers 38 E3
Brough 8 C5
Brough Hd. 10 B5
Brown, Pt. 32 B1
Brown Willy 9 G3
Brownfield 41 J3
Browning 38 B7
Brownsville, Oreg., U.S.A. 38 D2
Brownsville, Tenn., U.S.A. 41 H10
Brownsville, Tex., U.S.A. 41 N6
Brownwood 41 K5
Bruay-la-Buissière 12 A5
Bruce, Mt. 30 E2
Brue → 9 F5
Bruges = Brugge 16 C1
Brugge 16 C1
Bruneau 38 E6
Bruneau → 38 E6
Brunei ■ 23 C3
Brunner, L. 33 K3
Brunswick = Braunschweig 16 B5
Brunswick, Ga., U.S.A. 43 K5
Brunswick, Maine, U.S.A. 43 D11
Brunswick, Md., U.S.A. 42 F7
Brunswick, Mo., U.S.A. 40 F8
Brush 40 E3
Brussel 16 C2
Bruthen 32 C4
Bruxelles = Brussel 16 C2
Bryan, Ohio, U.S.A. 42 E3
Bryan, Tex., U.S.A. 41 K6
Bryan, Mt. 32 B2
Bryansk 18 D4
Bryce Canyon △ 39 H7
Bryson City 43 H4
Bucaramanga 46 B4
Buchan 10 D6
Buchan Ness 10 D7
Buchanan, L. 41 K5
Bucharest = Bucureşti 15 B12
Buckhannon 42 F5
Buckhaven 10 E5
Buckie 10 D6
Buckingham 9 F7
Buckinghamshire □ 9 F7
Buckleboo 32 B2
Buckley 8 D4
Bucklin 41 G5
Bucureşti 15 B12
Bucyrus 42 E4
Budapest 16 E9
Bude 9 G3
Budgewoi 32 B5
Buena Vista, Colo., U.S.A. 39 G10
Buena Vista, Va., U.S.A. 42 G6
Buena Vista Lake Bed 39 J4
Buenaventura 46 C3
Buenos Aires 48 C5
Buffalo, Mo., U.S.A. 41 G8
Buffalo, N.Y., U.S.A. 42 D6
Buffalo, Okla., U.S.A. 41 G5
Buffalo, S. Dak., U.S.A. 40 C3
Buffalo, Wyo., U.S.A. 38 D10
Buffalo △ 41 G8
Buford 43 H4
Bug → 7 G8
Bugun Shara 20 B5
Buhl 38 E6
Builth Wells 9 E4
Buir Nur 21 B6
Buji 21 F11
Bujumbura 28 E5
Bukavu 28 E5
Bukhoro 18 F7
Bukittinggi 23 D2
Bulahdelah 32 B5
Bulawayo 29 J5
Bulgaria ■ 15 C11
Bull Shoals L. 41 G8
Bullhead City 39 J6
Bulloo → 32 A3
Bulloo L. 32 A3
Bulls 33 J5
Bunbury 30 G2
Bunclody 11 D5
Buncrana 11 A4
Bundaberg 32 A5
Bundjalung △ 32 A5
Bundoran 11 B3
Bungay 9 E9
Bungil Cr. → 32 A4
Bunkie 41 K8
Bunnell 43 L5
Bunya Mts. △ 32 A5
Buon Ma Thuot 23 B2
Bur Acaba 24 E3
Bûr Sa'îd 27 B12
Bûr Sûdân 27 E13
Burao 24 E3
Buraydah 24 C3
Burbank 39 J4
Bure → 8 E9
Burgas 15 C12
Burghead 10 D5
Burgos 13 A4
Burgundy = Bourgogne □ 12 C6
Burkburnett 41 H5
Burkina Faso ■ 26 F5
Burley 38 E7
Burlington, Colo., U.S.A. 40 F3
Burlington, Iowa, U.S.A. 40 E9
Burlington, Kans., U.S.A. 40 F7
Burlington, N.C., U.S.A. 43 G6
Burlington, Vt., U.S.A. 42 C9
Burlington, Wash., U.S.A. 38 B2
Burlington, Wis., U.S.A. 42 D1
Burlyu-Tyube 18 E8
Burma ■ 25 C8
Burnet 41 K5
Burney 38 F3
Burnham-on-Sea 9 F5
Burnie 32 D4
Burnley 8 D5
Burns 38 E4
Burns Junction 38 E5
Burnside → 36 C9
Burnsville 40 C8
Burra 32 B2
Burray 10 C6
Burren 11 C2
Burren △ 11 C3
Burren Junction 32 B4
Burrinjuck Res. 32 C4
Burrow Hd. 10 G4
Burrum Coast △ 32 A5
Burry Port 9 F3
Bursa 15 D13
Burton 43 J5
Burton upon Trent 8 E6
Buru 23 D4
Burundi ■ 28 E5
Burwell 40 E5
Burwick 10 C5
Bury 8 D5
Bury St. Edmunds 9 E8
Buryatia □ 19 D11
Busan 21 C7
Būshehr 24 C4
Butaritari 34 G9
Bute 10 F3
Butha Qi 21 B7
Butler, Mo., U.S.A. 40 F7
Butler, Pa., U.S.A. 42 E6
Buton 23 D4
Butte, Mont., U.S.A. 38 C7
Butte, Nebr., U.S.A. 40 D5
Butterworth 23 C2
Buttevant 11 D3
Butuan 23 C4
Buxton 8 D6
Buzău 15 B12
Bydgoszcz 16 B9
Byers 40 F2
Bylas 39 K8
Bylot I. 37 B12
Byrock 32 B4
Byron, C. 32 A5
Byron Bay 32 A5
Byrranga, Gory 19 B11
Bytom 16 C9

C

C.W. McConaughy, L. 40 E4
Ca Mau 23 C2
Ca Mau, Mui 23 C2
Cabanatuan 23 B4
Cabimas 46 A4
Cabinda □ 28 F2
Cabinet Mts. 38 C6
Cabonga, Réservoir 37 E12
Cabool 41 G8
Caboolture 32 A5
Cabot Str. 37 E14
Čačak 15 C9
Cáceres 13 C2
Cachoeira do Sul 48 C6
Cachoeiro de Itapemirim 47 H10
Caddo 41 H6
Cader Idris 9 E4
Cadibarrawirracanna, L. 32 A2
Cadillac 42 C3
Cádiz 13 D2
Cadiz L. 39 J6
Cadney Park 32 A1
Caen 12 B3
Caernarfon 8 D3
Caernarfon B. 8 D3
Caerphilly 9 F4
Cagayan de Oro 23 C4
Cágliari 14 E3
Caguas 45 d
Caha Mts. 11 E2
Caher 11 D4
Caherciveen 11 E1
Cahore Pt. 11 D5
Cahors 12 D4
Cairn Gorm 10 D5
Cairngorm Mts. 10 D5
Cairngorms △ 10 D5
Cairnryan 10 G3
Cairns 30 D8
Cairo = El Qâhira 27 B12
Cairo, Ga., U.S.A. 43 K3
Cairo, Ill., U.S.A. 41 G10
Caithness 10 C5
Caithness, Ord of 10 C5
Caja de Muertos, I. 45 d
Cajamarca 46 E3
Calabar 26 H7
Calábria □ 14 E7
Calais, France 12 A4
Calais, U.S.A. 43 C12
Calamian Group 23 B3
Calapan 23 B4
Calbayog 23 B4
Calcasieu L. 41 L8
Calcutta = Kolkata 25 C7
Calder → 8 D6
Caldwell, Idaho, U.S.A. 38 E5
Caldwell, Kans., U.S.A. 41 G6
Caldwell, Tex., U.S.A. 41 K6
Caledon → 29 L5
Calexico 39 K6
Calf of Man 8 C3
Calgary 36 D8
Calhoun 43 H3
Cali 46 C3
Calicut 25 D6
Caliente 39 H6
California 40 F8
California □ 39 H4
California, G. de 44 B2
Calipatria 39 K6
Calistoga 38 G2
Callabonna, L. 32 A3
Callan 11 D4
Callander 10 E4
Callao 46 F3
Calne 9 F6
Caloundra 32 A5
Caltanissetta 14 F6
Calvi 12 E8
Calvinia 29 L3
Cam → 9 E8
Cam Ranh 23 B2
Camagüey 45 C9
Camas 38 D2
Camas Valley 38 E2
Cambodia ■ 23 B2
Camborne 9 G2
Cambrai 12 A5
Cambria 39 J3
Cambrian Mts. 9 E4
Cambridge, Jamaica 44 a
Cambridge, N.Z. 33 G5
Cambridge, U.K. 9 E8
Cambridge, Mass., U.S.A. 42 D10
Cambridge, Minn., U.S.A. 40 C8
Cambridge, Nebr., U.S.A. 40 E4
Cambridge, Ohio, U.S.A. 42 E5
Cambridgeshire □ 9 E7
Camden, Ala., U.S.A. 43 K2
Camden, Ark., U.S.A. 41 J8
Camden, Maine, U.S.A. 43 C11
Camden, N.J., U.S.A. 42 F8
Camden, S.C., U.S.A. 43 H5
Camdenton 41 F8
Camelford 9 G3
Cameron, Ariz., U.S.A. 39 J8
Cameron, La., U.S.A. 41 L8
Cameron, Mo., U.S.A. 40 F7
Cameron, Tex., U.S.A. 41 K6
Cameroon ■ 27 G7
Cameroun, Mt. 28 D1
Camilla 43 K3
Camino 38 G3
Camira Creek 32 A5
Camp Hill 42 E7
Camp Verde 39 J8
Camp Wood 41 L5
Campánia □ 14 D6
Campbell I. 34 N8
Campbell River 36 D7
Campbell Town 32 D4
Campbellsville 42 G3
Campbellton 37 E13
Campbelltown 32 B5
Campbeltown 10 F3
Campeche 44 D6
Campeche, Golfo de 44 D6
Camperdown 32 C3
Campina Grande 47 E11
Campinas 47 H9
Campo Grande 47 H8
Campos 47 H10
Camrose 36 D8
Can Tho 23 B2
Canada ■ 36 D10
Canadian 41 H4
Canadian → 41 H7
Çanakkale Boğazı 15 D12
Canandaigua 42 D7
Cananea 44 A2
Canarias, Is. 26 C2
Canaries 45 f
Canary Is. = Canarias, Is. 26 C2
Canaveral △ 43 L5
Canaveral, C. 43 L5
Canberra 32 C4
Canby, Calif., U.S.A. 38 F3
Canby, Minn., U.S.A. 40 C6
Canby, Oreg., U.S.A. 38 D2
Cancún 44 C7
Candelo 32 C4
Cando 40 A5
Caniapiscau → 37 D13
Caniapiscau, L. de 37 D13
Cann River 32 C4
Canna 10 D2
Cannes 12 E7
Cannock 9 E5
Cannonball → 40 B4
Canoas 48 B6
Cañon City 40 F2
Canora 36 D9
Canowindra 32 B4
Cantabria □ 13 A4
Cantábrica, Cordillera 13 A3
Canterbury 9 F9
Canterbury Bight 33 L3
Canterbury Plains 33 K3
Canton = Guangzhou 21 D6
Canton, Ga., U.S.A. 43 H3
Canton, Ill., U.S.A. 40 E9
Canton, Miss., U.S.A. 41 J9
Canton, Mo., U.S.A. 40 E9
Canton, N.Y., U.S.A. 42 C8
Canton, Ohio, U.S.A. 42 E5
Canton, S. Dak., U.S.A. 40 D6
Canton L. 41 G5
Canutillo 39 L10
Canvey 9 F8
Canyon 41 H4
Canyon De Chelly △ 39 H9
Canyonlands △ 39 G9
Canyons of the Ancients △ 39 H9
Canyonville 38 E2
Cap-Haïtien 45 D10
Cap Pt. 45 f
Cape Barren I. 32 D4
Cape Breton I. 37 E13
Cape Charles 42 G8
Cape Coast 26 G5
Cape Cod △ 42 E10
Cape Coral 43 M5
Cape Dorset 37 C12
Cape Fear → 43 H6
Cape Girardeau 41 G10
Cape Hatteras △ 43 H8
Cape Lookout △ 43 H7
Cape May 42 F8
Cape May Point 42 F8
Cape Town 29 L3
Cape Verde Is. ■ 4 D8
Cape York Peninsula 30 C7
Capesterre-Belle-Eau 44 b
Capesterre-de-Marie-Galante 44 b
Capitan 39 K11
Capitol Reef △ 39 G8
Capri 14 D6
Captain's Flat 32 C4
Capulin Volcano △ 41 G3
Caquetá → 46 D5
Caracas 46 A5
Caratasca, L. 45 D8
Caratinga 47 G10
Caravelle, Presqu'île de la 44 c
Carbondale, Colo., U.S.A. 38 G10
Carbondale, Ill., U.S.A. 41 G10
Carbondale, Pa., U.S.A. 42 E8
Carbonear 37 E14
Carcassonne 12 E5
Carcross 36 C6
Cárdenas 45 C8
Cardiff 9 F4
Cardigan 9 E3
Cardigan B. 9 E3
Cardston 36 E8
Carey 38 E7
Cariacica 47 H10
Caribbean Sea 45 E10
Cariboo Mts. 36 D7
Caribou 43 B12
Caribou Mts. 36 D8
Carinda 32 B4
Carlin 38 F5
Carlingford L. 11 B5
Carlinville 40 F10
Carlisle, U.K. 8 C5
Carlisle, U.S.A. 42 E7
Carlisle B. 45 g
Carlow 11 D5
Carlow □ 11 D5
Carlsbad, Calif., U.S.A. 39 K5
Carlsbad, N. Mex., U.S.A. 41 J2
Carlsbad Caverns △ 41 J2
Carluke 10 F5
Carmacks 36 C6
Carmarthen 9 F3
Carmarthen B. 9 F3
Carmarthenshire □ 9 F3
Carmaux 12 D5
Carmi 42 F1
Carn Ban 10 D4
Carn Eige 10 D3
Carnarvon, Australia 30 E1
Carnarvon, S. Africa 29 L4
Carncastle 11 B6
Carndonagh 11 A4
Carnegie, L. 30 F3
Carnegie Ridge 35 H19
Carnot, C. 32 B2
Carnoustie 10 E6
Carnsore Pt. 11 D5
Caro 42 D4
Carol City 43 N5
Carolina, Brazil 47 E9
Carolina, Puerto Rico 45 d
Caroline I. 35 H12
Caroline Is. 34 G7
Carondelet 31 B16
Caroona 32 B5
Carpathians 17 A2
Carpații Meridionali 15 B11
Carpentaria, G. of 30 C6
Carpentras 12 D6
Carpinteria 39 J4
Carra, L. 11 C2
Carrabelle 43 L3
Carrauntoohill 11 D2
Carrick-on-Shannon 11 C3
Carrick-on-Suir 11 D4
Carrickfergus 11 B6
Carrickmacross 11 C5
Carrieton 32 B2
Carrington 40 B5
Carrizo Cr. → 41 G3
Carrizo Plain △ 39 J4
Carrizo Springs 41 L5
Carrizozo 39 K11
Carroll 40 D7
Carrollton, Ga., U.S.A. 43 J3
Carrollton, Ill., U.S.A. 40 F9
Carrollton, Ky., U.S.A. 42 F3
Carrollton, Mo., U.S.A. 40 F8
Carron → 10 D4
Carron, L. 10 D3
Carson 40 B4
Carson City 38 G4
Carson Sink 38 G4
Cartagena, Colombia 46 A3
Cartagena, Spain 13 D5
Cartersville 43 H3
Carterton 33 J5
Carthage, Ill., U.S.A. 40 E9
Carthage, Mo., U.S.A. 41 G7
Carthage, N.Y., U.S.A. 42 D8
Carthage, Tex., U.S.A. 41 J7
Cartwright 37 D14
Caruaru 47 E11
Carúpano 46 A6
Caruthersville 41 G10
Cary 43 H6
Casa Grande 39 K8
Casablanca 26 B4
Cascade, Idaho, U.S.A. 38 D5
Cascade, Mont., U.S.A. 38 C8
Cascade Locks 38 D3
Cascade Ra. 38 C3
Cascade Res. 38 D5
Cascavel 47 H8
Casco B. 43 D10
Cashel 11 D4
Casino 32 A5
Casiquiare → 46 C5
Casper 38 E10
Caspian Sea 18 E6
Cass Lake 40 B7
Casselton 40 B6
Cassiar Mts. 36 D6
Cassville 41 G8
Castelló de la Plana 13 C5
Castelsarrasin 12 E4
Casterton 32 C3
Castilla-La Mancha □ 13 C4
Castilla y Leon □ 13 B3
Castle Dale 38 G8
Castle Douglas 10 G5
Castle Rock 40 F2
Castlebar 11 C2
Castlebay 10 E1
Castleblaney 11 B5
Castlederg 11 B4
Castleford 8 D6
Castlemaine, Australia 32 C3
Castlemaine, Ireland 11 D2
Castlepollard 11 C4
Castlerea 11 C3
Castlereagh → 32 B4
Castletown 8 C3
Castletown Bearhaven 11 E2
Castres 12 E5
Castries 45 f
Cat I. 45 C9
Catalina 39 K8
Cataluña □ 13 B6
Catanduanes □ 23 B4
Catània 14 F6
Catanzaro 14 E7
Caterham 9 F7
Cathlamet 38 C2
Catlettsburg 42 F4
Catoche, C. 44 C7
Catskill 42 D9
Catskill △ 42 D8
Catskill Mts. 42 D8
Catterick 8 C6
Caucasus Mountains 18 E5
Cavalier 40 A6
Cavan 11 B4
Cavan □ 11 C4
Cave Creek 39 K7
Cavendish 32 C3
Cawndilla L. 32 B3
Caxias 47 D10
Caxias do Sul 48 B6
Cayenne 47 B8
Cayey 45 d
Cayman Is. ☑ 45 D8
Cayuga L. 42 D7
Ceanannus Mor 11 C5
Cebu 23 B4
Cecil Plains 32 A5
Cedar → 40 E9
Cedar City 39 H7
Cedar Creek Res. 41 J6
Cedar Falls 40 D8
Cedar Key 43 L4
Cedar L. 36 D10
Cedar Park 41 K6
Cedar Rapids 40 E9
Cedartown 43 H3
Ceduna 32 B1
Cegléd 16 E9
Celaya 44 C4
Celebes = Sulawesi 23 D4
Celebes Sea 23 C4
Celina 42 E3
Cenderwasih, Teluk 23 D5
Center, N. Dak., U.S.A. 40 B4
Center, Tex., U.S.A. 41 K7
Centerville, Iowa, U.S.A. 40 E8
Centerville, Tenn., U.S.A. 43 H2
Centerville, Tex., U.S.A. 41 K7
Central, Cordillera, Colombia 46 C4
Central, Cordillera, Puerto Rico 45 d
Central African Rep. ■ 27 G9
Central America 2 D5
Central City, Colo., U.S.A. 38 G11
Central City, Ky., U.S.A. 42 G2
Central City, Nebr., U.S.A. 40 E6
Central Makran Range 24 C5
Central Pacific Basin 34 G10
Central Point 38 E2
Centralia, Ill., U.S.A. 40 F10
Centralia, Mo., U.S.A. 40 F8
Centralia, Wash., U.S.A. 38 C2
Cephalonia = Kefalonia 15 E9
Ceredigion □ 9 E3
Cerignola 14 D6
České Budějovice 16 D7
Českomoravská Vrchovina 16 D7
Cessnock 32 B5
Ceuta 13 E3
Ceve-i-Ra 31 E13
Cévennes 12 D5
Ceylon = Sri Lanka ■ 25 E7
Chaco → 39 H9
Chaco Culture △ 39 H10
Chad ■ 27 F8
Chadron 40 D3
Chagos Arch. ☑ 5 E14
Chāh Bahar 24 C5
Chai Wan 21 G11
Chalky Inlet 33 M1
Challenger Deep 34 F6
Challenger Fracture Zone 35 L17
Challis 38 D6
Chalmette 41 L10
Chalon-sur-Saône 12 C6
Châlons-en-Champagne 12 B6
Chama 39 H10
Chambal → 25 C6
Chamberlain 40 D5
Chamberlain L. 43 B11
Chambers 39 J9
Chambersburg 42 F7
Chambéry 12 D6
Champagne 12 B6
Champaign 42 E1
Champlain 42 C9
Champlain, L. 42 C9
Chancery Lane 45 g
Chandeleur Is. 41 L10
Chandeleur Sd. 41 L10
Chandigarh 25 B6
Chandler, Australia 32 A1
Chandler, Ariz., U.S.A. 39 K8
Chandler, Okla., U.S.A. 41 H6
Chang Jiang → 21 C7
Changan 21 F10
Changchun 21 B7
Changde 21 D6
Changhua 21 D7
Changjiang Shuiku 21 G10
Changsha 21 D6
Changzhi 21 C6
Changzhou 21 C6
Chania 15 G11
Channel Is., U.K. 9 H5
Channel Is., U.S.A. 39 K4
Channel Islands △ 39 J3
Channel-Port aux Basques 37 E14
Channel Tunnel 9 F9
Channing 41 H3
Chantrey Inlet 36 C10
Chanute 41 G7
Chaozhou 21 D6
Chapala, L. de 44 C4
Chapel Hill 43 H6
Chapleau 37 E11
Chappell 40 E3
Chard 9 G5
Chari → 27 F8
Chariton 40 E8
Chariton → 40 F8
Charleroi 16 C2
Charles, C. 42 G8
Charles City 40 D8
Charles Town 42 F7
Charlesbourg 42 B10
Charleston, Ill., U.S.A. 42 F1
Charleston, Miss., U.S.A. 41 H9
Charleston, Mo., U.S.A. 41 G10
Charleston, S.C., U.S.A. 43 J6
Charleston, W. Va., U.S.A. 42 F5
Charlestown, Ireland 11 C3
Charlestown, U.S.A. 42 F3
Charlestown of Aberlour 10 D5
Charleville 32 A4
Charleville-Mézières 12 B6
Charlevoix 42 C3
Charlotte, Mich., U.S.A. 42 D3
Charlotte, N.C., U.S.A. 43 H5
Charlotte Amalie 45 e
Charlotte Harbor 43 M4
Charlottesville 42 F6
Charlottetown 37 E13
Charlton 32 C3
Charlton I. 37 D12
Charolles 12 C6
Charters Towers 30 E8
Chartres 12 B4
Châteaubriant 12 C3
Châteaulin 12 B1
Châteauroux 12 C4
Châteaux, Pte. des 44 b
Châtellerault 12 C4
Chatham 9 F8
Chatham Is. 31 J15
Chatham Rise 34 M10
Chattahoochee 43 K3
Chattahoochee → 43 K3
Chattanooga 43 H3
Chatteris 9 E8
Chaumont 12 B6
Cheb 16 C6
Cheboksary 18 D5
Cheboygan 42 C3
Checotah 41 H7
Cheduba I. 25 D8
Cheepie 32 A4
Chehalis 38 C2
Chelan 38 C4
Chelan, L. 38 B3
Chelmsford 9 F8
Cheltenham 9 F5
Chelyabinsk 18 D7
Chelyuskin, Mys 19 B11
Chemnitz 16 C6
Chemult 38 E3
Chenab → 25 B6
Cheney 38 C5
Chengde 21 B6
Chengdu 20 C5
Chengjiang 20 D5
Chennai 25 D7
Chepstow 9 F5
Chequamegon B. 40 B9
Cher → 12 C4
Cheraw 43 H6
Cherbourg 12 B3
Cheremkhovo 19 D11
Cherepovets 18 D4
Cherkasy 18 E4
Chernihiv 18 D4
Chernivtsi 17 A3
Cherokee, Iowa, U.S.A. 40 D7
Cherokee, Okla., U.S.A. 41 G5
Cherokee Village 41 G9
Cherokees, Grand Lake O' The 41 G7
Cherskogo Khrebet 19 C15
Cherwell → 9 F6
Chesapeake 42 G7
Chesapeake B. 42 G7
Cheshire □ 8 D5
Cheshunt 9 F7
Chesil Beach 9 G5
Chester, U.K. 8 D5
Chester, Calif., U.S.A. 38 F3
Chester, Ill., U.S.A. 41 G10
Chester, Mont., U.S.A. 38 B8
Chester, Pa., U.S.A. 42 F8
Chester, S.C., U.S.A. 43 H5
Chester-le-Street 8 C6
Chesterfield 8 D6
Chesterfield, Îs. 31 D10
Chesterfield Inlet 36 C10
Chesterton Ra. 32 A4
Chesterton Range △ 32 A4
Chesuncook L. 43 C11
Chetumal 44 D7
Chetwynd 36 D7
Cheviot, The 8 B5
Cheviot Hills 8 B5
Chewelah 38 B5
Cheyenne, Okla., U.S.A. 41 H5
Cheyenne, Wyo., U.S.A. 40 E2
Cheyenne → 40 C4
Cheyenne Wells 40 F3
Chhapra 25 C7
Chhattisgarh □ 25 C7
Chi → 23 B2
Chiai 21 D7
Chiang Mai 23 B1
Chiba 22 F7
Chibougamau 37 E12
Chicago 42 E2
Chicago Heights 42 E2
Chichagof I. 36 D6
Chichester 9 G7
Chickasaw △ 41 H6
Chickasha 41 H6
Chiclayo 46 E3
Chico 38 G3
Chicopee 42 D9
Chicoutimi 37 E12
Chidley, C. 37 C13
Chieti 14 C6
Chigwell 9 F8
Chihuahua 44 B3
Chilapa 44 D5
Childers 32 A5
Childress 41 H4
Chile ■ 48 D2
Chile Basin 35 L20
Chile Rise 35 L18
Chillán 48 D2
Chillicothe, Ill., U.S.A. 40 E10
Chillicothe, Mo., U.S.A. 40 F8
Chillicothe, Ohio, U.S.A. 42 F4
Chilliwack 36 E7
Chiloé, I. de 48 E2
Chilpancingo 44 D5
Chiltern Hills 9 F7
Chilton 42 C1
Chilung 21 D7
Chimayo 39 H11
Chimborazo 46 D3
Chimbote 46 E3
China ■ 21 C6
Chinandega 44 E7
Chinati Peak 41 L2
Chincha Alta 46 F3
Chinchilla 32 A5
Chincoteague 42 G8
Chindwin → 25 C8
Chingola 29 G5
Chinle 39 H9
Chino Valley 39 J7
Chinon 12 C4
Chinook 38 B9
Chinook Trough 34 C10
Chipata 29 G6
Chipley 43 K3
Chippenham 9 F5
Chippewa → 40 C8
Chippewa Falls 40 C9
Chipping Norton 9 F6
Chiputneticook Lakes 43 C11
Chirchiq 18 E7
Chiricahua △ 39 K9
Chiricahua Peak 39 L9
Chisasibi 37 D12
Chisholm 40 B8
Chişinău 17 A3
Chisos Mts. 41 L3
Chita 19 D12
Chitral 25 B6
Chittagong 25 C8
Chocolate Mts. 39 K6
Choctawhatchee → 43 K3
Choiseul, St. Lucia 45 f
Choiseul, Solomon Is. 31 B10
Choke Canyon Res. 41 L5
Cholet 12 C3
Choluteca 44 E7
Chon Buri 23 B2
Ch'ŏngjin 21 B7
Chongqing 20 D5
Chongqing Shi □ 20 C5
Chonos, Arch. de los 48 F2
Chorley 8 D5
Chorzów 16 C9
Choteau 38 C7
Chowchilla 39 H3
Choybalsan 21 B6
Christchurch, N.Z. 33 K4
Christchurch, U.K. 9 G6
Christmas I. 23 E2
Chubbuck 38 E7
Chubut → 48 E3
Chudskoye, Ozero 7 F9
Chugwater 40 E2
Chukotskoye Nagorye 19 C18
Chula Vista 39 K5
Chuncheon 21 C7
Chur 12 C8
Church Stretton 9 E5
Churchill 36 D10
Churchill →, Man., Canada 36 D10
Churchill →, Nfld. & L., Canada 37 D13
Churchill, C. 36 D10
Churchill Falls 37 D13
Churchill L. 36 D9
Churchill Pk. 36 D7
Chuska Mts. 39 H9
Chuuk 34 G7
Cicero 42 E2
Ciechanów 16 B10
Ciego de Ávila 45 C9
Ciénaga 46 A4
Cienfuegos 45 C8
Cimarron, Kans., U.S.A. 41 G4
Cimarron, N. Mex., U.S.A. 41 G2
Cimarron → 41 G6
Cincinnati 42 F3
Cinto, Mte. 12 E8
Circle, Alaska, U.S.A. 36 C5
Circle, Mont., U.S.A. 40 B2
Circleville 42 F4
Cirebon 23 D2
Cirencester 9 F6
Cisco 41 J5
Citlaltépetl = Orizaba, Pico de 44 D5
Ciudad Bolívar 46 B6
Ciudad de México 44 D5
Ciudad del Carmen 44 D6
Ciudad Guayana 46 B6
Ciudad Guzmán 44 D4
Ciudad Juárez 44 A3
Ciudad Madero 44 C5
Ciudad Mante 44 C5
Ciudad Obregón 44 B3
Ciudad Real 13 C4
Ciudad Victoria 44 C5
Clackmannanshire □ 10 E5
Clacton-on-Sea 9 F9
Claire, L. 36 D8
Clanton 43 J2
Clara 11 C4
Clare, Australia 32 B2
Clare, U.S.A. 42 D3
Clare □ 11 D3
Clare → 11 C2
Clare I. 11 C1
Claremont 42 D9
Claremore 41 G7
Claremorris 11 C3
Clarence →, Australia 32 A5
Clarence →, N.Z. 33 K4
Clarendon 41 H4
Clarinda 40 E7
Clarington 42 D6
Clarion, Iowa, U.S.A. 40 D8
Clarion, Pa., U.S.A. 42 E6
Clarion Fracture Zone 35 F15
Clark 40 C6
Clark Fork 38 B5
Clark Fork → 38 B5
Clarkdale 39 J7
Clarke I. 32 D4
Clarks Fork Yellowstone → 38 D9
Clarksburg 42 F5
Clarksdale 41 H9
Clarkston 38 C5
Clarksville, Ark., U.S.A. 41 H8
Clarksville, Tenn., U.S.A. 43 G2
Clarksville, Tex., U.S.A. 41 J7
Claude 41 H4
Clay Center 40 F6
Claypool 39 K8
Clayton, N. Mex., U.S.A. 41 G3
Clayton, N.Y., U.S.A. 42 C7
Clear, C. 11 E2
Clear I. 11 E2
Clear L. 38 G2
Clear Lake, Iowa, U.S.A. 40 D8
Clear Lake, S. Dak., U.S.A. 40 C6
Clear Lake Res. 38 F3
Clearfield, Pa., U.S.A. 42 E6
Clearfield, Utah, U.S.A. 38 F8
Clearlake 38 G2
Clearwater 43 M4
Clearwater Mts. 38 C6
Cleburne 41 J6
Clee Hills 9 E5
Cleethorpes 8 D7
Cleeve Cloud 9 F6
Clemson 43 H4
Clermont 43 L5
Clermont-Ferrand 12 D5
Clevedon 9 F5
Cleveland, Miss., U.S.A. 41 J9
Cleveland, Ohio, U.S.A. 42 E5
Cleveland, Okla., U.S.A. 41 G6
Cleveland, Tenn., U.S.A. 43 H3
Cleveland, Tex., U.S.A. 41 K7
Cleveland, Mt. 38 B7
Cleveland Heights 42 E5
Clew B. 11 C2
Clewiston 43 M5
Clifden, Ireland 11 C1
Clifden, N.Z. 33 M1
Clifton, Australia 32 A5
Clifton, Ariz., U.S.A. 39 K9
Clifton, Colo., U.S.A. 39 G9
Clifton, Tex., U.S.A. 41 K6
Clinch → 43 H3
Clingmans Dome 43 H4
Clint 39 L10
Clinton, N.Z. 33 M2
Clinton, Ark., U.S.A. 41 H8
Clinton, Ill., U.S.A. 40 E10
Clinton, Ind., U.S.A. 42 F2
Clinton, Iowa, U.S.A. 40 E9
Clinton, Miss., U.S.A. 41 J9
Clinton, Mo., U.S.A. 40 F8
Clinton, N.C., U.S.A. 43 H6
Clinton, Okla., U.S.A. 41 H5
Clinton, S.C., U.S.A. 43 H5
Clinton, Tenn., U.S.A. 43 G3
Clinton Colden L. 36 C9
Clintonville 40 C10
Clipperton, I. 35 F17
Clipperton Fracture Zone 35 G16
Clisham 10 D2
Clitheroe 8 D5
Clogher Hd. 11 C5
Clonakilty 11 E3
Clonakilty B. 11 E3
Cloncurry, Australia 30 E7
Cloncurry, Ireland 11 C5
Clondalkin 11 C5
Clones 11 B4
Clonmel 11 D4
Cloquet 40 B8
Cloud Peak 38 D10
Cloudcroft 39 K11
Cloverdale 38 G2
Clovis, Calif., U.S.A. 39 H4
Clovis, N. Mex., U.S.A. 41 H3
Cluj-Napoca 17 A2
Clunes 32 C3
Clutha → 33 M2
Clwyd → 8 D4
Clyde 33 L2
Clyde → 10 F4
Clyde, Firth of 10 F3
Clyde Muirshiel △ 10 F4
Clyde River 37 B13
Clydebank 10 F4
Coachella 39 K5
Coachella Canal 39 K6
Coahoma 41 J4
Coalgate 41 H6
Coalinga 39 H3
Coalisland 11 B5
Coalville, U.K. 8 E6
Coalville, U.S.A. 38 F8
Coamo 45 d
Coast Mts. 36 D7
Coast Ranges 38 F2
Coatbridge 10 F4
Coatesville 42 F8
Coats I. 37 C11
Coats Land 6 E5
Coatzacoalcos 44 D6
Cobán 44 D6
Cobar 32 B4
Cóbh 11 E3
Cobleskill 42 D8
Cobram 32 C4
Cochabamba 46 G5
Cochin 25 E6
Cochran 43 J4
Cochrane 37 E11
Cockburn 32 B3
Cockburn, Canal 48 G2
Cockermouth 8 C4
Cockpit Country, The 44 a
Coco → 45 E8
Coco, I. del 35 G19
Cocoa 43 L5
Cocos Is. 23 E1
Cocos Ridge 35 G19
Cod, C. 42 D10
Codó 47 D10
Cody 38 D9
Coeur d'Alene 38 C5
Coeur d'Alene L. 38 C5
Coffeyville 41 G7
Coffin B. 32 B2
Coffin Bay 32 B2
Coffin Bay △ 32 B2
Coffin Bay Peninsula 32 B2
Coffs Harbour 32 B5
Cognac 12 D3
Cohuna 32 C3
Coigeach, Rubha 10 C3
Coimbatore 25 D6
Coimbra 13 B1
Cokeville 38 E8
Colac 32 C3
Colatina 47 G10
Colby 40 F4
Colchester 9 F8
Coldstream 10 F6
Coldwater, Kans., U.S.A. 41 G5
Coldwater, Mich., U.S.A. 42 E3
Colebrook 42 C10
Coleman 41 K5
Coleraine, Australia 32 C3
Coleraine, U.K. 11 A5
Coleridge, L. 33 K3
Colesberg 29 L5
Colfax, La., U.S.A. 41 K8
Colfax, Wash., U.S.A. 38 C5
Colima 44 D4
Coll 10 E2
Collarenebri 32 A4
College Park 43 J3
College Station 41 K6
Collierville 41 H10
Collingwood 33 J4
Collooney 11 B3
Colmar 12 B7
Colo → 32 B5
Cologne = Köln 16 C3
Colombia ■ 46 C4
Colombo 25 E6
Colón, Arch. de 35 H18
Colón Ridge 35 G18
Colonial Beach 42 F7
Colonsay 10 E2
Colorado □ 39 G10
Colorado →, N. Amer. 39 L6
Colorado →, U.S.A. 41 L7
Colorado City 41 J4
Colorado Plateau 39 H8
Colorado River Aqueduct 39 J6
Colorado Springs 40 F2
Colstrip 38 D10
Columbia, Ky., U.S.A. 42 G3
Columbia, La., U.S.A. 41 J8
Columbia, Miss., U.S.A. 41 K10
Columbia, Mo., U.S.A. 40 F8
Columbia, Pa., U.S.A. 42 E7
Columbia, S.C., U.S.A. 43 J5
Columbia, Tenn., U.S.A. 43 H2
Columbia → 38 C1
Columbia, C. 37 A11
Columbia, District of □ 42 F7
Columbia Basin 38 C4
Columbia Falls 38 B6
Columbia Plateau 38 D5
Columbus, Ga., U.S.A. 43 J3
Columbus, Ind., U.S.A. 42 F3
Columbus, Kans., U.S.A. 41 G7
Columbus, Miss., U.S.A. 43 J1
Columbus, Mont., U.S.A. 38 D9
Columbus, N. Mex., U.S.A. 39 L10
Columbus, Nebr., U.S.A. 40 E6
Columbus, Ohio, U.S.A. 42 F4
Columbus, Tex., U.S.A. 41 L6
Colusa 38 G2
Colville 38 B5
Colville → 36 B4
Colville, C. 33 G5
Colville Ridge 31 G15
Colwyn Bay 8 D4
Comanche 41 K5
Combahee → 43 J5
Combe Martin 9 F3
Comber 11 B6
Comeragh Mts. 11 D4
Commerce, Ga., U.S.A. 43 H4
Commerce, Tex., U.S.A. 41 J7
Committee B. 37 C11
Commoron Cr. → 32 A5
Como 12 D8
Como, Lago di 12 D8
Comodoro Rivadavia 48 F3
Comorin, C. 25 E6
Comoros ■ 5 E13
Compiègne 12 B5
Con Son 23 C2
Conakry 26 G3
Conara 32 D4
Concepción 48 D2
Concepción del Oro 44 C4
Conception, Pt. 39 J3
Conchas Dam 41 H2
Concho 39 J9
Concho → 41 K5
Conchos → 44 B4
Concord, Calif., U.S.A. 38 H2
Concord, N.C., U.S.A. 43 H5
Concord, N.H., U.S.A. 42 D10
Concordia 40 F6
Concrete 38 B3
Condamine 32 A5
Conde 40 C5
Condobolin 32 B4
Condon 38 D3
Congleton 8 D5
Congo ■ 28 E3
Congo → 28 F2
Congo, Dem. Rep. of the ■ 28 E4
Congo Basin 28 E4
Congress 39 J7
Conn, L. 11 B2
Connacht □ 11 C2
Conneaut 42 E5
Connecticut □ 42 E9
Connecticut → 42 E9
Connell 38 C4
Connellsville 42 E6
Connemara 11 C2
Connemara △ 11 C2
Connersville 42 F3
Conrad 38 B8
Conran, C. 32 C4
Conroe 41 K7
Consett 8 C6
Constance, L. = Bodensee 12 C8
Constanța 15 B13
Constantine 26 A7
Contact 38 F6
Contwoyto L. 36 C8
Conway, Ark., U.S.A. 41 H8
Conway, N.H., U.S.A. 42 D10
Conway, S.C., U.S.A. 43 J6
Conway, L. 32 A2
Conwy 8 D4
Conwy → 8 D4
Coober Pedy 32 A1
Cook 40 B8
Cook, Mt. = Aoraki Mount Cook 33 K3
Cook Inlet 36 D4
Cook Is. 35 J12
Cook Strait 33 J5
Cookeville 43 G3
Cookstown 11 B5
Cooktown 30 D8
Coolabah 32 B4
Cooladdi 32 A4
Coolah 32 B4
Coolamon 32 B4
Coolidge 39 K8
Coolidge Dam 39 K8
Cooloola △ 32 A5
Cooma 32 C4
Coon Rapids 40 C8
Coonabarabran 32 B4

Coonamble 32 B4
Cooninnie, L. 32 A2
Cooper 41 J7
Cooper Cr. → 32 A2
Cooper Ridge 35 F12
Cooperstown, *N. Dak., U.S.A.* 40 B5
Cooperstown, *N.Y., U.S.A.* 42 D8
Coorong, The 32 C2
Cooroy 32 A5
Coos Bay 38 E1
Coosa → 43 J2
Cootamundra 32 B4
Cootehill 11 B4
Cope 40 F3
Copenhagen = København 7 F6
Copper Harbor 42 B2
Copperas Cove 41 K6
Coppermine → 36 C8
Coquet → 8 B6
Coquille 38 E1
Coraki 32 A5
Coral Gables 43 N5
Coral Harbour 37 C11
Coral Sea 30 C9
Coral Sea Basin 34 J7
Coral Sea Islands Terr. □ 30 D9
Coral Springs 43 M5
Corbin 42 G3
Corby 9 E7
Corcoran 39 H4
Cordele 43 K4
Cordell 41 H5
Córdoba, *Argentina* 48 C4
Córdoba, *Mexico* 44 D5
Córdoba, *Spain* 13 D3
Córdoba, Sierra de 48 C4
Cordova 36 C5
Corfu = Kerkyra 15 E8
Corinth 43 H1
Corinth, G. of = Korinthiakos Kolpos 15 E10
Cork 11 E3
Cork □ 11 E3
Cork Harbour 11 E3
Corner Brook 37 E14
Corning, *Ark., U.S.A.* 41 G9
Corning, *Calif., U.S.A.* 38 G2
Corning, *Iowa, U.S.A.* 40 E7
Corning, *N.Y., U.S.A.* 42 D7
Cornwall 37 E12
Cornwall □ 9 G3
Cornwall I. 37 A11
Cornwallis I. 37 B10
Corny Pt. 32 B2
Coro 46 A5
Coromandel 33 G5
Coromandel Coast 25 D7
Corona, *Calif., U.S.A.* 39 K5
Corona, *N. Mex., U.S.A.* 39 J11
Coronation Gulf 36 C9
Corowa 32 C4
Corpus Christi 41 M6
Corpus Christi, L. 41 L6
Corraun Pen. 11 C2
Corrib, L. 11 C2
Corrientes 48 B5
Corrientes, C. 44 C3
Corrigan 41 K7
Corry 42 E6
Corse □ 12 F8
Corse, C. 12 E8
Corsica = Corse □ 12 F8
Corsicana 41 J6
Corte 12 E8
Cortez 39 H9
Cortland 42 D7
Corumbá 46 G7
Corunna = A Coruña 13 A1
Corvallis 38 D2
Corydon 40 E8
Cosenza 14 E7
Coshocton 42 E5
Costa Blanca 13 C5
Costa Brava 13 B7
Costa del Sol 13 D3
Costa Dorada 13 B6
Costa Rica ■ 45 F8
Cotabato 23 C4
Côte d'Azur 12 E7
Côte-d'Ivoire = Ivory Coast ■ 26 G4
Coteau des Prairies 40 C6
Coteau du Missouri 40 B4
Cotentin 12 B3
Cotonou 26 G6
Cotopaxi 46 D3
Cotswold Hills 9 F5
Cottage Grove 38 E2
Cottbus 16 C7
Cottonwood 39 J7
Cotulla 41 L5
Coudersport 42 E6
Couedic, C. du 32 C2
Coulee City 38 C4
Council 38 D5
Council Bluffs 40 E7
Council Grove 40 F6
Courantyne → 46 B7
Courtenay 36 E7
Coushatta 41 J8
Coutts Crossing 32 A5
Coventry 9 E6
Covington, *Ga., U.S.A.* 43 J4
Covington, *Ky., U.S.A.* 42 F3
Covington, *Tenn., U.S.A.* 41 H10
Covington, *Va., U.S.A.* 42 G5
Cowal, L. 32 B4
Cowangie 32 C3
Coward Springs 32 A2
Cowdenbeath 10 E5
Cowell 32 B2
Cowes 9 G6
Cowra 32 B4
Cozad 40 E5
Cozumel, Isla 44 C7
Crab Hill 45 g
Cracow 32 A5
Cradle Mt.-Lake St. Clair △ 32 D4
Cradock, *Australia* 32 B2
Cradock, *S. Africa* 29 L5
Craig 38 F10
Craigavon 11 B5
Craiova 15 B10
Cranbrook 36 E8
Crandon 40 C10
Crane, *Oreg., U.S.A.* 38 E4
Crane, *Tex., U.S.A.* 41 K3
Crane, The 45 g
Crater L. 38 E2
Crater Lake △ 38 E2
Craters of the Moon △ 38 E7
Crawford 40 D3
Crawfordsville 42 E2
Crawley 9 F7
Crazy Mts. 38 C8
Crediton 9 G4
Cree →, *Canada* 36 D9
Cree →, *U.K.* 10 G4
Cree L. 36 D9
Creede 39 H10
Creighton 40 D6
Cremona 12 D9
Crescent City 38 F1
Creston 40 E7
Crestview 43 K2
Crete = Kriti 15 G11
Crete 40 E6
Creuse → 12 C4
Crewe 8 D5
Crewkerne 9 G5
Crianlarich 10 E4
Crieff 10 E5
Crimean Pen. = Krymskyy Pivostriv 17 B4
Croagh Patrick 11 C2
Croatia ■ 14 B7
Crockett 41 K7
Crohy Hd. 11 B3
Croker, C. 30 C5
Cromarty 10 D4
Cromer 8 E9
Cromwell 33 L2
Crook 8 C6
Crooked → 38 D3
Crooked I. 45 C10
Crookston, *Minn., U.S.A.* 40 B6
Crookston, *Nebr., U.S.A.* 40 D4
Crookwell 32 B4
Crosby, *U.K.* 8 D4
Crosby, *U.S.A.* 40 A3
Crosbyton 41 J4
Cross City 43 L4
Cross Fell 8 C5
Cross Sound 36 D6
Crossett 41 J9
Crosshaven 11 E3
Crossmaglen 11 B5
Crossmolina 11 B2
Crossville 43 G3
Crow Agency 38 D10
Crow Hd. 11 E1
Crowell 41 J5
Crowley 41 K8
Crown Point 42 E2
Crownpoint 39 J9
Crows Nest 32 A5
Crowsnest Pass 36 E8
Croydon □ 9 F7
Crozet, Is. 5 G13
Crusheen 11 D3
Cruz Bay 45 e
Cruzeiro do Sul 46 E4
Crystal Brook 32 B2
Crystal City 41 L5
Crystal Falls 42 B1
Crystal River 43 L4
Crystal Springs 41 K9
Cuando → 29 H4
Cuanza → 28 F2
Cuauhtémoc 44 B3
Cuba 39 J10
Cuba ■ 45 C9
Cubango → 29 H4
Cuckfield 9 F7
Cúcuta 46 B4
Cuenca, *Ecuador* 46 D3
Cuenca, *Spain* 13 B4
Cuernavaca 44 D5
Cuero 41 L6
Cuiabá 47 G7
Cuihangcun 21 G10
Cuillin Hills 10 D2
Cuillin Sd. 10 D2
Culbertson 40 A2
Culcairn 32 C4
Culebra 45 d
Culgoa → 32 A4
Culgoa Flood Plain △ 32 A4
Culiacán 44 C3
Cullarin Ra. 32 B4
Cullen 10 D6
Cullman 43 H2
Cullompton 9 G4
Culpeper 42 F7
Culverden 33 K4
Cumaná 46 A6
Cumberland 42 F6
Cumberland → 43 G2
Cumberland, L. 43 G3
Cumberland Gap △ 43 G4
Cumberland I. 43 K5
Cumberland Island △ 43 K5
Cumberland Pen. 37 C13
Cumberland Plateau 43 H3
Cumberland Sd. 37 C13
Cumbernauld 10 F5
Cumborah 32 A4
Cumbria □ 8 C5
Cumbrian Mts. 8 C5
Cummins 32 B2
Cumnock, *Australia* 32 B4
Cumnock, *U.K.* 10 F4
Cunene → 29 H2
Cúneo 12 D7
Cunnamulla 32 A4
Cupar 10 E5
Curaçao 45 E11
Curitiba 48 B7
Currabubula 32 B5
Currane, L. 11 E1
Currant 38 G6
Currawinya △ 32 A3
Current → 41 G9
Currie, *Australia* 32 C3
Currie, *U.S.A.* 38 F6
Curtis 40 E4
Curtis Group 32 C4
Curtis I. 31 G15
Cushendall 11 A5
Cushing 41 H6
Custer 40 D3
Cut Bank 38 B7
Cuthbert 43 K3
Cuttaburra → 32 A3
Cuttack 25 C7
Cuvier I. 33 G5
Cuxhaven 16 B4
Cuyahoga Falls 42 E5
Cuzco 46 F4
Cwmbran 9 F4
Cyclades 15 F11
Cygnet 32 D4
Cynthiana 42 F3
Cyprus ■ 17 D4
Cyrenaica 27 C10
Czech Rep. ■ 16 D7
Częstochowa 16 C9

D

Da Hinggan Ling 21 B7
Da Lat 23 B2
Da Nang 23 B2
Da Qaidam 20 C4
Daba Shan 21 C5
Dacca = Dhaka 25 C8
Dade City 43 L4
Daegu 21 C7
Daejeon 21 C7
Dagupan 23 B4
Dahlak Kebir 24 D3
Dahlonega 43 H4
Daingean 11 C4
Dajarra 30 E6
Dakar 26 F2
Dakhla 26 D2
Dakota City 40 D6
Dalandzadgad 20 B5
Dalap-Uliga-Darrit 34 G9
Dalbeattie 10 G5
Dalby 32 A5
Dale City 42 F7
Dale Hollow L. 43 G3
Dalhart 41 G3
Dali 20 D5
Dalian 21 C7
Daliang Shan 20 D5
Dalkeith 10 F5
Dallas, *Oreg., U.S.A.* 38 D2
Dallas, *Tex., U.S.A.* 41 J6
Dalles, The 38 D3
Dalmacija 14 C7
Dalmatia = Dalmacija 14 C7
Dalmellington 10 F4
Daloa 26 G4
Dalry 10 F4
Dalrymple, L. 30 E8
Dalton, *Ga., U.S.A.* 43 H3
Dalton, *Nebr., U.S.A.* 40 E3
Dalton-in-Furness 8 C4
Daly Waters 30 D5
Damanhûr 27 B12
Damaraland 29 H2
Damascus = Dimashq 24 B2
Damāvand, Qolleh-ye 24 B4
Dampier 30 E2
Danbury 42 E9
Danby L. 39 J6
Dandenong 32 C4
Dandong 21 B7
Daniel 38 E8
Dannemora 42 C9
Dannevirke 33 J6
Dansville 42 D7
Danube = Dunărea → 15 B13
Danville, *Ill., U.S.A.* 42 E2
Danville, *Ky., U.S.A.* 42 G3
Danville, *Va., U.S.A.* 43 G6
Danzig = Gdańsk 16 A9
Dar es Salaam 28 F7
Darbhanga 25 C7
Dardanelle 41 H8
Dardanelles = Çanakkale Boğazı 15 D12
Dargaville 33 F4
Darhan 20 B5
Darién, G. del 46 B3
Darjiling 25 C7
Darling → 32 B3
Darling Downs 32 A5
Darling Ra. 30 G2
Darlington, *U.K.* 8 C6
Darlington, *U.S.A.* 43 H6
Darmstadt 16 D4
Darnley, C. 6 D10
Darnley B. 36 C7
Darrington 38 B3
Dart → 9 G4
Dartford 9 F8
Dartmoor 9 G4
Dartmoor △ 9 G4
Dartmouth, *Canada* 37 E13
Dartmouth, *U.K.* 9 G4
Dartmouth Res. 32 A4
Darwen 8 D5
Darwin 30 C5
Dashen, Ras 28 B7
Dashoguz 24 A4
Dasht → 24 C5
Dasht-i-Tahlab 24 C5
Datong 21 B6
Daugavpils 18 D3
Dauphin 36 D9
Dauphiné 12 D6
Davangere 25 D6
Davao 23 C4
Davao G. 23 C4
Davenport, *Iowa, U.S.A.* 40 E9
Davenport, *Wash., U.S.A.* 38 C4
Daventry 9 E6
David 46 B2
David City 40 E6
Davis 38 G3
Davis Dam 39 J6
Davis Mts. 41 K2
Davis Str. 6 C4
Dawlish 9 G4
Dawros Hd. 11 B3
Dawson, *Canada* 36 C6
Dawson, *U.S.A.* 43 K3
Dawson Creek 36 D7
Dax 12 E3
Daxian 20 C5
Daxue Shan 20 C5
Daylesford 32 C3
Dayr az Zawr 24 B3
Dayton, *Ohio, U.S.A.* 42 F3
Dayton, *Tenn., U.S.A.* 43 H3
Dayton, *Wash., U.S.A.* 38 C4
Dayton, *Wyo., U.S.A.* 38 D10
Daytona Beach 43 L5
Dayville 38 D4
De Aar 29 L4
De Funiak Springs 43 K2
De Land 43 L5
De Leon 41 J5
De Pere 42 C1
De Queen 41 H7
De Quincy 41 K8
De Smet 40 C6
De Soto 40 F9
De Tour Village 42 C4
De Witt 41 H9
Dead Sea 17 D5
Deadwood 40 C3
Deal 9 F9
Deal I. 32 C4
Dean, Forest of 9 F5
Dease → 36 D7
Dease Lake 36 D6
Death Valley 39 H5
Death Valley △ 39 H5
Death Valley Junction 39 H5
Debrecen 17 A2
Decatur, *Ala., U.S.A.* 43 H2
Decatur, *Ga., U.S.A.* 43 J3
Decatur, *Ill., U.S.A.* 40 F10
Decatur, *Ind., U.S.A.* 42 E3
Decatur, *Tex., U.S.A.* 41 J6
Deccan 25 D6
Deception Bay 32 A5
Decorah 40 D9
Dee →, *Aberds., U.K.* 10 D6
Dee →, *Dumf. & Gall., U.K.* 10 G4
Dee →, *Wales, U.K.* 8 D4
Deepwater 32 A5
Deer Lake 37 E14
Deer Lodge 38 C7
Deer Park 38 C5
Deer River 40 B8
Defiance 42 E3
Dehiwala 25 E6
Dehra Dun 25 B6
DeKalb 40 E10
Del Norte 39 H10
Del Rio 41 L4
Delano 39 J4
Delano Peak 39 G7
Delavan 40 D10
Delaware 42 E4
Delaware □ 42 F8
Delaware B. 42 F8
Delegate 32 C4
Delgado, C. 28 G8
Delhi, *India* 25 C6
Delhi, *U.S.A.* 41 J9
Delicias 44 B3
Déline 36 C7
Dell City 39 L11
Dell Rapids 40 D6
Deloraine 32 D4
Delphi 42 E2
Delphos 42 E3
Delray Beach 43 M5
Delta, *Colo., U.S.A.* 39 G9
Delta, *Utah, U.S.A.* 38 G7
Delta Junction 36 C5
Deltona 43 L5
Delungra 32 A5
Deming 39 K10
Demopolis 43 J2
Den Haag = 's-Gravenhage 16 B2
Den Helder 16 B2
Denali = McKinley, Mt. 36 C4
Denbigh 8 D4
Denbighshire □ 8 D4
Denham, Mt. 44 a
Denial B. 32 B1
Deniliquin 32 C3
Denison, *Iowa, U.S.A.* 40 E7
Denison, *Tex., U.S.A.* 41 J6
Denizli 17 C3
Denmark ■ 7 F6
Denmark Str. 6 C5
Dennery 45 f
Denny 10 E5
Denpasar 23 D3
Denton, *Mont., U.S.A.* 38 C9
Denton, *Tex., U.S.A.* 41 J6
D'Entrecasteaux, Îs. 31 D11
D'Entrecasteaux Is. 30 B9
Denver 40 F2
Denver City 41 J3
Dera Ismail Khan 25 B6
Derby, *Australia* 30 D3
Derby, *U.K.* 8 E6
Derby, *U.S.A.* 41 G6
Derbyshire □ 8 D6
Dereham 9 E8
Derg → 11 B4
Derg, L. 11 D3
Deridder 41 K8
Dermott 41 J9
Derry = Londonderry 11 B4
Derryveagh Mts. 11 B3
Derwent →, *Cumb., U.K.* 8 C4
Derwent →, *Derby, U.K.* 8 E6
Derwent →, *N. Yorks., U.K.* 8 D7
Derwent Water 8 C4
Des Moines, *Iowa, U.S.A.* 40 E8
Des Moines, *N. Mex., U.S.A.* 41 G3
Des Moines → 40 E9
Deschutes → 38 D3
Dese 24 D2
Desert Center 39 K6
Dessau 16 C6
D'Estrees B. 32 C2
Detour, Pt. 42 C2
Detroit 42 D4
Detroit Lakes 40 B7
Deutsche Bucht 16 A4
Deventer 16 B3
Deveron → 10 D6
Devils Lake 40 A5
Devils Tower 40 C2
Devils Tower △ 40 C2
Devine 41 L5
Devizes 9 F6
Devon □ 9 G4
Devon I. 37 B10
Devonport, *Australia* 32 D4
Devonport, *N.Z.* 33 G5
Dewey 45 d
Dexter, *Maine, U.S.A.* 43 C11
Dexter, *Mo., U.S.A.* 41 G10
Dexter, *N. Mex., U.S.A.* 41 J2
Dezfūl 24 B3
Dezhneva, Mys 19 C19
Dhahran = Az Zahrān 24 C4
Dhaka 25 C8
Dhamār 24 D3
Dhanbad 25 C7
Dharwad 25 D6
Dhaulagiri 25 C7
Dhule 25 C6
Diamantina → 32 A2
Diamond Mts. 38 G6
Dibrugarh 25 C8
Dickens 41 J4
Dickinson 40 B3
Dickson 43 G2
Diefenbaker, L. 36 D9
Dieppe 12 B4
Dierks 41 H8
Digby 37 E13
Dighton 40 F4
Digne-les-Bains 12 D7
Dijlah, Nahr → 24 B3
Dijon 12 C6
Dili 23 D4
Dilley 41 L5
Dillingham 36 D4
Dillon, *Mont., U.S.A.* 38 D7
Dillon, *S.C., U.S.A.* 43 H6
Dimashq 24 B2
Dimboola 32 C3
Dimitrovgrad 15 C11
Dimmitt 41 H3
Dinan 12 B2
Dinant 16 C2
Dinara Planina 14 C7
Dingle 11 D1
Dingle B. 11 D1
Dingwall 10 D4
Dinin → 11 D4
Dinosaur △ 38 F9
Dinuba 39 H4
Dipolog 23 C4
Dire Dawa 24 E3
Dirranbandi 32 A4
Disappointment, C. 38 C2
Disappointment, L. 30 E3
Disaster B. 32 C4
Discovery B., *Australia* 32 C3
Discovery B., *China* 21 G11
Diss 9 E9
District of Columbia □ 42 F7
Divide 38 D7
Dixon 40 E10
Dixon Entrance 36 D6
Diyarbakır 17 C6
Djakarta = Jakarta 23 D2
Djerid, Chott 26 B7
Djibouti 24 D3
Djibouti ■ 24 D3
Dnepr = Dnipro → 17 A4
Dnestr = Dnister → 18 E4
Dnipro → 17 A4
Dniprodzerzhynsk 17 A4
Dnipropetrovsk 17 A5
Dnister → 18 E4
Doberai, Jazirah 23 D5
Dobrich 15 C12
Dodecanese 15 F12
Dodge City 41 G5
Dodgeville 40 D9
Dodoma 28 F7
Dodson 38 B9
Doha = Ad Dawhah 24 C4
Dolbeau-Mistassini 37 E12
Dole 12 C6
Dolgellau 8 E4
Dolo 24 E3
Dolomiti 14 A4
Dolores 39 H9
Dolores → 39 G9
Dolphin and Union Str. 36 C8
Dominica ■ 45 D12
Dominican Rep. ■ 45 D10
Domville, Mt. 32 A5
Don →, *Russia* 18 E4
Don →, *Aberds., U.K.* 10 D6
Don →, *S. Yorks., U.K.* 8 D7
Don Figuerero Mts. 44 a
Donaghadee 11 B6
Donaghmore 11 D4
Donald 32 C3
Donaldsonville 41 K9
Donalsonville 43 K3
Doncaster 8 D6
Dondra Head 25 E7
Donegal 11 B3
Donegal □ 11 B4
Donegal B. 11 B3
Donetsk 17 A5
Dong Hoi 23 B2
Dongbei 21 B7
Dongchuan 20 D5
Dongting Hu 21 D6
Donington, C. 32 B2
Doniphan 41 G9
Donna 41 M5
Donnelly's Crossing 33 F4
Donostia-San Sebastián 13 A5
Doon → 10 F4
Dorchester 9 G5
Dorchester, C. 37 C12
Dordogne → 12 D3
Dordrecht 16 C2
Dorking 9 F7
Dornie 10 D3
Dornoch 10 D4
Dornoch Firth 10 D4
Döröö Nuur 20 B4
Dorrigo 32 B5
Dorris 38 F3
Dorset □ 9 G5
Dortmund 16 C3
Dothan 43 K3
Douai 12 A5
Douala 28 D1
Double Island Pt. 32 A5
Double Mountain Fork → 41 J4
Doubs → 12 C6
Doubtful Sd. 33 L1
Doubtless B. 33 F4
Douglas, *I. of Man* 8 C3
Douglas, *Ariz., U.S.A.* 39 L9
Douglas, *Ga., U.S.A.* 43 K4
Douglas, *Wyo., U.S.A.* 40 D2
Douglas Apsley △ 32 D4
Douglasville 43 J3
Dounreay 10 C5
Dourados 47 H8
Douro → 13 B1
Dove → 8 E6
Dove Creek 39 H9
Dover, *Australia* 32 D4
Dover, *U.K.* 9 F9
Dover, *Del., U.S.A.* 42 F8
Dover, *N.H., U.S.A.* 42 D10
Dover, *Ohio, U.S.A.* 42 E5
Dover, Str. of 9 G9
Dover-Foxcroft 43 C11
Dovrefjell 7 E5
Dowagiac 42 E2
Down □ 11 B5
Downey 38 E7
Downham Market 9 E8
Downieville 38 G3
Downpatrick 11 B6
Downpatrick Hd. 11 B2
Draguignan 12 E7
Drain 38 E2
Drake 40 B4
Drake Passage 6 B
Drakensberg 29 L5
Drammen 7 F6
Drava → 15 B8
Dresden 16 C6
Dreux 12 B4
Driffield 8 C7
Driggs 38 E8
Drina → 15 B8
Drobeta-Turnu Severin 15 B10
Drogheda 11 C5
Droichead Nua 11 C5
Droitwich 9 E5
Dromedary, C. 32 C5
Dromore 11 B4
Dromore West 11 B3
Dronfield 8 D6
Dronning Maud Land 6 E7
Drumcliff 11 B3
Drumheller 36 D8
Drummond 38 C7
Drummond I. 42 C4
Drummond Pt. 32 B2
Drumright 41 H6
Dry Harbour Mts. 44 a
Dryden 36 E10
Drygalski I. 6 D11
Du Quoin 40 G10
Dubai = Dubayy 24 C4
Dubawnt → 36 C9
Dubawnt L. 36 C9
Dubayy 24 C4
Dubbo 32 B4
Dublin, *Ireland* 11 C5
Dublin, *Ga., U.S.A.* 43 J4
Dublin, *Tex., U.S.A.* 41 J5
Dublin □ 11 C5
Dublin (DUB) 11 C5
Dubois, *Idaho, U.S.A.* 38 D7
Dubois, *Pa., U.S.A.* 42 E6
Dubrovnik 15 C8
Dubuque 40 D9
Duchesne 38 F8
Ducie I. 35 K15
Duck → 43 G2
Dudinka 19 C9
Dudley 9 E5
Duff Is. 31 B12
Dufftown 10 D5
Duisburg 16 C3
Dulce 39 H10
Duluth 40 B8
Dumaguete 23 C4
Dumas, *Ark., U.S.A.* 41 J9
Dumas, *Tex., U.S.A.* 41 H4
Dumbarton 10 F4
Dumfries 10 F5
Dumfries & Galloway □ 10 F5
Dumyât 27 B12
Dún Laoghaire 11 C5
Dunărea → 15 B13
Dunback 33 L3
Dunbar 10 E6
Dunblane 10 E5
Duncan, *Ariz., U.S.A.* 39 K9
Duncan, *Okla., U.S.A.* 41 H6
Duncansby Head 10 C5
Dundalk, *Ireland* 11 B5
Dundalk, *U.S.A.* 42 F7
Dundalk Bay 11 C5
Dundas 42 D6
Dundee 10 E6
Dundrum 11 B6
Dundrum B. 11 B6
Dunedin, *N.Z.* 33 L3
Dunedin, *U.S.A.* 43 L4
Dunfanaghy 11 A4
Dunfermline 10 E5
Dungannon 11 B5
Dungarvan 11 D4
Dungarvan Harbour 11 D4
Dungeness 9 G8
Dunglow 11 B3
Dungog 32 B5
Dunhuang 20 B4
Dunkeld, *Australia* 32 B4
Dunkeld, *U.K.* 10 E5
Dunkerque 12 A5
Dunkery Beacon 9 F4
Dunkirk = Dunkerque 12 A5
Dunkirk 42 D6
Dunleer 11 C5
Dunmanus B. 11 E2
Dunmanway 11 E2
Dunmore 42 E8
Dunmore East 11 D5
Dunmore Hd. 11 D1
Dunn 43 H6
Dunnellon 43 L4
Dunnet Hd. 10 C5
Dunning 40 E4
Dunolly 32 C3
Dunoon 10 F4
Duns 10 F6
Dunseith 40 A4
Dunshaughlin 11 C5
Dunsmuir 38 F2
Dunstable 9 F7
Dunstan Mts. 33 L2
Dunvegan 10 D2
Dupree 40 C4
Dupuyer 38 B7
Durance → 12 E6
Durand 40 C9
Durango, *Mexico* 44 C4
Durango, *U.S.A.* 39 H10
Durant, *Miss., U.S.A.* 41 J10
Durant, *Okla., U.S.A.* 41 J6
Durban 29 K6
Düren 16 C3
Durham, *U.K.* 8 C6
Durham, *U.S.A.* 43 H6
Durham □ 8 C6
Durness 10 C4
Durrës 15 D8
Durrow 11 D4
Dursey I. 11 E1
Dursley 9 F5
D'Urville I. 33 J4
Dushanbe 18 F7
Dusky Sd. 33 L1
Düsseldorf 16 C3
Dutch Harbor 36 D3
Duyun 20 D5
Dvina, Severnaya → 18 C5
Dwight 42 E1
Dyce 10 D6
Dyer, C. 37 C13
Dyersburg 41 G10
Dyfi → 9 E3
Dzhugdzur, Khrebet 19 D14
Dzungarian Gate 20 B3
Dzuumod 20 B5

E

Eads 40 F3
Eagar 39 J9
Eagle, *Alaska, U.S.A.* 36 C5
Eagle, *Colo., U.S.A.* 38 G10
Eagle Butte 40 C4
Eagle Grove 40 D8
Eagle L., *Calif., U.S.A.* 38 F3
Eagle L., *Maine, U.S.A.* 43 B11
Eagle Lake, *Maine, U.S.A.* 43 B11
Eagle Lake, *Tex., U.S.A.* 41 L6
Eagle Nest 39 H11
Eagle Pass 41 L4
Eagle River, *Mich., U.S.A.* 42 B1
Eagle River, *Wis., U.S.A.* 40 C10
Eaglehawk 32 C3
Ealing □ 9 F7
Earle 41 H9
Earlimart 39 J4
Earn → 10 E5
Earn, L. 10 E4
Earnslaw, Mt. 33 L2
Earth 41 H3
Easley 43 H4
East Anglia 8 E9
East Ayrshire □ 10 F4
East C. 33 G7
East Caroline Basin 34 G6
East Chicago 42 E2
East China Sea 21 D7
East Dunbartonshire □ 10 F4
East Falkland 48 G5
East Grand Forks 40 B6
East Grinstead 9 F8
East Helena 38 C8
East Kilbride 10 F4
East Lamma Channel 21 G11
East Lansing 42 D3
East Liverpool 42 E5
East London 29 L5
East Lothian □ 10 F6
East Mariana Basin 34 F7
East Orange 42 E8
East Pacific Rise 35 J17
East Point 43 J3
East Pt. 45 e
East Renfrewshire □ 10 F4
East Riding of Yorkshire □ 8 D7
East St. Louis 40 F9
East Sea = Japan, Sea of 22 D4
East Siberian Sea 19 B17
East Stroudsburg 42 E8
East Sussex □ 9 G8
East Tasman Plateau 34 M7
East Tawas 42 C4
East Timor ■ 23 D4
East Toorale 32 B4
Eastbourne, *N.Z.* 33 J5
Eastbourne, *U.K.* 9 G8
Easter Fracture Zone 35 K16
Easter I. = Pascua, I. de 35 K17
Eastern Ghats 25 D6
Eastland 41 J5
Eastleigh 9 G6
Eastmain 37 D12
Eastmain → 37 D12
Eastman 43 J4
Easton, *Md., U.S.A.* 42 F7
Easton, *Pa., U.S.A.* 42 E8
Eastport 43 C12
Eaton 40 E2
Eatonton 43 J4
Eau Claire 40 C9
Eau Claire, L. à l' 37 D12
Eauripik Rise 34 G6
Ebbw Vale 9 F4
Ebro → 13 B6
Ech Chéliff 26 A6
Echo Bay 36 C8
Eclipse Sd. 37 B12
Ecuador ■ 46 D3
Eday 10 B6
Eddrachillis B. 10 C3
Eddystone 9 G3
Eddystone Pt. 32 D4
Eden, *Australia* 32 C4
Eden, *N.C., U.S.A.* 43 G6
Eden, *Tex., U.S.A.* 41 K5
Eden → 8 C4
Edenderry 11 C4
Edenton 43 G7
Edgar 40 E6
Edge Hill 9 E6
Edgefield 43 J5
Edgeley 40 B5
Edgemont 40 D3
Edievale 33 L2
Edina 40 E8
Edinburg 41 M5
Edinburgh 10 F5
Edinburgh (EDI) 10 F5
Edithburgh 32 C2
Edmond 41 H6
Edmonds 38 C2
Edmonton 36 D8
Edmundston 37 E13
Edna 41 L6
Edson 36 D8
Edward → 32 C3
Edward, L. 28 E5
Edward VII Land 6 F17
Edwards Plateau 41 K4
Efate, I. 31 D12
Effigy Mounds △ 40 D9
Effingham 42 F1
Egan Range 38 G6
Eglinton I. 37 A10
Egmont △ 33 H5
Egmont, C. 33 H4
Egypt ■ 27 C12
Eidsvold 32 A5
Eifel 16 C3
Eigg 10 E2
Eil 24 E3
Eil, L. 10 E3
Eildon, L. 32 C4
Eindhoven 16 C2
Eire = Ireland ■ 11 C4
Eivissa 13 C6
Ekalaka 40 C2
Eketahuna 33 J5
El Aaiún 26 C3
El Cajon 39 K5
El Campo 41 L6
El Centro 39 K6
El Djouf 26 D4
El Dorado, *Ark., U.S.A.* 41 J8
El Dorado, *Kans., U.S.A.* 41 G6
El Dorado Springs 41 G8
El Faiyûm 27 C12
El Fâsher 27 F11
El Fuerte 44 B3
El Gîza 27 C12
El Iskandarîya 27 B11
El Jadida 26 B4
El Khârga 27 C12
El Khartûm 27 E12
El Khartûm Bahrî 27 E12
El Mahalla el Kubra 27 B12
El Malpais △ 39 J10
El Mansûra 27 B12
El Minyâ 27 C12
El Obeid 27 F12
El Paso 39 L10
El Qâhira 27 B12
El Salvador ■ 44 E7
El Suweis 27 C12
Elâzığ 17 C5
Elba, *Italy* 14 C4
Elba, *U.S.A.* 43 K2
Elbasan 15 D9
Elbe → 16 B4
Elbert, Mt. 39 G10
Elberton 43 H4
Elbeuf 12 B4
Elbląg 16 A9
Elbrus 18 E5
Elche 13 C5
Eldon 40 F8
Eldora 40 D8
Eldorado, *Ill., U.S.A.* 42 G1
Eldorado, *Tex., U.S.A.* 41 K4
Eldoret 28 D7
Elefantes → 29 J6
Elephant Butte Res. 39 K10
Elephant I. 6 D4
Eleuthera 45 C9
Elgin, *U.K.* 10 D5
Elgin, *Ill., U.S.A.* 42 D1
Elgin, *N. Dak., U.S.A.* 40 B4
Elgin, *Oreg., U.S.A.* 38 D5
Elgin, *Tex., U.S.A.* 41 K6
Elgon, Mt. 28 D6
Elizabeth, *Australia* 32 B2
Elizabeth, *U.S.A.* 42 E8
Elizabeth City 43 G7
Elizabethton 43 G4
Elizabethtown 42 G3
Elk → 43 H2
Elk City 41 H5
Elk River, *Idaho, U.S.A.* 38 C5
Elk River, *Minn., U.S.A.* 40 C8
Elkhart, *Ind., U.S.A.* 42 E3
Elkhart, *Kans., U.S.A.* 41 G4
Elkhorn → 40 E6
Elkin 43 G5
Elkins 42 F6
Elko 38 F6
Ellef Ringnes I. 37 B10
Ellendale 40 B5
Ellensburg 38 C3
Ellenville 42 E8
Ellerton 45 g
Ellery, Mt. 32 C4
Ellesmere, L. 33 M4
Ellesmere I. 37 B10
Ellesmere Port 8 D5
Ellice Is. = Tuvalu ■ 31 B14
Elliot Lake 37 E11
Ellis 40 F5
Elliston 32 B1
Ellisville 41 K10
Ellon 10 D6
Ellsworth, *Kans., U.S.A.* 40 F5
Ellsworth, *Maine, U.S.A.* 43 C11
Ellsworth Land 6 E2
Elma 38 C2
Elmhurst 42 E2
Elmira 42 D7
Elmore 32 C3
Eloy 39 K8
Eltham 33 H5
Eluru 25 D7
Elwood, *Ind., U.S.A.* 42 E3
Elwood, *Nebr., U.S.A.* 40 E5
Ely, *U.K.* 9 E8
Ely, *Minn., U.S.A.* 40 B9
Ely, *Nev., U.S.A.* 38 G6
Elyria 42 E4
Emāmrūd 24 B4
Emden 16 B3
Emerald 30 E8
Emmen 16 B3
Emmetsburg 40 D7
Emmett 38 E5
Emmonak 36 C3
Empalme 44 B2
Empangeni 29 K6
Emperor Seamount Chain 34 D9
Emperor Trough 34 C9
Emporia, *Kans., U.S.A.* 40 F6
Emporia, *Va., U.S.A.* 43 G7
Emporium 42 E6
Ems → 16 B3
Enard B. 10 C3
Encampment 38 F10
Encino 39 J11
Encounter B. 32 C2
Ende 23 D4
Enderbury I. 31 A16
Enderby Land 6 D9
Enderlin 40 B6
Endicott 42 D7
Enewetak Atoll 34 F8
Enfer, Pte. d' 44 c
Enfield 43 G7
Engadin 12 C9
Engels 18 D5
Enggano 23 D2
England 41 H9
England □ 9 E5
Englewood 40 F2
English → 36 D10
English Channel 9 G6
Enid 41 G6
Ennadai L. 36 C9
Enngonia 32 A4
Ennis, *Ireland* 11 D3
Ennis, *Mont., U.S.A.* 38 D8
Ennis, *Tex., U.S.A.* 41 J6
Enniscorthy 11 D5
Enniskillen 11 B4
Ennistimon 11 D2
Enns → 16 D7
Enschede 16 B3
Ensenada 44 A1
Entebbe 28 D6
Enterprise, *Ala., U.S.A.* 43 K3
Enterprise, *Oreg., U.S.A.* 38 D5
Enugu 26 G7
Enumclaw 38 C3
Épernay 12 B5
Ephraim 38 G8
Ephrata 38 C4
Epi 31 D12
Épinal 12 B7
Epsom 9 F7
Equatorial Guinea ■ 28 D1
Erdenet 20 B5
Erebus, Mt. 6 E15
Erfurt 16 C5
Eriboll, L. 10 C4
Erie 42 D5
Erie, L. 42 D5
Erigavo 24 D3
Eriskay 10 D1
Eritrea ■ 24 D2
Erlangen 16 D5
Erne → 11 B3
Erne, Lower L. 11 B4
Erne, Upper L. 11 B4
Eromanga 32 A3
Errigal 11 A3
Erris Hd. 11 B1
Erromango 31 D12
Erskine 40 B7
Erwin 43 G4
Erzgebirge 16 C6
Erzurum 17 C6
Es Sahrâ' Esh Sharqîya 27 C12
Esbjerg 7 F5
Escalante 39 H8
Escalante → 39 H8
Escambia → 43 K2
Escanaba 42 C2
Esch-sur-Alzette 12 B6
Escondido 39 K5
Escuinapa de Hidalgo 44 C3
Escuintla 44 E6
Eşfahān 24 B4
Esha Ness 10 A7
Esher 9 F7
Esk →, *Cumb., U.K.* 10 G5
Esk →, *N. Yorks., U.K.* 8 C7
Esker 37 D13
Eskilstuna 7 F7
Eskişehir 17 C4
Esmeraldas 46 C3
Espanola 39 H10
Esperance 30 G3
Esperance Harbour 45 f
Esperanza 45 d
Espinhaço, Serra do 47 G10
Espíritu Santo 31 D12
Espoo 7 E8
Essen 16 C3
Essequibo → 46 B7
Essex □ 9 F8
Estancia 39 J10
Estevan 36 E9
Estherville 40 D7
Estrela, Serra da 13 B2
Etawah 25 C6
eThekwini = Durban 29 K6
Ethiopia ■ 28 B7
Ethiopian Highlands 3 D12
Etive, L. 10 E3
Etna 14 F6
Etowah 43 H3
Etrek 24 B4
Ettrick Water → 10 F6
Eua 31 E16
Euclid 42 E5
Eucumbene, L. 32 C4
Eudora 41 J9
Eufaula, *Ala., U.S.A.* 43 K3
Eufaula, *Okla., U.S.A.* 41 H7
Eufaula L. 41 H7
Eugene 38 E2
Eugowra 32 B4
Eulo 32 A4
Eunice, *La., U.S.A.* 41 K8
Eunice, *N. Mex., U.S.A.* 41 J3
Euphrates = Furāt, Nahr al → 24 B3
Eureka, *Canada* 37 B10
Eureka, *Calif., U.S.A.* 38 F1
Eureka, *Kans., U.S.A.* 41 G6
Eureka, *Mont., U.S.A.* 38 B6
Eureka, *Nev., U.S.A.* 38 G5
Eureka, *S. Dak., U.S.A.* 40 C5
Euroa 32 C4
Europe 3 B11
Eustis 43 L5
Evans 40 E2
Evans Head 32 A5
Evanston, *Ill., U.S.A.* 42 E2
Evanston, *Wyo., U.S.A.* 38 F8
Evansville 42 G2
Eveleth 40 B8
Everard, L. 32 B2
Everest, Mt. 25 C7
Everett 38 C2
Everglades △ 43 N5
Everglades, The 43 N5
Everglades City 43 N5
Evergreen, *Ala., U.S.A.* 43 K2
Evergreen, *Mont., U.S.A.* 38 B6
Evesham 9 E6
Evia 15 E11
Évora 13 C2
Évreux 12 B4
Ewe, L. 10 D3
Ewing 40 D5
Excelsior Springs 40 F7
Exe → 9 G4
Exeter, *U.K.* 9 G4
Exeter, *U.S.A.* 39 H4
Exmoor 9 F4
Exmoor △ 9 F4
Exmouth 9 G4
Exmouth Plateau 34 J3
Expedition △ 32 A4
Extremadura □ 13 C2
Eye Pen. 10 C2
Eyemouth 10 F6
Eyre (North), L. 32 A2
Eyre (South), L. 32 A2
Eyre, L. 30 F6
Eyre Mts. 33 L2
Eyre Pen. 32 B2

F

F.Y.R.O.M. = Macedonia ■ 15 D9
Fabens 39 L10
Færoe Is. = Føroyar ☒ 4 A9
Fair Haven 42 D9
Fair Hd. 11 A5
Fairbanks 36 C5
Fairbury 40 E6
Fairfield, *Ala., U.S.A.* 43 J2
Fairfield, *Calif., U.S.A.* 38 G2
Fairfield, *Idaho, U.S.A.* 38 E6
Fairfield, *Ill., U.S.A.* 42 F1
Fairfield, *Iowa, U.S.A.* 40 E9
Fairfield, *Tex., U.S.A.* 41 K7
Fairhope 43 K2
Fairlie 33 L3
Fairmont, *Minn., U.S.A.* 40 D7
Fairmont, *W. Va., U.S.A.* 42 F5
Fairmount 42 D7
Fairplay 39 G11
Fairport 42 D7
Fairview, *Mont., U.S.A.* 40 B2
Fairview, *Okla., U.S.A.* 41 G5
Fairweather, Mt. 36 D6
Faisalabad 25 B6
Faith 40 C3
Fajardo 45 d
Fakaofo 31 B16
Fakenham 8 E8
Fakfak 23 D5
Falcon Res. 41 M5
Falfurrias 41 M5
Falkirk 10 F5
Falkland 10 E5
Falkland Is. ☒ 48 G5
Fall River 42 E10
Fallon 38 G4
Falls City 40 E7
Falmouth, *Jamaica* 44 a
Falmouth, *U.K.* 9 G2
Falun 7 E7
Fanad Hd. 11 A4
Fanling 21 F11
Fannich, L. 10 D4
Farāh 24 B5
Farāh → 24 B5
Farasān, Jazā'ir 24 D3
Fareham 9 G6
Farewell, C. 33 J4
Farghona 18 E8
Fargo 40 B6
Faribault 40 C8
Faridabad 25 C6
Farina 32 B2
Farmerville 41 J8
Farmington, *Maine, U.S.A.* 43 C10
Farmington, *Mo., U.S.A.* 41 G9
Farmington, *N. Mex., U.S.A.* 39 H9
Farmington, *Utah, U.S.A.* 38 F8
Farmville 42 G6
Farne Is. 8 B6
Faro 36 C6
Farson 38 E9
Fartak, Ra's 24 D4
Farwell 41 H3
Fastnet Rock 11 E2
Fataka 31 C12
Faulkton 40 C5
Fayette, *Ala., U.S.A.* 43 J2
Fayette, *Mo., U.S.A.* 40 F8
Fayetteville, *Ark., U.S.A.* 41 G7
Fayetteville, *N.C., U.S.A.* 43 H6
Fayetteville, *Tenn., U.S.A.* 43 H2
Fdérik 26 D3
Feakle 11 D3
Feale → 11 D2
Fear, C. 43 J7
Feather → 38 G3
Featherston 33 J5
Fécamp 12 B4
Feilding 33 J5
Feira de Santana 47 F11
Felipe Carrillo Puerto 44 D7
Felixstowe 9 F9
Fens, The 8 E7
Fenton 42 D4
Fenyang 21 C6
Ferbane 11 C4
Fergus 42 D5
Fergus Falls 40 B6
Fermanagh □ 11 B4
Fermont 37 D13
Fermoy 11 D3
Fernandina Beach 43 K5
Fernando Póo = Bioko 28 D1
Ferndale 38 B2
Fernley 38 G4
Ferrara 14 B4
Ferret, C. 12 D3
Ferriday 41 K9
Ferron 39 G8
Fertile 40 B6
Fès 26 B5
Fessenden 40 B5
Festus 40 F9
Fetlar 10 A8
Feuilles → 37 D12
Feyzābād 25 B6
Fez = Fès 26 B5
Fezzan 27 C8
Fianarantsoa 29 J9
Fife △, *U.K.* 10 E5
Fife □, *U.K.* 10 E5
Fife Ness 10 E6
Figeac 12 D5
Fiji ■ 33 C8
Filey 8 C7
Filey B. 8 C7
Fillmore 39 G7
Findhorn → 10 D5
Findlay 42 E4
Finisterre, C. = Fisterra, C. 13 A1
Finland ■ 7 E9
Finland, G. of 7 F9
Finlay → 36 D7
Finley, *Australia* 32 C4
Finley, *U.S.A.* 40 B6
Finn → 11 B4
Finniss, C. 32 B1
Fiordland △ 33 L1
Firenze 14 C4
Fish → 29 K3
Fishguard 9 E3
Fisterra, C. 13 A1
Fitchburg, *Mass., U.S.A.* 42 D10
Fitchburg, *Wis., U.S.A.* 40 D10
Fitzgerald 43 K4
Flagstaff 39 J8
Flagstaff L. 43 C10
Flambeau → 40 C9
Flamborough Hd. 8 C7
Flaming Gorge △ 38 F9
Flaming Gorge Res. 38 F9
Flandre 12 A5
Flandreau 40 C6
Flannan Is. 10 C1
Flathead L. 38 C7
Flattery, C. 38 B1
Flatwoods 42 F4
Fleetwood 8 D4
Flensburg 16 A4
Flers 12 B3
Fleurieu Pen. 32 C2
Flin Flon 36 D9
Flinders → 30 D7
Flinders I., *S. Austral., Australia* 32 B1
Flinders I., *Tas., Australia* 32 D4
Flinders Ranges 32 B2
Flint, *U.K.* 8 D4
Flint, *U.S.A.* 42 D4
Flint → 43 K3
Flint I. 35 J12
Flintshire □ 8 D4
Flodden 8 B5
Floodwood 40 B8
Flora 42 F1
Florala 43 K2
Florence = Firenze 14 C4
Florence, *Ala., U.S.A.* 43 H2
Florence, *Ariz., U.S.A.* 39 K8
Florence, *Colo., U.S.A.* 40 F2
Florence, *Oreg., U.S.A.* 38 E1
Florence, *S.C., U.S.A.* 43 H6
Florence, L. 32 A2
Flores 23 D4
Flores Sea 23 D4
Floresville 41 L5
Florianópolis 48 B7
Florida □ 43 L5
Florida, Straits of 45 C9
Florida Is. 31 B11
Florida Keys 43 N5
Florissant 40 F9
Florø 7 E5
Floydada 41 J4
Fly → 30 B7
Fochabers 10 D5
Focşani 15 B12
Fóggia 14 D6
Foix 12 E4
Foley 43 K2
Folkestone 9 F9
Folkston 43 K5
Fond-du-Lac, *Canada* 36 D9
Fond du Lac, *U.S.A.* 40 D10
Fongafale 31 B14
Fontainebleau 12 B5
Fontenay-le-Comte 12 C3
Fontenelle Res. 38 E8
Forbes 32 B4
Fords Bridge 32 A4
Fordyce 41 J8
Forel, Mt. 6 C5
Forest 41 J10
Forest City, *Iowa, U.S.A.* 40 D8
Forest City, *N.C., U.S.A.* 43 H5
Forest Grove 38 D2
Forestier Pen. 32 D4
Forfar 10 E6
Forks 38 C1
Forlì 14 B5
Forman 40 B6
Formby Pt. 8 D4
Føroyar ☒ 4 A9
Forres 10 D5
Forrest City 41 H9
Forsayth 30 D7
Forsyth 38 C10
Fort Albany 37 D11
Fort Augustus 10 D4
Fort Beaufort 29 L5
Fort Benton 38 C8
Fort Bragg 38 G2
Fort Bridger 38 F8
Fort Chipewyan 36 D8
Fort Collins 40 E2
Fort Davis 41 K3
Fort-de-France 44 c
Fort Defiance 39 J9
Fort Dodge 40 D7
Fort Fairfield 43 B12
Fort Garland 39 H11
Fort Good Hope 36 C7
Fort Hancock 39 L11
Fort Kent 43 B11
Fort Klamath 38 E3
Fort Laramie 40 D2
Fort Lauderdale 43 M5
Fort Liard 36 C7
Fort Lupton 40 E2
Fort MacKay 36 D8
Fort Macleod 36 E8
Fort McMurray 36 D8
Fort McPherson 36 C6
Fort Madison 40 E9
Fort Meade 43 M5
Fort Morgan 40 E3
Fort Myers 43 M5
Fort Nelson 36 D7
Fort Nelson → 36 D7
Fort Payne 43 H3
Fort Peck 38 B10
Fort Peck Dam 38 C10
Fort Peck L. 38 C10
Fort Pierce 43 M5
Fort Pierre 40 C4
Fort Providence 36 C8
Fort Resolution 36 C8
Fort St. John 36 D7
Fort Scott 41 G7
Fort Simpson 36 C7
Fort Smith, *Canada* 36 D8
Fort Smith, *U.S.A.* 41 H7
Fort Stockton 41 K3
Fort Sumner 41 H2
Fort Thompson 40 C5
Fort Union △ 41 H2
Fort Valley 43 J4
Fort Walton Beach 43 K2
Fort Wayne 42 E3
Fort William 10 E3
Fort Worth 41 J6
Fort Yates 40 B4
Fort Yukon 36 C5
Fortaleza 47 D11
Forth → 10 E5
Forth, Firth of 10 E6
Fortrose 10 D4
Fortuna, *Calif., U.S.A.* 38 F1
Fortuna, *N. Dak., U.S.A.* 40 A3
Foshan 21 D6
Fossil 38 D3
Fossil Butte △ 38 F8
Fostoria 42 E4
Fougères 12 B3
Foula 10 A6
Foulness I. 9 F8
Fountain 40 F2
Fountain Hills 39 K8
Fouta Djallon 26 F3
Foveaux Str. 33 M2
Fowey 9 G3
Fowler 40 F3
Foxe Basin 37 C12
Foxe Chan. 37 C12
Foxe Pen. 37 C12
Foxford 11 C2
Foxton 33 J5
Foyle, Lough 11 A4
Foynes 11 D2
Franca 47 H9
France ■ 12 C5
Frances 32 C3
Franche-Comté □ 12 C6
Francis Case, L. 40 D5
Francistown 29 J5
François L. 36 D7
Francs Pk. 38 E9
Frankfort, *Ind., U.S.A.* 42 E2
Frankfort, *Kans., U.S.A.* 40 F6
Frankfort, *Ky., U.S.A.* 42 F3
Frankfurt, *Brandenburg, Germany* 16 B7
Frankfurt, *Hessen, Germany* 16 C4
Franklin, *Ky., U.S.A.* 43 G2
Franklin, *La., U.S.A.* 41 L9
Franklin, *N.H., U.S.A.* 42 D10
Franklin, *Nebr., U.S.A.* 40 E5
Franklin, *Pa., U.S.A.* 42 E6
Franklin, *Va., U.S.A.* 43 G7
Franklin, *W. Va., U.S.A.* 42 F6
Franklin B. 36 C7
Franklin D. Roosevelt L. 38 B4
Franklin-Gordon Wild Rivers △ 32 D4
Franklin L. 38 F6
Franklin Mts. 36 C7
Franklin Str. 36 B10
Franklinton 41 K9
Frankston 32 C4
Frantsa Iosifa, Zemlya 18 A6
Fraser → 36 E7
Fraser I. 32 A5
Fraserburgh 10 D6
Frederick, *Md., U.S.A.* 42 F7
Frederick, *Okla., U.S.A.* 41 H5
Frederick, *S. Dak., U.S.A.* 40 C5
Fredericksburg, *Tex., U.S.A.* 41 K5
Fredericksburg, *Va., U.S.A.* 42 F7
Fredericktown 41 G9
Fredericton 37 E13
Frederikshavn 7 F6
Fredonia, *Ariz., U.S.A.* 39 H7
Fredonia, *Kans., U.S.A.* 41 G7
Fredonia, *N.Y., U.S.A.* 42 D6
Fredrikstad 7 F6
Free State □ 29 K5
Freeman 40 D6
Freeport, *Bahamas* 45 B9
Freeport, *Ill., U.S.A.* 40 D10
Freeport, *N.Y., U.S.A.* 42 E9
Freeport, *Tex., U.S.A.* 41 L7
Freetown 26 G3
Freiburg 16 E3
Fremont, *Calif., U.S.A.* 39 H2
Fremont, *Mich., U.S.A.* 42 D3
Fremont, *Nebr., U.S.A.* 40 E6
Fremont, *Ohio, U.S.A.* 42 E4
Fremont → 39 G8
French Guiana ☒ 47 C8
French Polynesia ☒ 35 K13
Frenchman Cr. →, *N. Amer.* 38 B10
Frenchman Cr. →, *U.S.A.* 40 E4
Fresnillo 44 C4
Fresno 39 H4
Fresno Res. 38 B9
Freycinet △ 32 D4
Freycinet Pen. 32 D4
Fria, C. 29 H2
Frio → 41 L5
Friona 41 H3
Fritch 41 H4
Frobisher B. 37 C13
Frobisher L. 36 D9
Frome 9 F5
Frome →, *Australia* 32 A2
Frome →, *U.K.* 9 G5
Frome, L. 32 B2
Front Royal 42 F6
Frostburg 42 F6
Frýdek-Místek 16 D9
Fuchū 22 F3
Fuerte → 44 B3
Fuhai 20 B3
Fuji 22 F6
Fuji-San 22 F6
Fujian □ 21 D6
Fukui 22 E5
Fukuoka 22 G2
Fukushima 22 E7
Fukuyama 22 F3
Fulda 16 C4
Fulda → 16 C4
Fullerton 40 E6
Fulton, *Mo., U.S.A.* 40 F9
Fulton, *N.Y., U.S.A.* 42 D7
Funabashi 22 F7
Funafuti 31 B14
Fundy, B. of 37 E13
Furāt, Nahr al → 24 B3
Furneaux Group 32 D4
Fürth 16 D5
Fury and Hecla Str. 37 C11
Fushun 21 B7
Fustic 45 g
Futian 21 F11
Futuna 33 B8
Fuxin 21 B7
Fuyong 21 F10
Fuyu 21 B7
Fuzhou 21 D6
Fylde 8 D5
Fyn 7 F6
Fyne, L. 10 F3

G

Gabès, G. de 27 B8
Gabon ■ 28 E2
Gaborone 29 J5
Gābrīk 24 C4
Gabrovo 15 C11
Gadag 25 D6
Gadsden 43 H3
Gaffney 43 H5
Gagnon 37 D13

Gail 41 J4
Gainesville, Fla., U.S.A. 43 L4
Gainesville, Ga., U.S.A. 43 H4
Gainesville, Mo., U.S.A. 41 G8
Gainesville, Tex., U.S.A. 41 J6
Gainsborough 8 D7
Gairdner, L. 32 B2
Gairloch 10 D3
Gairloch, L. 10 D3
Galápagos = Colón, Arch. de 35 H18
Galapagos Fracture Zone 35 G17
Galapagos Rise 35 J18
Galashiels 10 F6
Galaţi 15 B13
Galax 43 G5
Galcaio 24 E3
Galdhøpiggen 7 E5
Galela 23 C4
Galena 36 C4
Galesburg 40 E9
Galicia □ 13 A2
Galina Pt. 44 a
Galiuro Mts. 39 K8
Gallan Hd. 10 C1
Gallatin 43 G2
Galle 25 E7
Galley Hd. 11 E3
Gallipoli = Gelibolu 15 D12
Gallipolis 42 F4
Gällivare 7 D8
Galloway 10 F4
Galloway △ 10 F4
Galloway, Mull of 10 G4
Gallup 39 J9
Galty Mts. 11 D3
Galtymore 11 D3
Galva 40 E9
Galveston 41 L7
Galveston B. 41 L7
Galway 11 C2
Galway □ 11 C2
Galway B. 11 C2
Gambia ■ 26 F2
Gambia → 26 F2
Gambier, Îs. 35 K14
Gambier Is. 32 C2
Gammon Ranges △ 32 B2
Gan Jiang → 21 D6
Ganado 39 J9
Gäncä 17 B7
Gander 37 E14
Ganga → 25 C8
Ganges = Ganga → 25 C8
Gani 23 D4
Gannett Peak 38 E9
Gansu □ 20 C5
Gantheaume, C. 32 C2
Ganzhou 21 D6
Gao 26 E5
Gap 12 D7
Gar 20 C2
Gara, L. 11 C3
Garagum 18 F6
Garah 32 A4
Garberville 38 F2
Garda, L. di 14 B4
Garden City, Ga., U.S.A. 43 J5
Garden City, Kans., U.S.A. 41 G4
Garden City, Tex., U.S.A. 41 K4
Gardēz 25 B5
Gardiner, Maine, U.S.A. 43 C11
Gardiner, Mont., U.S.A. 38 D8
Gardnerville 38 G4
Gardo 24 E3
Garfield 38 C5
Garforth 8 D6
Gargantua, C. 42 B3
Garland, Tex., U.S.A. 41 J6
Garland, Utah, U.S.A. 38 F7
Garner 40 D8
Garnett 40 F7
Garoe 24 E3
Garonne → 12 D3
Garrison, Mont., U.S.A. 38 C7
Garrison, N. Dak., U.S.A. 40 B4
Garron Pt. 11 A6
Garry → 10 E5
Garry, L. 36 C9
Garstang 8 D5
Garvie Mts. 33 L2
Gary 42 E2
Garzê 20 C5
Gascogne 12 E4
Gascogne, G. de 12 D2
Gaspé 37 E13
Gaspésie, Pén. de la 37 E13
Gastonia 43 H5
Gatehouse of Fleet 10 G4
Gateshead 8 C6
Gatesville 41 K6
Gatineau 42 C8
Gatton 32 A5
Gatwick, London (LGW) 9 F7
Gau 33 D8
Gaua 31 C12
Gävle 7 E7
Gawler 32 B2
Gaxun Nur 20 B5
Gaya 25 C7
Gaylord 42 C3
Gayndah 32 A5
Gaza 17 D4
Gaza Strip ■ 24 B2
Gaziantep 17 C5
Gcuwa 29 L5
Gdańsk 16 A9
Gdańska, Zatoka 16 A9
Gdynia 16 A9
Gebe 23 C4
Gedser 7 G6
Geelong 32 C3
Gejiu 20 D5
Gelib 24 E3
Gelibolu 15 D12
Gelsenkirchen 16 C3
General Santos 23 C4
Genesee 38 C5
Genesee → 42 D7
Geneseo, Ill., U.S.A. 40 E9
Geneseo, N.Y., U.S.A. 42 D7
Geneva = Genève 12 C7
Geneva, Ala., U.S.A. 43 K3
Geneva, N.Y., U.S.A. 42 D7
Geneva, Nebr., U.S.A. 40 E6
Geneva, Ohio, U.S.A. 42 E5
Genève 12 C7
Gennargentu, Mti. del 14 D3
Genoa = Génova 12 D8
Genoa, Australia 32 C4
Genoa, U.S.A. 40 E6
Génova 12 D8
Gent 16 C1
George 29 L4
George → 37 D13
George, L., N.S.W., Australia 32 C4
George, L., S. Austral., Australia 32 C3
George, L., Fla., U.S.A. 43 L5
George, L., N.Y., U.S.A. 42 D9
George Sound 33 L1
George Town, Australia 32 D4
George Town, Malaysia 23 C2
George V Land 6 D14
George West 41 L5
Georgetown, Guyana 46 B7
Georgetown, Colo., U.S.A. 38 G11
Georgetown, Ky., U.S.A. 42 F3
Georgetown, Ohio, U.S.A. 42 F4
Georgetown, S.C., U.S.A. 43 J6
Georgetown, Tex., U.S.A. 41 K6
Georgia □ 43 K5
Georgian B. 37 E11
Gera 16 C6
Geraldine 38 C8
Geraldton 30 F1
Gereshk 24 B5
Gering 40 E3
Gerlach 38 F4
Germantown 41 M10
Germany ■ 16 C5
Germiston 29 K5
Gerona = Girona 13 B7
Getafe 13 B4
Gettysburg, Pa., U.S.A. 42 F7
Gettysburg, S. Dak., U.S.A. 40 C5
Geyser 38 C8
Ghana ■ 26 G5
Ghanzi 29 J4
Ghats, Eastern 25 D6
Ghats, Western 25 D6
Ghazâl, Bahr el → 27 G12
Ghaziabad 25 C6
Ghaznī 24 B5
Ghent = Gent 16 C1
Giant Sequoia △ 39 J4
Giants Causeway 11 A5
Gibbon 40 E5
Gibraltar ⊠ 13 D3
Gibraltar, Str. of 13 E3
Gibraltar Range △ 32 A5
Gibson Desert 30 E4
Giddings 41 K6
Gifu 22 F5
Gigha 10 F3
Gijón 13 A3
Gila → 39 K6
Gila Bend 39 K7
Gila Bend Mts. 39 K7
Gila Cliff Dwellings △ 39 K9
Gilbert Is. 31 A14
Gilgandra 32 B4
Gilgit 25 B6
Gillam 36 D10
Gilles, L. 32 B2
Gillette 40 C2
Gillingham 9 F8
Gilmer 41 J7
Gilroy 39 H3
Gimie, Mt 45 f
Gin Gin 32 A5
Giohar 24 E3
Girard 41 G7
Girdle Ness 10 D6
Girona 13 B7
Gironde → 12 D3
Girraween △ 32 A5
Girvan 10 F4
Gisborne 33 H7
Giuba → 24 E3
Giza = El Gîza 27 C12
Gizhiga 19 C17
Gjoa Haven 36 C10
Glace Bay 37 E14
Glacier △ 38 B7
Glacier Peak 38 B3
Gladewater 41 J7
Gladstone, Queens., Australia 30 E9
Gladstone, S. Austral., Australia 32 B2
Gladstone, U.S.A. 42 C2
Gladwin 42 D3
Glamorgan, Vale of □ 9 F4
Glasco 40 F6
Glasgow, U.K. 10 F4
Glasgow, Ky., U.S.A. 42 G3
Glasgow, Mont., U.S.A. 38 B10
Glasgow Int. (GLA) 10 F4
Glastonbury 9 F5
Glen Affric 10 D3
Glen Canyon 39 H8
Glen Canyon △ 39 H8
Glen Canyon Dam 39 H8
Glen Coe 10 E3
Glen Garry 10 D3
Glen Innes 32 A5
Glen Mor 10 D4
Glen More △ 10 D5
Glen Moriston 10 D4
Glen Spean 10 E4
Glen Ullin 40 B4
Glenallen 36 C5
Glenariff △ 11 A5
Glenbeigh 11 D2
Glencoe 40 C7
Glencolumbkille 11 B3
Glendale, Ariz., U.S.A. 39 K7
Glendale, Calif., U.S.A. 39 J4
Glendive 40 B2
Glendo 40 D2
Glenelg → 32 C3
Glengad Hd. 11 A4
Glengarriff 11 E2
Glenmorgan 32 A4
Glennamaddy 11 C3
Glenns Ferry 38 E6
Glenreagh 32 B5
Glenrock 38 E11
Glenrothes 10 E5
Glens Falls 42 D9
Glenties 11 B3
Glenveagh △ 11 A3
Glenville 42 F5
Glenwood, Ark., U.S.A. 41 H8
Glenwood, Iowa, U.S.A. 40 E7
Glenwood, Minn., U.S.A. 40 C7
Glenwood Springs 38 G10
Glin 11 D2
Gliwice 16 C9
Globe 39 K8
Głogów 16 C8
Glomma → 7 F6
Glossop 8 D6
Gloucester, Australia 32 B5
Gloucester, U.K. 9 F5
Gloucester Point 42 G7
Gloucestershire □ 9 F5
Gniezno 16 B8
Goa □ 25 D6
Goalen Hd. 32 C5
Goat Fell 10 F3
Gobabis 29 J3
Gobi 21 B5
Godalming 9 F7
Godavari → 25 D7
Gods → 36 D10
Gods L. 36 D10
Gogebic, L. 40 B10
Goiânia 47 G9
Goio-Erê 48 A6
Golconda 38 F5
Gold Beach 38 E1
Gold Coast, Australia 30 F9
Gold Coast, W. Afr. 26 H5
Gold Hill 38 E2
Golden B. 33 J4
Golden Gate 38 H2
Golden Spike △ 38 F7
Golden Vale 11 D3
Goldendale 38 D3
Goldfield 39 H5
Goldsboro 43 H7
Goldsmith 41 K3
Goldthwaite 41 K5
Goliad 41 L6
Golspie 10 D5
Gómez Palacio 44 B4
Gonābād 24 B4
Gonaïves 45 D10
Gongbei 21 G10
Gongga Shan 25 C9
Gonghe 20 C5
Gongming 21 F10
Gongolgon 32 B4
Gonzales, Calif., U.S.A. 39 H3
Gonzales, Tex., U.S.A. 41 L6
Good Hope, C. of 29 L3
Gooding 38 E6
Goodland 40 F4
Goodooga 32 A4
Goole 8 D7
Goolgowi 32 B4
Goomeri 32 A5
Goondiwindi 32 A5
Goose Creek 43 J5
Goose L. 38 F3
Gorakhpur 25 C7
Gordon 40 D3
Gordon → 32 D4
Gore 33 M2
Gorey 11 D5
Gorgān 24 B4
Gorleston 9 E9
Görlitz 16 C7
Gorontalo 23 C4
Gort 11 C3
Gorzów Wielkopolski 16 B7
Gosford 32 B5
Goshen 42 E3
Gosport 9 G6
Göta kanal 7 F7
Göteborg 7 F6
Gotha 16 C5
Gothenburg = Göteborg 7 F6
Gothenburg 40 E4
Gotland 7 F7
Göttingen 16 C4
Gouda 16 B2
Gouin, Rés. 37 E12
Goulburn 32 B4
Gourock 10 F4
Gouverneur 42 C8
Governador Valadares 47 G10
Gowanda 42 D6
Gower 9 F3
Gowna, L. 11 C4
Goyder Lagoon 32 A2
Gozo 14 F6
Graaff-Reinet 29 L4
Gracias a Dios, C. 45 E8
Grady 41 H3
Grafham Water 9 E7
Grafton, Australia 32 A5
Grafton, N. Dak., U.S.A. 40 A6
Grafton, W. Va., U.S.A. 42 F5
Graham 41 J5
Graham, Mt. 39 K9
Graham Land 6 D3
Grahamstown 29 L5
Grain Coast 26 H3
Grampian Mts. 10 E5
Grampians, The 32 C3
Gran Canaria 26 C2
Gran Chaco 48 B4
Gran Sasso d'Itália 14 C5
Granada, Nic. 44 E7
Granada, Spain 13 D4
Granada, U.S.A. 41 F3
Granard 11 C4
Granbury 41 J6
Granby, Canada 37 E12
Granby, U.S.A. 38 F11
Grand →, Mo., U.S.A. 40 F8
Grand →, S. Dak., U.S.A. 40 C4
Grand Bahama I. 45 B9
Grand-Bourg 44 b
Grand Canyon 39 H7
Grand Canyon △ 39 H7
Grand Canyon-Parashant △ 39 H7
Grand Cayman 45 D8
Grand Coulee 38 C4
Grand Coulee Dam 38 C4
Grand Falls 37 E13
Grand Falls-Windsor 37 E14
Grand Forks 40 B6
Grand Haven 42 D2
Grand I. 42 B2
Grand Island 40 E5
Grand Isle 41 L9
Grand Junction 39 G9
Grand L. 41 L8
Grand Lake 38 F11
Grand Marais 42 B3
Grand Portage 40 B10
Grand Prairie 41 J6
Grand Rapids, Canada 36 D10
Grand Rapids, Mich., U.S.A. 42 D2
Grand Rapids, Minn., U.S.A. 40 B8
Grand St-Bernard, Col du 12 D7
Grand Staircase-Escalante △ 39 H8
Grand Teton 38 E8
Grand Teton △ 38 D8
Grand Union Canal 9 E7
Grand-Vigie, Pte. de la 44 b
Grande, Rio → 41 N6
Grande Baleine, R. de la → 37 D12
Grande Prairie 36 D8
Grande-Terre 44 b
Grandfalls 41 K3
Grandview 38 C4
Grangemouth 10 E5
Granger 38 F9
Grangeville 38 D5
Granite City 40 F9
Granite Falls 40 C7
Granite Pk. 38 D9
Granity 33 J3
Grant 40 E4
Grant, Mt. 38 G4
Grant City 40 E7
Grant Range 39 G6
Grantham 8 E7
Grantown-on-Spey 10 D5
Grants 39 J10
Grants Pass 38 E2
Grantsville 38 F7
Granville, N. Dak., U.S.A. 40 A4
Granville, N.Y., U.S.A. 42 D9
Grass Range 38 C9
Grass Valley, Calif., U.S.A. 38 G3
Grass Valley, Oreg., U.S.A. 38 D3
Grasse 12 E7
Grassy 32 D3
Graulhet 12 E4
's-Gravenhage 16 B2
Gravesend, Australia 32 A5
Gravesend, U.K. 9 F8
Grayling 42 C3
Grays 9 F8
Grays Harbor 38 C1
Grays L. 38 E8
Graz 16 E7
Great Australian Bight 30 G5
Great Bahama Bank 44 B4
Great Barrier I. 33 G5
Great Barrier Reef 30 D8
Great Basin 38 G5
Great Basin △ 38 G6
Great Bear → 36 C7
Great Bear L. 36 C8
Great Bend 40 F5
Great Blasket I. 11 D1
Great Camanoe 45 e
Great Channel 25 E8
Great Dividing Ra. 30 E8
Great Exuma I. 45 C9
Great Falls 38 C8
Great Inagua I. 45 C10
Great Karoo 29 L4
Great Lake 32 D4
Great Malvern 9 E5
Great Miami → 42 F3
Great Ormes Head 8 D4
Great Ouse → 8 E8
Great Pedro Bluff 44 a
Great Pee Dee → 43 J6
Great Plains 2 C5
Great Salt L. 38 F7
Great Salt Lake Desert 38 F7
Great Salt Plains L. 41 G5
Great Sand Dunes △ 39 H11
Great Sandy △ 32 A5
Great Sandy Desert 30 E3
Great Skellig 11 E1
Great Slave L. 36 C8
Great Smoky Mts. △ 43 H4
Great Snow Mt. 36 D7
Great Victoria Desert 30 F4
Great Wall 21 C5
Great Whernside 8 C6
Great Yarmouth 9 E9
Greater Antilles 45 D10
Greater London □ 9 F7
Greater Manchester □ 8 D5
Greater Sunda Is. 23 D3
Greece ■ 15 E9
Greeley, Colo., U.S.A. 40 E2
Greeley, Nebr., U.S.A. 40 E5
Greely Fd. 37 B10
Greem-Bell, Ostrov 18 A7
Green →, Ky., U.S.A. 42 G2
Green →, Utah, U.S.A. 39 G9
Green B. 42 C2
Green Bay 42 C2
Green C. 32 C5
Green Cove Springs 43 L5
Green River, Utah, U.S.A. 39 G8
Green River, Wyo., U.S.A. 38 F9
Green Valley 39 L8
Greenbush 40 A6
Greencastle 42 F2
Greeneville 43 G4
Greenfield, Ind., U.S.A. 42 F3
Greenfield, Iowa, U.S.A. 40 E7
Greenfield, Mass., U.S.A. 42 D9
Greenfield, Mo., U.S.A. 41 G8
Greenland ⊠ 6 C4
Greenland Sea 6 B6
Greenock 10 F4
Greenore 11 B5
Greenore Pt. 11 D5
Greensboro, Ga., U.S.A. 43 J4
Greensboro, N.C., U.S.A. 43 G6
Greensburg, Ind., U.S.A. 42 F3
Greensburg, Kans., U.S.A. 41 G5
Greensburg, Pa., U.S.A. 42 E6
Greenstone Pt. 10 D3
Greenville, Ala., U.S.A. 43 K2
Greenville, Calif., U.S.A. 38 F3
Greenville, Maine, U.S.A. 43 C11
Greenville, Mich., U.S.A. 42 D3
Greenville, Miss., U.S.A. 41 J9
Greenville, Mo., U.S.A. 41 G9
Greenville, N.C., U.S.A. 43 H7
Greenville, Ohio, U.S.A. 42 E3
Greenville, Pa., U.S.A. 42 E5
Greenville, S.C., U.S.A. 43 H4
Greenville, Tex., U.S.A. 41 J6
Greenwich □ 9 F8
Greenwood, Ark., U.S.A. 41 H7
Greenwood, Ind., U.S.A. 42 F2
Greenwood, Miss., U.S.A. 41 J9
Greenwood, S.C., U.S.A. 43 H4
Gregory 40 D5
Gregory, L. 32 A2
Grenada 41 J10
Grenada ■ 45 E12
Grenfell 32 B4
Grenoble 12 D6
Gresham 38 D2
Gretna, U.K. 10 F5
Gretna, U.S.A. 41 L9
Grey → 33 K3
Grey Ra. 32 A3
Greybull 38 D9
Greymouth 33 K3
Greystones 11 C5
Greytown 33 J5
Gridley 38 G3
Griffin 43 J3
Griffith 32 B4
Grimsay 10 D1
Grimsby 8 D7
Grinnell 40 E8
Gris-Nez, C. 12 A4
Grise Fiord 37 B10
Groesbeck 41 K6
Groningen 16 B3
Groom 41 H4
Groote Eylandt 30 C6
Gros Islet 45 f
Gros Piton 45 f
Gros Piton Pt. 45 f
Grossglockner 16 E6
Groton 40 C5
Grove Hill 43 K2
Groves 41 L8
Groveton 42 C10
Groznyy 17 B7
Grudziądz 16 B9
Gruinard B. 10 D3
Grundy Center 40 D8
Gruver 41 G4
Guadalajara, Mexico 44 C4
Guadalajara, Spain 13 B4
Guadalcanal 31 B11
Guadalete → 13 D2
Guadalquivir → 13 D2
Guadalupe 39 J3
Guadalupe → 41 L6
Guadalupe Mts. △ 41 K2
Guadalupe Peak 41 K2
Guadarrama, Sierra de 13 B4
Guadeloupe ⊠ 44 b
Guadiana → 13 D2
Guadix 13 D4
Guam ⊠ 34 F6
Guamúchil 44 B3
Guana I. 45 e
Guanajuato 44 C4
Guane 45 C8
Guangdong □ 21 D6
Guangxi Zhuangzu Zizhiqu □ 21 D5
Guangyuan 25 B9
Guangzhou 21 D6
Guanica 45 d
Guantánamo 45 C9
Guaporé → 46 F5
Guarapuava 48 B6
Guatemala 44 E6
Guatemala ■ 44 D6
Guatemala Basin 35 F18
Guatemala Trench 35 F18
Guaviare → 46 C5
Guayama 45 d
Guayaquil 46 D3
Guayaquil, G. de 46 D2
Guaymas 44 B2
Guéret 12 C4
Guernsey, U.K. 9 H5
Guernsey, U.S.A. 40 D2
Guildford 9 F7
Guilin 21 D6
Guinea ■ 26 F3
Guinea, Gulf of 4 D10
Guinea-Bissau ■ 26 F3
Güines 45 C8
Guingamp 12 B2
Guiyang 20 D5
Guizhou □ 20 D5
Gujarat □ 25 C6
Gujranwala 25 C6
Gulbarga 25 D6
Gulf Islands △ 43 E2
Gulfport 41 K10
Gulgong 32 B4
Gunnbjørn Fjeld 6 C5
Gunnedah 32 B5
Gunnewin 32 A4
Gunningbar Cr. → 32 B4
Gunnison, Colo., U.S.A. 39 G10
Gunnison, Utah, U.S.A. 38 G8
Gunnison → 39 G9
Guntersville 43 H2
Guntur 25 D7
Gurdon 41 J8
Gurley 32 A4
Gusinoozersk 19 D11
Gustine 39 H3
Guthrie, Okla., U.S.A. 41 H6
Guthrie, Tex., U.S.A. 41 J4
Guttenberg 40 D9
Guwahati 20 D4
Guy Fawkes River △ 32 A5
Guyana ■ 46 C7
Guyenne 12 D4
Guymon 41 G4
Guyra 32 B5
Gwabegar 32 B4
Gwādar 24 C5
Gwalior 25 C6
Gwangju 21 C7
Gweebarra B. 11 B3
Gweedore 11 A3
Gweru 29 H5
Gwinn 42 B2
Gwydir → 32 A4
Gwynedd □ 8 E3
Gyaring Hu 20 C4
Gympie 32 A5
Győr 16 E8
Gyumri 17 B6

H

Ha Tinh 23 B2
Ha'apai Group 31 D16
Haarlem 16 B2
Haast → 33 K2
Hachinohe 22 C7
Ḥadd, Ra's al 24 C4
Haddington 10 F6
Ḥaḍramawt 24 D3
Hadrian's Wall 8 B5
Haeju 21 C7
Hafar al Bāṭin 24 C3
Hagen 16 C3
Hagerman 41 J2
Hagerman Fossil Beds △ 38 E6
Hagerstown 42 F7
Hagondange 12 B7
Hags Hd. 11 D2
Hague, C. de la 12 B3
Hague, The = 's-Gravenhage 16 B2
Haguenau 12 B7
Haifa = Ḥefa 17 D5
Haikou 21 D6
Ḥā'il 24 C3
Hailar 21 B6
Hailey 38 E6
Hainan □ 21 E5
Haines 38 D5
Haines City 43 L5
Haines Junction 36 C6
Haiphong 20 D5
Haiti ■ 45 D10
Ḥajjah 24 D3
Hakodate 22 C7
Ḥalab 24 B2
Halberstadt 16 C5
Halcombe 33 J5
Halden 7 F6
Halesowen 9 E5
Halesworth 9 E9
Haleyville 43 H2
Halfmoon Bay 33 M2
Halifax, Canada 37 E13
Halifax, U.K. 8 D6
Halīl → 24 C4
Halkirk 10 C5
Hall Pen. 37 C13
Hallāniyat, Jazā'ir al 24 D4
Halle 16 C5
Hallett 32 B2
Hallettsville 41 L6
Hallock 40 A6
Halls Creek 30 D4
Halmahera 23 C4
Halmstad 7 F6
Halstead 9 F8
Halton □ 8 D5
Haltwhistle 8 C5
Hamadān 24 B3
Ḥamāh 24 B2
Hamamatsu 22 F5
Hamar 7 E6
Hamburg, Germany 16 B4
Hamburg, Ark., U.S.A. 41 J9
Hamburg, N.Y., U.S.A. 42 D6
Hämeenlinna 7 E8
Hameln 16 B4
Hamersley Ra. 30 E2
Hami 20 B4
Hamilton, Australia 32 C3
Hamilton, Canada 37 E12
Hamilton, N.Z. 33 G5
Hamilton, U.K. 10 F4
Hamilton, Ala., U.S.A. 43 H1
Hamilton, Mont., U.S.A. 38 C6
Hamilton, N.Y., U.S.A. 42 D8
Hamilton, Ohio, U.S.A. 42 F3
Hamilton, Tex., U.S.A. 41 K5
Hamilton → 32 A2
Hamlet 43 H6
Hamley Bridge 32 B2
Hamlin 41 J4
Hamm 16 C3
Hammerfest 7 C8
Hammond, Ind., U.S.A. 42 E2
Hammond, La., U.S.A. 41 K9
Hammonton 42 F8
Hampden 33 L3
Hampshire □ 9 F6
Hampshire Downs 9 F6
Hampton, Ark., U.S.A. 41 J8
Hampton, Iowa, U.S.A. 40 D8
Hampton, S.C., U.S.A. 43 J5
Hampton, Va., U.S.A. 42 G7
Hancock 40 B10
Handan 21 C6
Hanford 39 H4
Hanford Reach △ 38 C4
Hangayn Nuruu 20 B4
Hangzhou 21 C7
Hangzhou Wan 21 C7
Hankinson 40 B6
Hankö 7 F8
Hanksville 39 G8
Hanmer Springs 33 K4
Hanna, Canada 36 D8
Hanna, U.S.A. 38 F10
Hannibal 40 F9
Hannover 16 B4
Hanoi 20 D5
Hanover, N.H., U.S.A. 42 D9
Hanover, Pa., U.S.A. 42 F7
Hans Lollik I. 45 e
Hanson, L. 32 B2
Hanzhong 20 C5
Haora 25 C7
Haparanda 7 D8
Happy 41 H4
Happy Camp 38 F2
Happy Valley-Goose Bay 37 D13
Har Hu 20 C4
Har Us Nuur 20 B4
Ḥaraḍ 24 C3
Harare 29 H6
Harbin 21 B7
Harbor Beach 42 D4
Hardangerfjorden 7 E5
Hardin 38 D10
Hardy, Pte. 45 f
Harer 24 E3
Hargeisa 24 E3
Hari → 23 D2
Haridwar 25 C6
Harīrūd → 24 B5
Harlan, Iowa, U.S.A. 40 E7
Harlan, Ky., U.S.A. 43 G4
Harlech 8 E3
Harlem 38 B9
Harlingen 41 M6
Harlow 9 F8
Harlowton 38 C9
Harney Basin 38 E4
Harney L. 38 E4
Harney Peak 40 D3
Härnösand 7 E7
Haroldswick 10 A8
Harricana → 37 D12
Harriman 43 H3
Harris 10 D2
Harris, L. 32 B2
Harris, Sd. of 10 D1
Harrisburg, Ill., U.S.A. 41 G10
Harrisburg, Nebr., U.S.A. 40 E3
Harrisburg, Pa., U.S.A. 42 E7
Harrison, Ark., U.S.A. 41 G8
Harrison, Nebr., U.S.A. 40 D3
Harrison, C. 37 D14
Harrisonburg 42 F6
Harrisonville 40 F7
Harrisville 42 C4
Harrodsburg 42 G3
Harrogate 8 C6
Harrow □ 9 F7
Harry S. Truman Res. 40 F7
Hart 42 D2
Hart, L. 32 B2
Hartford, Conn., U.S.A. 42 E9
Hartford, Ky., U.S.A. 42 G2
Hartford, S. Dak., U.S.A. 40 D6
Hartford, Wis., U.S.A. 40 D10
Hartford City 42 E3
Hartland Pt. 9 F3
Hartlepool 8 C6
Hartselle 43 H2
Hartshorne 41 H7
Hartsville 43 H5
Hartwell 43 H4
Harvey, Ill., U.S.A. 42 E2
Harvey, N. Dak., U.S.A. 40 B5
Harwich 9 F9
Haryana □ 25 C6
Harz 16 C5
Hasa 24 C3
Haskell 41 J5
Haslemere 9 F7
Hastings, N.Z. 33 H6
Hastings, U.K. 9 G8
Hastings, Mich., U.S.A. 42 D3
Hastings, Minn., U.S.A. 40 C8
Hastings, Nebr., U.S.A. 40 E5
Hastings Ra. 32 B5
Hat Yai 23 C2
Hatay 17 C4
Hatch 39 K10
Hatfield P.O. 32 B3
Hatgal 20 A5
Hattah 32 B3
Hatteras, C. 43 H8
Hattiesburg 41 K10
Haugesund 7 F5
Hauraki G. 33 G5
Haut Atlas 26 B4
Havana = La Habana 44 B3
Havana 40 E9
Havant 9 G7
Havasu, L. 39 J6
Havel → 16 B6
Havelock, N.Z. 33 J4
Havelock, U.S.A. 43 H7
Haverfordwest 9 F3
Haverhill, U.K. 9 E8
Haverhill, U.S.A. 42 D10
Havre 38 B9
Havre-St.-Pierre 37 D13
Haw → 43 H6
Hawaiian Is. 35 E12
Hawaiian Ridge 35 E11
Hawarden 40 D6
Hawea, L. 33 L2
Hawera 33 H5
Hawick 10 F6
Hawke B. 33 H6
Hawker 32 B2
Hawkinsville 43 J4
Hawley 40 B6
Hawthorne 38 G4
Hay 32 B3
Hay → 36 C8
Hay-on-Wye 9 E4
Hay River 36 C8
Hay Springs 40 D3
Hayden 38 F10
Hayes 40 C4
Hayes → 36 D10
Hayle 9 G2
Hayling I. 9 G7
Haymā' 24 D4
Hays 40 F5
Hayward, Calif., U.S.A. 39 G2
Hayward, Wis., U.S.A. 40 B9
Haywards Heath 9 G7
Hazard 42 G4
Hazelton 40 B4
Hazen 40 B4
Hazlehurst, Ga., U.S.A. 43 K4
Hazlehurst, Miss., U.S.A. 41 K9
Hazleton 42 E8
Healdsburg 38 G2
Healdton 41 H6
Healesville 32 C4
Heard I. 5 G14
Hearne 41 K6
Hearst 37 E11
Heart → 40 B4
Heathrow, London (LHR) 9 F7
Heavener 41 H7
Hebbronville 41 M5
Hebei □ 21 C6
Hebel 32 A4
Heber Springs 41 H9
Hebgen L. 38 D8
Hebrides, Sea of the 10 D2
Hebron, Canada 37 D13
Hebron, N. Dak., U.S.A. 40 B3
Hebron, Nebr., U.S.A. 40 E6
Hecate Str. 36 D6
Hechi 20 D5
Hechuan 20 C5
Hecla 40 C5
Heerlen 12 A6
Ḥefa 17 D5
Hefei 21 C6
Hegang 21 B8
Hei Ling Chau 21 G11
Heidelberg 16 D4
Heilbronn 16 D4
Heilongjiang □ 21 B7
Hejaz = Ḥijāz 24 C3
Hekou 20 D5
Helena, Ark., U.S.A. 41 H9
Helena, Mont., U.S.A. 38 C7
Helensburgh 10 E4
Helensville 33 G5
Helgoland 16 A3
Hells Canyon △ 38 D5
Helmand → 24 B5
Helmsdale 10 C5
Helmsdale → 10 C5
Helper 38 G8
Helsingborg 7 F6
Helsinki 7 E9
Helston 9 G2
Helvellyn 8 C4
Hemel Hempstead 9 F7
Hemet 39 K5
Hemingford 40 D3
Hempstead 41 K6
Henan □ 21 C6
Henderson, Ky., U.S.A. 42 G2
Henderson, N.C., U.S.A. 43 G6
Henderson, Nev., U.S.A. 39 H6
Henderson, Tenn., U.S.A. 43 H1
Henderson, Tex., U.S.A. 41 J7
Henderson I. 35 K15
Hendersonville, N.C., U.S.A. 43 H4
Hendersonville, Tenn., U.S.A. 43 G2
Henggang 21 F11
Hengmen 21 F10
Hengqin Dao 21 G10
Hengyang 21 D6
Henley-on-Thames 9 F7
Henlopen, C. 42 F8
Hennessey 41 G6
Henrietta 41 J5
Henrietta Maria, C. 37 D11
Henry 40 E10
Henryetta 41 H7
Hentiyn Nuruu 21 B5
Henty 32 C4
Henzada 25 D8
Heppner 38 D4
Herāt 24 B5
Hereford, U.K. 9 E5
Hereford, U.S.A. 41 H3
Herefordshire □ 9 E5
Herford 16 B4
Herington 40 F6
Herkimer 42 D8
Herm 9 H5
Hermann 40 F9
Hermidale 32 B4
Hermiston 38 D4
Hermosillo 44 B2
Hernando 41 H10
Herne Bay 9 F9
Herreid 40 C4
Herrin 41 G10
Hertford 9 F7
Hertfordshire □ 9 F7
's-Hertogenbosch 16 C2
Hesperia 39 J5
Hessen □ 16 C4
Hettinger 40 C3
Hewitt 41 K6
Hexham 8 C5
Heysham 8 C5
Heywood 32 C3
Hialeah 43 N5
Hiawatha 40 F7
Hibbing 40 B8
Hibbs B. 32 D4
Hickman 41 G10
Hickory 43 H5
Hicks, Pt. 32 C4
Hidalgo del Parral 44 B3
Higashiōsaka 22 F4
Higgins 41 G4
High Island Res. 21 G11
High Level 36 D8
High Point 43 H6
High Prairie 36 D8
High River 36 D8
High Wycombe 9 F7
Highland □ 10 D4
Highland Park 42 D2
Highmore 40 C5
Ḥijāz 24 C3
Hiko 39 H6
Hikurangi, Gisborne, N.Z. 33 H6
Hikurangi, Northland, N.Z. 33 F5
Hildesheim 16 B4
Hill City, Idaho, U.S.A. 38 E6
Hill City, Kans., U.S.A. 40 F5
Hill City, Minn., U.S.A. 40 B8
Hill City, S. Dak., U.S.A. 40 D3
Hillaby, Mt. 45 g
Hillcrest 45 g
Hillsboro, Kans., U.S.A. 40 F6
Hillsboro, N. Dak., U.S.A. 40 B6
Hillsboro, Ohio, U.S.A. 42 F4
Hillsboro, Tex., U.S.A. 41 J6
Hillsborough 42 D10
Hillsdale 42 E3
Hillston 32 B4
Hilton Head Island 43 J5
Hilversum 16 B2
Himachal Pradesh □ 25 B6
Himalaya 25 C7
Himeji 22 F4
Ḥimṣ 24 B2
Hinckley, U.K. 9 E6
Hinckley, U.S.A. 40 B8
Hindmarsh, L. 32 C3
Hindu Kush 25 B6
Hinesville 43 K5
Hingham 38 B8
Hinton 42 G5
Hios 15 E12
Hirosaki 22 C7
Hiroshima 22 F3
Hispaniola 45 D10
Hitachi 22 E7
Hitchin 9 F7
Hiva Oa 35 H14
Hjälmaren 7 F7
Hoa Binh 23 A2
Hoare B. 37 C13
Hobart, Australia 32 D4
Hobart, U.S.A. 41 H5
Hobbs 41 J3
Hobe Sound 43 M5
Hodgson 36 D10
Hōfu 22 F2
Hogan Group 32 C4
Hohenwald 43 H2
Hohhot 21 B6
Hoisington 40 F5
Hokianga Harbour 33 F4
Hokitika 33 K3
Hokkaidō □ 22 B8
Holbrook, Australia 32 C4
Holbrook, U.S.A. 39 J8
Holden 38 G7
Holdenville 41 H6
Holdrege 40 E5
Holetown 45 g
Holguín 45 C9
Holland 42 D2
Hollandale 41 J9
Hollidaysburg 42 E6
Hollis 41 H5
Hollister, Calif., U.S.A. 39 H3
Hollister, Idaho, U.S.A. 38 E6
Holly Hill 43 L5
Holly Springs 41 H10
Hollywood 43 N5
Holman 36 B8
Holmen 40 D9
Holsworthy 9 G3
Holton 40 F7
Holtville 39 K6
Holy I., Anglesey, U.K. 8 D3
Holy I., Northumberland, U.K. 8 B6
Holyhead 8 D3
Holyoke, Colo., U.S.A. 40 E3
Holyoke, Mass., U.S.A. 42 D9
Home B. 37 C13
Homedale 38 E5
Homer, Alaska, U.S.A. 36 D4
Homer, La., U.S.A. 41 J8
Homestead 43 N5
Homestead △ 40 E6
Homs = Ḥimṣ 24 B2
Homyel 18 D4
Hondo 41 L5
Honduras ■ 44 E7
Honduras, G. de 44 D7
Honey L. 38 F3
Hong → 20 D5
Hong Gai 23 A2
Hong Kong □ 21 G11
Hong Kong I. 21 G11
Hong Kong Int. (HKG) 21 G10
Hongjiang 21 D5
Hongshui He → 21 D5
Hongze Hu 21 C6
Honiara 31 B10
Honiton 9 G4
Honolulu 35 E12
Honshū 22 F6
Hood, Mt. 38 D3
Hood River 38 D3
Hoodsport 38 C2
Hook Hd. 11 D5
Hooker 41 G4
Hooper Bay 36 C3
Hoopeston 42 E2
Hoorn 16 B2
Hoover 43 J2
Hoover Dam 39 J6
Hope 41 J8
Hope, L. 32 A2
Hopedale 37 D13
Hopetoun 32 C3
Hopewell 42 G7
Hopkinsville 43 G2
Hopland 38 G2
Hoquiam 38 C2
Horlivka 17 A5
Hormuz, Str. of 24 C4
Horn, Cape = Hornos, C. de 48 H3
Horn, Is. 31 C15
Horn Head 11 A3
Hornavan 7 D7
Hornbeck 41 K8
Hornbrook 38 F2
Horncastle 8 D7
Hornell 42 D7
Hornos, C. de 48 H3
Hornsea 8 D7
Horqin Youyi Qianqi 21 B7
Horse Cr. → 40 E3
Horsham, Australia 32 C3
Horsham, U.K. 9 F7
Horton 40 F7
Horton → 36 C7
Hot Creek Range 38 G6
Hot Springs, Ark., U.S.A. 41 H8
Hot Springs, S. Dak., U.S.A. 40 D3
Hot Springs △ 41 H8
Hotan 20 C2
Hotchkiss 39 G10
Hou Hai 21 F10
Houghton 40 B10
Houghton L. 42 C3
Houghton-le-Spring 8 C6
Houhora Heads 33 F4
Houlton 43 B12
Houma 41 L9
Houston, Mo., U.S.A. 41 G9
Houston, Tex., U.S.A. 41 L7
Hovd □ 20 B4
Hove 9 G7
Hovenweep △ 39 H9
Hövsgöl Nuur 20 A5
Howard, Australia 32 A5
Howard, U.S.A. 40 C6
Howe 38 E7
Howe, C. 32 C5
Howell 42 D4
Howitt, L. 32 A2
Howland I. 34 G10
Howrah = Haora 25 C7
Howth 11 C5
Howth Hd. 11 C5
Hoy 10 C5
Høyanger 7 E5
Hoylake 8 D4
Hradec Králové 16 C7
Hrodna 18 D3
Hron → 16 E9
Hsinchu 21 D7
Hua Hin 23 B1
Huahine, Î. 35 J12
Huai He → 21 C6
Huainan 21 C6
Huaiyin 21 C6
Hualapai Peak 39 J7
Huambo 29 G3
Huancayo 46 F3
Huang He → 21 C6
Huangshan 21 D6
Huangshi 21 C6
Huánuco 46 E3
Huascarán, Nevado 46 E3
Huatabampo 44 B3
Hubbard 41 K6
Hubei □ 21 C6
Hubli 25 D6
Hucknall 8 D6
Huddersfield 8 D6
Hudiksvall 7 E7
Hudson, N.Y., U.S.A. 42 D9
Hudson, Wis., U.S.A. 40 C8
Hudson, Wyo., U.S.A. 38 E9
Hudson → 42 E8
Hudson Bay 37 D11
Hudson Falls 42 D9
Hudson Str. 37 C13
Hue 23 B2
Huelva 13 D2
Huesca 13 A5
Hughenden 30 E7
Hugo, Colo., U.S.A. 40 F3
Hugo, Okla., U.S.A. 41 H7
Hugoton 41 G4
Huize 20 D5
Hull 37 E12
Hull → 8 D7
Hulun Nur 21 B6
Humacao 45 d
Humber → 8 D7
Humboldt, Canada 36 D9
Humboldt, Iowa, U.S.A. 40 D7
Humboldt, Tenn., U.S.A. 41 H10
Humboldt → 38 F4
Hume, L. 32 C4
Humen 21 F10
Humphreys Peak 39 J8
Hunan □ 21 D6
Hungary ■ 16 E9
Hungerford 32 A3
Hŭngnam 21 C7
Hunsrück 16 D3
Hunstanton 8 E8
Hunter I. 32 D3
Hunter Ra. 32 B5
Hunterville 33 H5
Huntingburg 42 F2
Huntingdon, U.K. 9 E7
Huntingdon, U.S.A. 42 E7
Huntington, Ind., U.S.A. 42 E3
Huntington, Oreg., U.S.A. 38 D5
Huntington, Utah, U.S.A. 38 G8
Huntington, W. Va., U.S.A. 42 F4
Huntington Beach 39 K5
Huntly, N.Z. 33 G5
Huntly, U.K. 10 D6
Huntsville, Canada 37 E12
Huntsville, Ala., U.S.A. 43 H2
Huntsville, Tex., U.S.A. 41 K7
Huonville 32 D4
Hurghada 24 C2
Hurley, N. Mex., U.S.A. 39 K9
Hurley, Wis., U.S.A. 40 B9
Huron 40 C5
Huron, L. 42 C4
Hurricane 39 H7
Hurunui → 33 K4
Hutchinson, Kans., U.S.A. 41 F6
Hutchinson, Minn., U.S.A. 40 C7
Hutton, Mt. 32 A4
Huzhou 21 C7
Hwang Ho = Huang He → 21 C6
Hyannis, Mass., U.S.A. 42 E10
Hyannis, Nebr., U.S.A. 40 E4
Hyargas Nuur 20 B4
Hyderabad, India 25 D6
Hyderabad, Pakistan 24 C5
Hyères 12 E7
Hyères, Îs. d' 12 E7
Hyndman Peak 38 E6
Hyrum 38 F8
Hysham 38 C10
Hythe 9 F9

I

Ialomiţa → 15 B12
Iaşi 17 A3
Ibadan 26 G6
Ibagué 46 C3
Ibb 24 D3
Iberian Peninsula 2 B9
Ibiza = Eivissa 13 C6
'Ibrī 24 C4
Ica 46 F3
İçel 17 C4
Iceland ■ 7 B2
Ichihara 22 F7
Ichinomiya 22 F5
Ida Grove 40 D7
Idabel 41 J7
Idaho □ 38 D7
Idaho City 38 E6
Idaho Falls 38 E7
Idar-Oberstein 16 D3
Ife 26 G6
Igarka 18 C9
Iglésias 14 E3
Igloolik 37 C11
Iguaçu, Cat. del 48 B6
Iguala 44 D5
Iisalmi 7 E9
IJsselmeer 16 B2
Ikaluktutiak 36 C9
Ikeda 22 F3
Ilagan 23 B4
Ile → 18 E8
Île-de-France □ 12 B5
Ilesha 26 G6
Ilfracombe 9 F3
Ilhéus 47 F11
Iliamna L. 36 D4
Iligan 23 C4
Ilkeston 8 E6
Ilkley 8 D6
Iller → 16 D4
Illinois □ 40 E10
Illinois → 40 F9
Iloilo 23 B4
Ilorin 26 G6
Imabari 22 F3
Imbil 32 A5
imeni Ismail Samani, Pik 18 F8
Imi 24 E3
Imlay 38 F4
Immingham 8 D7
Immokalee 43 M5
Imperatriz 47 E9
Imperial 40 E4
Imperial Dam 39 K6
Imphal 25 C8
Inangahua 33 J3
Inari 7 D9
Inarijärvi 7 D9
Incheon 21 C7
Incline Village 38 G4
Incomáti → 29 K6
Indalsälven → 7 E7
Independence, Calif., U.S.A. 39 H4
Independence, Iowa, U.S.A. 40 D9
Independence, Kans., U.S.A. 41 G7
Independence, Ky., U.S.A. 42 F3
Independence, Mo., U.S.A. 40 F7
Independence Mts. 38 F5
India ■ 25 C6
Indian → 43 M5
Indian Ocean 3 E14
Indian Springs 39 G6
Indiana 42 E6
Indiana □ 42 F3
Indianapolis 42 F2
Indianola, Iowa, U.S.A. 40 E8
Indianola, Miss., U.S.A. 41 J9
Indigirka → 19 B15
Indio 39 K5
Indo-China 23 B2
Indonesia ■ 23 D3
Indore 25 C6
Indravati → 25 D7
Indre → 12 C4
Indulkana 32 A1
Indus → 24 C5
Indus, Mouths of the 24 C5
Ingleborough 8 C5
Inglewood, Queens., Australia 32 A5
Inglewood, Vic., Australia 32 C3
Inglewood, N.Z. 33 H5
Inglewood, U.S.A. 39 K4
Ingolstadt 16 D5
Ingomar 38 C10
Inishbofin 11 C1
Inisheer 11 C2
Inishfree B. 11 A3
Inishkea North 11 B1
Inishkea South 11 B1
Inishmaan 11 C2
Inishmore 11 C2
Inishmurray I. 11 B3
Inishowen Pen. 11 A4
Inishshark 11 C1
Inishturk 11 C1
Inishvickillane 11 D1
Injune 32 A4
Inland Kaikoura Ra. 33 J4
Inn → 16 D6
Innamincka 32 A3
Inner Hebrides 10 E2
Inner Mongolia = Nei Monggol Zizhiqu □ 21 B6
Inner Sound 10 D3
Innsbruck 16 E5
Inny → 11 C4
Inowrocław 16 B9
Insein 25 D8
Interlaken 12 C7
International Falls 40 A8
Inukjuak 37 D12
Inuvik 36 C6
Inveraray 10 E3
Inverbervie 10 E6
Invercargill 33 M2
Inverclyde □ 10 F4
Inverell 32 A5
Invergordon 10 D4
Inverloch 32 C4
Inverness, U.K. 10 D4
Inverness, U.S.A. 43 L4
Inverurie 10 D6
Investigator Group 32 B1
Investigator Str. 32 C2
Inyo Mts. 39 H5
Inyokern 39 J5
Iola 41 G7
Iona 10 E2
Ione 38 G3
Ionia 42 D3
Ionian Is. = Ionioi Nisoi 15 E9
Ionian Sea 15 E7
Ionioi Nisoi 15 E9
Iowa □ 40 D8
Iowa → 40 E9
Iowa City 40 E9
Iowa Falls 40 D8
Iowa Park 41 J5
Ipatinga 47 G10
Ipoh 23 C2
Ipswich, Australia 32 A5
Ipswich, U.K. 9 E9
Ipswich, U.S.A. 40 C5
Iqaluit 37 C13
Iquique 46 H4
Iquitos 46 D4
Iraklio 15 G11
Iran ■ 24 B4
Irapuato 44 C4
Iraq ■ 24 B3
Ireland ■ 11 C4
Iringa 28 F7
Irish Republic ■ 11 C4
Irish Sea 8 D3
Irkutsk 19 D11
Iron Baron 32 B2
Iron Knob 32 B2
Iron Mountain 42 C1
Iron River 40 B10
Ironton, Mo., U.S.A. 41 G9
Ironton, Ohio, U.S.A. 42 F4
Ironwood 40 B9
Ironwood Forest △ 39 K8
Irrara Cr. → 32 A4
Irrawaddy → 25 D8
Irtysh → 18 C7
Irvine, U.K. 10 F4
Irvine, U.S.A. 42 G4
Irvinestown 11 B4
Irving 41 J6
Irymple 32 B3
Isabel 40 C4
Isabela 45 d
Isar → 16 D6
Isère → 12 D6
Isfahan = Eşfahān 24 B4
Ishim → 18 D8
Ishinomaki 22 D7
Ishpeming 42 B2
İskenderun 17 C5
Isla → 10 E5
Islamabad 25 B6
Island L. 36 D10
Island Lagoon 32 B2
Island Pond 42 C10
Islands, B. of 33 F5
Islay 10 F2
Isle of Wight □ 9 G6
Isle Royale △ 42 B1
Ismâ'ilîya 27 B12
Israel ■ 17 D4
Issoire 12 D5
İstanbul 15 D13
İstanbul Boğazı 15 D13
Istokpoga, L. 43 M5
Istra 14 B6
Istres 12 E6
Istria = Istra 14 B6
Itabuna 47 F11
Itaipú, Reprêsa de 48 B6
Italy ■ 14 C5
Itapipoca 47 D11
Itchen → 9 G6
Ithaca 42 D7
Ivanhoe, Australia 32 B3
Ivanhoe, U.S.A. 40 C6
Ivano-Frankivsk 18 E3
Ivanovo 18 D5
Ivory Coast ■ 26 G4
Ivujivik 37 C12
Ivybridge 9 G4
Iwaki 22 E7
Iwakuni 22 F3
Iwo 26 G6
Izhevsk 18 D6
Izkī 24 C4
İzmir 15 E12

J

J. Strom Thurmond L. 43 J4
Jabalpur 25 C6
Jaboatão 47 E11
Jackman 43 C10
Jacksboro 41 J5
Jackson, Barbados 45 g
Jackson, Ala., U.S.A. 43 K2
Jackson, Calif., U.S.A. 38 G3
Jackson, Ky., U.S.A. 42 G4
Jackson, Mich., U.S.A. 42 D3
Jackson, Minn., U.S.A. 40 D7
Jackson, Miss., U.S.A. 41 J9
Jackson, Mo., U.S.A. 41 G10
Jackson, Ohio, U.S.A. 42 F4
Jackson, Tenn., U.S.A. 43 H1
Jackson, Wyo., U.S.A. 38 E8
Jackson B. 33 K2
Jackson L. 38 E8
Jacksons 33 K3
Jacksonville, Ala., U.S.A. 43 J3
Jacksonville, Ark., U.S.A. 41 H8
Jacksonville, Fla., U.S.A. 43 K5
Jacksonville, Ill., U.S.A. 40 F9
Jacksonville, N.C., U.S.A. 43 H7
Jacksonville, Tex., U.S.A. 41 K7
Jacksonville Beach 43 K5
Jacmel 45 D10
Jacob Lake 39 H7
Jaén 13 D4
Jaffa = Tel Aviv-Yafo 17 D4
Jaffa, C. 32 C2
Jaffna 25 E7
Jagdalpur 25 D7
Jahrom 24 C4
Jaipur 25 C6
Jakarta 23 D2
Jal 41 J3
Jalna 25 D6
Jaluit I. 34 G8
Jamaica ■ 44 a
Jambi 23 D2
James →, S. Dak., U.S.A. 40 D6
James →, Va., U.S.A. 42 G7
James B. 37 D12
Jamestown, Australia 32 B2
Jamestown, N. Dak., U.S.A. 40 B5
Jamestown, N.Y., U.S.A. 42 D6
Jammu 25 B6
Jammu & Kashmir □ 25 B6
Jamnagar 25 C6
Jamshedpur 25 C7
Jan Mayen 6 B6
Jandowae 32 A5
Janesville 40 D10
Japan ■ 22 F5
Japan, Sea of 22 D4
Japan Trench 34 D6
Japurá → 46 D5
Jarvis I. 35 H12
Jäsk 24 C4
Jasper, Canada 36 D8
Jasper, Ala., U.S.A. 43 J2
Jasper, Fla., U.S.A. 43 K4
Jasper, Ind., U.S.A. 42 F2
Jasper, Tex., U.S.A. 41 K8
Jaunpur 25 C7
Java = Jawa 23 D3
Java Sea 23 D2
Java Trench 23 D2
Jawa 23 D3
Jaya, Puncak 23 D5
Jayton 41 J4
Jean 39 J6
Jeanerette 41 L9
Jebel, Bahr el → 27 G12
Jedburgh 10 F6
Jedda = Jiddah 24 C2
Jefferson, Iowa, U.S.A. 40 D7
Jefferson, Tex., U.S.A. 41 J7
Jefferson, Mt., Nev., U.S.A. 38 G5
Jefferson, Mt., Oreg., U.S.A. 38 D3
Jefferson City, Mo., U.S.A. 40 F8
Jefferson City, Tenn., U.S.A. 43 G4
Jeffersontown 42 F3
Jeffersonville 42 F3
Jeffrey City 38 E10
Jeju-do 21 C7
Jekyll I. 43 K5
Jelenia Góra 16 C7
Jena, Germany 16 C5
Jena, U.S.A. 41 K8
Jenkins 42 G4
Jennings 41 K8
Jeonju 21 C7
Jeparit 32 C3
Jequié 47 F10
Jérémie 45 D10
Jerez de la Frontera 13 D2
Jerilderie 32 C4
Jerome 38 E6
Jersey 9 H5
Jersey City 42 E8
Jersey Shore 42 E7
Jerseyville 40 F9
Jerusalem 17 D5
Jervis B. 32 C5
Jesup 43 K5
Jetmore 41 F5
Jhansi 25 C6
Jharkhand □ 25 C7
Jhelum → 25 B6

K

L

M

Manila, Phil. 23 B4
Manila, U.S.A. 38 F9
Manila B. 23 B4
Manilla 32 B5
Manipur □ 25 C8
Manistee 42 C2
Manistee → 42 C2
Manistique 42 C2
Manitoba □ 36 D10
Manitoba, L. 36 D10
Manitou Is. 42 C2
Manitou Springs 40 F2
Manitoulin I. 37 E11
Manitowoc 42 C2
Manizales 46 B3
Mankato, Kans., U.S.A. 40 F5
Mankato, Minn., U.S.A. 40 C8
Mannahill 32 B3
Mannar 25 E6
Mannar, G. of 25 E6
Mannheim 16 D4
Manning, Canada 36 D8
Manning, U.S.A. 43 J5
Mannum 32 B2
Manokwari 23 D5
Manorhamilton 11 B3
Manosque 12 E6
Manra 31 A16
Mansel I. 37 C12
Mansfield, Australia 32 C4
Mansfield, U.K. 8 D6
Mansfield, La., U.S.A. 41 J8
Mansfield, Ohio, U.S.A. 42 E4
Mansfield, Tex., U.S.A. 41 J6
Mantalingajan, Mt. 23 C3
Manteca 39 H3
Manteo 43 H8
Mantes-la-Jolie 12 B4
Manti 38 G8
Manton 42 C3
Mántova 14 B4
Manu'a Is. 33 B14
Manukau 33 G5
Many 41 K8
Manzanillo, Cuba 45 C9
Manzanillo, Mexico 44 D4
Manzano Mts. 39 J10
Manzhouli 21 B6
Maoming 21 D6
Mapam Yumco 20 C3
Mapia, Kepulauan 23 C5
Mapleton 38 D2
Maputo 29 K6
Maquoketa 40 D9
Mar Chiquita, L. 48 C4
Mar del Plata 48 D5
Marabá 47 E9
Maracaibo 46 A4
Maracaibo, L. de 46 B4
Maracay 46 A5
Marajó, I. de 47 D9
Marana 39 K8
Maranoa → 32 A4
Marañón → 46 D4
Marathon 41 K3
Marbella 13 D3
Marble Falls 41 K5
March 9 E8
Marche 12 C4
Marco Island 43 N5
Mardan 25 B6
Maré, Î. 31 E12
Maree, L. 10 D3
Marengo 40 E8
Marfa 41 K2
Margarita, I. de 46 A6
Margate 9 F9
Mārgow, Dasht-e 24 B5
Maria I. 32 D4
Maria Island △ 32 D4
Maria van Diemen, C. 33 F4
Mariala △ 32 A4
Mariana Trench 34 F6
Marianna, Ark., U.S.A. 41 H9
Marianna, Fla., U.S.A. 43 K3
Marias → 38 C8
Maribor 14 A6
Maricopa, Ariz., U.S.A. 39 K7
Maricopa, Calif., U.S.A. 39 J4
Marie Byrd Land 6 E18
Marie-Galante 44 b
Mariental 29 J3
Marietta, Ga., U.S.A. 43 J3
Marietta, Ohio, U.S.A. 42 F5
Marília 47 H9
Marinette 42 C2
Maringá 48 A6
Marion, Ala., U.S.A. 43 J2
Marion, Ill., U.S.A. 41 G10
Marion, Ind., U.S.A. 42 E3
Marion, Iowa, U.S.A. 40 D9
Marion, Kans., U.S.A. 40 F6
Marion, N.C., U.S.A. 43 H5
Marion, Ohio, U.S.A. 42 E4
Marion, S.C., U.S.A. 43 H6
Marion, Va., U.S.A. 43 G5
Marion, L. 43 J5
Mariposa 39 H4
Maritimes, Alpes 12 D7
Mariupol 17 A5
Marked Tree 41 H9
Market Drayton 8 E5
Market Harborough 9 E7
Market Rasen 8 D7
Markham, Mt. 6 F15
Marksville 41 K8
Marla 32 A1
Marlborough 9 F6
Marlborough Downs 9 F6
Marlin 41 K6
Marlow, U.K. 9 F7
Marlow, U.S.A. 41 H6
Marmara Denizi 15 D13
Marne → 12 B5
Maroochydore 32 A5
Maroona 32 C3
Marquesas Fracture Zone 35 H15
Marquette 42 B2
Marquis 45 f
Marquises, Îs. 35 H14
Marrakech 26 B4
Marrawah 32 D3
Marree 32 A2
Marrero 41 L9
Marrowie Cr. → 32 B4
Mars Hill 43 B12
Marsden 32 B4
Marseille 12 E6
Marsh I. 41 L9
Marshall, Ark., U.S.A. 41 H8
Marshall, Mich., U.S.A. 42 D3
Marshall, Minn., U.S.A. 40 C7
Marshall, Mo., U.S.A. 40 F8
Marshall, Tex., U.S.A. 41 J7
Marshall Is. ■ 34 G9
Marshalltown 40 D8
Marshfield, Mo., U.S.A. 41 G8
Marshfield, Wis., U.S.A. 40 C9
Mart 41 K6
Martaban, G. of 25 D8
Martapura 23 D3
Martha's Vineyard 42 E10
Martigues 12 E6
Martin, S. Dak., U.S.A. 40 D4
Martin, Tenn., U.S.A. 41 G10
Martin L. 43 J3
Martinborough 33 J5
Martinez 43 J4
Martinique ☑ 44 c
Martin's Bay 45 g
Martins Ferry 42 E5
Martinsburg 42 F7
Martinsville, Ind., U.S.A. 42 F2
Martinsville, Va., U.S.A. 43 G6
Marton 33 J5
Maryborough, Queens., Australia 32 A5
Maryborough, Vic., Australia 32 C3
Maryland □ 42 F7
Maryport 8 C4
Marystown 37 E14
Marysville, Calif., U.S.A. 38 G3
Marysville, Kans., U.S.A. 40 F6
Marysville, Ohio, U.S.A. 42 E4
Maryville, Mo., U.S.A. 40 E7
Maryville, Tenn., U.S.A. 43 H4
Masan 21 C7
Masaya 44 E7
Masbate 23 B4
Maseru 29 K5
Mashhad 24 B4
Maşīrah 24 C4
Mask, L. 11 C2
Mason 41 K5
Mason City 40 D8
Masqat 24 C4
Massachusetts □ 42 D10
Massena 42 C8
Massiah Street 45 g
Massif Central 12 D5
Massillon 42 E5
Masterton 33 J5
Masvingo 29 J6
Mata Utu 31 C15
Matadi 28 F2
Matagalpa 44 E7
Matagami 37 E12
Matagami, L. 37 E12
Matagorda B. 41 L6
Matagorda I. 41 L6
Matamoros, Coahuila, Mexico 44 B5
Matamoros, Tamaulipas, Mexico 44 B5
Matane 37 E13
Matanzas 45 C8
Mataram 23 D3
Mataró 13 B7
Mataura 33 M2
Matehuala 44 C4
Matera 14 D7
Mathis 41 L6
Mathura 25 C6
Mati 23 C4
Matiri Ra. 33 J4
Matlock 8 D6
Mato Grosso □ 47 F8
Mato Grosso, Planalto do 47 G8
Matopo Hills 29 J5
Maţruḩ 24 C4
Matsue 22 F3
Matsumoto 22 E6
Matsusaka 22 F5
Matsuyama 22 G3
Mattagami → 37 D11
Mattancheri 25 E6
Matterhorn 12 D7
Matthew, Î. 31 E13
Mattoon 42 F1
Maturín 46 B6
Maubeuge 12 A6
Maubin 25 D8
Maude 32 B3
Maudin Sun 25 D8
Maughold Hd. 8 C3
Maumee 42 E4
Maumee → 42 E4
Maumere 23 D4
Maun 29 H4
Maupin 38 D3
Maurepas, L. 41 K9
Mauritania ■ 26 E3
Mauritius ■ 5 F13
Mauston 40 D9
Max 40 B4
May, C. 42 F8
May Pen 44 a
Mayaguana 45 C10
Mayagüez 45 d
Maybell 38 F9
Maybole 10 F4
Maydena 32 D4
Mayer 39 J7
Mayfield 43 G1
Mayhill 39 K11
Maykop 17 B6
Maynooth 11 C5
Mayo 36 C6
Mayo □ 11 C2
Mayor I. 33 G6
Maysville 42 F4
Mayville 40 B6
Mazār-e Sharīf 24 B5
Mazatlán 44 C3
Mazurski, Pojezierze 16 B10
Mbabane 29 K6
Mbandaka 28 D3
Mbanza Ngungu 28 F2
Mbeya 28 F6
Mbuji-Mayi 28 F4
McKean 31 A16
Mead, L. 39 H6
Meade 41 G4
Meadow Lake 36 D9
Meadow Valley Wash → 39 H6
Meadville 42 E5
Meares, C. 38 D2
Meath □ 11 C5
Meaux 12 B5
Mecca = Makkah 24 C2
Mechelen 16 C2
Mecklenburg 16 B5
Medan 23 C1
Médéa 26 A6
Medellín 46 B3
Medford, Oreg., U.S.A. 38 E2
Medford, Wis., U.S.A. 40 C9
Medicine Bow 38 F10
Medicine Bow Mts. 38 F10
Medicine Bow Pk. 38 F10
Medicine Hat 36 E8
Medicine Lake 40 A2
Medicine Lodge 41 G5
Medina = Al Madīnah 24 C2
Medina, N. Dak., U.S.A. 40 B5
Medina, N.Y., U.S.A. 42 D6
Medina, Ohio, U.S.A. 42 E5
Medina → 41 L5
Medina L. 41 L5
Mediterranean Sea 3 C11
Médoc 12 D3
Medway □ 9 F8
Medway → 9 F8
Meekatharra 30 F2
Meeker 38 F10
Meerut 25 C6
Meeteetse 38 D9
Meghalaya □ 25 C8
Mehlville 40 F9
Meighen I. 37 A10
Meiktila 25 C8
Meizhou 21 D6
Mekele 24 D2
Meknès 26 B4
Mekong → 23 C2
Melaka 23 C2
Melanesia 31 A10
Melanesian Basin 34 G8
Melbourne, Australia 32 C4
Melbourne, U.S.A. 43 L5
Mélèzes → 37 D12
Melfort 36 D9
Melitopol 17 A5
Mellen 40 B9
Mellette 40 C5
Melrose, Australia 32 B4
Melrose, U.K. 10 F6
Melrose, Minn., U.S.A. 40 C7
Melrose, N. Mex., U.S.A. 41 H3
Melstone 38 C10
Melton Mowbray 8 E7
Melun 12 B5
Melville 36 D9
Melville I., Australia 30 C5
Melville I., Canada 37 B9
Melville Pen. 37 C11
Melvin, Lough 11 B3
Memphis, Tenn., U.S.A. 41 H10
Memphis, Tex., U.S.A. 41 H4
Mena 41 H7
Menai Strait 8 D3
Menard 41 K5
Menard Fracture Zone 35 M18
Mendaña Fracture Zone 35 J18
Mende 12 D5
Mendip Hills 9 F5
Mendocino 38 G2
Mendocino, C. 38 F1
Mendocino Fracture Zone 35 D13
Mendota, Calif., U.S.A. 39 H3
Mendota, Ill., U.S.A. 40 E10
Mendoza 48 C3
Mengzi 20 D5
Menindee 32 B3
Menindee L. 32 B3
Meningie 32 C2
Menominee 42 C2
Menominee → 42 C2
Menomonie 40 C9
Menorca 13 C8
Mentawai, Kepulauan 23 D1
Mentor 42 E5
Merbein 32 B3
Merca 24 E3
Merced 39 H3
Mercer 33 G5
Mercy, C. 37 C13
Mere 9 F5
Meredith, L. 41 H4
Mergui 25 D8
Mérida, Mexico 44 C7
Mérida, Spain 13 C2
Mérida, Venezuela 46 B4
Mérida, Cord. de 46 B4
Meriden, U.K. 9 E6
Meriden, U.S.A. 42 E9
Meridian, Idaho, U.S.A. 38 E5
Meridian, Miss., U.S.A. 43 J1
Merkel 41 J5
Merrick 10 F4
Merrill, Oreg., U.S.A. 38 E3
Merrill, Wis., U.S.A. 40 C10
Merriman 40 D4
Merritt 36 D7
Merritt Island 43 L5
Merriwa 32 B5
Merryville 41 K8
Mersea I. 9 F8
Mersey → 8 D4
Merseyside □ 8 D4
Mersin = İçel 17 C4
Merthyr Tydfil 9 F4
Mertzon 41 K4
Mesa 39 K8
Mesa Verde △ 39 H9
Mesopotamia = Al Jazirah 24 B3
Mesquite 39 H6
Messina 14 E6
Messina, Str. di 14 F6
Meta → 46 B5
Meta Incognita Pen. 37 C13
Metairie 41 L9
Metaline Falls 38 B5
Methven 33 K3
Metlakatla 36 D6
Metropolis 41 G10
Metz 12 B7
Meuse → 12 A6
Mexia 41 K6
Mexicali 44 A1
Mexican Water 39 H9
México, Mexico 44 D5
Mexico, U.S.A. 40 F9
Mexico ■ 44 C4
México, Ciudad de 44 D5
Mexico, G. of 44 C7
Meymaneh 24 B5
Mezen → 18 C5
Miami, Fla., U.S.A. 43 N5
Miami, Okla., U.S.A. 41 G7
Miami, Tex., U.S.A. 41 H4
Miami Beach 43 N5
Mianwali 25 B6
Miass 18 D7
Michigan □ 42 C3
Michigan, L. 42 D2
Michigan City 42 E2
Michurinsk 18 D5
Micoud 45 f
Micronesia 34 G7
Micronesia, Federated States of ■ 34 G7
Mid-Pacific Seamounts 34 F10
Middelburg 29 L5
Middle Alkali L. 38 F3
Middle East 24 B2
Middle Loup → 40 E5
Middleburg 43 K5
Middlebury 42 C9
Middleport 42 F4
Middlesboro 43 G4
Middlesbrough 8 C6
Middletown, U.K. 11 B5
Middletown, N.Y., U.S.A. 42 E8
Middletown, Ohio, U.S.A. 42 F3
Midhurst 9 G7
Midi, Canal du → 12 E4
Midland, Mich., U.S.A. 42 D3
Midland, Tex., U.S.A. 41 K3
Midleton 11 E3
Midlothian □ 10 F5
Midway Is. 34 E10
Midwest 38 E10
Midwest City 41 H6
Mieres 13 A3
Milaca 40 C8
Milan, Mo., U.S.A. 40 E8
Milan, Tenn., U.S.A. 43 H1
Milano 12 D8
Milbank 40 C6
Mildenhall 9 E8
Mildura 32 B3
Miles 32 A5
Miles City 40 B2
Milford, Del., U.S.A. 42 F8
Milford, Utah, U.S.A. 39 G7
Milford Haven 9 F2
Milford Sd. 33 L1
Milford Sound 33 L1
Millau 12 D5
Millbrook 43 J2
Mille Lacs L. 40 B8
Milledgeville 43 J4
Millen 43 J5
Millennium I. = Caroline I. 35 H12
Miller 40 C5
Millet 45 f
Millicent 32 C3
Millington 41 H10
Millinocket 43 C11
Millmerran 32 A5
Millom 8 C4
Millstreet 11 D2
Milltown Malbay 11 D2
Millville 42 F8
Millwood L. 41 J8
Milo 43 C11
Milparinka 32 A3
Milton, N.Z. 33 M2
Milton, Fla., U.S.A. 43 K2
Milton, Pa., U.S.A. 42 E7
Milton-Freewater 38 D4
Milton Keynes 9 E7
Milwaukee 42 D2
Milwaukee Deep 2 D6
Milwaukie 38 D2
Min Jiang →, Fujian, China 21 D6
Min Jiang →, Sichuan, China 20 D5
Minami-Tori-Shima 34 E7
Minas Gerais □ 47 G9
Minatitlán 44 D6
Minbu 25 C8
Mindanao 23 C4
Mindanao Trench 23 B4
Minden, La., U.S.A. 41 J8
Minden, Nev., U.S.A. 38 G4
Mindoro 23 B4
Mindoro Str. 23 B4
Minehead 9 F4
Mineola 41 J7
Mineral Wells 41 J5
Minidoka 38 E7
Minneapolis, Kans., U.S.A. 40 F6
Minneapolis, Minn., U.S.A. 40 C8
Minnesota □ 40 B8
Minnesota → 40 C8
Minnewaukan 40 A5
Minnipa 32 B2
Minorca = Menorca 13 C8
Minot 40 A4
Minsk 18 D3
Mintabie 32 A1
Minto, L. 37 D12
Minturn 38 G10
Minzhong 21 F10
Miramichi 37 E13
Mirbāţ 24 D4
Miri 23 C3
Mīrjāveh 24 C5
Mirzapur 25 C7
Mishan 21 B8
Mishawaka 42 E2
Misool 23 D5
Mişrātah 27 B9
Missinaibi → 37 D11
Mission, S. Dak., U.S.A. 40 D4
Mission, Tex., U.S.A. 41 M5
Mission Viejo 39 K5
Mississippi □ 41 J10
Mississippi → 41 L10
Mississippi River Delta 41 L9
Mississippi Sd. 41 K10
Missoula 38 C7
Missouri □ 40 F8
Missouri → 40 F9
Missouri City 41 L7
Missouri Valley 40 E7
Mistassini, L. 37 D12
Mitchell, Australia 32 A4
Mitchell, Nebr., U.S.A. 40 E3
Mitchell, Oreg., U.S.A. 38 D3
Mitchell, S. Dak., U.S.A. 40 D6
Mitchell → 30 D7
Mitchell, Mt. 43 H4
Mitchelstown 11 D3
Mito 22 E7
Mitsiwa 24 D2
Mittagong 32 B5
Mitumba, Mts. 28 F5
Miyakonojō 22 H2
Miyazaki 22 H2
Mizen Hd., Cork, Ireland 11 E2
Mizen Hd., Wicklow, Ireland 11 D5
Mizoram □ 25 C8
Mjøsa 7 E6
Mmabatho 29 K5
Mo i Rana 7 D6
Moa, I. 30 C7
Moab 39 G9
Moala 33 D8
Moama 32 C3
Moate 11 C4
Moberly 40 F8
Mobile 43 K1
Mobile B. 43 K2
Mobridge 40 C4
Mochudi 29 J5
Moclips 38 C1
Módena, Italy 14 B4
Modena, U.S.A. 39 H7
Modesto 39 H3
Modimolle 29 J5
Moe 32 C4
Moffat 10 F5
Mogadishu = Muqdisho 24 E3
Mogi das Cruzes 48 A7
Mogollon Rim 39 J8
Mohall 40 A4
Mohave, L. 39 J6
Moher, Cliffs of 11 D2
Moidart, L. 10 E3
Moisie → 37 D13
Mojave 39 J4
Mojave △ 39 J6
Mojave Desert 39 J5
Mokai 33 H5
Mokau 33 H5
Mokopane 29 J5
Mold 8 D4
Moldavia = Moldova ■ 17 A3
Molde 7 E5
Moldova ■ 17 A3
Mole → 9 F7
Mole Creek 32 D4
Molepolole 29 J5
Moline 40 E9
Mollendo 46 G4
Molokai Fracture Zone 35 E15
Molong 32 B4
Molopo → 29 K4
Molucca Sea 23 D4
Moluccas = Maluku 23 D4
Mombasa 28 E7
Mona Passage 45 D11
Monaco ■ 12 E7
Monadhliath Mts. 10 D4
Monaghan 11 B5
Monaghan □ 11 B5
Monahans 41 K3
Monar, L. 10 D3
Monasterevin 11 C4
Mönchengladbach 16 C3
Moncks Corner 43 J5
Monclova 44 B4
Moncton 37 E13
Mondeodo 23 D4
Moneague 44 a
Monessen 42 E6
Monett 41 G8
Moneymore 11 B5
Mongolia ■ 20 B5
Mongu 29 H4
Monifieth 10 E6
Monmouth, U.K. 9 F5
Monmouth, Ill., U.S.A. 40 E9
Monmouth, Oreg., U.S.A. 38 D2
Monmouthshire □ 9 F5
Mono L. 39 H4
Monroe, Ga., U.S.A. 43 J4
Monroe, La., U.S.A. 41 J8
Monroe, Mich., U.S.A. 42 E4
Monroe, N.C., U.S.A. 43 H5
Monroe, Utah, U.S.A. 39 G7
Monroe, Wis., U.S.A. 40 D10
Monroe City 40 F9
Monroeville 43 K2
Monrovia 26 G3
Mons 16 C1
Mont-de-Marsan 12 E3
Mont-Laurier 37 E12
Montana □ 38 C9
Montargis 12 C5
Montauban 12 D4
Montauk Pt. 42 E10
Montbéliard 12 C7
Montceau-les-Mines 12 C6
Monte-Carlo 12 E7
Monte Cristi 45 D10
Monte Vista 39 H10
Montego Bay 44 a
Montélimar 12 D6
Montello 40 D10
Montemorelos 44 B5
Montenegro □ 15 C8
Monterey 39 H3
Montería 46 B3
Monterrey 44 B4
Montes Claros 47 G10
Montesano 38 C2
Montevideo, Uruguay 48 C5
Montevideo, U.S.A. 40 C7
Montezuma 40 E8
Montezuma Castle △ 39 J8
Montgomery, U.K. 9 E4
Montgomery, Ala., U.S.A. 43 J2
Montgomery, W. Va., U.S.A. 42 F5
Montgomery City 40 F9
Monticello, Ark., U.S.A. 41 J9
Monticello, Fla., U.S.A. 43 K4
Monticello, Ind., U.S.A. 42 E2
Monticello, Iowa, U.S.A. 40 D9
Monticello, Ky., U.S.A. 43 G3
Monticello, Minn., U.S.A. 40 C8
Monticello, Miss., U.S.A. 41 K9
Monticello, Utah, U.S.A. 39 H9
Montluçon 12 C5
Montpelier, Idaho, U.S.A. 38 E8
Montpelier, Vt., U.S.A. 42 C9
Montpellier 12 E5
Montréal 37 E12
Montreux 12 C7
Montrose, U.K. 10 E6
Montrose, U.S.A. 39 G10
Montserrat ☑ 45 D12
Monywa 25 C8
Monza 12 D8
Moonie 32 A5
Moonie → 32 A4
Moonta 32 B2
Moorcroft 40 C2
Moorefield 42 F6
Moorfoot Hills 10 F5
Moorhead 40 B6
Moorreesburg 29 L3
Moose Jaw 36 D9
Moose Lake 40 B8
Moosehead L. 43 C11
Mooselookmeguntic L. 43 C10
Moosomin 36 D9
Moosonee 37 D11
Mopti 26 F5
Mora, Sweden 7 E6
Mora, Minn., U.S.A. 40 C8
Mora, N. Mex., U.S.A. 39 J11
Moradabad 25 C6
Moran, Kans., U.S.A. 41 G7
Moran, Wyo., U.S.A. 38 E8
Morant Bay 44 a
Morant Pt. 44 a
Morar, L. 10 E3
Moratuwa 25 E6
Morava →, Serbia & M. 15 B9
Morava →, Slovak Rep. 16 D8
Moray □ 10 D5
Moray Firth 10 D5
Morden 36 E10
Moreau → 40 C4
Morecambe 8 C5
Morecambe B. 8 C5
Moree 32 A4
Morehead 42 F4
Morehead City 43 H7
Morelia 44 D4
Morena, Sierra 13 C3
Moresby I. 36 D6
Moreton I. 32 A5
Moreton Island △ 32 A5
Morgan 38 F8
Morgan City 41 L9
Morganfield 42 G2
Morganton 43 H5
Morgantown 42 F6
Moriarty 39 J10
Morioka 22 D7
Morlaix 12 B2
Mornington 32 C4
Moro G. 23 C4
Morocco ■ 26 B4
Morogoro 28 F7
Morón 45 C9
Moroni 38 G8
Morotai 23 C4
Morpeth 8 B6
Morrilton 41 H8
Morrinsville 33 G5
Morris, Ill., U.S.A. 40 E10
Morris, Minn., U.S.A. 40 C7
Morristown, Ariz., U.S.A. 39 K7
Morristown, Tenn., U.S.A. 43 G4
Morro Bay 39 J3
Mortlake 32 C3
Morton, Tex., U.S.A. 41 J3
Morton, Wash., U.S.A. 38 C2
Morundah 32 B4
Moruya 32 C5
Morven 32 A4
Morvern 10 E3
Morwell 32 C4
Moscow = Moskva 18 D4
Moscow 38 C5
Mosel → 12 A7
Moses Lake 38 C4
Mosgiel 33 L3
Moshi 28 E7
Moskva 18 D4
Mosquero 41 H3
Moss Vale 32 B5
Mossburn 33 L2
Mosselbaai 29 L4
Mossgiel 32 B3
Mossoró 47 E11
Most 16 C6
Mostaganem 26 A6
Mostar 15 C7
Mosul = Al Mawşil 24 B3
Motherwell 10 F5
Mott 40 B3
Motueka 33 J4
Motueka → 33 J4
Moulamein 32 C3
Moule à Chique, C. 45 f
Moulins 12 C5
Moulmein 25 D8
Moultrie 43 K4
Moultrie, L. 43 J5
Mound City, Mo., U.S.A. 40 E7
Mound City, S. Dak., U.S.A. 40 C4
Moundsville 42 F5
Mount Airy 43 G5
Mount Aspiring △ 33 L2
Mount Barker 32 C2
Mount Bellew Bridge 11 C3
Mount Burr 32 C3
Mount Carmel 42 F2
Mount Desert I. 43 C11
Mount Dora 43 L5
Mount Field △ 32 D4
Mount Gambier 32 C3
Mount Hagen 30 B7
Mount Hope, N.S.W., Australia 32 B4
Mount Hope, S. Austral., Australia 32 B2
Mount Isa 30 E6
Mount Kaputar △ 32 B5
Mount Lofty Ranges 32 B2
Mount Magnet 30 F2
Mount Maunganui 33 G6
Mount Perry 32 A5
Mount Pleasant, Iowa, U.S.A. 40 E9
Mount Pleasant, Mich., U.S.A. 42 D3
Mount Pleasant, S.C., U.S.A. 43 J6
Mount Pleasant, Tenn., U.S.A. 43 H2
Mount Pleasant, Tex., U.S.A. 41 J7
Mount Pleasant, Utah, U.S.A. 38 G8
Mount Rainier △ 38 C3
Mount St. Helens △ 38 C2
Mount Shasta 38 F2
Mount Sterling, Ill., U.S.A. 40 F9
Mount Sterling, Ky., U.S.A. 42 F4
Mount Vernon, Ill., U.S.A. 42 F1
Mount Vernon, Ind., U.S.A. 40 F10
Mount Vernon, Ohio, U.S.A. 42 E4
Mount Vernon, Wash., U.S.A. 38 B2
Mount William △ 32 D4
Mountain Ash 9 F4
Mountain City, Nev., U.S.A. 38 F6
Mountain City, Tenn., U.S.A. 43 G5
Mountain Grove 41 G8
Mountain Home, Ark., U.S.A. 41 G8
Mountain Home, Idaho, U.S.A. 38 E6
Mountain Iron 40 B8
Mountain View 41 H8
Mountainair 39 J10
Mountmellick 11 C4
Mountrath 11 D4
Mourne → 11 B4
Mourne Mts. 11 B5
Moville 11 A4
Moy → 11 B2
Moyen Atlas 26 B4
Mozambique ■ 29 H7
Mozambique Chan. 3 E13
Mpumalanga 29 K6
Mthatha 29 L5
Mu Us Shamo 21 C5
Muar 23 C2
Muck 10 E2
Muckadilla 32 A4
Muckle Flugga 10 A8
Mudanjiang 21 B7
Muddy Cr. → 39 H8
Mudgee 32 B4
Mufulira 29 G5
Muhammad Qol 24 C2
Mui Wo 21 G10
Muine Bheag 11 D5
Muir of Ord 10 D4
Mulde → 16 C6
Mule Creek Junction 40 D2
Muleshoe 41 H3
Mulhacén 13 D4
Mulhouse 12 C7
Mull 10 E3
Mull, Sound of 10 E3
Mullen 40 D4
Mullens 42 G5
Muller, Pegunungan 23 C3
Mullet Pen. 11 B1
Mullingar 11 C4
Mullins 43 H6
Mullumbimby 32 A5
Mulroy B. 11 A4
Multan 25 B6
Mulvane 41 G6
Mumbai 25 D6
Muna 23 D4
München 16 D5
Muncie 42 E3
Mundabbera 32 A5
Munday 41 J5
Mungallala 32 A4
Mungallala Cr. → 32 A4
Munich = München 16 D5
Munising 42 B2
Münster 16 C3
Munster □ 11 D3
Muong Sai 23 A2
Muqdisho 24 E3
Murchison → 30 F1
Murcia 13 D5
Murdo 40 D4
Mureş → 17 A2
Murfreesboro, N.C., U.S.A. 43 G7
Murfreesboro, Tenn., U.S.A. 43 H2
Murgon 32 A5
Müritz 16 B6
Murmansk 7 D10
Murom 18 D5
Murphy 38 E5
Murray, Ky., U.S.A. 43 G1
Murray, Utah, U.S.A. 38 F8
Murray → 32 C2
Murray, L. 43 H5
Murray Bridge 32 C2
Murray Fracture Zone 35 D14
Murray River △ 32 B3
Murrumbidgee → 32 B3
Murrumburrah 32 B4
Murrurundi 32 B5
Murtoa 32 C3
Mururoa 35 K14
Murwillumbah 32 A5
Mûsa, Gebel 27 C12
Muscat = Masqat 24 C4
Muscatine 40 E9
Muscle Shoals 43 H2
Musgrave Ranges 30 F5
Musi → 23 D2
Musina 29 J6
Muskegon 42 D2
Muskegon → 42 D2
Muskegon Heights 42 D2
Muskogee 41 H7
Musselburgh 10 F5
Musselshell → 38 C10
Muswellbrook 32 B5
Mutare 29 H6
Mutton I. 11 D2
Mwanza 28 E6
Mweelrea 11 C2
Mweru, L. 28 F5
My Tho 23 B2
Myanmar = Burma ■ 25 C8
Myeik Kyunzu 25 D8
Myingyan 25 C8
Myitkyina 25 C8
Mykolayiv 17 A4
Mynydd Du 9 F4
Myrtle Beach 43 J6
Myrtle Creek 38 E2
Myrtle Point 38 E1
Mysore 25 D6

N

Naab → 16 D6
Naas 11 C5
Naberezhnyye Chelny 18 D6
Naches 38 C3
Nacimiento, L. 39 J3
Nacogdoches 41 K7
Nacozari de García 44 A3
Nadi 33 C7
Naga 23 B4
Nagaland □ 25 C8
Nagano 22 E6
Nagaoka 22 E6
Nagasaki 22 G1
Nagercoil 25 E6
Nagles Mts. 11 D3
Nagoya 22 F5
Nagpur 25 C6
Naguabo 45 d
Naha 21 D7
Nain 37 D13
Nairn 10 D5
Nairobi 28 E7
Najd 24 C3
Najrān 24 D3
Nakhodka 19 E14
Nakhon Ratchasima 23 B2
Nakhon Sawan 25 D9
Nakhon Si Thammarat 23 C2
Nakina 37 D11
Nakuru 28 E7
Nalchik 17 B6
Nam Co 20 C4
Nam Dinh 23 A2
Namaland 29 K3
Namangan 18 E8
Nambour 32 A5
Nambucca Heads 32 B5
Namcha Barwa 20 D4
Namib Desert 29 J3
Namibe 29 H2
Namibia ■ 29 J3
Namlea 23 D4
Namoi → 32 B4
Nampa 38 E5
Namp'o 21 C7
Nampula 29 H7
Namumea 31 B14
Namur 16 C2
Nanaimo 36 E7
Nanango 32 A5
Nanchang 21 D6
Nanchong 20 C5
Nancy 12 B7
Nanded 25 D6
Nandewar Ra. 32 B5
Nanjing 21 C6
Nanking = Nanjing 21 C6
Nanlang 21 G10
Nanning 20 D5
Nanping 21 D6
Nansen Sd. 37 B9
Nansha 21 F10
Nantes 12 C3
Nanticoke 42 E7
Nantong 21 C7
Nantou 21 F10
Nantucket I. 42 E10
Nantwich 8 D5
Nanumanga 31 B14
Nanusa, Kepulauan 23 C4
Nanyang 21 C6
Napa 38 G2
Napier 33 H6
Naples = Nápoli 14 D6
Naples 43 M5
Napo → 46 D4
Napoleon, N. Dak., U.S.A. 40 B5
Napoleon, Ohio, U.S.A. 42 E3
Nápoli 14 D6
Nara Visa 41 H3
Naracoorte 32 C3
Naradhan 32 B4
Narberth 9 F3
Narbonne 12 E5
Narmada → 25 C6
Narooma 32 C5
Narrabri 32 B4
Narran → 32 A4
Narrandera 32 B4
Narromine 32 B4
Narvik 7 D7
Naryn 25 A6
Naseby 33 L3
Naser, Buheirat en 27 D12
Nashua, Mont., U.S.A. 38 B10
Nashua, N.H., U.S.A. 42 D10
Nashville, Ark., U.S.A. 41 J8
Nashville, Ga., U.S.A. 43 K4
Nashville, Tenn., U.S.A. 43 G2
Nasik 25 D6
Nassau 45 B9
Natal 47 E11
Natashquan 37 D13
Natashquan → 37 D13
Natchez 41 K9
Natchitoches 41 K8
Nathalia 32 C4
Natimuk 32 C3
Natuna Besar, Kepulauan 23 C2
Natuna Selatan, Kepulauan 23 C2
Natural Bridges △ 39 H8
Naturaliste, C. 32 D4
Naturaliste Plateau 30 G1
Nauru ■ 34 H8
Navajo Res. 39 H10
Navarra □ 13 A5
Navasota 41 K6
Naver → 10 C4
Navojoa 44 B3
Nawabshah 24 C5
Nawoiy 24 A5
Naxos 15 F11
Nazas → 44 B4
Nazca Ridge 35 K19
Naze, The 9 F9
Ndjamena 27 F8
Ndola 29 G5
Neagh, Lough 11 B5
Neah Bay 38 B1
Neales → 32 A2
Near Is. 36 D1
Neath 9 F4
Nebine Cr. → 32 A4
Nebraska □ 40 E5
Nebraska City 40 E7
Necedah 40 C9
Neches → 41 L8
Neckar → 16 D4
Needles 39 J6
Needles, The 9 G6
Neenah 42 C1
Neepawa 36 D10
Nefyn 8 E3
Negaunee 42 B2
Negril 44 a
Negro →, Argentina 48 E4
Negro →, Brazil 46 D7
Negros 23 C4
Nei Monggol Zizhiqu □ 21 B6
Neijiang 20 D5
Neilingding Dao 21 G10
Neillsville 40 C9
Neilton 38 C2
Neiva 46 C3
Neligh 40 D5
Nellore 25 D6
Nelson, Canada 36 E8
Nelson, N.Z. 33 J4
Nelson, U.K. 8 D5
Nelson, U.S.A. 39 J7
Nelson → 36 D10
Nelson, C. 32 C3
Nelson Lakes △ 33 J4
Nelspruit 29 K6
Nemunas → 18 D3
Nen Jiang → 21 B7
Nenagh 11 D3
Nendo 31 C12
Nene → 9 E8
Nenjiang 21 B7
Neodesha 41 G7
Neosho 41 G7
Neosho → 41 H7
Nepal ■ 25 C7
Nephi 38 G8
Nephin 11 B2
Nephin Beg Range 11 C2
Nerang 32 A5
Ness, L. 10 D4
Ness City 40 F5
Netherlands ■ 16 C2
Netherlands Antilles ☑ 45 E11
Nettilling L. 37 C12
Neuchâtel 12 C7
Neuchâtel, Lac de 12 C7
Neuse → 43 H7
Neusiedler See 16 E8
Neva → 7 E10
Nevada, Iowa, U.S.A. 40 D8
Nevada, Mo., U.S.A. 41 G7
Nevada □ 38 G5
Nevada City 38 G3
Nevers 12 C5
Nevertire 32 B4
Nevinnomyssk 17 B6
New → 42 F5
New Albany, Ind., U.S.A. 42 F3
New Albany, Miss., U.S.A. 41 H10
New Amsterdam 46 B7
New Angledool 32 A4
New Baltimore 42 D4
New Bedford 42 E10
New Bern 43 H7
New Boston 41 J7
New Braunfels 41 L5
New Brighton 33 K4
New Britain, Papua N. G. 30 B9
New Britain, U.S.A. 42 E9
New Britain Trench 30 J3
New Brunswick 42 E8
New Brunswick □ 37 E13
New Caledonia ☑ 31 E12
New Caledonia Trough 34 L8
New Castle, Ind., U.S.A. 42 F3
New Castle, Pa., U.S.A. 42 E5
New Delhi 25 C6
New England 40 B3
New England Ra. 32 B5
New Forest 9 G6
New Galloway 10 F4
New Georgia Is. 31 B10
New Glasgow 37 E13
New Guinea 30 B7
New Hampshire □ 42 D10
New Hampton 40 D8
New Haven 42 E9
New Hebrides = Vanuatu ■ 31 D12
New Iberia 41 K9
New Ireland 30 A9
New Jersey □ 42 E8
New Lexington 42 F4
New Liskeard 37 E12
New London, Conn., U.S.A. 42 E9
New London, Wis., U.S.A. 40 C10
New Madrid 41 G10
New Martinsville 42 F5
New Meadows 38 D5
New Mexico □ 39 J10
New Norfolk 32 D4
New Orleans 41 L9
New Philadelphia 42 E5
New Plymouth, N.Z. 33 H5
New Plymouth, U.S.A. 38 E5
New Port Richey 43 L4
New Providence 45 B9
New Quay 9 E3
New Radnor 9 E4
New Richmond 40 C8
New River Gorge △ 42 G5
New Roads 41 K9
New Rockford 40 B5
New Romney 9 G8
New Ross 11 D5
New Salem 40 B4
New Smyrna Beach 43 L5
New South Wales □ 32 B4
New Tecumseth 42 C6
New Town 40 B3
New Tredegar 9 F4
New Ulm 40 C7
New Westminster 38 B2
New York 42 E9
New York □ 42 D8
New Zealand ■ 33 J6
Newark, Del., U.S.A. 42 F8
Newark, N.J., U.S.A. 42 E8
Newark, N.Y., U.S.A. 42 D7
Newark, Ohio, U.S.A. 42 E4
Newark-on-Trent 8 D7
Newberg 38 D2
Newberry, Mich., U.S.A. 42 B3
Newberry, S.C., U.S.A. 43 H5
Newburgh 42 E8
Newbury 9 F6
Newburyport 43 D10
Newcastle, Australia 32 B5
Newcastle, S. Africa 29 K5
Newcastle, U.K. 11 B6
Newcastle, U.S.A. 40 D2
Newcastle Emlyn 9 E3
Newcastle-under-Lyme 8 D5
Newcastle-upon-Tyne 8 C6
Newcastle West 11 D2
Newell 40 C3
Newfoundland & Labrador □ 37 D14
Newhaven 9 G8
Newkirk 41 G6
Newlyn 9 G2
Newman 30 E2
Newmarket, Ireland 11 D2
Newmarket, U.K. 9 E8
Newnan 43 J3
Newport, Ireland 11 C2
Newport, I. of W., U.K. 9 G6
Newport, Newport, U.K. 9 F5
Newport, Ark., U.S.A. 41 H9
Newport, Ky., U.S.A. 42 F3
Newport, N.H., U.S.A. 42 D9
Newport, Oreg., U.S.A. 38 D1
Newport, R.I., U.S.A. 42 E10
Newport, Tenn., U.S.A. 43 H4
Newport, Vt., U.S.A. 42 C9
Newport, Wash., U.S.A. 38 B5
Newport Beach 39 K5
Newport News 42 G7
Newport Pagnell 9 E7
Newquay 9 G2
Newry 11 B5
Newton, Ill., U.S.A. 40 F10
Newton, Iowa, U.S.A. 40 E8
Newton, Kans., U.S.A. 41 F6
Newton, Mass., U.S.A. 42 D10
Newton, Miss., U.S.A. 41 J10
Newton, N.C., U.S.A. 43 H5
Newton, N.J., U.S.A. 42 E8
Newton, Tex., U.S.A. 41 K8
Newton Abbot 9 G4
Newton Aycliffe 8 C6
Newton Stewart 10 G4
Newtonmore 10 D4
Newtown 9 E4
Newtownabbey 11 B6
Newtownards 11 B6
Newtownstewart 11 B4
Neyshābūr 24 B4
Nezperce 38 C5
Ngapara 33 L3
Ngoring Hu 20 C4
Nha Trang 23 B2
Nhill 32 C3
Niagara Falls, Canada 37 E12
Niagara Falls, U.S.A. 42 D6
Niamey 26 F6
Nias 23 C1
Nicaragua ■ 44 E7
Nicaragua, L. de 44 E7
Nice 12 E7
Niceville 43 K2
Nicholasville 42 G3
Nicobar Is. 25 E8
Nicosia 17 C4
Nicoya, Pen. de 44 F7
Nidd → 8 D6
Niedersachsen □ 16 B4
Niemen = Nemunas → 18 D3
Niger ■ 26 E7
Niger → 26 G7
Nigeria ■ 26 G7
Nightcaps 33 L2
Niigata 22 E6
Nijmegen 16 C2
Nikiniki 23 D4
Nikolayevsk-na-Amur 19 D15
Nikumaroro 31 A16
Nikunau 31 A14
Nîl, Nahr en → 27 B12
Nîl el Abyad → 27 E12
Nîl el Azraq → 27 E12
Nile = Nîl, Nahr en → 27 B12
Niles 42 E2
Nîmes 12 E6
Nimmitabel 32 C4
Nindigully 32 A4
Ninepin Group 21 G11
Ningbo 21 D7
Ningjing Shan 20 D4
Ningxia Huizu Zizhiqu □ 20 C5
Niobrara 40 D6
Niobrara → 40 D6
Niort 12 C3
Nipawin 36 D9
Nipigon, L. 37 E11
Nipissing, L. 37 E12
Nipomo 39 J3
Niš 15 C9
Nishinomiya 22 F4
Niterói 47 H10
Nith → 10 F5
Nitra 16 D9
Nitra → 16 E9
Niua Group 31 D16
Niuafo'ou 33 B11
Niuatoputapu 31 D16
Niue 31 D17
Niulakita 31 C14
Niutao 31 B14
Nivernais 12 C5
Nixa 41 G8
Nixon 41 L6
Nizamabad 25 D6
Nizhnevartovsk 18 C8
Nizhniy Novgorod 18 D5
Nizhniy Tagil 18 D6
Nízké Tatry 16 D9
Nizwá 24 C4
Nkongsamba 28 D1
Nobeoka 22 G2
Noblesville 42 E3
Nocona 41 J6
Nogales, Mexico 44 A2
Nogales, U.S.A. 39 L8
Noirmoutier, Î. de 12 C2
Nome 36 C3
Nord-Ostsee-Kanal 16 A4
Nordfriesische Inseln 16 A4
Nordkapp 7 C9
Nordrhein-Westfalen □ 16 C3
Nordvik 19 B12
Nore → 11 D4
Norfolk, Canada 42 D5
Norfolk, Nebr., U.S.A. 40 D6
Norfolk, Va., U.S.A. 42 G7
Norfolk □ 9 E8
Norfolk Basin 31 G13
Norfolk I. 31 F12
Norfolk Ridge 34 K8
Norfork L. 41 G8
Norilsk 19 C9
Normal 40 E10
Norman 41 H6
Norman Wells 36 C7
Normandie 12 B4
Normanton 30 D7
Norristown 42 E8
Norrköping 7 F7
Norrland 7 E7
Norseman 30 G3
North, C. 37 E13
North Adams 42 D9
North America 2 B5
North Atlantic Ocean 2 C8
North Augusta 43 J5
North Australian Basin 30 C2
North Ayrshire □ 10 F4
North Battleford 36 D9
North Bay 37 E12
North Bend 38 E1
North Berwick 10 E6
North C. 33 F4
North Canadian → 41 H7
North Cape = Nordkapp 7 C9
North Carolina □ 43 H6
North Cascades △ 38 B3
North Channel 10 F3
North Charleston 43 J6
North Chicago 42 D2
North Dakota □ 40 B5
North Downs 9 F8
North East Lincolnshire □ 8 D7
North Esk → 10 E6
North European Plain 3 B12
North Foreland 9 F9
North Fork Grand → 40 C3
North Fork Red → 41 H5
North I. 33 H5
North Korea ■ 21 C7
North Lanarkshire □ 10 F5
North Las Vegas 39 H6
North Lincolnshire □ 8 D7
North Little Rock 41 H8
North Loup → 40 E5
North Magnetic Pole 37 B9
North Mankato 40 C8
North Minch 10 C3
North Myrtle Beach 43 J6
North Palisade 39 H4
North Platte 40 E4
North Platte → 40 E4
North Pole 6 A
North Powder 38 D5
North Pt. 45 g
North Ronaldsay 10 B6
North Saskatchewan → 36 D9
North Sea 3 B10
North Somerset □ 9 F5
North Taranaki Bight 33 H5
North Thompson → 36 D7
North Tonawanda 42 D6
North Tyne → 8 B5
North Uist 10 D1
North Vernon 42 F3
North Walsham 8 E9
North West C. 30 E1
North West Frontier □ 25 B6
North West Highlands 10 D4
North West River 37 D13
North Wildwood 42 F8
North York Moors 8 C7
North York Moors △ 8 C7
North Yorkshire □ 8 C6
Northallerton 8 C6
Northam 30 G2
Northampton, U.K. 9 E7
Northampton, U.S.A. 42 D9
Northamptonshire □ 9 E7
Northeast Pacific Basin 35 D13
Northern Ireland □ 11 B5
Northern Marianas ☑ 34 F6
Northern Territory □ 30 E5
Northfield 40 C8
Northland □ 33 F4
Northome 40 B7
Northport, Ala., U.S.A. 43 J2
Northport, Wash., U.S.A. 38 B5
Northumberland □ 8 B6
Northumberland, C. 32 C3
Northumberland Str. 37 E13
Northwest Pacific Basin 34 D8
Northwest Territories □ 36 C8
Northwich 8 D5
Northwood, Iowa, U.S.A. 40 D8
Northwood, N. Dak., U.S.A. 40 B6
Norton 40 F5
Norton Sd. 36 C3
Norwalk, Conn., U.S.A. 42 E9
Norwalk, Iowa, U.S.A. 40 E8
Norwalk, Ohio, U.S.A. 42 E4
Norway, Maine, U.S.A. 43 C10
Norway, Mich., U.S.A. 42 C2
Norway ■ 7 E6
Norway House 36 D10
Norwegian B. 37 B9
Norwegian Sea 4 A9
Norwich, U.K. 9 E9
Norwich, Conn., U.S.A. 42 E9
Norwich, N.Y., U.S.A. 42 D8
Noss Hd. 10 C5
Nossob → 29 K4
Notre Dame B. 37 E14
Nottaway → 37 D12
Nottingham 8 E6
Nottingham I. 37 C12
Nottinghamshire □ 8 D6
Nottoway → 42 G7
Nouâdhibou 26 D2
Nouâdhibou, Ras 26 D2
Nouakchott 26 E2
Nouméa 31 E12
Nouvelle Amsterdam, Î. 5 F14
Nova Friburgo 47 H10
Nova Iguaçu 48 A8
Nova Scotia □ 37 E13
Novara 12 D8
Novaya Zemlya 18 B6
Novgorod 18 D4
Novi Sad 15 B8
Novocherkassk 17 A6
Novokuznetsk 18 D9
Novomoskovsk 18 D4
Novorossiysk 17 B5
Novoshakhtinsk 17 A5
Novosibirsk 18 D9
Novosibirskiye Ostrova 19 B15
Novotroitsk 18 D6
Nowata 41 G7
Nowra 32 B5
Nu Jiang → 20 D4
Nu Shan 20 D4
Nûbîya, Es Sahrâ en 27 D12
Nueces → 41 M6
Nueltin L. 36 C10
Nueva Rosita 44 B4
Nuevitas 45 C9
Nuevo Laredo 44 B5
Nugget Pt. 33 M2
Nuhaka 33 H6
Nui 31 B14
Nukey Bluff 32 B2
Nuku Hiva 35 H13
Nuku'alofa 33 E12
Nukulaelae 31 B14
Nukunonu 31 B16
Nukus 18 E6
Nullarbor Plain 30 G4
Numalla, L. 32 A3
Numazu 22 F6
Numurkah 32 C4
Nunap Isua 6 D4
Nunavut □ 37 C11
Nuneaton 9 E6
Nunivak I. 36 D3
Nuremberg = Nürnberg 16 D5
Nuriootpa 32 B2
Nürnberg 16 D5
Nushki 24 C5
Nuuk 6 C4
Nuweveldberge 29 L4
Nuyts Arch. 32 B1
Nyainqentanglha Shan 20 D4
Nyasa, L. = Malawi, L. 29 G6
Nymagee 32 B4
Nymboida △ 32 A5
Nyngan 32 B4
Nysa 16 C8
Nyssa 38 E5

O

Oa, Mull of 10 F2
Oacoma 40 D5
Oahe, L. 40 C4
Oahe Dam 40 C4
Oak Harbor 38 B2
Oak Hill 42 G5
Oak Island 43 J6
Oak Ridge 43 G3
Oakdale 41 K8
Oakes 40 B5
Oakesdale 38 C5
Oakey 32 A5
Oakham 9 E7
Oakland 39 H2
Oakley, Idaho, U.S.A. 38 E7
Oakley, Kans., U.S.A. 40 F4
Oakridge 38 E2
Oamaru 33 L3
Oates Land 6 D15
Oatlands 32 D4
Oaxaca 44 D5
Ob → 18 C7
Oba 37 E11
Oban 10 E3
Obbia 24 E3
Oberhausen 16 C3
Oberlin, Kans., U.S.A. 40 F4
Oberlin, La., U.S.A. 41 K8
Oberon 32 B4
Obi 23 D4
Obihiro 22 B8
Obskaya Guba 18 C8
Ocala 43 L4
Occidental, Cordillera 46 C3
Ocean City, Md., U.S.A. 42 F8
Ocean City, N.J., U.S.A. 42 F8
Ocean Park 38 C1
Oceanside 39 K5
Ochil Hills 10 E5
Ocho Rios 44 a
Ocilla 43 K4
Ocmulgee → 43 K4
Oconee → 43 K4
Oconomowoc 40 D10
Oconto 42 C2
Oconto Falls 42 C1
Odawara 22 F6
Odense 7 F6
Oder → 16 B7
Odesa 17 A4
Odessa, Tex., U.S.A. 41 K3
Odessa, Wash., U.S.A. 38 C4
O'Donnell 41 J4
Oelrichs 40 D3
Oelwein 40 D9
Oeno I. 35 K14
Offa 26 G6
Offaly □ 11 C4
Offenbach 16 C4
Ogaden 24 E3
Ōgaki 22 F5
Ogallala 40 E4
Ogasawara Gunto 34 E6
Ogbomosho 26 G6
Ogden 38 F7
Ogdensburg 42 C8
Ogeechee → 43 K5
Ogooué → 28 E1
Ohai 33 L2
Ohakune 33 H5
Ohau, L. 33 L2
Ohio □ 42 E3
Ohio → 42 G1
Ohře → 16 C7
Ohridsko Jezero 15 D9
Oil City 42 E6
Oise → 12 B5
Oistins 45 g
Oistins B. 45 g
Ōita 22 G2
Ojai 39 J4
Ojos del Salado, Cerro 48 B3
Oka → 18 D5
Okahandja 29 J3
Okanogan 38 B4
Okanogan → 38 B4
Okavango Delta 29 H4
Okayama 22 F3
Okazaki 22 F5
Okeechobee 43 M5
Okeechobee, L. 43 M5
Okefenokee △ 43 K4
Okefenokee Swamp 43 K4
Okehampton 9 G4
Okha 19 D15
Okhotsk 19 D15
Okhotsk, Sea of 19 D15
Okinawa-Jima 21 D7
Oklahoma □ 41 H6
Oklahoma City 41 H6
Okmulgee 41 H7
Okolona 41 J10
Oktyabrskoy Revolyutsii, Ostrov 19 B10
Okuru 33 K2
Ola 41 H8
Olancha 39 H4
Öland 7 F7
Olary 32 B3

P

Q

R

S

St. Helier 9 H5
St-Hyacinthe 37 E12
St. Ignace 42 C3
St. Ignatius 38 C6
St. Ives, *Cambs., U.K.* 9 E7
St. Ives, *Corn., U.K.* 9 G2
St. James 40 D7
St-Jean, L. 37 E12
St. John, *Canada* 37 E13
St. John, *U.S.A.* 41 G5
St. John → 43 C12
St. John I. 45 e
St. John's, *Antigua & B.* 45 D12
St. John's, *Canada* 37 E14
St. Johns, *Ariz., U.S.A.* 39 J9
St. Johns, *Mich., U.S.A.* 42 D3
St. Johns → 43 K5
St. John's Pt. 11 B3
St. Johnsbury 42 C9
St-Joseph 44 c
St. Joseph, *La., U.S.A.* 41 K9
St. Joseph, *Mo., U.S.A.* 40 F7
St. Joseph → 42 D2
St. Joseph, L. 37 D10
St. Kitts & Nevis ■ 45 D12
St. Lawrence → 37 E13
St. Lawrence, Gulf of 37 E13
St. Lawrence I. 36 C2
St-Lô 12 B3
St-Louis 44 b
St. Louis, *Senegal* 26 E2
St. Louis, *U.S.A.* 40 F9
St. Louis → 40 B8
St. Lucia ■ 45 f
St. Lucia, L. 29 K6
St. Magnus B. 10 A7
St-Malo 12 B2
St-Marc 45 D10
St. Maries 38 C5
St-Martin ☑ 45 D12
St-Martin, C. 44 c
St. Martins 45 g
St. Mary Pk. 32 B2
St. Marys, *Australia* 32 D4
St. Mary's, *Corn., U.K.* 9 H1
St. Mary's, *Orkney, U.K.* 10 C6
St. Marys, *Ga., U.S.A.* 43 K5
St. Marys, *Pa., U.S.A.* 42 E6
St. Matthew I. 36 C2
St. Mawes 9 G2
St-Nazaire 12 C2
St. Neots 9 E7
St-Omer 12 A5
St. Paul, *Minn., U.S.A.* 40 C8
St. Paul, *Nebr., U.S.A.* 40 E5
St. Paul, I. 5 F14
St. Peter 40 C8
St. Peter Port 9 H5
St. Petersburg = Sankt-Peterburg 18 D4
St. Petersburg 43 M4
St-Pierre 44 c
St-Pierre-et-Miquelon ☑ 37 E14
St-Quentin 12 B5
St. Regis 38 C6
St. Simons I. 43 K5
St. Simons Island 43 K5
St. Thomas I. 45 e
St-Tropez 12 E7
St. Vincent, G. 32 C2
St. Vincent & the Grenadines ■ 45 E12
Ste-Anne 44 b
Ste. Genevieve 40 G9
Ste-Marie 44 c
Ste-Rose 44 b
Saintes 12 D3
Saintes, Îs. des 44 b
Saintfield 11 B6
Saintonge 12 D3
Saipan 34 F6
Sakakawea, L. 40 B4
Sakarya 17 B4
Sakata 22 D6
Sakha □ 19 C13
Sakhalin 19 D15
Sala 7 F7
Sala-y-Gómez 35 K17
Sala y Gómez Ridge 35 K18
Salada, L. 39 K6
Salado →, *Argentina* 48 C4
Salado →, *Mexico* 41 M5
Salālah 24 D4
Salamanca, *Spain* 13 B3
Salamanca, *U.S.A.* 42 D6
Salayar 23 D4
Salcombe 9 G4
Saldanha 29 L3
Sale, *Australia* 32 C4
Sale, *U.K.* 8 D5
Salekhard 18 C7
Salem, *India* 25 D6
Salem, *Ill., U.S.A.* 42 F1
Salem, *Ind., U.S.A.* 42 F2
Salem, *Mass., U.S.A.* 42 D10
Salem, *Mo., U.S.A.* 41 G9
Salem, *N.J., U.S.A.* 42 F8
Salem, *Ohio, U.S.A.* 42 E5
Salem, *Oreg., U.S.A.* 38 D2
Salem, *S. Dak., U.S.A.* 40 D6
Salem, *Va., U.S.A.* 42 G5
Salerno 14 D6
Salford 8 D5
Salina, *Kans., U.S.A.* 40 F6
Salina, *Utah, U.S.A.* 39 G8
Salina Cruz 44 D5
Salinas 39 H3
Salinas → 39 H3
Salinas Grandes 48 C4
Salinas Pueblo Missions △ 39 J10
Saline →, *Ark., U.S.A.* 41 J8
Saline →, *Kans., U.S.A.* 40 F6
Salisbury, *U.K.* 9 F6
Salisbury, *Md., U.S.A.* 42 F8
Salisbury, *N.C., U.S.A.* 43 H5
Salisbury I. 37 C12
Salisbury Plain 9 F6
Sallisaw 41 H7
Salluit 37 C12
Salmon 38 D7
Salmon → 38 D5
Salmon Arm 36 D8
Salmon River Mts. 38 D6
Salome 39 K7
Salon-de-Provence 12 E6
Salt → 39 K7
Salt Fork Red → 41 H5
Salt L. 32 B3
Salt Lake City 38 F8
Salta 48 A3
Saltash 9 G3
Saltburn by the Sea 8 C7
Saltcoats 10 F4
Saltee Is. 11 D5
Saltillo 44 B4
Salton Sea 39 K6
Saluda → 43 J5
Salvador 47 F11
Salvador, El ■ 44 E7
Salvador, L. 41 L9
Salween → 25 D8
Salzburg 16 E6
Salzgitter 16 B5
Sam Rayburn Res. 41 K7
Samar 23 B4
Samara 18 D6
Samarinda 23 D3
Samarqand 18 F7
Samoa ■ 33 B13
Samoan Is. 33 A13
Samos 15 F12
Samsun 17 B5
Samut Prakan 23 B2
San Agustin, C. 23 C4
San Ambrosio 35 K20
San Andreas 38 G3
San Andrés, I. de 45 E8
San Andres Mts. 39 K10
San Andrés Tuxtla 44 D5
San Angelo 41 K4
San Antonio, *N. Mex., U.S.A.* 39 K10
San Antonio, *Tex., U.S.A.* 41 L5
San Antonio → 41 L6
San Augustine 41 K7
San Benito 41 M6
San Bernardino 39 J5
San Bernardino Str. 23 B4
San Blas, C. 43 L3
San Carlos, *Phil.* 23 B4
San Carlos, *U.S.A.* 39 K8
San Carlos L. 39 K8
San Clemente 39 K5
San Clemente I. 39 K4
San Cristóbal, *Solomon Is.* 31 C11
San Cristóbal, *Venezuela* 46 B4
San Cristóbal de las Casas 44 D6
San Diego, *Calif., U.S.A.* 39 K5
San Diego, *Tex., U.S.A.* 41 M5
San Félix 35 K20
San Francisco 39 H2
San Francisco → 39 K9
San Francisco de Macorís 45 D10
San German 45 d
San Gorgonio Mt. 39 J5
San Gottardo, P. del 12 C8
San Joaquin → 39 G3
San Jon 41 H3
San Jorge, G. 48 F3
San José, *Costa Rica* 45 F8
San Jose, *Phil.* 23 B4
San Jose, *U.S.A.* 39 H3
San Jose → 39 J10
San Juan, *Argentina* 48 C3
San Juan, *Dom. Rep.* 45 D10
San Juan, *Puerto Rico* 45 d
San Juan →, *Nic.* 45 E8
San Juan →, *U.S.A.* 39 H8
San Juan Mts. 39 H10
San Lucas, C. 44 C3
San Luis, *Ariz., U.S.A.* 39 K6
San Luis, *Colo., U.S.A.* 39 H11
San Luis Obispo 39 J3
San Luis Potosí 44 C4
San Manuel 39 K8
San Marcos 41 L6
San Marino ■ 14 C5
San Mateo 39 H2
San Matías, G. 48 E4
San Miguel, *El Salv.* 44 E7
San Miguel, *U.S.A.* 39 J3
San Miguel de Tucumán 48 B3
San Miguel I. 39 J3
San Nicolas I. 39 K4
San Pedro → 39 K8
San Pedro de las Colonias 44 B4
San Pedro de Macorís 45 D11
San Pedro Sula 44 D7
San Rafael, *Calif., U.S.A.* 38 H2
San Rafael, *N. Mex., U.S.A.* 39 J10
San Remo 12 E7
San Saba 41 K5
San Salvador 44 E7
San Salvador de Jujuy 48 A4
San Salvador I. 45 C10
San Sebastián 45 d
San Simon 39 K9
Sana' 24 D3
Sanandaj 24 B3
Sancti Spíritus 45 C9
Sancy, Puy de 12 D5
Sand Hills 40 D4
Sand Springs 41 G6
Sandakan 23 C3
Sanday 10 B6
Sanders 39 J9
Sanderson 41 K3
Sandersville 43 J4
Sandpoint 38 B5
Sandray 10 E1
Sandringham 8 E8
Sandusky, *Mich., U.S.A.* 42 D4
Sandusky, *Ohio, U.S.A.* 42 E4
Sandy 38 F8
Sandy C. 32 D3
Sandy Cr. → 38 F9
Sandy L. 36 D10
Sanford, *Fla., U.S.A.* 43 L5
Sanford, *Maine, U.S.A.* 43 D10
Sanford, *N.C., U.S.A.* 43 H6
Sanford, Mt. 36 C5
Sanger 39 H4
Sangihe, Pulau 23 C4
Sangkulirang 23 C3
Sangli 25 D6
Sangre de Cristo Mts. 41 G2
Sanibel 43 M4
Sanikiluaq 37 D12
Sanirajak 37 C11
Sankt Gallen 12 C8
Sankt Moritz 12 C8
Sankt-Peterburg 18 D4
Sankuru → 28 E4
Sanliurfa 17 C5
Sanmenxia 21 C6
Sanming 21 D6
Sanquhar 10 F5
Santa Ana, *El Salv.* 44 E7
Santa Ana, *U.S.A.* 39 K5
Santa Barbara 39 J4
Santa Catalina, Gulf of 39 K5
Santa Catalina I. 39 K4
Santa Clara, *Cuba* 45 C9
Santa Clara, *U.S.A.* 39 H7
Santa Clarita 39 J4
Santa Coloma de Gramenet 13 B7
Santa Cruz, *Bolivia* 46 G6
Santa Cruz, *U.S.A.* 39 H2
Santa Cruz de Tenerife 26 C2
Santa Cruz I. 39 K4
Santa Cruz Is. 31 C12
Santa Cruz Mts. 44 a
Santa Fé, *Argentina* 48 C4
Santa Fe, *U.S.A.* 39 J11
Santa Inés, I. 48 G2
Santa Isabel 31 B10
Santa Lucia Range 39 J3
Santa Maria, *Brazil* 48 B6
Santa Maria, *U.S.A.* 39 J3
Santa María → 44 A3
Santa Marta 46 A4
Santa Marta, Sierra Nevada de 46 A4
Santa Monica 39 K4
Santa Rosa, *Calif., U.S.A.* 38 G2
Santa Rosa, *N. Mex., U.S.A.* 41 H2
Santa Rosa and San Jacinto Mts. △ 39 K5
Santa Rosa I., *Calif., U.S.A.* 39 K3
Santa Rosa I., *Fla., U.S.A.* 43 K2
Santa Rosa Range 38 F5
Santai 20 C5
Santander 13 A4
Santaquin 38 G8
Santarém, *Brazil* 47 D8
Santarém, *Portugal* 13 C1
Santee → 43 J6
Santiago 48 C2
Santiago → 46 D3
Santiago de Compostela 13 A1
Santiago de Cuba 45 D9
Santiago de los Caballeros 45 D10
Santiago del Estero 48 B4
Santo Domingo 45 D11
Santo Domingo Pueblo 39 J10
Santorini 15 F11
Santos 48 A7
Sanxiang 21 G9
Sanya 23 B2
São Bernardo do Campo 48 A7
São Francisco → 47 F11
São José do Rio Prêto 47 H9
São Lourenço 47 H9
São Luís 47 D10
São Paulo 48 A7
São Roque, C. de 47 E11
São Tomé & Príncipe ■ 4 D10
Saône → 12 D6
Sapelo I. 43 K5
Sapporo 22 B7
Sapulpa 41 H6
Saqqez 24 B3
Saraburi 23 B2
Sarajevo 15 C8
Saran, Gunung 23 D3
Saranac Lakes 42 C8
Sarangani B. 23 C4
Saransk 18 D5
Sarapul 18 D6
Sarasota 43 M4
Saratoga 38 F10
Saratoga Springs 42 D9
Saratov 18 D5
Sarawak □ 23 C3
Sardegna □ 14 D3
Sardinia = Sardegna □ 14 D3
Sargasso Sea 35 D20
Sargodha 25 B6
Sārī 24 B4
Sarita 41 M6
Sark 9 H5
Sarlat-la-Canéda 12 D4
Sarnia 37 E11
Sarreguemines 12 B7
Sarthe → 12 C3
Sasebo 22 G1
Saskatchewan □ 36 D9
Saskatchewan → 36 D9
Saskatoon 36 D9
Sássari 14 D3
Sassnitz 16 A6
Satilla → 43 K5
Satpura Ra. 25 C6
Satu Mare 17 A2
Saudi Arabia ■ 24 C3
Saugerties 42 D9
Sauk Centre 40 C7
Sauk Rapids 40 C7
Sault Ste. Marie, *Canada* 37 E11
Sault Ste. Marie, *U.S.A.* 42 B3
Saumur 12 C3
Saunders, C. 33 L3
Sava → 15 B9
Savage 40 B2
Savage River 32 D4
Savai'i 33 A12
Savanna 40 D9
Savanna-la-Mar 44 a
Savannah, *Ga., U.S.A.* 43 J5
Savannah, *Mo., U.S.A.* 40 F7
Savannah, *Tenn., U.S.A.* 43 H1
Savannah → 43 J5
Savannakhet 23 B2
Savoie □ 12 D7
Savona 12 D8
Sawatch Range 39 G10
Sawel Mt. 11 B4
Sawtooth △ 38 D6
Sawtooth Range 38 E6
Sawu 23 E4
Sawu Sea 23 D4
Saxmundham 9 E9
Saxony = Sachsen □ 16 C6
Sayan, Zapadnyy 19 D10
Saydā 17 D5
Sayḥūt 24 D4
Saynshand 21 B6
Sayre, *Okla., U.S.A.* 41 H5
Sayre, *Pa., U.S.A.* 42 E7
Sázava → 16 D7
Scafell Pike 8 C4
Scalloway 10 A7
Scalpay 10 D3
Scandinavia 7 E6
Scapa Flow 10 C5
Scarba 10 E3
Scarborough 8 C7
Scariff I. 11 E1
Scarp 10 C1
Scebeli → 24 E3
Scebeli, Wabi → 24 E3
Schaffhausen 12 C8
Schefferville = Kawawachikamach 37 D13
Schelde → 16 C2
Schell Creek Ra. 38 G6
Schenectady 42 D9
Schleswig 16 A4
Schleswig-Holstein □ 16 A4
Schœlcher 44 c
Schouten I. 32 D4
Schurz 38 G4
Schuyler 40 E6
Schwäbische Alb 16 D4
Schwaner, Pegunungan 23 D3
Schwarzwald 16 D4
Schwerin 16 B5
Schwyz 12 C8
Scilly, Isles of 9 H1
Scioto → 42 F4
Scobey 40 A2
Scone, *Australia* 32 B5
Scone, *U.K.* 10 E5
Scotia 38 F1
Scotland □ 10 E5
Scott City 40 F4
Scottish Borders □ 10 F6
Scottsbluff 40 E3
Scottsboro 43 H3
Scottsburg 42 F3
Scottsdale, *Australia* 32 D4
Scottsdale, *U.S.A.* 39 K7
Scottsville 43 G2
Scottville 42 D2
Scranton 42 E8
Scunthorpe 8 D7
Seaford, *U.K.* 9 G8
Seaford, *U.S.A.* 42 F8
Seaforth, L. 10 D2
Seagraves 41 J3
Seaham 8 C6
Seal → 36 D10
Sealy 41 L6
Searchlight 39 J6
Searcy 41 H9
Searles L. 39 J5
Seascale 8 C4
Seaside, *Calif., U.S.A.* 39 G3
Seaside, *Oreg., U.S.A.* 38 D2
Seaspray 32 C4
Seattle 38 C2
Sebastián Vizcaíno, B. 44 B2
Sebewaing 42 D4
Sebring 43 M5
Sebuku, Teluk 23 C3
Secretary I. 33 L1
Security 40 F2
Sedalia 40 F8
Sedan, *France* 12 B6
Sedan, *U.S.A.* 41 G6
Sedbergh 8 C5
Seddon 33 J5
Seddonville 33 J4
Sedona 39 J8
Sedro-Woolley 38 B2
Segovia 13 B3
Seguin 41 L6
Seil 10 E3
Seiling 41 G5
Seine → 12 B4
Sekondi-Takoradi 26 H5
Selah 38 C3
Selaru 23 D5
Selby, *U.K.* 8 D6
Selby, *U.S.A.* 40 C4
Selden 40 F4
Selenge Mörön → 20 A5
Seligman 39 J7
Selkirk, *Canada* 36 D10
Selkirk, *U.K.* 10 F6
Selkirk Mts. 36 D8
Sellafield 8 C4
Sells 39 L8
Selma, *Ala., U.S.A.* 43 J2
Selma, *Calif., U.S.A.* 39 H4
Selma, *N.C., U.S.A.* 43 H6
Selmer 43 H1
Selsey Bill 9 G7
Selvas 46 E5
Selwyn L. 36 D9
Selwyn Mts. 36 C6
Semarang 23 D3
Semey 18 D9
Seminoe Res. 38 F10
Seminole, *Okla., U.S.A.* 41 H6
Seminole, *Tex., U.S.A.* 41 J3
Seminole Draw → 41 J3
Senatobia 41 H10
Sendai 22 D7
Seneca 43 H4
Seneca Falls 42 D7
Seneca L. 42 D7
Senegal ■ 26 F3
Sénégal → 26 E2
Senja 7 D7
Senkaku-Shotō 21 D7
Senlis 12 B5
Sens 12 B5
Sentinel 39 K7
Seoul 21 C7
Sept-Îles 37 D13
Sequim 38 B2
Sequoia △ 39 H4
Seram 23 D4
Seram Sea 23 D4
Serang 23 D2
Serbia □ 15 C9
Serbia & Montenegro ■ 15 B9
Seremban 23 C2
Serov 18 D7
Serowe 29 J5
Serpukhov 18 D4
Sète 12 E5
Sétif 26 A7
Settat 26 B4
Settle 8 C5
Settlement, The 45 e
Setúbal 13 C1
Seul, Lac 36 D10
Sevastopol 17 B4
Severn →, *Canada* 37 D11
Severn →, *U.K.* 9 F5
Severnaya Zemlya 19 B10
Severodvinsk 18 C4
Sevier → 39 G7
Sevier Desert 38 G7
Sevier L. 38 G7
Sevilla 13 D2
Seward, *Alaska, U.S.A.* 36 C5
Seward, *Nebr., U.S.A.* 40 E6
Seward Peninsula 36 C3
Seychelles ■ 5 E13
Seymour, *Australia* 32 C4
Seymour, *Ind., U.S.A.* 42 F3
Seymour, *Tex., U.S.A.* 41 J5
Sfântu Gheorghe 15 B11
Sfax 27 B8
Sha Tau Kok 21 F11
Sha Tin 21 G11
Shaanxi □ 21 C5
Shache 20 C2
Shafter 39 J4
Shaftesbury 9 F5
Shahjahanpur 25 C6
Shajing 21 F10
Shakhty 17 A6
Shaki 26 G6
Shaluli Shan 20 C4
Shām, Bādiyat ash 24 B3
Shamokin 42 E7
Shamrock 41 H4
Shan □ 25 C8
Shandong □ 21 C6
Shanghai 21 C7
Shangqiu 21 C6
Shangrao 21 D6
Shangshui 21 C6
Shanklin 9 G6
Shannon 33 J5
Shannon → 11 D2
Shannon (SNN) 11 D3
Shannon, Mouth of the 11 D2
Shannonbridge 11 C3
Shantar, Ostrov Bolshoy 19 D14
Shantou 21 D6
Shanxi □ 21 C6
Shaoguan 21 D6
Shaoxing 21 D7
Shaoyang 21 D6
Shap 8 C5
Shapinsay 10 B6
Shaqrā' 24 D3
Shark B. 30 F1
Sharm el Sheikh 24 C2
Sharon 42 E5
Sharon Springs 40 F4
Shashi 21 C6
Shasta, Mt. 38 F2
Shasta L. 38 F2
Shatsky Rise 34 D7
Shatt al Arab 24 C3
Shawano 42 C1
Shawinigan 37 E12
Shawnee 41 H6
Sheberghān 24 B5
Sheboygan 42 D2
Sheelin, L. 11 C4
Sheep Haven 11 A4
Sheerness 9 F8
Sheffield, *U.K.* 8 D6
Sheffield, *U.S.A.* 43 H2
Shekou 21 G10
Shelby, *Mich., U.S.A.* 42 D2
Shelby, *Miss., U.S.A.* 41 J9
Shelby, *Mont., U.S.A.* 38 B8
Shelby, *N.C., U.S.A.* 43 H5
Shelbyville, *Ill., U.S.A.* 40 F10
Shelbyville, *Ind., U.S.A.* 42 F3
Shelbyville, *Ky., U.S.A.* 42 F3
Shelbyville, *Tenn., U.S.A.* 43 H2
Sheldon 40 D7
Shelikhova, Zaliv 19 D16
Shellharbour 32 B5
Shelton 38 C2
Shenandoah, *Iowa, U.S.A.* 40 E7
Shenandoah, *Pa., U.S.A.* 42 E7
Shenandoah, *Va., U.S.A.* 42 F6
Shenandoah △ 42 F6
Shenandoah → 42 F7
Shenyang 21 B7
Shenzhen 21 F10
Shenzhen (SZX) 21 F10
Shenzhen Shuiku 21 F11
Shenzhen Wan 21 G10
Shepherd Is. 31 D12
Shepparton 32 C4
Sheppey, I. of 9 F8
Shepton Mallet 9 F5
Sherborne 9 G5
Sherbrooke 37 E12
Sheridan, *Ark., U.S.A.* 41 H8
Sheridan, *Wyo., U.S.A.* 38 D10
Sheringham 8 E9
Sherkin I. 11 E2
Sherman 41 J6
Sherwood Forest 8 D6
Shetland Is. 10 A7
Sheung Shui 21 F11
Sheyenne → 40 B6
Shibām 24 D3
Shiel, L. 10 E3
Shihezi 20 B3
Shijiazhuang 21 C6
Shikarpur 24 C5
Shikoku □ 22 G3
Shiliguri 25 C7
Shillelagh 11 D5
Shimoga 25 D6
Shimonoseki 22 G2
Shin, L. 10 C4
Shiping 20 D5
Shippensburg 42 E7
Shiprock 39 H9
Shīrāz 24 C4
Shire → 29 H7
Shirshov Ridge 34 B8
Shiyan 21 F10
Shiyan Shuiku 21 F10
Shizuoka 22 F6
Shkodër 15 C8
Shoreham by Sea 9 G7
Shortland Is. 31 B10
Shoshone 38 E6
Shoshone L. 38 D8
Shoshone Mts. 38 G5
Shoshoni 38 E9
Show Low 39 J9
Shreveport 41 J8
Shrewsbury 9 E5
Shropshire □ 9 E5
Shuangliao 21 B7
Shuangyashan 21 B8
Shule 20 C2
Shumagin Is. 36 D4
Shwebo 25 C8
Shymkent 18 E7
Sialkot 25 B6
Siam = Thailand ■ 23 B2
Šiauliai 7 F8
Siberia 3 A15
Siberut 23 D1
Sibi 24 C5
Sibiu 15 B11
Sibley 40 D7
Sibolga 23 C1
Sibsagar 25 C8
Sibu 23 C3
Sibuyan Sea 23 B4
Siccus → 32 B2
Sichuan □ 20 C5
Sicilia 14 F6
Sidi-bel-Abbès 26 A5
Sidlaw Hills 10 E5
Sidmouth 9 G4
Sidney, *Mont., U.S.A.* 40 B2
Sidney, *N.Y., U.S.A.* 42 D8
Sidney, *Nebr., U.S.A.* 40 E3
Sidney, *Ohio, U.S.A.* 42 E3
Sidney Lanier, L. 43 H4
Siegen 16 C4
Siena 14 C4
Sierra Blanca 39 L11
Sierra Blanca Peak 39 K11
Sierra Leone ■ 26 G3
Sierra Madre Occidental 44 B3
Sierra Madre Oriental 44 C5
Sierra Nevada, *Spain* 13 D4
Sierra Nevada, *U.S.A.* 38 G3
Sierra Vista 39 L8
Sikeston 41 G10
Sikhote Alin, Khrebet 19 E14
Sikkim □ 25 C7
Silchar 25 C8
Siler City 43 H6
Silesia = Śląsk 16 C8
Siling Co 20 C3
Silloth 8 C4
Siloam Springs 41 G7
Silsbee 41 K7
Silver City 39 K9
Silver Cr. → 38 E4
Silver Lake 38 E3
Silvermine Mts. 11 D3
Silverton, *Colo., U.S.A.* 39 H10
Silverton, *Tex., U.S.A.* 41 H4
Silvies → 38 E4
Simao 25 C9
Simbirsk 18 D5
Simeulue 23 C1
Simferopol 17 B4
Simi Valley 39 J4
Simplonpass 12 C8
Simpson Desert 30 F6
Simpson Pen. 37 C11
Sinai, Mt. = Mûsa, Gebel 27 C12
Sinclair 38 F10
Sinclair's B. 10 C5
Sindh □ 25 C5
Singapore ■ 23 C2
Singaraja 23 D3
Singkawang 23 C2
Singleton 32 B5
Sinkiang = Xinjiang Uygur Zizhiqu □ 20 C3
Sinton 41 L6
Sion 12 C7
Sion Mills 11 B4
Sioux Center 40 D6
Sioux City 40 D6
Sioux Falls 40 D6
Sioux Lookout 36 D10
Siping 21 B7
Sipura 23 D1
Sir James MacBrien, Mt. 36 C7
Siracusa 14 F6
Siren 40 C8
Sīrjān 24 C4
Sisseton 40 C6
Sīstān, Daryācheh-ye 24 B5
Sisters 38 D3
Sitito-Ozima Ridge 34 E6
Sitka 36 D6
Sittingbourne 9 F8
Sittwe 25 C8
Sivas 17 C5
Sîwa 27 C11
Six Cross Roads 45 g
Sixmilebridge 11 D3
Sjælland 7 F6
Skagerrak 7 F5
Skagway 36 D6
Skeena → 36 D6
Skegness 8 D8
Skellefteå 7 E8
Skellefteälven → 7 E8
Skerries, The 8 D3
Skiathos 15 E10
Skibbereen 11 E2
Skiddaw 8 C4
Skien 7 F5
Skikda 26 A7
Skipton 8 D5
Skopje 15 C9
Skowhegan 43 C11
Skull 11 E2
Skunk → 40 E9
Skye 10 D2
Skykomish 38 C3
Slane 11 C5
Slaney → 11 D5
Śląsk 16 C8
Slatina 15 B11
Slaton 41 J4
Slave → 36 C8
Slave Coast 26 G6
Slave Lake 36 D8
Sleaford 8 D7
Sleaford B. 32 B2
Sleat, Sd. of 10 D3
Sleeper Is. 37 D11
Sleeping Bear Dunes △ 42 C2
Sleepy Eye 40 C7
Slidell 41 K10
Slieve Aughty 11 C3
Slieve Bloom 11 C4
Slieve Donard 11 B6
Slieve Gamph 11 B3
Slieve Gullion 11 B5
Slieve League 11 B3
Slieve Mish 11 D2
Slievenamon 11 D4
Sligo 11 B3
Sligo □ 11 B3
Sligo B. 11 B3
Sliven 15 C12
Slough 9 F7
Slovak Rep. ■ 16 D9
Slovenia ■ 14 B6
Slovenské Rudohorie 16 D10
Slovyansk 17 A5
Slyne Hd. 11 C1
Smallwood Res. 37 D13
Smederevo 15 B9
Smerwick Harbour 11 D1
Smith Center 40 F5
Smith River △ 38 F2
Smith Sd. 6 B3
Smithfield, *N.C., U.S.A.* 43 H6
Smithfield, *Utah, U.S.A.* 38 F8
Smithton 32 D4
Smithville 41 K6
Smoky → 36 D8
Smoky Bay 32 B1
Smoky Hill → 40 F6
Smoky Hills 40 F5
Smolensk 18 D4
Smyrna 42 F8
Snaefell 8 C3
Snake → 38 C4
Snake I. 32 C4
Snake Range 38 G6
Snake River Plain 38 E7
Sneem 11 E2
Snizort, L. 10 D2
Snøhetta 7 E5
Snohomish 38 C2
Snow Hill 42 F8
Snowdon 8 D3
Snowdonia △ 8 D4
Snowflake 39 J8
Snowshoe Pk. 38 B6
Snowtown 32 B2
Snowville 38 F7
Snowy → 32 C4
Snowy Mts. 32 C4
Snyder, *Okla., U.S.A.* 41 H5
Snyder, *Tex., U.S.A.* 41 J4
Sobral 47 D10
Soc Trang 23 C2
Socastee 43 J6
Sochi 17 B5
Société, Is. de la 35 J12
Socorro, *N. Mex., U.S.A.* 39 J10
Socorro, *Tex., U.S.A.* 39 L10
Socotra 24 D4
Soda L. 39 J5
Soda Springs 38 E8
Soddy-Daisy 43 H3
Söderhamn 7 E7
Sofiya 15 C10
Sognefjorden 7 E5
Sohâg 27 C12
Soissons 12 B5
Sokhumi 17 B6
Soko Is. 21 G10
Sokoto 26 F7
Solander I. 33 M1
Solapur 25 D6
Soldotna 36 C4
Soledad 39 H3
Solent, The 9 G6
Solihull 9 E6
Solikamsk 18 D6
Solimões = Amazonas → 47 D8
Solingen 16 C3
Solomon, N. Fork → 40 F5
Solomon, S. Fork → 40 F5
Solomon Is. ■ 31 B10
Solomon Rise 34 G7
Solomon Sea 30 B9
Solon 21 B7
Solon Springs 40 B9
Solothurn 12 C7
Solvang 39 J3
Solvay 42 D7
Solway Firth 8 C4
Somali Rep. ■ 24 E3
Somaliland □ 24 E3
Sombrerete 44 C4
Somers 38 B6
Somerset, *Ky., U.S.A.* 42 G3
Somerset, *Pa., U.S.A.* 42 E6
Somerset □ 9 F5
Somerset I. 36 B10
Somerton 39 K6
Somme → 12 A4
Son La 23 A2
Songgang 21 F10
Songhua Jiang → 21 B8
Songkhla 23 C2
Songpan 20 C5
Sonora, *Calif., U.S.A.* 39 H3
Sonora, *Tex., U.S.A.* 41 K4
Sonora → 44 B2
Sonoran Desert 39 K6
Sonoyta 44 A2
Sonsonate 44 E7
Sopot 16 A9
Soria 13 B4
Sorocaba 48 A7
Sorong 23 D5
Sørøya 7 C8
Sorrell 32 D4
Sosnowiec 16 C9
Soufrière, *Guadeloupe* 44 b
Soufrière, *St. Lucia* 45 f
Soufrière Bay 45 f
Sound, The 9 G3
Souris → 40 A4
Sousse 27 A8
South Africa ■ 29 L4
South America 2 E7
South Atlantic Ocean 2 F9
South Australia □ 32 B2
South Australian Basin 34 L4
South Ayrshire □ 10 F4
South Baldy Pk. 39 J10
South Bend 42 E2
South Boston 43 G6
South Bruny I. 32 D4
South Carolina □ 43 J5
South Charleston 42 F5
South China Sea 23 C3
South Dakota □ 40 C5
South Downs 9 G7
South East C. 32 D4
South Esk → 10 E6
South Fiji Basin 34 K9
South Foreland 9 F9
South Fork Grand → 40 C3
South Fork Milk → 38 B10
South Fork Republican → 40 E4
South Georgia 48 G9
South Gloucestershire □ 9 F5
South Haven 42 D2
South I. 33 L3
South Invercargill 33 M2
South Korea ■ 21 C7
South Lake Tahoe 38 G3
South Lanarkshire □ 10 F5
South Loup → 40 E5
South Magnetic Pole 6 D13
South Milwaukee 42 D2
South Molton 9 F4
South Nahanni → 36 C7
South Negril Pt. 44 a
South New Hebrides Trench 31 E13
South Orkney Is. 6 D4
South Pittsburg 43 H3
South Platte → 40 E4
South Pole 6 F
South Portland 43 D10
South Pt. 45 g
South Ronaldsay 10 C6
South Sandwich Is. 4 G8
South Saskatchewan → 36 D9
South Shetland Is. 6 D4
South Shields 8 C6
South Sioux City 40 D6
South Sister 38 D3
South Solomon Trench 31 C11
South Taranaki Bight 33 H5
South Tasman Rise 34 M6
South Tyne → 8 C5
South Uist 10 D1
South Valley 39 J10
South West C., *Australia* 32 D4
South West C., *N.Z.* 33 M1
South Yorkshire □ 8 D6
Southampton, *U.K.* 9 G6
Southampton, *U.S.A.* 42 E9
Southampton I. 37 C11
Southaven 41 H9
Southbridge 33 K4
Southend-on-Sea 9 F8
Southern Alps 33 K3
Southern Indian L. 36 D10
Southern Ocean 3 G12
Southern Pines 43 H6
Southern Uplands 10 F5
Southland □ 33 L1
Southport, *Australia* 32 A5
Southport, *U.K.* 8 D4
Southwest △ 32 D4
Southwest Pacific Basin 31 G17
Southwold 9 E9
Southwood △ 32 A5
Soweto 29 K5
Spain ■ 13 B4
Spalding, *Australia* 32 B2
Spalding, *U.K.* 8 E7
Spanish Fork 38 F8
Spanish Town, *Br. Virgin Is.* 45 e
Spanish Town, *Jamaica* 44 a
Sparks 38 G4
Sparta, *Mich., U.S.A.* 42 D3
Sparta, *Wis., U.S.A.* 40 D9
Spartanburg 43 H5
Spartivento, C. 14 F7
Spean → 10 E4
Spearfish 40 C3
Spearman 41 G4
Speightstown 45 g
Spencer, *Idaho, U.S.A.* 38 D7
Spencer, *Iowa, U.S.A.* 40 D7
Spencer, *Nebr., U.S.A.* 40 D5
Spencer, C. 32 C2
Spencer G. 32 B2
Spennymoor 8 C6
Spenser Mts. 33 K4
Sperrin Mts. 11 B5
Spey → 10 D5
Spiddle 11 C2
Spithead 9 G6
Spitzbergen = Svalbard 6 B7
Split 14 C7
Spofford 41 L4
Spokane 38 C5
Spooner 40 C9
Sprague 38 C5
Spratly Is. 23 C3
Spray 38 D4
Spree → 16 B6
Spring Creek 38 F6
Spring Hall 45 g
Spring Hill 43 L4
Spring Mts. 39 H6
Springbok 29 K3
Springdale 41 G7
Springer 41 G2
Springerville 39 J9
Springfield, *N.Z.* 33 K3
Springfield, *Colo., U.S.A.* 41 G3
Springfield, *Ill., U.S.A.* 40 F10
Springfield, *Mass., U.S.A.* 42 D9
Springfield, *Mo., U.S.A.* 41 G8
Springfield, *Ohio, U.S.A.* 42 F4
Springfield, *Oreg., U.S.A.* 38 D2
Springfield, *Tenn., U.S.A.* 43 G2
Springfield, *Vt., U.S.A.* 42 D9
Springhill 41 J8
Springs 29 K5
Springville 38 F8
Spruce Knob-Seneca Rocks △ 42 F6
Spur 41 J4
Spurn Hd. 8 D8
Srebrenica 15 B8
Sredinnyy Khrebet 19 D16
Srednekolymsk 19 C16
Srepok → 23 B2
Sri Lanka ■ 25 E7
Srinagar 25 B6
Staffa 10 E2
Stafford, *U.K.* 8 E5
Stafford, *U.S.A.* 41 G5
Staffordshire □ 8 E5
Staines 9 F7
Stalybridge 8 D5
Stamford, *U.K.* 9 E7
Stamford, *Conn., U.S.A.* 42 E9
Stamford, *Tex., U.S.A.* 41 J5
Stamps 41 J8
Standish 42 D4
Stanford 38 C8
Stanley, *Australia* 32 D4
Stanley, *China* 21 G11
Stanley, *Falk. Is.* 48 G5
Stanley, *U.K.* 8 C6
Stanley, *Idaho, U.S.A.* 38 D6
Stanley, *N. Dak., U.S.A.* 40 A3
Stanovoy Khrebet 19 D13
Stansted, London (STN) 9 F8
Stanthorpe 32 A5
Stanton 41 J4
Staples 40 B7
Stapleton 40 E4
Stara Planina 15 C10
Stara Zagora 15 C11
Starbuck I. 35 H12
Starke 43 L4
Starkville 41 J10
Start Pt. 9 G4
State College 42 E7
Statesboro 43 J5
Statesville 43 H5
Staunton, *Ill., U.S.A.* 40 F10
Staunton, *Va., U.S.A.* 42 F6
Stavanger 7 F5
Staveley 33 K3
Stavropol 17 A6
Stawell 32 C3
Stayton 38 D2
Steamboat Springs 38 F10
Steele 40 B5
Steens Mt. 38 E4
Steiermark □ 16 E7
Steinkjer 7 E6
Stellenbosch 29 L3
Stephens Creek 32 B3
Stephenville, *Canada* 37 E14
Stephenville, *U.S.A.* 41 J5
Sterling, *Colo., U.S.A.* 40 E3
Sterling, *Ill., U.S.A.* 40 E10
Sterling, *Kans., U.S.A.* 40 F5
Sterling City 41 K4
Sterling Heights 42 D4
Sterlitamak 18 D6
Stettler 36 D8
Steubenville 42 E5
Stevenage 9 F7
Stevens Point 40 C10
Stevenson → 32 A2
Stevensville 38 C6
Stewart 36 D7
Stewart → 36 C6
Stewart I. 33 M1
Stewartville 40 D8
Steyr 16 D7
Stigler 41 H7
Stikine → 36 D6
Stillwater, *N.Z.* 33 K3
Stillwater, *U.S.A.* 41 G6
Stillwater Range 38 G4
Stilwell 41 H7
Stirling 10 E5
Stirling □ 10 E4
Stockholm 7 F7
Stockport 8 D5
Stocksbridge 8 D6
Stockton, *Calif., U.S.A.* 39 H3
Stockton, *Kans., U.S.A.* 40 F5
Stockton, *Mo., U.S.A.* 41 G8
Stockton-on-Tees 8 C6
Stockton Plateau 41 K3
Stoeng Treng 23 B2
Stoer, Pt. of 10 C3
Stoke-on-Trent 8 D5
Stokes Pt. 32 D3
Stone 8 E5
Stonehaven 10 E6
Stonehenge 9 F6
Stora Lulevatten 7 D7
Storavan 7 D7
Store Bælt 7 F6
Storm B. 32 D4
Storm Lake 40 D7
Stornoway 10 C2
Storsjön 7 E6
Storuman 7 D7
Stour →, *Dorset, U.K.* 9 G6
Stour →, *Kent, U.K.* 9 F9
Stour →, *Suffolk, U.K.* 9 F9
Stourbridge 9 E5
Stowmarket 9 E9
Strabane 11 B4
Strahan 32 D4
Stralsund 16 A6
Strand 29 L3
Strangford L. 11 B6
Stranorlar 11 B4
Stranraer 10 G3
Strasbourg 12 B7
Stratford, *N.Z.* 33 H5
Stratford, *U.S.A.* 41 G3
Stratford-upon-Avon 9 E6
Strath Spey 10 D5
Strathalbyn 32 C2
Strathaven 10 F4
Strathmore 10 E5
Strathpeffer 10 D4
Strathy Pt. 10 C4
Strawberry → 38 F8
Streaky B. 32 B1
Streaky Bay 32 B1
Streator 40 E10
Strokestown 11 C3
Stroma 10 C5
Strómboli 14 E6
Stromeferry 10 D3
Stromness 10 C5
Stromsburg 40 E6
Stronsay 10 B6
Stroud 9 F5
Stroud Road 32 B5
Stryker 38 B6
Strzelecki Cr. → 32 A2
Stuart, *Fla., U.S.A.* 43 M5
Stuart, *Nebr., U.S.A.* 40 D5
Stuart L. 36 D7
Stuart Ra. 32 A1
Sturgeon Bay 42 C2
Sturgis, *Mich., U.S.A.* 42 E3
Sturgis, *S. Dak., U.S.A.* 40 C3
Sturt △ 32 A3
Sturt Stony Desert 30 F6
Stuttgart, *Germany* 16 D4
Stuttgart, *U.S.A.* 41 H9
Subotica 15 A8
Suck → 11 C3
Sucre 46 G5
Sudan 41 H3
Sudan ■ 27 E11
Sudbury, *Canada* 37 E11
Sudbury, *U.K.* 9 E8
Sudeten Mts. = Sudety 16 C8
Sudety 16 C8
Suez = El Suweis 27 C12
Suffolk 42 G7
Suffolk □ 9 E9
Şuḩār 24 C4
Suihua 21 B7
Suining 25 B9
Suir → 11 D4
Sukabumi 23 D2
Sukadana 23 D3
Sukkur 25 C5
Sulaiman Range 25 B5
Sulawesi 23 D4
Sullivan, *Ill., U.S.A.* 40 F10
Sullivan, *Ind., U.S.A.* 42 F2
Sullivan, *Mo., U.S.A.* 40 F9
Sullom Voe 10 A7
Sulphur, *La., U.S.A.* 41 K8
Sulphur, *Okla., U.S.A.* 41 H6
Sulphur Springs 41 J7
Sulu Arch. 23 C4
Sulu Sea 23 C4
Sumatera 23 C2
Sumba 23 D3
Sumba, Selat 23 D3
Sumbawa 23 D3
Sumburgh Hd. 10 B7
Sumenep 23 D3
Summer L. 38 E3
Summerside 37 E13
Summersville 42 F5
Summerville, *Ga., U.S.A.* 43 H3
Summerville, *S.C., U.S.A.* 43 J5
Summit Peak 39 H10
Sumner 40 D8
Sumqayıt 17 B7
Sumter 43 J5
Sumy 18 D4
Sun City 39 K7
Sun City Center 43 M4
Sun Lakes 39 K8
Sun Valley 38 E6
Sunart, L. 10 E3
Sunburst 38 B8
Sunbury, *Australia* 32 C3
Sunbury, *U.S.A.* 42 E7
Sunda, Selat 23 D2
Sunda Is. 34 H2
Sundance 40 C2
Sundarbans 25 C7
Sunderland 8 C6
Sundown △ 32 A5
Sundsvall 7 E7
Sungaipenuh 23 D2
Sunland Park 39 L10
Sunnyside 38 C3
Sunnyvale 39 H2
Sunrise Manor 39 H6
Sunshine Coast 30 F9
Supai 39 H7
Superior, *Ariz., U.S.A.* 39 K8
Superior, *Mont., U.S.A.* 38 C6
Superior, *Nebr., U.S.A.* 40 E5
Superior, *Wis., U.S.A.* 40 B8
Superior, L. 37 E11
Supiori 23 D5
Şūr 24 C4
Sur, Pt. 39 H3
Surabaya 23 D3
Surakarta 23 D3
Surat, *Australia* 32 A4
Surat, *India* 25 C6
Surat Thani 23 C1
Surfers Paradise 30 F9
Surgut 18 C8
Surigao 23 C4
Suriname ■ 47 C7
Surrey □ 9 F7
Susanville 38 F3
Susquehanna → 42 F7
Sussex, E. □ 9 G8
Sussex, W. □ 9 G7
Sutherland, *S. Africa* 29 L4
Sutherland, *U.K.* 10 C4
Sutherland, *U.S.A.* 40 E4
Sutherland Falls 33 L1
Sutherlin 38 E2
Sutlej → 25 C6
Sutton, *Nebr., U.S.A.* 40 E6
Sutton, *W. Va., U.S.A.* 42 F5
Sutton Coldfield 9 E6
Sutton in Ashfield 8 D6
Suva 33 D8
Suwannee → 43 L4
Suwarrow Is. 35 J11
Suzhou 21 C7
Svalbard 6 B7
Svealand □ 7 E7
Sverdrup Chan. 37 B8
Sverdrup Is. 37 B8
Swaffham 9 E8
Swains I. 35 J11
Swainsboro 43 J4
Swakopmund 29 J2
Swale → 8 C6
Swan Hill 32 C3
Swan Ra. 38 C7
Swan River 36 D9
Swanage 9 G6
Swansea, *Australia* 32 D4
Swansea, *U.K.* 9 F4
Swaziland ■ 29 K6
Sweden ■ 7 F7
Sweet Grass 38 B8
Sweet Home 38 D2
Sweetwater, *Tenn., U.S.A.* 43 H3
Sweetwater, *Tex., U.S.A.* 41 J4
Sweetwater → 38 E10
Swellendam 29 L4
Swift Current 36 D9
Swilly, L. 11 A4
Swindon 9 F6
Swinford 11 C3
Switzerland ■ 12 C8
Swords 11 C5
Sydney, *Australia* 32 B5
Sydney, *Canada* 37 E13
Syktyvkar 18 C6
Sylacauga 43 J2
Sylhet 25 C8
Sylvania, *Ga., U.S.A.* 43 J5
Sylvania, *Ohio, U.S.A.* 42 E4
Sylvester 43 K4
Syracuse, *Kans., U.S.A.* 41 G4
Syracuse, *N.Y., U.S.A.* 42 D7
Syracuse, *Nebr., U.S.A.* 40 E6
Syrdarya → 18 E7
Syria ■ 24 B2
Syrian Desert = Shām, Bādiyat ash 24 B3
Syzran 18 D5
Szczecin 16 B7
Szechwan = Sichuan □ 20 C5
Szeged 16 E10
Székesfehérvár 16 E9
Szekszárd 16 E9
Szolnok 16 E10
Szombathely 16 E8

T

Ţabas 24 B4
Tabiteuea 31 A13
Tablas I. 23 B4
Table Mt. 29 L3
Table Rock L. 41 G8
Tabora 28 F6
Tabrīz 24 B3
Tabuaeran 35 G12
Tabūk 24 C2
Tacheng 20 B3
Tacloban 23 B4
Tacna 46 G4
Tacoma 38 C2
Tacuarembó 48 C5
Tadmor 33 J4
Taft 39 J4
Taganrog 17 A5
Tagus = Tejo → 13 C1
Tahakopa 33 M2
Tahan, Gunung 23 C2
Tahiti 35 J13
Tahlequah 41 H7
Tahoe, L. 38 G3
Tahoe City 38 G3
Tahoka 41 J4
Tai Au Mun 21 G11
Tai Mo Shan 21 G11
Tai O 21 G10
Tai Pang Wan 21 F11
Tai Po 21 G11
Taibei = T'aipei 21 D7
T'aichung 21 D7
Taieri → 33 M3
Taihape 33 H5
Tailem Bend 32 C2
Tain 10 D4
T'ainan 21 D7
Taipa 21 G10
T'aipei 21 D7
Taiping 23 C2
Taitao, Pen. de 48 F2
T'aitung 21 D7
Taiwan ■ 21 D7
Taiyuan 21 C6
Ta'izz 24 D3
Tajikistan ■ 18 F8
Tak 23 B1
Takaka 33 J4
Takamatsu 22 F4
Takaoka 22 E5
Takapuna 33 G5
Takasaki 22 E6
Takla Makan 20 C3
Talaud, Kepulauan 23 C4
Talbragar → 32 B4
Talca 48 D2
Talcahuano 48 D2
Taliabu 23 D4
Talihina 41 H7
Talladega 43 J2
Tallahassee 43 K3
Tallangatta 32 C4
Tallinn 18 D3
Tallulah 41 J9
Taloyoak 36 C10
Talwood 32 A4
Talyawalka Cr. → 32 B3
Tama 40 E8
Tamale 26 G5
Tamana 31 A14
Tamar → 9 G3
Tambov 18 D5
Tamil Nadu □ 25 D6
Tamo Abu, Banjaran 23 C3
Tampa 43 M4
Tampa B. 43 M4
Tampere 7 E8
Tampico 44 C5
Tamworth, *Australia* 32 B5
Tamworth, *U.K.* 9 E6
Tana →, *Kenya* 28 E8
Tana →, *Norway* 7 C9
Tana, L. 27 F13
Tanami Desert 30 D5
Tanana → 36 C4
Tandou L. 32 B3
Tandragee 11 B5
Taneatua 33 H6
Tanga 28 F7
Tanganyika, L. 28 F6
Tanger 26 A4
Tanggula Shan 20 C4
Tangier = Tanger 26 A4
Tangjia 21 G10
Tangjia Wan 21 G10
Tangshan 21 C6
Tanimbar, Kepulauan 23 D5
Tanjungbalai 23 C1
Tanjungkarang Telukbetung 23 D2
Tanjungpandan 23 D2
Tanjungredeb 23 C3
Tanna 31 D12
Tanta 27 B12
Tanunda 32 B2
Tanzania ■ 28 F6
Tanzhou 21 G9
Taos 39 H11
Tapachula 44 E6
Tapajós → 47 D8
Tapanui 33 L2
Tapuae-o-Uenuku 33 K4
Tara 32 A5
Tarābulus, *Lebanon* 17 D5
Tarābulus, *Libya* 27 B8
Tarakan 23 C3
Taranaki □ 33 H5
Taranaki, Mt. 33 H5
Taransay 10 D1
Táranto 14 D7
Táranto, G. di 14 D7
Tararua Ra. 33 J5
Tarawa 34 G9
Tarawera 33 H6
Tarawera, L. 33 H6
Taraz 18 E8
Tarbagatay, Khrebet 18 E9
Tarbat Ness 10 D5
Tarbert, *Ireland* 11 D2
Tarbert, *Argyll & Bute, U.K.* 10 F3
Tarbert, *W. Isles, U.K.* 10 D2
Tarbes 12 E4
Tarboro 43 H7
Tarcoola 32 B1
Tarcoon 32 B4
Taree 32 B5
Târgovişte 15 B11
Târgu-Jiu 15 B10
Tarim He → 20 C3
Tarim Pendi 20 B3
Tarn → 12 E4
Tarnów 7 G8
Taroom 32 A4
Tarpon Springs 43 L4
Tarragona 13 B6
Tarraleah 32 D4
Tarsus 17 C4
Tartu 18 D3
Tashkent = Toshkent 18 E7
Tasikmalaya 23 D2
Tasman Abyssal Plain 30 G9
Tasman B. 33 J4
Tasman Basin 34 M7
Tasman Mts. 33 J4
Tasman Pen. 32 D4
Tasman Sea 31 H10
Tasmania □ 32 D4
Tassili n'Ajjer 26 C7
Tatarsk 18 D8
Tathra 32 C4
Tatnam, C. 37 D10
Tatry 16 D10
Tatum 41 J3
Tauern 16 E6
Taumarunui 33 H5
Taunggyi 25 C8
Taunton, *U.K.* 9 F4
Taunton, *U.S.A.* 42 E10
Taunus 16 C4
Taupo 33 H6
Taupo, L. 33 H5
Tauranga 33 G6
Tauranga Harb. 33 G6
Taurus Mts. = Toros Dağları 17 C4
Taveuni 33 C9
Tavistock 9 G3
Tavoy 25 D8
Taw → 9 F3
Tawas City 42 C4
Tawau 23 C3
Tay △ 10 E5
Tay → 10 E5
Tay, Firth of 10 E5
Tay, L. 10 E4
Taylor, *Nebr., U.S.A.* 40 E5
Taylor, *Tex., U.S.A.* 41 K6
Taylor, Mt. 39 J10
Taylorville 40 F10
Taymā 24 C2
Taymyr, Poluostrov 19 B11
Tayport 10 E6
Tbilisi 17 B6
Te Anau, L. 33 L1
Te Aroha 33 G5
Te Awamutu 33 H5
Te Kuiti 33 H5
Te Puke 33 G6
Te Waewae B. 33 M1
Teague 41 K6
Tecumseh, *Mich., U.S.A.* 42 D4
Tecumseh, *Okla., U.S.A.* 41 H6
Tees → 8 C6
Tees B. 8 C6
Tegal 23 D2
Tegucigalpa 44 E7
Tehachapi 39 J4
Tehachapi Mts. 39 J4
Tehrān 24 B4
Tehuantepec 44 D5
Tehuantepec, G. de 44 D5
Tehuantepec, Istmo de 44 D6
Tehuantepec Fracture Zone 35 F18
Teifi → 9 E3
Teign → 9 G4
Teignmouth 9 G4
Tejo → 13 C1
Tekamah 40 E6
Tekapo, L. 33 K3
Tekoa 38 C5
Tel Aviv-Yafo 17 D4
Tela 44 D7
Telegraph Creek 36 D6
Teles Pires → 46 E7
Telescope Pk. 39 H5
Telford 9 E5
Tell City 42 G2
Telluride 39 H10
Teluk Intan 23 C2
Tema 26 G5
Temba 29 K5
Teme → 9 E5
Temecula 39 K5
Temirtau 18 D8
Tempe 39 K8
Temple 41 K6
Templemore 11 D4
Temuco 48 D2
Temuka 33 L3
Ten Degree Channel 25 E8
Tenaha 41 K7
Tenaro, Akra 15 F10
Tenasserim □ 25 D8
Tenby 9 F3
Tenerife 26 C2
Tengchong 20 D4
Tennant Creek 30 D5
Tennessee □ 43 H2
Tennessee → 42 G1
Tenterden 9 F8
Tenterfield 32 A5
Teófilo Otoni 47 G10
Tepic 44 C4
Teraina 35 G11
Téramo 14 C5
Terang 32 C3
Terek → 17 B7
Teresina 47 E10
Terewah, L. 32 A4
Teridgerie Cr. → 32 B4
Ternate 23 C4
Terni 14 C5
Terowie 32 B2
Terrace 36 D7
Terrassa 13 B7
Terre Haute 42 F2
Terrebonne B. 41 L9
Terrell 41 J6
Terry 40 B2
Teruel 13 B5
Teryaweynya L. 32 B3
Tesiyn Gol → 20 A4
Teslin 36 C6
Test → 9 G6
Teton → 38 C8
Tétouan 26 A4
Tetovo 15 C9
Teutoburger Wald 16 B4
Tevere → 14 D5
Teviot → 10 F6
Tewantin 32 A5
Tewkesbury 9 F5
Texarkana, *Ark., U.S.A.* 41 J8
Texarkana, *Tex., U.S.A.* 41 J7
Texas 32 A5
Texas □ 41 K5
Texas City 41 L7
Texel 16 B2
Texline 41 G3
Texoma, L. 41 J6
Tezpur 25 C8
Thabana Ntlenyana 29 K5
Thabazimbi 29 J5
Thai Binh 23 A2
Thailand ■ 23 B2
Thailand, G. of 23 B2
Thallon 32 A4
Thames 33 G5
Thames → 9 F8
Thames Estuary 9 F8
Thane 25 D6
Thanet, I. of 9 F9
Thanh Hoa 23 B2
Thanh Pho Ho Chi Minh 23 B2
Thar Desert 25 C6
Thargomindah 32 A3
Thatcher, *Ariz., U.S.A.* 39 K9
Thatcher, *Colo., U.S.A.* 41 G2
Thayer 41 G9
The Broads 8 E9
The Everglades 43 N5
The Pas 36 D9

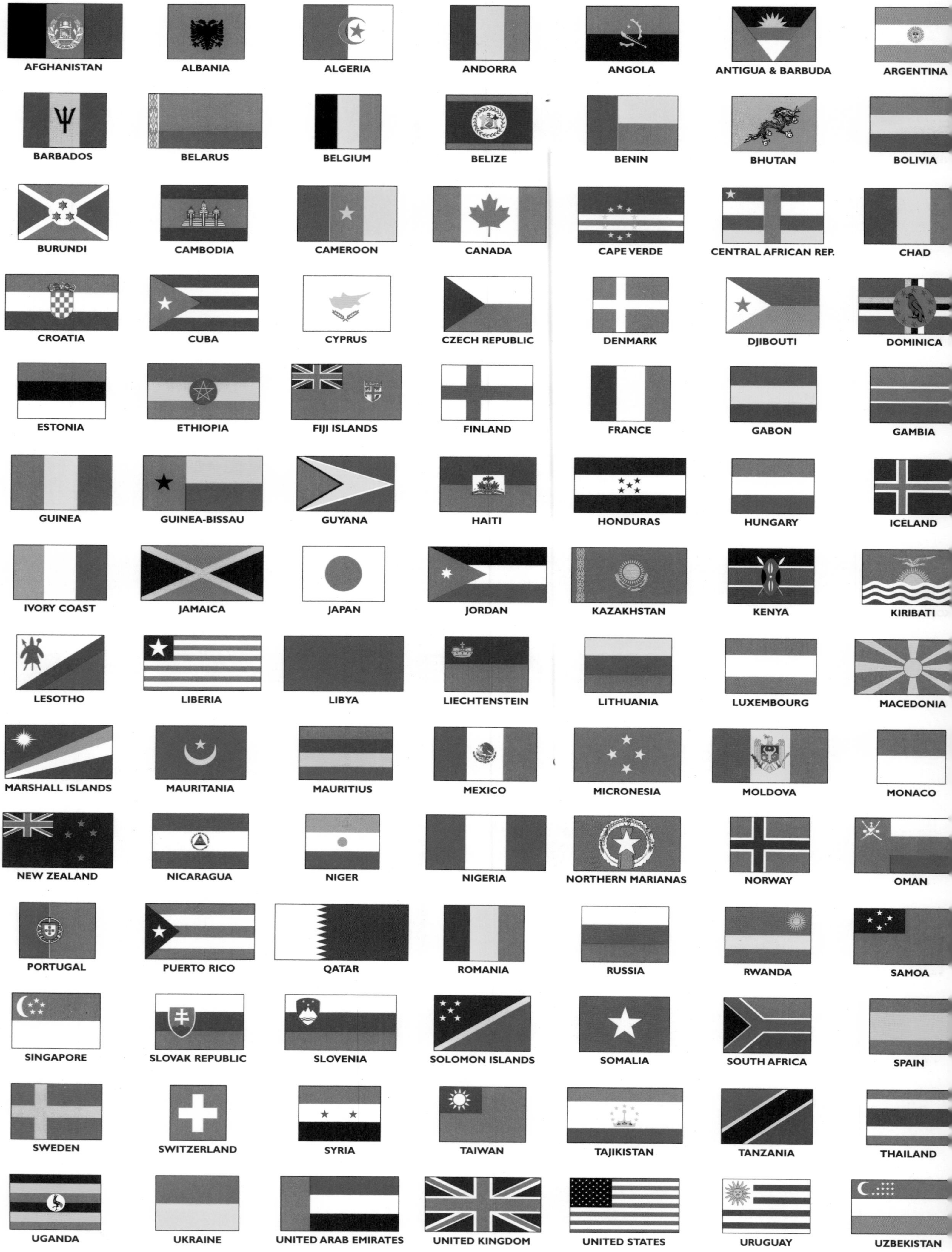
AFGHANISTAN
ALBANIA
ALGERIA
ANDORRA
ANGOLA
ANTIGUA & BARBUDA
ARGENTINA
BARBADOS
BELARUS
BELGIUM
BELIZE
BENIN
BHUTAN
BOLIVIA
BURUNDI
CAMBODIA
CAMEROON
CANADA
CAPE VERDE
CENTRAL AFRICAN REP.
CHAD
CROATIA
CUBA
CYPRUS
CZECH REPUBLIC
DENMARK
DJIBOUTI
DOMINICA
ESTONIA
ETHIOPIA
FIJI ISLANDS
FINLAND
FRANCE
GABON
GAMBIA
GUINEA
GUINEA-BISSAU
GUYANA
HAITI
HONDURAS
HUNGARY
ICELAND
IVORY COAST
JAMAICA
JAPAN
JORDAN
KAZAKHSTAN
KENYA
KIRIBATI
LESOTHO
LIBERIA
LIBYA
LIECHTENSTEIN
LITHUANIA
LUXEMBOURG
MACEDONIA
MARSHALL ISLANDS
MAURITANIA
MAURITIUS
MEXICO
MICRONESIA
MOLDOVA
MONACO
NEW ZEALAND
NICARAGUA
NIGER
NIGERIA
NORTHERN MARIANAS
NORWAY
OMAN
PORTUGAL
PUERTO RICO
QATAR
ROMANIA
RUSSIA
RWANDA
SAMOA
SINGAPORE
SLOVAK REPUBLIC
SLOVENIA
SOLOMON ISLANDS
SOMALIA
SOUTH AFRICA
SPAIN
SWEDEN
SWITZERLAND
SYRIA
TAIWAN
TAJIKISTAN
TANZANIA
THAILAND
UGANDA
UKRAINE
UNITED ARAB EMIRATES
UNITED KINGDOM
UNITED STATES
URUGUAY
UZBEKISTAN